T5-CVQ-054

CHRISTIANIZING KINSHIP

CHRISTIANIZING KINSHIP

❦

RITUAL SPONSORSHIP IN ANGLO-SAXON ENGLAND

Joseph H. Lynch

Cornell University Press

ITHACA AND LONDON

First published 1998 by Cornell University Press.

Printed in the United States of America.

Cornell University Press strives to utilize environmentally responsible suppliers and materials to the fullest extent possible in the publishing of its books. Such materials include vegetable-based, low-VOC inks and acid-free papers that are also either recycled, totally chlorine-free, or partly composed of nonwood fibers.

Lynch, Joseph H., 1943–
Christianizing kinship : ritual sponsorship in Anglo-Saxon England / Joseph H. Lynch.
p. cm.
Includes bibliographical references and index.
ISBN 0-8014-3527-7 (alk. paper)
1. Sponsors—England. 2. Anglo-Saxons—Kinship. 3. England—Religious life and customs. 4. England—Church history—449–1066.
I. Title.
BR747.L86 1998
274.2′02—dc21 98-3806

Cloth printing 10 9 8 7 6 5 4 3 2 1

Dedicated to my favorite people:

Ann, Elizabeth and Tyler, Michael and Christine, and Matthew

Contents

Acknowledgments

The origins of this book go back more than thirty-five years. My interest in medieval history was encouraged by William M. Daly, professor emeritus at Boston College, with whom I began my training in the field. Bill is a meticulous scholar, a helpful mentor, and a lifelong friend. At Harvard University, I had the great privilege of working with historians who are at once masters of their craft and good human beings, Giles Constable and Jocelyn Hillgarth.

I studied Old English with generous, helpful colleagues at Ohio State, Alan Brown and Nicholas Howe, each of whom read a version of this book. Nick also gave me advice on translations from Old English, although errors and infelicities are mine. Graduate students, past and present, have raised questions, suggested approaches, and critiqued my work. I am grateful particularly to Philip Adamo, David Blanks, Leigh Ann Craig, Louis Haas, R. J. Stansbury, Elizabeth Todd, and Sanford Zale.

Books—at least my books—take a long time to reach completion. Institutional support and patience have been a great help. I want to thank especially the College of Humanities and its longtime dean, Micheal Riley for support and encouragement. Likewise, my colleagues Franklin J. Pegues, James Kittelson, Marvin Zahniser, and Michael Hogan, chair of the department, have been unfailingly supportive over the course of many years. William Childs, a colleague in American Business History, also read a version of the manuscript and offered helpful suggestions.

My children, Elizabeth and Tyler, Michael and Chris, and Matt, who are not interested in things medieval, have nonetheless sustained my efforts by their accomplishments. Finally, I must acknowledge the love and support of my wife and best friend, Ann Lynch. She never let discouragement or problems deflect me for long from this book. Without her, it could never have been written.

J.H.L.

Abbreviations

AESC	*Annales. Economies, Sociétés, Civilisations*
AKKR	*Archiv für Katholisches Kirchenrecht*
ASC	*Anglo-Saxon Chronicle*
ASC(A)	Edited by Janet Bately, vol. 3 of *The Anglo-Saxon Chronicle. A Collaborative Edition,* general editors, David Dumville and Simon Keynes (Cambridge, 1986)
ASC(B)	Edited by Simon Taylor, vol. 4 of ibid. (Cambridge, 1983)
ASC(C)	Edited by Harry August Rositzke, *The C-Text of the Old English Chronicles,* Beiträge zur englischen Philologie 34 (Bochum, 1940)
ASC(D)	Edited by G. B. Cubbin, vol. 6 of *The Anglo-Saxon Chronicle: A Collaborative Edition,* general editors, David Dumville and Simon Keynes (Cambridge, 1996)
ASC(E)	Edited by Charles Plummer, *Two of the Saxon Chronicles Parallel,* on the basis of the edition by John Earle, vol. 1 (Oxford, 1892)
ASC(F)	Edited by Benjamin Thorpe, *The Anglo-Saxon Chronicle,* 2 vols., Rolls Series (London, 1861)
ASC(G)	Edited by Angelika Lutz, *Die Version G der Angelsächsischen Chronik,* Münchener Universitäts-Schriften, Philosophische Fakultät, Texte und Untersuchungen zur Englischen Philologie 11 (Munich, 1981)

The Peterborough Chronicle, 1070–1154	Edited by Cecily Clark (Oxford, 1970)
ASE	*Anglo-Saxon England*
Ausgewählte	*Ausgewählte Quellen zur deutschen Geschichte des Mittelalters*
BAP	Bibliothek der angelsächsischen Prosa
Bede, *HE*	Bede, *Historia Ecclesiastica gentis Anglorum,* in *The Ecclesiastical History of the English People,* edited and translated by Bertram Colgrave and R. A. B. Mynors (Oxford, 1969).
c.	chapter/canon
CCCC	Cambridge, Corpus Christ College
CCSL	*Corpus christianorum, Series latina*
CSAE	Cambridge Studies in Anglo-Saxon England
CSEL	Corpus scriptorum ecclesiasticorum latinorum
CSMLT	Cambridge Studies in Medieval Life and Thought
CTSEEH	Collection de textes pour servir à l'étude et à l'enseignement de l'histoire
CUA	The Catholic University of America
DAEM	*Deutsches Archiv für Erforschung des Mittelalters*
EETS	Early English Text Society
OS	Original Series
SS	Supplementary Series
EHD	*English Historical Documents,* vol. 1, *c. 500–1042,* 2d ed. by Dorothy Whitelock (London and New York, 1979)
EHR	*English Historical Review*
EME	*Early Medieval Europe*
ES	*Englische Studien*
FS	*Frühmittelalterliche Studien*
Gregory, *HF*	Gregory of Tours, *Historia Francorum,* 2d ed. by Bruno Krusch, Wilhelm Levison, and Walther Holtzmann, *MGH SRM* 1/1 (Hanover 1951)
HBS	The Henry Bradshaw Society
Mansi	J. D. Mansi, *Sacrorum conciliorum nova et amplissima collectio,* 31 vols. (Florence, 1759–98)
MGH	*Monumenta Germaniae Historica*
AA	*Auctores Antiquissimi*
Capitularia	*Capitularia regum francorum*
SRG	*Scriptores rerum germanicarum in usum scholarum*
SRM	*Scriptores rerum merovingicarum*

PL	*Patrologia latina*
QLP	*Questions Liturgiques et Paroissiales*
RB	*Revue Bénédictine*
RHE	*Revue d'Histoire Ecclésiastique*
RQCAKG	*Römische Quartalschrift für Christliche Altertumskunde und Kirchengeschichte*
S	Peter Sawyer, *Anglo-Saxon Charters: An Annotated List and Bibliography,* Royal Historical Society Guides and Handbooks, 8 (London, 1968)
SC	*Sources chrétiennes*
SSAM	*Settimane di studio del Centro Italiano di studi sull'alto medioevo*
ST	*Studi e testi*
Typologie	Typologie des sources du moyen âge occidental
ZSSRG	*Zeitschrift der Savigny-Stiftung für Rechtsgeschichte*

CHRISTIANIZING KINSHIP

Introduction

What difference did it make for an early medieval people to "convert" to Christianity? We assume that changes, perhaps profound changes, occurred but it is an issue worth examining. The conversion of Germanic, Celtic, Slavic, and other non-Mediterranean peoples is especially interesting. Traditional Christian institutions took shape within the Roman Empire, and many of those institutions presupposed the existence of Greco-Roman society. For example, by the fifth century, bishops resided in cities and exercised their authority over defined territory, which often included the rural part of the *civitas* within which they lived; the higher clergy were generally of the same social class as the people who filled high government positions; secular schools were taken for granted, in which the higher clergy and bureaucrats were educated; writing was an instrument of government and collective memory in both church and state; law was an abstract, respected force; the media for promoting religious and political messages were more or less the same—public speeches, mosaics, statues, coins, ceremonies, symbolic clothing. The list could go on, but the main point is that Christianity and late Greco-Roman culture were so intertwined that it is difficult to see where one broke off and the other began. When Christianity spread to peoples beyond the borders of the Roman Empire, whether they were Celts, Slavs, Ethiopians, or Germans, adaptations were inevitable because conditions were so different. The successes, failures, and compromises of Christianity in those regions offer varying test cases of what it meant to convert to Christianity.

The Anglo-Saxon kingdoms provide an interesting laboratory of change. The Angles, Saxons, Jutes, and others who lived along the shores of the North Sea were among the least romanized of the peoples beyond the borders of the Roman Empire. In the fifth century they began to migrate into Britain, which Rome had ruled for four hundred years. Over the course of four centuries, in fitful, uncoordinated warfare, they conquered lowland Britain, subjugating, enslaving, driving out, or killing the Christian Romano-British population, which survived in the west of the island, in Cornwall, Wales, and Strathclyde. By A.D. 597, when the first Christian missionaries arrived, there was a Germanic society in lowland Britain, relatively untouched by Roman/Christian civilization. The inhabitants of lowland Britain differed markedly from their Romano-British predecessors. They spoke Germanic languages, worshiped their own gods, were preliterate, without coinage, practiced their own styles of art, and were divided into numerous warring kingdoms and subkingdoms. Through channels to be discussed later, the Anglo-Saxon kings and upper classes accepted Christianity during the seventh century. There were episodes of apostasy and pagan reaction, but Anglo-Saxon societies became officially Christian within a century of the missionaries' arrival.

Official conversion was only a first step in a process of profound cultural transformation. In large ways and small, Christianity brought with it a special way of doing things: it was a religion with a lot of cultural baggage in its train. The changes that christianization brought about are sometimes quite visible. The Anglo-Saxons were gradually brought into the wider world of the Mediterranean and northern Gaul. Anglo-Saxon clerics traveled across Frankish Gaul to Rome and must have been amazed at what they saw. They brought back objects and ideas. The most prominent visible change was the introduction of Christian material things: buildings, books, personnel, rituals, and objects. Traditional Anglo-Saxon architecture was based on wooden construction, but Christianity favored stone for its churches. Christian worship demanded many small, perishable objects—made of cloth, bone, ivory, glass, wood—which we have a difficult time imagining outside a museum case. When we enter the relatively small surviving Anglo-Saxon churches today, their drab interiors leave us with a misleading impression of dullness. In their heyday, however, they were decorated with wall hangings, pictures, vestments, glass objects, chalices, patens, elaborate book covers, votive offerings, candles, and reliquaries. They must have been quite impressive to contemporaries.

Christianity was also a religion based on books; not just the Bible, but books to guide the performance of the liturgy, to administer the canon law, to understand the church fathers, and to preach the faith. For such a book-bound religion to function, some of the clergy had to be literate in Latin, and others had to be literate at least in the vernacular, a need which led to formal schooling on late Roman and monastic models.[1] Christianity had its own sacred people, distinguished by their clothes, their hairstyles, and their behavior. Bishops, priests, deacons, monks, and nuns constituted new social categories that had to be integrated into an already complex social hierarchy. Christianity introduced new rituals—baptism and the Eucharist—but also blessings, consecrations, veneration of relics, and new forms of prayers.

The introduction of Christianity had an impact on individual behavior as well. Burial practices changed gradually as the churchyard became the usual place of burial, and the grave goods of pagans times diminished in quantity or vanished altogether. Traditional Anglo-Saxon legal forms, such as ordeals and oaths, were carried out in a Christian context. Slavery did not disappear, but the freeing of slaves became a pious act, as did almsgiving. Pilgrimage became a valued, pious act: many Anglo-Saxons went to Rome, but some reached other important shrines on the Continent and in the Near East.[2] Even magic and medicine were influenced, as Christian formulas entered the repertoire of healers and singers of incantations.

The introduction of Christianity also brought changes in government. Christianity generally supported the power of early medieval kings on both theological and practical grounds. The authority of kings was ratified in the Old and New Testaments, whereas that of dukes, counts, ealdormen, and thegns was not. As a practical matter, bishops and abbots found it more convenient and more stable to deal with a few kings than with scores of fractious nobles. When the Anglo-Saxon kings adopted Christianity, they took on some of the trappings of proper kings, that is, the Frankish kings and Roman emperors. They issued written laws in imitation of Christian Roman and Germanic rulers. Bede said that the earliest laws, those of King Æthelberht of Kent, were issued after the example of the Romans (*iuxta exempla Romanorum*).[3] They issued coins of silver or, much less often, gold.

1. Michael Lapidge, "The School of Theodore and Hadrian," *ASE* 15 (1986), investigated the subjects taught in the school and the surviving manuscript evidence. Pierre Riché, *Education and Culture in the Barbarian West,* trans. John J. Contreni (Columbia, S.C., 1976), pp. 314–23 and 369–99, remains a useful introduction to the diversity of Christian schools in early Anglo-Saxon England.
2. Huneberc, *The Hodoeporicon of St. Willibald,* in *The Anglo-Saxon Missionaries in Germany,* trans. C. H. Talbot (New York, 1954), recorded Willibald's travels to shrines in Italy, the eastern Mediterranean, and the Holy Land.
3. Bede, *HE,* 2.5, p. 150. H. G. Richardson and G. O. Sayles, *Law and Legislation from Æthelberht to Magna Carta* (Edinburgh, 1966), pp. 1–12, discussed Christian influence on the appearance of written law.

With the encouragement of the clergy, they used written charters based on Continental notarial practice in order to guarantee the stability of gifts to churches.[4] Under church influence, kings sanctioned the transfer of wealth to churches through gifts after death, pious donations, and written wills, which had no place in the customary division of property among heirs.[5] The Christian Anglo-Saxon kings entered more readily into the alliance network of Christian Europe.

These examples emphasize that conversion to Christianity had multiple, significant consequences, some of them visible in objects, and others, less visible but no less real, in behavior and belief. Change in deep-rooted belief and behavior was slow, particularly in the countryside, where the mass of people lived. The Anglo-Saxon church only gradually acquired the personnel and estates to put churches and other permanent institutions in the countryside. The survival of pagan practices, such as divination and worship at springs and rocks, was a persistent theme in Anglo-Saxon legislation and sermons.[6] It is also true that personal relationships, such as marriage, changed only slowly under Christian influence. Christianity had a great interest in regulating sexual behavior, but polygamy, "incestuous" unions, divorce, adultery, and married clergy persisted, probably because they were at the core of personal behavior and of popular culture.[7]

Modern scholars have an easier time grasping changes represented in surviving objects that can be seen or touched—buildings, manuscript books, charters, coins, and the like. But Christianity also introduced new ideas, attitudes, and values, which are more difficult to grasp. Even dreams and visions were christianized. Bede recorded visions of the other world—and it was a decidedly Christian other world—which were experienced by the Irishman Fursa, by Drychthelm, by an unnamed layman, and by a

4. Margaret Deanesly, "Canterbury and Paris in the Reign of Æthelberht," *History* 26 (1941); Jacob Braude, *Die Familiengemeinschaften der Angelsachsen* (Leipzig, 1932) stressed the church's role in the creation of *bocland,* which was a landed estate guaranteed by a royal grant recorded in a charter.

5. Michael Sheehan, *The Will in Medieval England: From the Conversion of the Anglo-Saxons to the End of the Thirteenth Century* (Toronto, 1963), pp. 12–66.

6. Audrey Meaney, "Ælfric and Idolatry," *Journal of Religious History* 13 (1984); David R. Wilson, *Anglo-Saxon Paganism* (London and New York, 1992).

7. On the criticism of Anglo-Saxon sexual practices, see Alcuin's letter (c. 797) to the Mercian ealdorman Osbert in *EHD,* pp. 855–56; Pope John VIII's letter (late 877 or early 878) to Ethelred, archbishop of Canterbury, ibid., pp. 881–82; Archbishop Fulk of Reims's letter (c. 890) to Archbishop Plegmund of Canterbury, ibid., p. 887. On Germanic marriage customs, particularly the preference for unions considered incestuous by Mediterranean Christians, see Jack Goody, *The Development of the Family and Marriage in Europe* (Cambridge, 1983), pp. 34–48. Margaret Clunies Ross, "Concubinage in Anglo-Saxon England," *Past and Present* 108 (1985), analyzed Anglo-Saxon marital strategies.

monk. In Boniface's correspondence, there is a fragment of a vision of the next world in which identifiable Anglo-Saxon persons are named.[8] In a society where "heroic" values of strength, daring, vengeance, and individual martial prowess were highly valued, the Christian message of peace and nonresistance posed a challenge that had a difficult time being understood, let alone implemented. Christianity introduced new heroes, including saints who had been ascetics, virgins, martyrs, monks, and nuns. They did not displace the traditional warrior heroes; the two kinds of hero coexisted in tension.

Christianity introduced into Anglo-Saxon society at least one more institution, that of spiritual kinship arising out of sacramental sponsorship. This was not a development unique to England. Wherever Christianity was accepted, a new form of kinship based on sponsorship had to be integrated into native mores.[9] In 1986, I published a book on sponsorship and godparentage in the early medieval west.[10] The focus of my research was Frankish Gaul, with some attention to Italy and Byzantium. I found Anglo-Saxon sources referring to sponsorship, but because they did not fit the patterns of development discernible in Continental Christianity, I did not investigate them in detail. Subsequent research has convinced me that the Anglo-Saxon appropriation of sponsorship and spiritual kinship needs its own treatment. In Anglo-Saxon society, sponsorship became a nodal point where liturgy and theology intersected with politics and personal relationships. This book is an investigation of the introduction and assimilation of sponsorship and spiritual kinship in Anglo-Saxon England, a long, complicated process in which the Anglo-Saxons proved quite innovative. They created a distinct version of the "godparent complex," which I explore in the following chapters.

8. Bede, *HE,* 3.19, 5.12, 5.13, and 5.14. Boniface, *Epistola* 115, in *S. Bonifatii et Lullii epistolae,* ed. Michael Tangl, *MGH Epistolae selectae* 1 (Berlin, 1916), pp. 247–50.

9. On the introduction of spiritual kinship to the recently converted Bulgars, see Pope Nicholas I, *Epistola* 99, ed. E. Perels, *MGH Epistolae* 6. (Hanover, 1925), pp. 568–600. The prohibition on marriage between spiritual kin created problems, as when Saint Methodius criticized a ruler who had married his comother; see A. Vaillant, "Une homélie de Méthode," *Revue des Etudes Slaves* 23 (1947). On the spread of spiritual kinship in Slavic lands, see Evelyne Patlagean, "Christianisation et parentés rituelles: Le domaine de Byzance" *AESC* 33 (1978), 625–28, and Eve Levin, *Sex and Society in the World of the Orthodox Slavs, 900–1700* (Ithaca, N.Y., 1989), pp. 150–53.

10. Joseph H. Lynch, *Godparents and Kinship in Early Medieval Europe* (Princeton, N.J., 1986).

CHAPTER I

The Godparent Complex

Every baptism in medieval Europe had the potential to create a familylike relationship that theologians and canonists called "spiritual kinship" and that some anthropologists have called "fictive kinship" or a "godparent complex." A key figure in the new family was the baptismal sponsor, who became a godparent to the person who had been sponsored and a coparent to that person's parents. There can be baptismal sponsorship with few or no consequences. Such is the situation in much of the modern West, where sponsorship creates an insignificant godparent complex or none at all. But that has not been the historical norm. In traditional Christian societies past and present, everyone would recognize that in addition to kinship by common descent and kinship by marriage, they had a third sort of relative, the spiritual kinsman from sponsorship. Wherever Christianity took root, whether in seventh-century England, tenth-century Russia, or sixteenth-century Latin America, it introduced this new form of kinship. But within the shared framework of sponsorship/spiritual kinship, there have been significant variations. In modern America, for instance, most baptismal sponsors know they are somehow tied to the child they sponsored but are often unaware that in earlier times and in some contemporary societies their sponsorship would also have created a strong kinlike bond to the infant's parents. Many readers will be only marginally familiar with the theological, liturgical, and social importance of sponsorship in premodern and some contemporary Christian communities, the latter primarily in southern Europe and Latin America. Before sponsorship and spiritual kinship can be studied in Anglo-Saxon England, they must be explained in a wider context. Where did Christian sponsorship and spiritual kinship come from and what were their purposes?

Baptism was the first sacrament in Christian life and long regarded as the most important because it rescued sinful humans from the grip of Satan and admitted them to full membership in the Christian church. Christians understood baptism as more than a "ceremony," which is a weak and slightly pejorative term in English. They believed it changed the inner being of a person by wiping away original sin, freeing the neophyte (literally, "the newly planted") from demonic powers, and giving him or her a new life. Traditional Christian language, based on Scripture, described the change in various ways: the baptized person had "died" and "risen" with Christ[1]; had been taken from darkness and "enlightened"; had been made an "adopted" child of God[2]; or had been "reborn."[3]

The Sponsorship of Adults

The early Christian communities around the shores of the Mediterranean were rigorist in their demands on those who wished to join them. One consequence of that rigorism was that baptism was not easily granted. By the later second century, a process, called in modern literature "Christian initiation," was developing to prepare adults in a structured way for baptism. The person undergoing the long, theatrical initiation passed from paganism or Judaism to Christianity in three stages. The first stage in the transition was that from outsider to catechumen (from a Greek word meaning "one who is under instruction"). The second stage was that from catechumen to *competens* or *electus* (from Latin words meaning, respectively, "one who seeks" and "one who is chosen") or *photizomenos* (a Greek word meaning "one who is being enlightened"). The third stage was that from *competens* to *fidelis* ("one of the faithful"), when a person achieved full membership in the Christian community through completion of initiation in baptism.

The Catechumen

Catechumenos was a Greek Christian word for a person preparing for baptism. From it, modern scholars coined the word *catechumenate* to de-

1. See Romans 6:1–6.
2. See Romans 8:14–17; Galatians 4:5–6.
3. J. Ysebaert, *Greek Baptismal Terminology: Its Origin and Early Development,* Graecitas Christianorum primaeva 1 (Nijmegen, 1962). Walter Bedard, *The Symbolism of the Baptismal Font in*

scribe the process by which a person was initiated into Christianity.[4] By the early third century, unbaptized people who sought admission to a Christian community were investigated carefully and needed Christians in good standing to testify to their suitability "to hear the word."[5] Those who testified were sponsors who helped the unbeliever to cross the threshold into the community. If the persons requesting admission were accepted, they became catechumens in a ceremony that generally included making the sign of the cross on the candidates, giving them a taste of salt, and praying over them. The catechumens were in an intermediate state—they were Christians of a sort, no longer completely in the grip of demonic forces but not yet full members of the church. It is indicative of the catechumens' situation that the third-century writer Hippolytus warned that they should not exchange the kiss of peace with one another or with baptized members of the church because their "kiss was not yet holy."[6] Catechumens had no right to know the deeper mysteries—the *arcana*—of the faith, which were contained particularly in the eucharistic service and in the exact words of the Creed and the Lord's Prayer.[7] They could attend church services to hear the Scripture readings and sermons—"the Mass of the Catechumens"—but had to leave when the Eucharist began, which was reserved for the baptized, the *fideles.*

In the third century, admission of new members was serious business. The reluctance of most Christian churches to grant quick baptism meant that a person could be a catechumen for a long time. Hippolytus recommended a catechumenate of three years, although he granted that exceptional zeal could shorten the time.[8] During their period of testing, catechumens received religious instruction, but initiation was not merely a matter of the intellect. They were exorcised frequently to expel the demons who

---

Early Christian Thought (Washington, D.C., 1951), traced the view of the baptismal font as a tomb from which the spiritually dead arose and as a womb from which new Christians were born.

4. On Christian initiation, see the translated documents and commentary in Thomas M. Finn, *Early Christian Baptism and the Catechumenate: West and East Syria* (Collegeville, Minn., 1992) and *Early Christian Baptism and the Catechumenate: Italy, North Africa, and Egypt* (Collegeville, Minn. 1992). See also Michel Dujarier, *Le parrainage des adultes aux trois premiers siècles de l'Eglise: Recherche historique sur l'évolution des garanties et des étapes catéchuménales avant 313* (Paris, 1962); and Bernard de Guchteneëre, "Le parrainage des adultes aux ive et ve siècles de l'Eglise" (Excerpta ex dissertatione ad Lauream in Facultate Theologica Pontificiae Universitatis Gregorianae, Louvain, 1964).

5. Hippolytus, *The Apostolic Tradition,* c. 15–16, in *La Tradition Apostolique d'après les anciennes versions,* 2d ed. Bernard Botte, *SC* 11bis (Paris, 1968), pp. 68–74.

6. Ibid. c. 18, p. 70.

7. On the *disciplina arcani,* see *The Study of Liturgy,* rev. ed. by Cheslyn Jones, Geoffrey Wainwright, Edward Yarnold, and Paul Bradshaw (London and New York, 1992), pp. 141–42.

8. Hippolytus, *Apostolic Tradition,* c. 17, pp. 74–75.

were thought to possess the unbaptized. In addition, their personal behavior was closely observed. When a catechumen eventually sought baptism, another sponsor testified to his or her good intentions and honorable behavior during the catechumenate.

The nature of the catechumenate changed significantly during the fourth and fifth centuries, when the Roman Empire legalized and subsequently favored Catholic Christianity. Pagans poured into the Christian churches, which still required them to become catechumens. The pressure of numbers, however, forced a relaxation in the traditional rigor of the catechumenate, which continued to function in an increasingly vestigial form. By the late fourth century, there was no instruction for catechumens beyond that which they might get by attending the religious services open to them, and there was no deadline as to when they had to be baptized. Some people remained catechumens for years or even a lifetime, especially men, whose expected sexual sins made them reluctant to take on the moral burden of baptism. The penitential system was very demanding on the baptized but less so on catechumens, whose sins, however enormous, would be washed away whenever they chose to be baptized.[9] In his *Confessions,* Augustine of Hippo described just such an attitude toward baptism in the middle decades of the fourth century in North Africa. His pious mother, Monica, had enrolled him in the catechumenate "from birth" but had delayed his baptism on the grounds that he would "defile" himself with sin and that "after baptism, the guilt of pollution would be greater":

> When I was still a boy, I had heard about eternal life promised to us through the humility of our Lord God, coming down to our pride, and I was already signed with the sign of His cross and seasoned with salt from the time I came from my mother's womb. She greatly put her trust in you. You saw, Lord, how one day, when I was still a small boy, pressure on the chest suddenly made me hot with fever and almost at death's door. You saw, my God, because you were already my guardian, with what fervour of mind and with what faith I then begged for the baptism of your Christ, my God and Lord, urging it on the devotion of my mother and of the mother of us all, your Church. My physical mother [Monica] was distraught. With a pure heart and faith in you she even more lovingly travailed in labour for my eternal salvation. She hastily made arrangements for me to be initiated and washed in the sacraments of salvation, confessing you, Lord Jesus, for the remission of sins. But suddenly I recovered. My cleansing was deferred on the assump-

9. On the rigors of public penance for serious sins committed after baptism, see Cyrille Vogel, *La discipline pénitentielle en Gaule des origines à la fin du viie siècle* (Paris, 1952), pp. 29–67.

> tion that, if I lived, I would be sure to soil myself; and after that solemn washing the guilt would be greater and more dangerous if I then defiled myself with sins.[10]

Like many other fourth-century males, including Ambrose of Milan, Augustine remained a catechumen until his mid-thirties, when he had a religious conversion in the Pauline sense and Ambrose baptized him at Milan on Easter, 387.

The *Competens*

Faced with large numbers of catechumens who delayed baptism, fourth- and fifth-century bishops concentrated their efforts on intensive preparation of those who wished to proceed to baptism. Except for catechumens threatened by an emergency, such as life-threatening illness, all were baptized at one of the great religious festivals, normally Easter or Pentecost. About forty days before Easter or Pentecost, the catechumens who wanted to be baptized "gave in their names" and received a new status, in Greek areas that of *photizomenos,* at Rome *electus,* and elsewhere in Latin-speaking areas *competens.* Modern scholars have called the period of intense preparation for baptism the "competentate." There was considerable variation in the competentate from one region to another, but the basic structure was fixed by the mid-fourth century. The *competentes* put aside their ordinary lives for the weeks of preparation, which were sometimes called the Forty Days, and later Lent. If the *competentes* lived in the countryside, they might come to the bishop's city to participate in baptismal preparation, which included fasting, sexual abstinence, frequent exorcisms, instruction in Scripture, and daily church services.[11]

To become a *competens,* a catechumen needed a sponsor who would testify to his or her worthiness to be baptized and accompany the catechumen during the weeks of initiation. It must have been a burdensome duty for the sponsors, who had to disrupt their own lives for several weeks.[12] Egeria, a fourth-century female pilgrim from somewhere in the west, perhaps Spain, wrote for her sisters at home an informative account of her travels in

10. Augustine, *Confessionum libri xiii,* 1.11, ed. L. Verheijen, *CCSL* 27 (Turnhout, 1981), pp. 9–10: Trans. Henry Chadwick, *Confessions* (Oxford, 1991), pp. 13–14.
11. On the baptismal preparation for adults during Augustine's episcopate at Hippo, see F. Van der Meer, *Augustine the Bishop,* trans. Brian Battershaw and G. R. Lamb (London, 1961), pp. 353–61. See also Robert de Latte, "Saint Augustin et le baptême: Etude liturgico-historique du rituel baptismal des adultes chez Saint Augustin," *QLP* 56 (1976).
12. Lynch, *Godparents,* pp. 83–116.

the eastern Mediterranean.[13] She was at Jerusalem for Easter in the last decade of the fourth century and recorded her observations, which included an unparalleled account of the competentate. At Jerusalem, early in Lent, those who wished to be baptized "gave in their names," which were recorded on a list. The bishop and his clergy then examined each candidate in a solemn, public gathering. Those whom they accepted for baptism were instructed and exorcised daily during the weeks preceding Easter. Egeria's eyewitness account is worth quoting.

> Once the priest has all the names, on the second day of Lent at the start of the eight weeks, the bishop's chair is placed in the middle of the Great Church. . . , the presbyters sit in chairs on either side of him, and all [the rest of] the clergy stand. Then one by one those seeking baptism are brought up, men coming with their fathers and women with their mothers. As they come in one by one, the bishop asks their neighbors questions about them: "Is this person leading a good life? Does he respect his parents? Is he a drunkard or a boaster?" He asks about all the serious human vices. And if his inquiries show him that someone has not committed any of these misdeeds, he himself puts down his name; but if someone is guilty he is told to go away, and the bishop tells him that he is to amend his ways before he may come to the font. He asks the men and the women the same questions. But it is not too easy for a stranger to come to baptism if he has no witnesses who are acquainted with him.[14]

In Egeria's account, catechumens who wanted to give in their names for baptism needed the favorable testimony of sponsors, who included neighbors and persons called "mothers" for the female candidates and "fathers" for the male candidates. For some catechumens, these might have been their biological parents, but that is unlikely when they were from pagan or Jewish families or persons whose biological parents were absent or dead. Whether biological parent or not, all sponsors could be called mothers and fathers in a spiritual sense: they were participating in the spiritual gestation and baptismal rebirth of the *competens*.[15]

Mothers, fathers, and neighbors shared in the sponsorship of adult candidates by providing testimony to the bishop about the behavior of the candidates during the catechumenate. Egeria reported that after the *competentes* were accepted for baptism and were enrolled by name on the bap-

13. Egeria, *Itinerarium,* ed. A. Franceschini and R. Weber, *CCSL* 175 (Turnhout, 1965) Trans. John Wilkinson, *Egeria's Travels* (London, 1971).

14. Ibid., c. 45.2–4, p. 87 and trans., pp. 143–44.

15. A. A. R. Bastiaensen, *Observations sur le vocabulaire liturgique dans l'Itineraire d'Egérie* (Nijmegen and Utrecht, 1962), pp. 17–19, interpreted *patres* and *matres* as fourth-century terms for sponsors.

tismal list, they came to church with their "mothers" and "fathers" every day during Lent for exorcisms and instruction by the bishop: "During the forty days, he goes through the whole Bible, beginning with Genesis, and first relating the literal meaning of each passage, and then interpreting its spiritual meaning."[16] During the final week of Lent, called the Great Week, the preparation for baptism intensified. Among other things, accompanied by their "mothers" and "fathers," the candidates personally recited to the bishop the Creed, which they had been given to memorize.

Perhaps because Egeria wanted to respect the traditional Christian reluctance to describe the religious mysteries, she wrote nothing about the actual baptism, which took place on Easter morning. She did note that the newly baptized came to sermons during the following week in their white baptismal robes, accompanied by their "mothers" and "fathers." During the week after baptism the bishop instructed them about the deeper meaning of the ceremonies they had experienced. Egeria noted that the applause of the newly baptized listeners could be heard through the closed doors of the church. No unbaptized person, including a catechumen, was allowed to hear these sermons, called mystagogic because the hearer was led into the meaning of the baptismal mysteries.[17]

Thus, from the third century, sponsors for adults testified twice in Christian initiation, first at the admission to the catechumenate and second at the admission to the competentate. They also accompanied the *competentes* when they passed into the third stage as baptized Christians. Even though Egeria's "mothers" and "fathers" accompanied the *competens* during the preparation, the adult candidates made personal commitments, which they expressed in their own words and gestures, as for example when each *competens* recited the Creed.

The Sponsorship of Infants

The structured process of Christian initiation had been developed for adults, who could understand religious instruction and make personal commitments. Even the relatively young could be initiated in the traditional liturgy. For instance, Augustine thought that by age seven, children

16. Egeria, *Itinerarium*, c. 46.1–3, pp. 87–88; Wilkinson, p. 144.

17. Egeria, *Itinerarium*, cc. 46–47, pp. 88–89. On the mystagogic sermons delivered to the newly baptized, see Hugh M. Riley, *Christian Initiation: A Comparative Study of the Interpretation of the Baptismal Liturgy in the Mystagogical Writings of Cyril of Jerusalem, John Chrysostom, Theodore of Mopsuestia, and Ambrose of Milan* (Washington, D.C., 1974). There is a clear account of Christian initiation at Antioch in Thomas M. Finn, *The Liturgy of Baptism in the Baptismal Instructions of St. John Chrysostom* (Washington, D.C., 1967).

could distinguish truth from falsehood, recite the Creed, and respond for themselves to the baptismal questions. Hence they could participate as adults in their own baptism.[18]

The acceptance of infant baptism posed a challenge to the traditional initiation. The origins of infant baptism are disputed but lie partly in changing views of the moral status of infants. The earliest Christians seem to have had an optimistic view; for in 1 Corinthians 7:12–14, Paul advised Christian spouses married to unbelievers to remain in the marriage: "This is because the unbelieving husband is made one with the saints through his wife, and the unbelieving wife is made one with the saints through her husband. *If this were not so, your children would be unclean, whereas in fact they are holy.*" But as the conviction grew that all human beings, including infants, were polluted by Adam's sin and consequently damned without baptism, parents were reluctant to allow their children to die unbaptized, a real danger in a world with high rates of infant mortality.[19] An unbaptized child's serious illness must have forced some parents to seek baptism, as in the case of Augustine cited above, who would have been baptized if he had not recovered from illness. By the late second or early third century, some Christian families were deciding to have their children baptized young, whether they were ill or not. The older, optimistic view of the young still had its supporters. Tertullian (c. 160–c. 225) urged the delay of baptism of the very young, in part because those who spoke on their behalf—whom he called *sponsores*—could not in reality guarantee that the youngsters would be good Christians when they grew older.[20] In third-century North Africa, where infant baptism may already have been widespread, the debate seems to have been about how soon after birth an infant might be baptized. A certain bishop had forbidden newborn infants to be baptized before the eighth day after birth, on analogy to the circumcision rule in Leviticus 12:3. Bishop Cyprian of Carthage (248–258), supported by a council of sixty-six North African bishops, rebuked him and declared that newborns could be baptized immediately after birth.[21] By the late fourth century, infant baptism was firmly rooted in Christian practice.

18. Robert de Latte, "Saint Augustin et le baptême: Etude liturgico-historique du rituel baptismal des enfants chez Saint Augustin," *QLP* 57(1976) pp. 42–43.

19. Lynch, *Godparents,* pp. 117–21. Although Joachim Jeremias, *Infant Baptism in the First Four Centuries,* trans. David Cairns (Philadelphia, 1962), argued that infant baptism could be found in the New Testament, Kurt Aland, *Did the Early Church Baptize Infants?* trans. G. R. Beasley-Murray (London, 1961), made a stronger case that the first secure references to the practice come from around the year 200.

20. Tertullian, *De baptismo,* c. 5, ed. R. F. Refoulé in collaboration with M. Drouzy, *SC* 35 (Paris, 1952), pp. 93–94.

21. Cyprian, *Epistola* 64, in *S. Thasci Caecili Cypriani opera omnia,* ed. Guilelmus Haertel, *CSEL* 3/2 (Vienna, 1871), pp. 718–21.

The traditional system of initiation, created for adults, had to be adapted to the baptism of infants and children younger than about seven. In his *Apostolic Tradition,* Hippolytus was primarily concerned with the sponsorship and baptism of adults, which he described in detail. As an afterthought, he briefly described the sponsorship of the very young at Rome in the early third century: "First baptize the little ones. Let all [the little ones] who are able to speak for themselves speak. However if they are not able to speak for themselves, let their parents or someone from their kin speak for them."[22] The main consideration for Hippolytus was whether the child could speak for itself. If it could, such a child was to be baptized as an adult. If it could not speak on its own behalf, then it needed helpers, whom Hippolytus identified as parents or kinsmen. In order to baptize the very young in liturgies intended for adults, a second kind of sponsorship developed, which coexisted for a time with that of adults. The sponsors for infants acted on behalf of and made promises about the *future* behavior of the youngster who was being baptized. They were distinct from the sponsors for adults, who testified about the *past* behavior of catechumens and *competentes.*[23]

If Hippolytus had written in A.D. 530 instead of A.D. 230, he might have reversed his emphasis, describing infant baptism in detail and giving cursory treatment to adult baptism. By then, a profound change in the sociology of Christianity had shifted the focus of baptism from adults to infants. In the Christian communities of the fifth and sixth centuries, the ordinary candidates for baptism were the infants and young children of Christian families. The liturgy was conservative and not substantially revised for those so young they could neither speak, memorize and recite the Creed, nor make personal commitments. Instead the liturgy for adults was retained but, as in Hippolytus's day, an adult acted, spoke, and promised on behalf of each child. Because they made promises about the infant's future behavior, the sponsors were committing themselves to a long-term relationship with the child. If they were the child's parents, which was usually the case in the church of the later Roman Empire, then religious and familial obligations reinforced one another. If they were not the child's biological parents, as might happen for orphans, foundlings, and slave children, a quasi-parental relationship was potentially created.[24]

22. Hippolytus, *Apostolic Tradition,* c. 21, p. 80.

23. Latte, "Saint Augustin et le baptême . . . des enfants."

24. Christianne Brusselmans, "Les fonctions de parrainage des enfants aux premiers siècles de l'Eglise, 100–550" (Ph.D. diss., CUA, 1964), is an excellent treatment of the sources on the sponsorship of infants. Augustine, *Epistola* 98.6, in *S. Aureli Augustini hipponiensis episcopi epistulae,* ed. A. Goldbacher, *CSEL* 34 (Vienna, 1895), pp. 527–28, noted that as a form of piety, consecrated virgins offered slaves, orphans, and abandoned children for baptism.

For a time, the two sorts of sponsorship coexisted, but as the baptism of adults became uncommon, infant baptism predominated, with its particular kind of sponsor. The sponsorship of adults survived in fossilized form in liturgical prayers and was sometimes revived temporarily when missionary activity led to the conversion of adults. But in Christianized regions during the Middle Ages, the sponsorship of infants was the dominant practice, with its implication of a personal relationship that continued after baptism, perhaps for the lifetime of sponsor and child. In those circumstances, the sponsors for adults came to resemble those for infants. It was primarily out of infant sponsorship that spiritual kinship and the godparent complex arose, although sponsorship alone did not create a godparent complex. A theology of sponsorship was needed to transform liturgical actions into a pattern of social behavior.

The Theology of Sponsorship

As often happens in the development of theology, sponsorship was a fact before it attracted the attention of theologians, who tried to give it a meaning within their understanding of baptism. When late ancient and early medieval churchmen wrote about baptism, they often used imagery and analogies drawn from family life. They taught that human beings came from their mothers' wombs physically alive but spiritually dead because of original sin. In baptism they were born a second time—in a spiritual way. A second birth naturally suggested a second set of parents. In some instances God was said to be the father, and the Church the mother, in the second, spiritual birth.[25] But there was a competing interpretation that saw the sponsor as the spiritual parent at the second birth. When biological parents sponsored their own children, they were both natural and spiritual parents. In a letter to Bishop Boniface of Cataquas, written between 408 and 411, Augustine argued that there was an appropriate symmetry in parental sponsorship: biological parents who had transmitted original sin to their child should participate in its removal by baptism.[26]

Between the third and the seventh centuries, writers concerned with canon law or theology did not express interest in whether the sponsor was a parent or nonparent, as long as some adult helped the child to go through Christian initiation. Some infants, for example foundlings and orphans, had necessarily to be sponsored by nonparents.[27] But the participation of

25. Bedard, *Symbolism of the Baptismal Font,* pp. 17–36.
26. Augustine, *Epistula* 98.6, p. 527.
27. Ibid., pp. 527–28.

biological parents was gradually undermined and eventually abandoned entirely. At least three factors contributed to the imposition of a taboo on parents sponsoring their own child. The strongest reason for the exclusion of parents was a change in the view of sexual contact among baptismal participants. During the seventh and eighth centuries, there was a remarkable change in attitude about the sexual significance of spiritual kinship. The physical and spiritual births were no longer regarded as complementary; they were opposites. Physical birth was rooted in sexual relations and accompanied by pain and blood; spiritual birth was rooted in God's grace and accompanied by blessed water and prayers. Biological and spiritual parents became polar opposites—the former responsible for carnal birth and the latter for spiritual rebirth.[28] Second, in sixth- and seventh-century Byzantium, Italy, and Frankish Gaul, biological parents and the sponsors of their children came to be regarded as related to one another in spiritual kinship through the child. They were literally "coparents" of their common child and as such were forbidden to marry one another in order to prevent sexual relations among spiritual kin, which were regarded as a kind of incest.[29] This view made the centuries-old practice of biological parents sponsoring their own child dangerous, because if parents sponsored, they became coparents to their own spouses, with whom subsequent sexual relations were forbidden. To guarantee a distinction between physical and spiritual birth and to prevent spouses from becoming coparents to one another, biological parents were formally forbidden to sponsor their own child in the Byzantine Empire about 727 and in the Frankish kingdom in 813.[30] In about 840 the Frankish scholar Walafrid Strabo explained the matter thus. "A father or mother must not receive their own offspring [in baptism], so that there may be a distinction between spiritual and carnal generation. If by chance that [sponsorship] happens, they who have taken the spiritual bond of coparenthood in their common child will not henceforth have the sharing of carnal intercourse."[31] The third factor was that

28. Lynch, *Godparents,* pp. 219–57.

29. The earliest texts that explicitly or by implication forbade coparents to marry are: for Byzantium, Council in Trullo (692), c. 53, in *Iuris ecclesiastici Graecorum historia et monumenta,* vol. 2, ed. J. B. Pitra (Rome, 1868), p. 51, and in Mansi 11, col. 967; for Italy, Roman Council of 721, c. 4, in Mansi 12, col. 263; for Frankish Gaul, *Liber historiae francorum* (about 735), c. 31, ed. Bruno Krusch, *MGH SRM* 2 (Hanover 1888), pp. 292–93, and Boniface, *Epistolae* 32, 33, and 34 (about 735), pp. 55–59.

30. Leo III and Constantine V, *Novella* (31 March 726–30 March 727), in Dieter Simon, "Zur Ehegesetzgebung der Isaurier," in *Fontes minores,* vol. 1, Forschungen zur byzantinischen Rechtsgeschichte 1 (Frankfurt am Main, 1976), pp. 22–23; Council of Mainz (813), c. 55, in *Concilia aevi Karolini,* ed. Albert Werminghoff, *MGH Concilia* 2/1 (Hanover, 1906), p. 273: "Nullus igitur proprium filium vel filiam de fonte baptismatis suscipiat."

31. Walafrid Strabo, *Libellus de exordiis et incrementis quarundam in observationibus ecclesiae,* c. 27, *MGH Capitularia* 2 (Hanover, 1897), p. 512.

biological parents saw an advantage to be gained by inviting as sponsor an outsider, who would be a friend, patron, and kinsman to their child and to themselves.

As parents withdrew or were pushed from sponsorship of their own children, baptismal sponsorship moved from being a liturgical detail to a social force. By the mid-eighth century, every baptized person had two distinct kinds of parents, natural and spiritual. The bond linking the spiritual parent to the child was what modern scholars call godparenthood. The bond linking the biological and spiritual parent to one another was what they call coparenthood. Until the later ninth century there was only one sponsor per child, so that the status of sponsor was a scarce and valued commodity.[32] Although they lost the right to sponsor their own child, biological parents gained the opportunity to bestow an honor and to create a kinsman when they chose a sponsor. All responsible adults could expect to be asked. A web of spiritual kin paralleled that of blood kin and of affinal kin. Since at least the eighth century, godparent complexes flourished in Byzantium and most of the Latin west.

The Proliferation of Spiritual Kin

The relationship of godparent to godchild and that of coparents to one another did not exhaust the social possibilities of sponsorship. The spiritual family tended to expand to resemble the biological family. In Byzantium and Italy, the children of the sponsor became the spiritual kin of the sponsored child: spiritual siblings (*spiritalis germani*).[33] In addition, the cleric who baptized, whether bishop, priest, or deacon, also entered the spiritual family as a spiritual father.[34] Finally, in some circumstances married sponsors could transmit their godparenthood and coparenthood to their spouses;

32. The earliest councils to oppose the multiplication of baptismal sponsors are the Council of Metz (893), c. 6, in Mansi 18, col. 79, and the Council of Coblenz (922), c. 3, in *Constitutiones et acta publica imperatorum et regum,* 1:630 ed. L. Weiland, *MGH Legum* 4 (Hanover, 1893), 1:630.

33. For Byzantium, see Ecloga 2.2, in *Ecloga: Das Gesetzbuch Leons III und Konstantinos V,* ed. Ludwig Burgmann (Frankfurt am Main, 1983), p. 170, which forbade the sponsor's son to marry the girl who had been sponsored or her mother. See also Ruth Macrides, "The Byzantine Godfather," *Byzantine and Modern Greek Studies* 11 (1987), 143–44. For Lombard Italy, see King Liutprand, *Leges Liutprandi regis,* 34, ed. Fr. Bluhme, *MGH Leges* 4 (Hanover, 1868), p. 124: "Item hoc censimus adque precipimus, ut nullus presumat cummatrem suam uxorem ducere, sed nec filiam, quam de sacro fonte levavit; neque filius eius presumat filiam illius uxorem ducere, qui eum de fonte suscipit, quia spiritualis germani esse noscuntur"; see also Zachary, *Epistola* to Theodore of Pavia (Jaffé 2306) in *Epistolae langobardicae collectae,* ed. Wilhelm Gundlach, *MGH Epistolae* 3 (Berlin, 1892), p. 710.

34. Lynch, *Godparents,* pp. 165–69.

who had not personally sponsored. The tendency of the spiritual family to expand was thus remarkable. However much it varied in extent from one godparent complex to another, the spiritual family became a permanent feature in the social interaction of medieval Christians.

Sponsorship and spiritual kinship also took root away from the Mediterranean when Germanic peoples adopted Christianity. Gerd Althoff has described early medieval Germanic societies as in principle *friedlos,* literally "peace-less," because conflict was assumed as the normal state of affairs.[35] Peace and cooperation were promoted by forms of association, such as a kin group (*Verwandtschaft*), a community (*Genossenschaft*), or a lordship (*Herrschaft*). If a peace-making form of association did not exist among those who wanted to cooperate, it had to be created by such practices as marriage, oaths, feudal commendation, and numerous forms of "adoption."[36] Sponsorship was integrated into Germanic societies in part because it created a particularly desirable form of kinship, which was religiously sanctioned.[37] Sponsorship could create kinship where none had previously existed or it could strengthen preexisting bonds, as when children were sponsored by their uncles or brothers. As the mid-ninth-century author of the *Vita Bertini* put it, Saint Bertin became coparent to a married couple by sponsoring their child "in accordance with that praiseworthy custom dedicated to joining the bonds of brotherly love among Christians."[38]

The Scope of Research

In the early Middle Ages, the interaction of the practice of sponsorship and the theology of baptismal rebirth gave rise to godparent complexes, which did not develop in a uniform way. Significant variations existed—and still exist—in the concrete manifestations. Anthropological research has emphasized that the complexes can differ significantly from one society to another and, within societies, from one social class to another. But some fundamental features are recognizable across wide spans of space and time:

35. Gerd Althoff, *Verwandte, Freunde, und Getreue: Zum politischen Stellenwert der Gruppenbindungen im früheren Mittelalter* (Darmstadt, 1990), p. 2.
36. Althoff, *Verwandte,* pp. 31–84; Max Pappenheim, "Über künstliche Verwandtschaft im germanischen Rechte," ZSSRG, Germanistische Abteilung 29 (1908).
37. Althoff, *Verwandte,* pp. 77–84.
38. *Vita Bertini,* c. 19, ed. Bruno Krusch and Wilhelm Levinson, *MGH SRM* 5 (Hanover, 1910), p. 765: "et compater fuit secundum laudabilem ritum, inter christianos ad coniungenda fraternae caritatis foedera consecratum."

1. The sponsorship of infants at baptism was the primary model, on which other forms of sponsorship were built.
2. The spiritual family always embraced sponsors and sponsored and might also include the parents of the sponsored child, spiritual siblings, and the baptizing clergyman.
3. The kinship created by sponsorship was sometimes regarded as more binding than other forms of kinship because it was rooted in baptismal grace.
4. Sex and grace came to be regarded as incompatible, so sexual relations between godparent and godchild were forbidden and the sexual prohibition often extended to coparents and to anyone classified as a spiritual relative.
5. Biological parents were excluded from sponsorship to prevent them from becoming spiritual kin to one another.
6. The obligation to invite outsiders to sponsor provided an opportunity to choose sponsors for social ends, which may be summarized as making new kinsmen for the child, for the child's parents, as well as for the sponsor, the sponsor's spouse, and the sponsor's children.

There is a vast literature on the godparent complexes of modern times, primarily in Latin America, Italy, Spain, and Greece.[39] The historical study of the godparent complexes in Europe is, however, less developed. Since my book on early medieval forms of the godparent complex appeared in 1986, a number of books and articles have been published. Bernhard Jussen analyzed evidence on the godparent complex both in sixth-century Frankish society and in the later Middle Ages.[40] Ruth Macrides provided an introduction to the Byzantine godparent complex.[41] Christiane Klapisch-Zuber has written extensively on sponsorship in late medieval and early

39. Hugo Nutini and Betty Bell, *Ritual Kinship: The Structure and Historical Development of the Compadrazgo System in Rural Tlaxcala* (Princeton, 1980), 1:405–28, surveyed 250 studies of the godparent complex in Latin America. Since 1980, many more have been published. On Italy, see Italo Signorini, *Padrini e compadri: Un'analisi antropologica della parentela spirituale* (Turin, 1981); on Spain, see George Foster, "Cofradría and Compadrazgo in Spain and Spanish America," *Southwestern Journal of Anthropology* 9 (1953), and Julian Pitt-Rivers, "Ritual Kinship in Spain," *Transactions of the New York Academy of Sciences*, 2d ser. 20 (1958); on Greece, see J. K. Campbell, *Honour, Family, and Patronage: A Study of Institutions and Moral Values in a Greek Mountain Community* (Oxford, 1962), pp. 217–24.

40. Bernhard Jussen, *Patenschaft und Adoption im frühen Mittelalter: Künstliche Verwandtschaft als soziale Praxis* (Göttingen, 1991), and "Le parrainage à la fin du Moyen Age: Savoir publique, attentes théologiques, et usages sociaux," *AESC* 47 (1992).

41. Macrides, "Byzantine Godfather," pp. 139–62.

modern Italy, primarily Florence.[42] Agnès Fine synthesized studies of the godparent complex in early modern and modern times, with an emphasis on France and Italy.[43] Local, regional, and topical studies are still needed, however, before a wide-ranging and complete history of the godparent complex in European history is possible.

The fully developed godparent complex, particularly with extensive sexual prohibitions, took shape in the Byzantine Empire in the sixth and seventh centuries. During the late seventh and eighth centuries it was transmitted to Frankish Gaul, where sponsorship and spiritual kinship were long known but had few clear sexual consequences. The eighth-century popes, with their ties to Byzantium and to the Frankish kingdom, were the primary conduits that brought the sexual prohibitions to the Franks. After the mid-eighth century the popes were supported by Frankish reformers.

The Anglo-Saxons practiced infant baptism, and hence sponsorship, from the moment their conversion began in the late sixth century. The transmission of the godparent complex with sexual prohibitions from east to west meant, however, that the Anglo-Saxon church, which was at the western edge of Latin Christendom, was late in adopting that sort of complex. Instead, the Anglo-Saxons adapted sponsorship and its potential for creating kinship to their own social structures and diplomatic needs, creating a unique form of the godparent complex with its own history and special features. In the early Anglo-Saxon church, from 597 to about 830, the godparent complex differed from that on the Continent in that it stressed the godparent/godchild bond, neglected the coparental bond, and acknowledged no sexual consequences from sponsorship.

The Viking incursions and settlements of the ninth century created a break in the written sources. Virtually nothing can be known about baptism, sponsorship, and spiritual kinship until the sources reappear after the 890s. When Anglo-Saxon society recovered its stability in the tenth century, a new phase began in the history of Anglo-Saxon Christianity, and of the godparent complex. The tenth- and eleventh-century religious revival of the Anglo-Saxon church drew heavily on Continental sources, which introduced into the late Anglo-Saxon church the "modern" Frankish form of the godparent complex; but even then the sexual taboos, so prominent on the Continent, made little headway in the face of Anglo-Saxon tradition. It

42. See, e.g., Christiane Klapisch-Zuber, "Compérage et clientélisme à Florence, 1360–1520," *Ricerche Storiche* 15 (1985), or "Parrains et filleuls: Une approche comparée de la France, l'Angleterre, et l'Italie médiévales," *Medieval Prosopography* 6 (1985).
43. Agnès Fine, *Parrains, marraines: La parenté spirituelle en Europe* (Paris, 1994).

was only after the Norman Conquest of 1066 that the godparent complex in England was assimilated to that of northern France, although it retained features that made it distinct from those of Italy and Byzantium. This book explores the nature, evolution, and impact of the godparent complex in Anglo-Saxon England.

CHAPTER 2

The Missionaries and Baptism

Christianity came to the Anglo-Saxons as a well-developed religion, but through the efforts of missionaries from different regions who brought significant variations that persisted for a long time. Missionaries from Rome and from Irish Iona, as well as a few bishops from Frankish Gaul, Italy, and even Byzantium, were active among the Anglo-Saxons between 597 and 690, after which the episcopate was entirely Anglo-Saxon. There are no surviving baptismal rituals from the missionary period, and baptismal practices must be tentatively reconstructed by comparison with contemporary Continental practices.[1] There is no evidence that Celtic Christians of the sixth and seventh centuries had a godparent complex, but the Roman and Frankish missionaries certainly knew about it because some form of it was traditional in their homelands. An examination of the baptismal practices in sixth- and seventh-century Rome and Frankish Gaul sheds light on the sponsoring practices and godparent complexes the missionaries might have brought to the Anglo-Saxons.

Baptism at Rome

Pope Gregory I (590–604) sent the earliest missionaries directly from Rome. When the Italian monk Augustine and his party landed in Kent in

1. Sarah Foot, " 'By Water in the Spirit': The Administration of Baptism in Early Anglo-Saxon England," in *Pastoral Care before the Parish,* ed. John Blair and Richard Sharpe (Leicester, 1992); on uncertainties about the earliest baptismal liturgies in England, see pp. 172–75.

597, they brought with them the Roman Christianity of their day. In view of the centrality of liturgy in early medieval Christian life, Augustine and subsequent missionaries certainly brought liturgical books, including some form of the prayers and gestures used to carry out a baptism.[2] Liturgical books must have been imported repeatedly, although information survives on only a few instances. Bede reported that when Pope Gregory sent a second group of missionaries in 601, he dispatched objects necessary for proper Christian worship and ministry: "sacred vessels, altar cloths and church ornaments, vestments for priests and clerics, relics of the holy apostles and martyrs, and also many books (*codices plurimos*)," though unfortunately he did not specify what the books were. The things sent were, however, entirely for liturgical purposes, and some of the books were certainly liturgical.[3] The Anglo-Saxon monastic founder Benedict Biscop (628–689) went to Rome five times, beginning in 653. On his fourth visit, he brought back religious books he had purchased or been given, along with relics, paintings, and liturgical objects.[4] Abbot Ceolfrith of Jarrow also brought back books from Rome.[5] When Archbishop Theodore of Tarsus and Abbot Hadrian arrived from Rome in 669, they too must have brought books, including liturgical ones.

No liturgical book used by Augustine and his successors is known to survive, but that gap in our knowledge is not unusual. Early medieval liturgical books must have existed in hundreds of copies, but they were practical books, used frequently, and prone to be worn out. Furthermore, older books became obsolete as liturgy changed, and many were destroyed or discarded. For those reasons, few liturgical texts survive from anywhere in western Europe before the eighth century.[6]

2. G. G. Willis, "Early English Liturgy from Augustine to Alcuin," in *Further Essays in Early Roman Liturgy* (London, 1968), pp. 191–97; Margaret Deanesly, *The Pre-Conquest Church in England* (New York, 1961), p. 59. David Dumville, "The Importation of Mediterranean Manuscripts into Theodore's England," in *Archbishop Theodore: Commemorative Studies on His Life and Influence,* ed. Michael Lapidge (Cambridge, 1995), believes hundreds of manuscripts came from southern Europe to Anglo-Saxon England in the seventh and eighth centuries, of which only eleven can now be identified.

3. Bede, *HE,* 1.29, pp. 105–6.

4. Bede, *Historia abbatum,* c. 4, in *Venerabilis Baedae opera historica,* ed. Charles Plummer (Oxford, 1896), 2: 367: "librosque omnis divinae eruditionis non paucos uel placito praetio emptos, uel amicorum dono largitos retulit." On Benedict Biscop's voyages to Rome and book collecting, see ibid., c. 6, p. 369, c. 9, p. 373, and c. 11, p. 375; and *HE,* 4.18 and 5.19.

5. *Vita Ceolfridi,* c. 20, in *Venerabilis Baedae opera historica,* 2: 395: "et bibliothecam, quam de Roma uel ipse, uel Benedictus adtulerat, nobiliter ita ampliavit."

6. On the development of the liturgy and the surviving texts from before the eighth century, see Cyrille Vogel, *Medieval Liturgy: An Introduction to the Sources,* trans. and rev. William G. Storey and Niels K. Rasmussen (Washington, D.C., 1986), pp. 31–59.

Conditions in Anglo-Saxon England, especially during the ninth century, were unfavorable to the survival of liturgical books. In his preface to the translation of Pope Gregory's *Pastoral Care,* King Alfred lamented that even before the Viking raids, there was a decline of literacy in Latin among the clergy, which might imply a slackening in copying books, including liturgical ones.[7] The absence of liturgical books from early Anglo-Saxon England was exacerbated by that region's violent history. In the ninth century, Viking raids and settlements inflicted severe troubles on the Anglo-Saxon kingdoms. The invaders looted churches and monasteries and destroyed libraries. As a consequence, no complete liturgical book from Anglo-Saxon England survives from before the Danish invasions.[8] When the military victories of the kings of Wessex made possible a religious and cultural recovery in the late ninth and tenth centuries, liturgical books were often imported from the Carolingian kingdom. Hence, traces of the pre-Viking Anglo-Saxon liturgy are very rare. As we do not know with certainty which baptismal ceremonies Augustine of Canterbury introduced into Kent, we must try to assess the possibilities.

Rome is the logical place to look for a general idea of Augustine's baptismal liturgy. Augustine was prior of St. Andrew's monastery in Rome when Pope Gregory sent him on his missionary journey. He encountered very unfamiliar circumstances in Kent, which was pagan in religion, Germanic in culture, nonliterate, and without cities. He seems to have consulted Pope Gregory on pressing issues. Bede incorporated into his *Ecclesiastical History* a *Libellus responsionum,* which was a set of answers from Pope Gregory I to questions posed by Augustine arising out of his experience in England. There has been much controversy about the authenticity of the *Libellus.*[9] In the second response, Gregory wrote: "My brother, you know the customs of the Roman church in which, of course, you were brought up. But it is my wish that if you have found any customs in the Roman or Gaulish church or any other church which may be more pleasing to Almighty God, you should make a careful selection of them and sedulously teach the Church of the English, which is still new in the faith, what you have been able to gather from other churches."[10]

7. *EHD,* pp. 887–88.
8. Willis, *Further Essays,* p. 192.
9. On the complicated transmission of the *Libellus* and doubts about its authenticity, see Paul Meyvaert, "Bede's Text of the *Libellus responsionum* of Gregory the Great to Augustine of Canterbury," in *England before the Conquest: Studies in Primary Sources Presented to Dorothy Whitelock* (Cambridge, 1971), who cautiously accepted its authenticity.
10. Bede, *HE,* 1.27, pp. 80–83. Willis, *Further Essays,* p. 197, argued for the authenticity of this section of the *Libellus responsionum.*

In the early Middle Ages, liturgical diversity was a deeply rooted fact. Although the bishops of Rome sought liturgical uniformity in the suburbicarian dioceses directly under their control in Italy, they did not expect it elsewhere.[11] Thus Augustine and his successors had some freedom in choosing a baptismal ritual or, as it is properly called, an *ordo,* although their Roman roots must have heavily influenced their choice.

Liturgical activity at Rome in the sixth and seventh centuries was vigorous. The liturgy was evolving but extant documents are scarce. As a consequence, precision about the baptismal liturgy is rarely possible, although approximations are. What do we know about sponsorship and the godparent complex at Rome in the late fifth or sixth centuries? Three important texts, one a century earlier than Augustine and two at least a half century later, provide a general idea.

John the Deacon's *Letter to Senarius*

In the last decade of the fifth century, John the Deacon, who might later have been Pope John I (523–526), wrote to a learned lay aristocrat, Senarius, who had posed written questions about the baptismal liturgy and other matters.[12] Senarius wanted to know what certain words meant and why certain rituals were performed. His inquiries indicate that the meanings of some elements of the baptismal liturgy were already obscure in the late fifth century. In his response, John the Deacon described the liturgy for baptizing adults, although his description is incomplete because he took some things for granted and did not specify the intervals of time between ceremonies. I shall not analyze all of John's explanations, which are quite elaborate. Instead I shall concentrate on his description of baptism and sponsorship at Rome in the late fifth or early sixth century, where the traditional catechumenate and competentate were still observed.

The Catechumen

Because all unbelievers were trapped in the snares of the devil, those who wished to be baptized had first to be exorcized. John noted that the candidates entered the *cathecumenorum auditorium,* perhaps a separate

11. Vogel, *Medieval Liturgy,* pp. 372–73, n. 31; Paul Meyvaert, "Diversity within Unity: A Gregorian Theme," *Heythrop Journal* 4 (1963).

12. John the Deacon, *Epistola Iohannis Diaconi ad Senarium,* in "Un florilège carolingien sur la symbolisme des cérémonies du baptême, avec un Appendice sur la lettre de Jean Diacre," ed. André Wilmart, in *Analecta Reginensia* (Vatican City, 1933), pp. 170–79. John the Deacon's letter is analyzed in A. Dondeyne, "La discipline des scrutins dans l'Eglise latine avant Charlemagne," *RHE* 28 (1932), pp. 751–59. There is a partial English translation of John's letter in E. C. Whitaker, *Documents of the Baptismal Liturgy* (London, 1960), pp. 144–48.

room where the admission to the catechumenate and subsequent services took place.[13] The reception into the catechumenate had three elements: the candidates were exorcized by being blown upon (*exsufflatus*) to drive out the devil; they then received salt that had been blessed; and finally they received frequent layings-on of hands accompanied by a threefold invocation of the Trinity. At that point they had become catechumens, freed from the devil's power and opened to the power of Christ.[14]

The *Competens* or *Electus*

After an unspecified interval of time, the catechumen, who had been purified by exorcism, was judged worthy to be given access to the mysteries of the Christian religion. The serious preparation for baptism at Rome began when the catechumen advanced to the competentate. The candidate was told the words of the Creed and "he who a little before was only called a *catechumenus* is now called a *competens* or *electus.*" John described the *electus* as a fetus conceived in the womb of Mother Church, although the time of the holy birth through baptism had not yet come.[15]

The elect participated in three liturgical gatherings, called "scrutinies" (*scrutinia*),[16] which John the Deacon described as moral and intellectual examinations: "We scrutinize their hearts through faith [to determine] whether the sacred words have fixed themselves in their minds after the renunciation of the devil, whether they understand the grace coming from the Redeemer, whether they confess that they believe in God the Father Almighty."[17] At the third scrutiny the ears and nostrils of the elect were touched with the "oil of sanctification" and their chests were anointed with the "oil of consecration." In preparation for immediate baptism, they removed their footwear and their "death-bringing and carnal clothing" (*morticinis et carnalibus indumentis*). With their old life symbolically stripped away and standing naked, the elect had been fully prepared for baptism.

Baptism

Immediately after the third scrutiny, the *electus* was baptized with a threefold immersion in the water. The new Christian was then anointed with chrism and clothed in symbolic garments. A covering was put on the

13. Charles Thomas, *Christianity in Roman Britain to AD 500* (London, 1981), p. 205, noted that some churches in the Mediterranean region had separate rooms for catechumens (*catechumenorium, exorcisterium*) and for postbaptismal anointing (*chrismarium*).
14. John the Deacon, *Epistola,* c. 3, pp. 171–72.
15. Ibid., c. 4, p. 173.
16. See Dondeyne, "La discipline des scrutins."
17. John the Deacon, *Epistola,* c. 4, p. 173.

head, in imitation of the priests of the Old Law. White clothing was put on the body in imitation of the risen Christ (Matt. 17:2), so that the "rags" (*pannus*) of the old error that darkened the first birth might be replaced by the clothing (*habitus*) of the second birth, which was a "garment of glory" (*gloriae indumentum*).[18]

Thus far, John was describing the baptism of adults. He did not mention sponsors, perhaps because Senarius had not asked about them and so no reply was needed. But the baptism of infants was common in the late fifth century, and John added the following: "However that point ought not to be passed over, that all these things are done even for little ones (*parvuli*) who understand nothing on account of their youth. Hence you ought to know that whether they are offered by parents or by any other persons (*a parentibus aut a quibus libet aliis offeruntur*), it is necessary that they who were damned by someone else's error should be saved by someone else's profession [of faith]."[19] The "parents or other persons" were the infants' sponsors who, in John's terms, offered the infants for baptism and professed faith for them. Sponsors at the baptism of infants raised theological questions about the propriety or possibility that one person could profess faith for another. John addressed that theological point briefly when he argued, as Augustine had, that it was appropriate that the infants who were damned because of someone else's sin (i.e., Adam's) should be cleansed because of someone else's profession of faith (i.e., that of their parents or other persons).[20]

John's letter illustrates four important points about sponsorship at Rome in approximately A.D. 500. First, John did not mention sponsors for adults, perhaps because Senarius had not asked about them or because they were taken for granted. Second, John shared the centuries-old view that young children required help to be baptized in a liturgy created for adults. He specified that the "little ones" were offered by parents or other persons and that adults made a profession of faith for the children. Third, those who offered the very young for baptism could be parents, as they had been earlier, but they did not have to be. The choice of sponsors was apparently open. Fourth, John identified the main liturgical task of the sponsor as the profession of faith on behalf of infants, who could not speak.

The *Old Gelasian Sacramentary*

In the early Middle Ages, differing liturgies coexisted, and the compilers of liturgical books often drew on diverse traditions. As a consequence, the

18. Ibid., c. 6, p. 174.
19. Ibid., c. 7, p. 175.
20. Augustine, *Epistola* 98.6, p. 527, where Augustine told Bishop Boniface that parents could offer their children for baptism, but their participation was not necessary.

few surviving early liturgical texts are almost always the product of the mixing of traditions: it is difficult to identify a "pure" Roman or Gallican liturgical book.[21] The earliest baptismal service that is substantially Roman is contained in the *Old Gelasian Sacramentary*, whose prototype was probably composed at Rome between 628 and 715. It survives in a unique copy (*Codex Vaticanus Reginensis latinus 316*), made around 750 at the nunnery of Chelles near Paris, with some additions from the Gallican liturgy.[22]

In its provisions for Christian initiation, the *Sacramentary* contains primarily the prayers used by the celebrants. The rubrics, which may be compared with stage directions for the many participants, are relatively few. The prayers refer to adults and make no explicit provision for children, although the skimpy rubrics occasionally refer to *infantes*, a term that must be interpreted in context. In baptismal terminology, *infans* is an ambiguous word. It can refer to actual infants or to recently baptized adults who were "newborns"—*neophyti* or *infantes*—in the faith. But adults were not called *infantes* until after they had been baptized, or born spiritually. If a rubric refers to an *infans* before baptism, one may presume that it refers to an actual infant. For instance, there can be no doubt that the *Sacramentary* referred to real infants or young children in the rubric that directed an acolyte to hold one of the *infantes* in his arms as he recited the Creed on their behalf.[23]

Baptism at Rome in the seventh century was still a grand drama, played out over the weeks of Lent preceding Easter. Rather than describe the whole set of ceremonies, I shall concentrate on what the *Old Gelasian Sacramentary* reveals about baptismal sponsors, who are identified in the rubrics as "those who are going to receive" (*eos qui suscepturi sunt*) because they took the baptized person as she or he emerged from the font.

What is most striking in the *Old Gelasian Sacramentary* is that the focus was not on the baptism of adults but on that of infants. The prayers and rituals generally came from the tradition of adult baptism, but the rubrics indicate that the recipients were infants. On Monday of the third week in

21. Vogel, *Medieval Liturgy*, pp. 62–64.

22. Antoine Chavasse, *Le sacramentaire gélasien (Vaticanus Reginensis 316): Sacramentaire presbytéral en usage dans les titres romains au viie siècle* (Paris and Tournai, 1958), pp. vi–viii. For a useful summary of scholarship on the *Old Gelasian Sacramentary*, see D. M. Hope and G. Wolfenden, "The Medieval Western Rites," in *Study of Liturgy*, pp. 270–71. The *Old Gelasian Sacramentary* is in *Liber sacramentorum Romanae aecclesiae ordinis anni circuli (Sacramentarium Gelasianum)*, ed. L. C. Mohlberg, L. Eizenhöfer, and P. Siffrin (Rome, 1960) and in *Liber sacramentorum Romanae ecclesiae*, ed. H. A. Wilson (Oxford, 1894). There is an English translation of the baptismal sections in Whitaker, *Documents*, pp. 156–86.

23. *Liber sacramentorum*, no. xxxv, ed. Wilson, p. 53: "Post haec, accipiens acolytus unum ex ipsis infantibus masculum, tenens eum in sinistro brachio ponens manum super caput eius. . . . Et dicit acolytus Symbolum Graece decantando, tenens manum super caput infantis." On the term *infans* or its equivalent, *neophytus*, see Bastiaensen, *Observations*, pp. 16–17.

Lent, the "elect" were summoned to the first of what were now seven scrutinies—three on Sundays, which are those described by John the Deacon more than 125 years earlier, and four on week days. The rubric for the first scrutiny says:

> When they have come to the church, the names of the infants will be written down by an acolyte, and they will be summoned into the church in the order in which the names are written. The males will stand on the right side and the females on the left side, and the priest gives a prayer over them.[24]

The compiler(s) of the sacramentary apparently no longer understood the difference between the statuses of catechumen and elect. The candidates are called elect at ceremonies in which in earlier times they would have been have called catechumens. For instance, the blessing of salt and its placement in the mouth of each infant was a very old part of the entry to the catechumenate, but in the *Old Gelasian Sacramentary* those actions occur after a prayer (*oratio super electos*) in which the candidates are already called the "elect."

The rubrics indicate the ways in which the adult liturgy was adapted to infants. For example, when the infants were "given" the Creed, the rubric is as follows:

> After these things an acolyte takes one of the male infants into his left arm and places his hand above his head. And the priest asks him: "In what language does he confess our lord Jesus Christ?" [The acolyte answers] "In Greek." The priest next says "Announce their faith which they believe." And the acolyte sings the Creed in Greek, holding his hand over the head of the infant. [He then does the same for "Latin-speaking" infants.][25]

During the scrutinies on the third, fourth, and fifth Sundays in Lent, the sponsors and the elect were named in the canon of the Mass. The *Memento* prayer asked the Lord to be mindful "of your male and female servants who are going to receive your elect at the holy grace of your baptism." In the rubric that follows immediately, the celebrant of the scrutinal Mass was told to be silent, "and may the names of the men and women who are going to receive those *infantes* be recited." In the three scrutinal Masses the names of the individual elect were recited in the *Hanc igitur oblationem* prayer, presumably from the list made by the acolyte at the first scrutiny.

24. *Liber sacramentorum,* no. xxix, ed. Wilson, p. 45.
25. Ibid., no. xxxv, pp. 53–55.

The Saturday before Easter was a day of intense liturgical activity, on which the elect were supposed to "return" (i.e., recite) the Creed. The first rubric for that day says, "In the morning the *infantes* return the Creed," which in reality they could not do. A later rubric addressed the celebrant thus: "But next you say the Creed, with your hand placed on the heads of [each of] them."[26] The elect were also "catechized" on Holy Saturday, but the instructional elements had receded in favor of exorcisms. The nostrils and ears of the elect were touched with saliva; their chests and backs were anointed with exorcized oil, and each was asked individually to renounce Satan, his works, and his pomps. Someone, not identified in the rubrics, responded for the child. There is no reference to the child's parents in the *Old Gelasian Sacramentary,* although it is possible that for many infants, the sponsor was the parent.

The baptismal service in the *Old Gelasian Sacramentary* reflects three realities of baptism in seventh-century Rome: the conservatism of the liturgical compilers, who retained rites and prayers originally composed for adults; the dominance of infants as the recipients of baptism, for whom clergy and other adults had to act and speak; and the fact that sponsors were singled out as "those who were going to receive the infants" after baptism.

Ordo Romanus XI

The third document that gives insight into baptism at Rome in the seventh century is the *Ordo Romanus XI.* Some liturgical events were elaborate, with numerous personnel, processions, liturgical objects, and prescribed gestures. To carry out such a public event properly, a book that contained only the prayers might not be sufficient. Liturgical events that happened regularly (e.g., the Mass) might be conducted more or less according to custom, but rarer ones, such as annual baptism at Easter, needed detailed directions. A liturgical *ordo* is such a set of directions, which choreographed complex liturgical events.[27]

Ordo Romanus XI, which has been dated between 650 and 700 and localized in Rome, described the steps of Christian initiation.[28] *Ordo XI* is clearly related to the baptismal service in the *Old Gelasian Sacramentary,*

26. Ibid., no. xlii, pp. 78–79.

27. See Aimé-Georges Martimort, *Les "ordines," les ordinaires, et les cérémoniaux,* Typologie, fascicule 56 (Turnhout, 1991), pp. 18–34; *Les ordines romani du Haut Moyen Age,* 5 vols., ed. Michel Andrieu, Spicilegium Sacrum Lovaniense 11, 23, 24, 28, 29 (Louvain, 1931–1961), contains fifty edited *ordines romani.*

28. *Ordo Romanus XI,* in *Les ordines,* 2:365–447. Andrieu analyzed the complex interrelations between the *Old Gelasian Sacramentary* and *Ordo Romanus XI,* 2:380–408. There is an English translation in Whitaker, *Documents,* pp. 186–94.

but there has been some debate about which came first. Antoine Chavasse argued convincingly that *Ordo XI* was composed at Rome after the baptismal service in the *Sacramentary* and was dependent on it.[29] *Ordo Romanus XI* is rich in rubrics because its chief purpose was to give the stage directions for a complex liturgical activity. It is also rich in information about sponsors. The following is a chronological summary of the sponsors' roles:

Date	Liturgical Action
Third week in Lent	Summon *electi* to the first scrutiny on Thursday of the third week.
Thursday of third week	An acolyte records the names of infants and sponsors (*eos qui ipsos suscepturi sunt*) and summons each child into church by name.
	At five points in the scrutiny, godfathers (*patrini*) and godmothers (*matrinae*) make the sign of the cross with their thumb on the infants' foreheads. The infant catechumens then wait outside the church doors until the scrutinal Mass is finished.
	The offerings at Mass are made by the infants' parents or "by those who are to receive them from the font."
	In the *Memento* prayer, the priest recites the names of "those who are going to receive the infants from the font."
	In the *Hanc igitur* prayer, the priest recites the names of the little *electi.*
	When the first scrutinal Mass ends, all receive communion, except for the unbaptized infants.
	The first scrutiny ends with a summons to the second scrutiny, which takes place the following Sunday.
Sunday of third week	The second scrutiny is the same as the first, described above.
Scrutiny of fourth week	The third scrutiny is the same as the first until the ceremonies of the "opening of the ears" and "handing over" (*traditiones*) to the *electi*

29. Chavasse, *Le sacramentaire gélasien,* pp. 166–68.

	of the four gospels, the Creed and the Lord's Prayer.
	"Parents go outside with their infants, and give them into somebody else's keeping."
	The parents and the sponsors reenter the church and make their offerings during Mass.
	The fourth scrutiny is announced.
Scrutiny of fifth week	Scrutiny of fifth week is the same as the first scrutiny.
Scrutiny of sixth week	Same as the first scrutiny.
Scrutiny of seventh week	Same as the first scrutiny.
Scrutiny of Holy Saturday	Infants are catechized; the infants "return" the Creed; the infants leave the church, and the bishop blesses the font; the bishop baptizes one or two infants and a deacon baptizes the rest.
	A priest anoints the newly baptized on their heads with chrism. "And those who are to receive them [the infants] are ready with towels in their hands and accept them from the bishop or the deacons who baptize them."
	The infants are brought before the bishop and "he gives to each a stole and chasuble and chrismal cloth and ten coins and they are robed [in white garments]."
	The infants are arranged in a circle according to their names on the list and are confirmed by the bishop's prayers and anointed by him with chrism.
	The infants, who are now baptized, attend their first Mass and receive communion for the first time.
The week after baptism	Infants come to church every day for a week, and their parents make the offering for them.

Ordo Romanus XI confirms that in the second half of the seventh century, infants were the usual candidates for baptism at Rome. The rubrics sometimes distinguish between sponsors and parents and bring to light the prominent role the sponsors had in helping the youngsters move through the traditional ceremonies. Significantly, the male and female sponsors now had special names, *patrinus* and *matrina,* based on the Latin words for father and mother, and which are attested for the first time in the *Ordo Romanus XI.*

The purpose of this analysis of Roman liturgical documents has been to throw light on what sponsoring rituals the Roman missionaries might have brought to Anglo-Saxon England. In John's *Letter* and in the *Ordo Romanus XI,* the presence of parents aiding their childrens' baptism is attested. John mentioned their profession of faith on behalf of their children, to which Bede also referred in his commentary on the Gospel of Mark 7:29: "Through the faith and confession of parents in baptism, the little ones, who can not yet on their own understand or do anything good or bad, are freed from the devil."[30] All three Roman sources indicated that nonparents, including clergy, also helped the infants through the rituals. Sponsors, identified as "those who are going to receive them," are present in the *Old Gelasian Sacramentary,* but in *Ordo Romanus XI* they are very active and have technical names, *patrinus* and *matrina.*

Sponsorship and Its Social Consequences

Did liturgical sponsorship in sixth- and seventh-century Rome have any social significance, with which the missionaries might have been familiar? In other words, did liturgical sponsorship at Rome in the sixth and seventh centuries create some sort of godparent complex? None of the Roman liturgical texts even hints that the sponsorship of infants had any subsequent social significance. After the sponsor had participated in the initiation of the infant, perhaps nothing more was expected. Or if the sponsor was the child's parent, he or she did what all Christian parents were expected to do. But it is likely that a liturgical *ordo,* which had a specific and practical purpose, is the wrong place to look for any postbaptismal consequences of sponsorship.

Texts about or by Pope Gregory I, who sent Augustine to Kent, do shed light on the social consequences of sponsorship. Some of Gregory's letters might argue against the existence of social consequences. Before he became pope, he was papal representative (*apocrisarius*) at the court of the Byzantine emperor Maurice (582–602). Gregory of Tours, who was Pope Gregory's contemporary, reported that the future pope sponsored the emperor's

30. Bede, *In Marci Evangelium expositio,* bk. 2, ad versum 7:29, ed. D. Hurst, *CCSL* 120 (Turnhout, 1960), p. 525: "per fidem et confessionem parentum in baptismo liberantur a diabolo paruuli qui necdum per se sapere uel aliquid agere boni possunt aut mali."

son, Theodosius, who was born 4 August 583.[31] In Gregory's eight extant letters to the emperor Maurice and in three letters to the empress Constantina, he never, however, alluded to a godparental or coparental bond. Gregory's relations with Maurice were strained by disagreements over the patriarch of Constantinople's claim to the title of Ecumenical Patriarch and other issues, but Gregory never reminded the emperor of their spiritual kinship as a way to persuade him.[32] When Phocas (602–610) deposed Maurice, killing him and his sons, including Theodosius, Gregory wrote a letter congratulating the new emperor on his accession, in which he saw God's hand at work.[33] Gregory's silence about his spiritual kinship with Maurice and his son contrasts sharply with papal letters of the eighth century. Over a period of forty years, Pope Stephen II,[34] Pope Paul I,[35] and Pope Hadrian I[36] sponsored Carolingian children and persistently reminded their fathers, kings Pepin, Carloman, and Charlemagne, that they were the popes' *compatres spiritales.*[37]

Gregory of Tours is the source of all subsequent reports that Pope Gregory sponsored Maurice's son. Perhaps he was mistaken about events in Constantinople, which was very far away. Or perhaps sponsorship in the 580s was not so important as it had become in the 780s. In any case, Pope Gregory did not in any extant letter invoke his spiritual kinship to Maurice, to Constantina, or to their son. No case for a godparent complex at Rome (or at Byzantium) about A.D. 600 can be made on the basis of Gregory's letters to Maurice and Constantina.

But other writings of Gregory do offer evidence that in Italy social relationships continued after the act of sponsorship. In 593/94, Gregory recounted in his *Dialogues* a story that Bishop Maximian of Syracuse had

31. Gregory *HF,* 10.1, p. 478: "epistulam ad imperatorem Mauricium dirigeret, cuius filium ex lavacro sancto susciperet." John the Deacon, *Vita sancti Gregorii magni,* 1.40, *PL* 75, col. 79, and Paul the Deacon, *Vita Gregorii,* c. 10, *PL* 75, col. 46, both quoted Gregory of Tours's account almost verbatim.

32. Gregory I, *Epistolae,* in *S. Gregorii Magni Registrum epistularum,* ed. Dag Norberg, *CCSL* 140 and 140A (Turnhout, 1982): to the emperor Maurice, 3.61, 5.30, 5.36, 5.37, 6.16, 6.64, 7.6, and 7.30; to the empress Constantina, 4.30, 5.38, and 5.39. On Gregory's sponsorship and subsequent relations with Maurice, see Michael Whitby, *The Emperor Maurice and His Historian: Theophylact Simocatta on Persian and Balkan Warfare* (Oxford, 1988), pp. 18 and 23–24, and Jeffrey Richards, *Consul of God: The Life and Times of Gregory the Great* (London, 1980), pp. 217–27.

33. Gregory I to Phocas (May 603), in Gregory, *Registrum,* 13.32, pp. 1033–34.

34. Pope Stephen II to King Pippin, no. 6 (755), no. 7 (755), no. 8 (756), and no. 11 (757), in *Codex Carolinus,* ed. Wilhelm Gundlach, *MGH Epistolae* 3 (Berlin, 1892), pp. 491–504 passim.

35. Pope Paul I to Pippin, written between 758 and 767, including nos. 14, 16–22, 24, 25, 27–32, 34, 36–38, and 40–43, in ibid., pp. 511–57.

36. Hadrian I to Charlemagne, nos. 66–94, in ibid., pp. 594–632.

37. On the spiritual kinships created by successive popes with Pepin, Carloman, and Charlemagne, see Arnold Angenendt, "Das geistliche Bündnis der Päpste mit den Karolingern, 754–796," *Historisches Jahrbuch* 100 (1980).

told him. On a Saturday before Easter a town official (*curialis*) in the province of Valeria sponsored a girl in baptism, after which the girl stayed the night in his home. The *curialis* drank too much wine and raped her. He did not subsequently repent. In fact he attended church each day for a week after Easter, perhaps as sponsors were expected to do while their godchildren were still dressed in their white clothes. The *curialis* came to a sudden death on the seventh day, and his body burned up in his grave as a sign of the fate of his soul.[38] This cautionary tale is almost a commentary on Justinian's decision of 530, which forbade a male sponsor to marry a female godchild or, by implication, to have sexual relations with her outside of marriage.[39] Gregory's tale indicates that in sixth-century Italy, the bond of godfather/goddaughter was presumed to be close enough for a young girl to be permitted to stay overnight at her godfather's house. The godparental bond also precluded sexual intimacy. It seemed right that a violator of the bond be punished in a public way.

Gregory also mentioned the coparental bond. In August 594, he wrote a letter to an unidentified abbot named Valentinus, in which he criticized him for allowing women to enter his monastery and "something even more serious, that your monks make comothers for themselves and as a consequence have imprudent contact with those women."[40] The letter indicates that Valentinus's monks sponsored children and maintained friendly contact with the children's mothers, a relationship Gregory thought "imprudent" and inappropriate for monks. The women were identified with the technical word *commatres,* which is an early use of that term and points to a recognized social relationship in late sixth-century Italy.

In these two texts, Gregory demonstrated the existence in sixth-century Italy of consequences from sponsorship which continued after the baptism. Some tentative conclusions can be drawn about both godparenthood and coparenthood. First, the cases of the *curialis* and the monks demonstrate that nonparents were invited to sponsor another person's child. Second, a male, the *curialis,* could sponsor a female, although it is unlikely that the reverse was customary.[41] I have found no example of a female sponsoring a

38. Gregory I, *Dialogi* 4.33, in *Dialogues,* ed. Adalbert de Vogüé and French trans., by Paul Antin, *SC* 265 (Paris, 1980), 3:108–12.

39. *Codex Iustinianus,* bk. 5, tit. 4, law 26, in *Corpus iuris civilis,* ed. Paul Krueger (Berlin, 1895), 2:197. See Lynch, *Godparents,* pp. 224–30.

40. Gregory I, *Registrum,* 4.40, p. 261: "et quod adhuc est gravius, monachos tuos mulieres sibi commatres facere, et ex hoc incautam cum eis communionem habere." Valentinus might have been abbot of a monastery in the diocese of Spoleto; see ibid., 9.108, pp. 660–61.

41. In 758, Pope Paul I sponsored by proxy Pepin's newborn daughter Gisela: see *Codex Carolinus,* letter 14, pp. 511–12. Archbishop Thomas of Milan sponsored Charlemagne's daughter, also named Gisela, at Milan in 781, *Annales regni Francorum,* s.a. 781, ed. Friedrich Kurze, in *Aus-*

male before the middle of the tenth century.[42] Third, sexual relations between the sponsor and the sponsored were regarded as a serious sin. Fourth, the relationship between coparents was close enough to draw Gregory's rebuke when monks created comothers by sponsorship and might be sexually tempted by the resulting contacts.

Without trying to be too precise, it seems likely that Augustine of Canterbury and other Roman missionaries brought from Italy to Kent something similar to Roman baptismal sponsorship and its social consequences, just as they imported many other Roman practices and values.

Baptism in Frankish Gaul

In spite of their geographic proximity, Frankish bishops had not tried to convert the Anglo-Saxons during the sixth century. Indeed, until Pope Gregory sent missionaries to Anglo-Saxon England, the western bishops did not have a strong tradition of missionary activity outside their own dioceses. Literary sources, numismatics, and archaeological evidence prove, however, that before the arrival of Augustine's party in Kent, there were long-standing economic and cultural relationships between southeastern England and northern Gaul.[43] There were also political alliances between the kings of Kent and the Merovingian kings at Paris, ratified by royal marriages. In 562/63, Æthelberht, king of Kent (about 560–about 616)[44] married a Merovingian princess, Bertha, who had as her chaplain a Frankish bishop, Liudhard. In 618, King Eadbald of Kent (about 618–640) married another Frankish princess, Emma. King Clovis II (639–657) married Balthild, an Anglo-Saxon captive, who might have been of high birth.[45] The Franks also had a supporting role in the success of Augustine of Canterbury's mission. Ian Wood has recently argued that when Gregory sent the missionaries to England, he wrote to some Frankish bishops and rulers,

gewählte 5 (Darmstadt) (1968), 40: "et ibi baptizata est filia eius domna Gisola ab archiepiscopo nomine Thoma, qui et ipse eam a sacro baptismo suscepit."

42. Rodulfus Glaber, *Vita domni Willelmi abbatis,* c. 1, in *Rodulfi Glabri Historiarum libri quinque,* ed. Neithard Bulst, trans. John France and Paul Reynolds (Oxford, 1989), p. 256: Adelaide, wife of Otto I, sponsored William of Volpiano at baptism; the same text in Neithard Bulst, "Rodulfus Glabers Vita domni Willelmi abbatis: Neue Edition nach einer Handschrift des 11. Jahrhunderts (Paris, Bibl. nat. lat 5390)," *DAEM* 30 (1974), 464.

43. Annethe Lohaus, *Die Merowinger und England* (Munich, 1974), esp. pp. 143–55.

44. Ian Wood, "The Mission of Augustine of Canterbury to the English," *Speculum* 69 (1994), 10–11, argued that Æthelberht succeeded to the Kentish throne much later than is usually thought, perhaps as late as 589.

45. Lohaus, *Die Merowinger und England,* p. 27. Ian Wood, *The Merovingian Kingdoms, 450–751* (London, 1994), pp. 212–13.

notably Queen Brunhild, with a request for support, which they apparently provided.[46]

Even though the first missionaries to the kingdom of Kent were Roman and those to the kingdom of Northumbria were Irish, the influence of Frankish Gaul on every aspect of Anglo-Saxon church life became important once missionary activity had begun.[47] Bede reported multiple ties with the Frankish church. Some losers in Anglo-Saxon dynastic struggles fled to Gaul, where they lived in exile among the Merovingians who were sometimes their kinsmen through earlier marriages. Some Anglo-Saxon exiles were baptized in Gaul.[48] Convents were scarce in England in the early years after the conversion, and some women became nuns at Frankish houses, for example at Chelles.[49] During a resurgence of paganism among the East Saxons between 618 and 625, Bishops Mellitus and Justus fled to Gaul to await the outcome of events.[50] Anglo-Saxon pilgrims to Rome passed across Frankish Gaul coming and going. Sometimes Anglo-Saxon clerics went to Gaul to obtain valid episcopal orders, as when Wilfrid of Ripon went to Compiègne for his episcopal consecration in about 665.[51]

The traffic was not all one way. Some Franks took part in the seventh-century missionary activity in England; Bishop Felix preached in Kent in 631/32, and Bishop Agilbert (later bishop of Paris) worked in Wessex in 649/50.[52] In short, the Frankish church was a model and stimulus (and sometimes a scandal) to the nascent Anglo-Saxon church. The many personal and institutional contacts between Christian Anglo-Saxons and Christian Franks make it important to understand the basic outlines of sponsorship and the godparent complex in sixth- and seventh-century Frankish society.

No baptismal liturgy survives from seventh-century Gaul. The extant eighth-century missals that embody the Gallican or hybrid Gallican-Roman baptismal liturgies refer only rarely to infants or to sponsors.[53] Some literary texts do throw light on baptism in sixth- and seventh-century

46. Ian Wood, "Mission of Augustine," pp. 4–10.

47. Ibid., pp. 1–17, stresses the importance of the Franks in Pope Gregory's plans for the conversion of Kent.

48. Bede, *HE,* 2.16, p. 190 and 3.18, p. 266: Sigeberht lived in exile in Gaul and was baptized there; *HE,* 2.20, p. 204: Queen Æthelfred sent her children to Gaul to be brought up by King Dagobert.

49. Bede, *HE,* 4.23, p. 406: Hilda, who was later abbess of Whitby, intended to go to Chelles, where her sister Hereswith was a nun.

50. Bede, *HE,* 2.5, p. 152.

51. Bede, *HE,* 4.2, p. 334 and 5.19, p. 522.

52. On Felix, see Bede, *HE,* 2.15 and 3.18; on Agilbert, see Bede, *HE,* 3.7 and 3.25.

53. Vogel, *Medieval Liturgy,* p. 108, listed editions of the *Missale Gothicum, Missale Bobbiense, Missale Francorum,* and *Missale Gallicanum Vetus.*

Gaul. The most famous baptism in Frankish history was that of King Clovis (481–511), and its date has given rise to a great deal of scholarly dispute. A letter of Bishop Avitus of Vienne to Clovis indicated that the latter was baptized at Christmas, but opinion is split over which Christmas between 496 and 506.[54] Although Bishop Gregory of Tours's account of Clovis's life is late and suspect,[55] his description of the baptism is useful, because it was based on a lost *vita* of Bishop Remigius of Reims, who baptized Clovis, and on Gregory's knowledge of how baptisms were generally performed in Frankish Gaul.[56]

Gregory wrote that Clovis's wife, Chlotild, was a Catholic Christian and her first two sons by him were baptized: one died in his baptismal robes and the other lived. Gregory reported that Clovis vowed to become a Christian if he defeated the Alamanni. After his victory, he was instructed in private by Bishop Remigius, until he could gain the assent of his warriors. The consent gained, the bishop

> commanded the font to be prepared. The streets were overshadowed with coloured hangings, the churches adorned with white hangings, the baptistery was set in order, smoke of incense spread in clouds, perfumed tapers gleamed, the whole church about the place of baptism was filled with divine fragrance. And now the king first demanded to be baptized by the bishop. Like a new Constantine, he moved forward to the water, to blot out the former leprosy, to wash away in this new stream the foul stains borne from the old days. . . . The King therefore, confessing Almighty God, three in one, was baptized in the name of the Father, the Son and the Holy Ghost and anointed with holy chrism, with the sign of the Cross of Christ. Of his army were baptized more than 3000.[57]

Gregory of Tours did not record the king's sponsor, but Hincmar of Reims asserted in his *Vita Remigii,* composed about 878, that Bishop

54. Ian Wood, *Merovingian Kingdoms,* pp. 41–49; Georges Tessier, *Le baptême de Clovis* (Paris, 1964), pp. 69–126. On the historiography concerning the date of Clovis's baptism, see Mark Spencer, "Dating the Baptism of Clovis, 1886–1993," *EME* 3 (1994), who reviewed modern debates about the date and argued for the period 496–499.

55. William M. Daly, "Clovis: How Barbaric, How Pagan?" *Speculum* 69 (1994), argued convincingly that late-fifth- and early-sixth-century sources about Clovis must be preferred to Gregory's colorful but legendary tales written eighty or ninety years later.

56. Gregory, *HF,* 2.31, p. 77, refers to a *liber vitae eius.* P. de Puniet, "La liturgie baptismale en Gaulle avant Charlemagne," *Revue des Questions Liturgiques,* nouvelle sér. 28 (1902), analyzed Gregory's description of Clovis's baptism.

57. Gregory, *HF,* 2.31, pp. 71–78, trans. by O. M. Dalton, *The History of the Franks by Gregory of Tours* (Oxford, 1927), 2:69–70.

Remigius himself had sponsored Clovis.[58] Hincmar based his statement on the *testamentum* of Remigius, which he incorporated into the *vita.* In the *testamentum,* Remigius disposed of a silver vessel given to him by King Clovis, "whom I received from the holy font of baptism."[59]

Aside from his description of Clovis's baptism, Gregory of Tours provided almost no information on the baptismal liturgy itself in his *History of the Franks,* which was finished about 592. But he was quite interested in sponsorship and spiritual kinship because they were politically and socially significant in his society. He provides unequivocal evidence of a vigorous Frankish godparent complex. Bernhard Jussen investigated the sponsoring practices of the Franks, primarily as recorded in Gregory of Tours's *History.*[60] Gregory referred sixteen times to spiritual kinship arising out of baptismal sponsorship in his own society and twice to sponsorships that took place in Byzantium. Aside from one early Frankish episode and the two Byzantine examples, his accounts of sponsorship and its consequences span the last twenty years of his own lifetime and refer to people high in the social hierarchy, most of whom he knew.

Gregory's evidence permits the following conclusions about sponsorship and spiritual kinship among the Franks. First, sponsorship was practiced only at baptism. Gregory referred in the account of Clovis's baptism to the postbaptismal anointing by Bishop Remigius, but anointing did not yet exist as a distinct sacrament of confirmation with its own sponsor. Second, Franks apparently invited one outsider, of the same sex as the child, to act as sponsor. Third, bishops baptized young Merovingian princes—that is to be expected—but what might be unexpected is that bishops also sponsored the infants; that is, a bishop might both baptize and lift the infant from the font, as Hincmar believed Bishop Remigius had done when Clovis was baptized. Fourth, in the bloody dynastic politics of the Merovingian family, sponsorship was used, not always successfully, to confirm alliances and to create amity. Fifth, because sponsorship was a scarce commodity and not to be wasted, some youngsters might be kept unbaptized for a relatively long time, seven years, for example, for Chlothar II, until his powerful uncle, King Gunthrum, agreed to sponsor him. This

58. Hincmar of Reims, *Vita Remigii episcopi remensis,* c. 15, ed. Bruno Krusch, *MGH SRM* 3 (Hanover, 1896), p. 297.

59. Remigius of Reims, *Testamentum sancti Remigii Remensis episcopi,* in ibid., pp. 336–47. A. H. M. Jones, P. Grierson, and J. A. Crook, "The Authenticity of the 'Testamentum S. Remigii,' " *Revue Belge de Philologie et d'Histoire* 35 (1957), defended the authenticity of the short version of the *Testamentum* incorporated into Hincmar's *Vita.*

60. Jussen, *Patenschaft.* For another analysis, see Lynch, *Godparents,* pp. 163–204.

case might have been unusual because there were doubts about the boy's legitimate birth. In sponsoring him, Gunthrum acknowledged his legitimacy.[61] Sixth, the bond between godparent and godchild could create warm, familial feelings that persisted long after the sponsorship itself. Bishop Praetextatus of Rouen justified his support of a young Merovingian prince against the boy's father by saying that the boy was a "spiritual son to me from the bath [of baptism]."[62] In two recorded instances, royal children were spared death by their relatives because of the bond of godparenthood.[63] Seventh, in the late sixth century, the Franks also recognized that sponsorship created coparenthood. It may already have been true that the uniting of adults through coparenthood was a major social goal of sponsorship.[64] Gregory of Tours' did not use the terms *compater* and *commater,* although roughly contemporary sources did, including Pope Gregory I.[65] He did once use a precise circumlocution that throws a beam of light on how Frankish coparents regarded one another: a person was a "common father to another man's son" (*pater communis filio eius*).[66]

Although Gregory of Tours and his Frankish contemporaries recognized godparenthood and coparenthood, they were silent about sexual taboos among spiritual kin. Frankish sources mentioned the sexual consequences of sponsorship only about 730, that is, about 140 years after Gregory's death. Jussen argued that even in 730 the incest taboos rooted in sponsorship were the creation of churchmen and without much practical impact until the twelfth century, if then.[67] In any case, the sexual taboos deriving from sponsorship are not attested in sixth- or seventh-century Gaul, from which the Frankish missionaries came.

61. Jussen, *Patenschaft,* pp. 229–70, provided a detailed analysis of the circumstances.

62. Gregory, *HF,* 5.18, pp. 221–22; "filius enim mihi erat, ut saepe dixi, spiritalis ex lavacro."

63. Gregory, *HF,* 3.23, p. 122: a child was spared by his godfather, who urged him to flee; Fredegar, *Chronicle,* c. 3, in *The Fourth Book of the Chronicle of Fredegar with Its Continuations,* ed. and trans. J. M. Wallace-Hadrill (London, 1960), p. 34: Chlothar II had two of his young relatives executed but spared their brother because he was his godson, for whom he felt *amor.*

64. Lynch, *Godparents,* pp. 192–201.

65. The word *compater:* Bertram of Le Mans, *Testamentum* (616), in *Actus pontificum Cenomannis in urbe degentium,* ed. Gustave Busson and Ambroise Ledru, *Archives Historiques du Maine* 2 (1901), 133. The word *commater:* Diocesan Synod of Auxerre (561–605), c. 25, in *Concilia Galliae, A. 511–A. 695,* ed. Carlo de Clercq, *CCSL* 148A (Turnhout, 1963), p. 268. On Pope Gregory's use of the word *commater,* see above, n. 40.

66. Gregory, *HF,* 9.10, p. 424. On the vocabulary of spiritual kinship, see Joseph H. Lynch, "*Spiritale Vinculum:* The Vocabulary of Spiritual Kinship in Early Medieval Europe," in *Religion, Culture, and Society in the Early Middle Ages: Studies in Honor of Richard E. Sullivan,* ed. Thomas F. X. Noble and John J. Contreni (Kalamazoo, Mich., 1987), pp. 181–204.

67. Jussen, *Patenschaft,* pp. 28–34.

Baptism among Celtic Christians

When the Anglo-Saxons invaded post-Roman Britain in the fifth century, they began generations of sporadic warfare with the romanized Celtic Christian inhabitants. The wars were localized and had many ups and downs, but over time the British Christians were conquered, enslaved, exterminated, or driven west into Cornwall, Devon, Wales, and Strathclyde or across the sea to Brittany. The British Christians made no known efforts to convert their bitter enemies, the Anglo-Saxons.

The Roman missionaries knew that in addition to the pagan Anglo-Saxons there were Christians on the island of Britain and made contact with some of them early. In the *Libellus responsionum,* Pope Gregory gave Augustine authority over "all the bishops of Britain, so that the unlearned may be taught, the weak may be strengthened by [your] persuasion, and the wicked corrected by [your] authority."[68] This negative assessment of the British Christians was not a promising start for uniting with them. Bede reported that Augustine met with British bishops twice in order to assert his authority over them, but he was unsuccessful, perhaps because, as Bede reported, he seemed disrespectful, or because he was regarded as an agent of their enemy, Æthelberht, the Anglo-Saxon king of Kent.[69]

There was something about the way the British Christians performed baptism that the Roman missionaries did not like, but no source says explicitly what it was. As Jane Stevenson noted, "Practically nothing specific can be said about the Romano-British liturgy."[70] But as one of the conditions for fellowship with the British bishops, Augustine asked them to "complete the ministry of baptism through which we are reborn again to God, according to the custom of the Holy and Apostolic Roman church."[71] It has been suggested that Augustine's criticism of British baptism might have been occasioned by a failure on the part of British Christians to invoke at baptism all three persons of the Trinity, or by their use of one rather than three immersions. Margaret Pepperdene argued that the matter at issue was the omission of the final anointing of the newly baptized with chrism, and hence the confirmation of the baptism. In her view,

68. Bede, *HE,* 1.27, response 7, p. 88.
69. Bede, *HE,* 2.3, pp. 134–42; see also Ian Wood, "Mission of Augustine," pp. 4–5.
70. Jane Stevenson, "Introduction" to the reprinting of Frederick E. Warren, *The Liturgy and Ritual of the Celtic Church* (Woodbridge, England, 1987), p. liii. There is also a useful bibliography and introduction to the Irish and other Celtic liturgies by Stevenson in ibid., pp. ix–cxxvii.
71. Bede, *HE,* 2.2, pp. 138–39: "ut ministerium baptizandi quo Deo renascimur iuxta morem sanctae Romanae et apostolicae ecclesiae conpleatis."

Bede chose his verb (*conpleatis*) carefully—the British bishops should "complete" baptism as the Romans did, with an episcopal anointing.[72]

Although the Christian Romano-Celts living in Britain did not try to convert the pagan Anglo-Saxons, the Irish, who lived at a safe distance from the Anglo-Saxons, sent missionaries to Northumbria. King Oswald (634–642), who had become a Christian while in exile in Ireland, invited Aidan, an Irish bishop from Iona, who arrived in Northumbria in 635. He preached and baptized for about fifteen years, but we do not know how he carried out baptism. Bede admired Aidan and recorded no negative comments on his baptism.[73] Other Irish missionaries were also active in Northumbria and elsewhere in the seventh century.

Because of a dearth of sources, it is not possible to know whether the Irish missionaries introduced forms of sponsorship and spiritual kinship. Irish Christianity had its origins from fifth-century Britain and Gaul, and as in those places, Irish Christians baptized their infants and must have had some sort of liturgical sponsorship for them, if only for practical problems associated with infant baptism. The only extant Irish baptismal liturgy, which survives in the *Stowe Missal,* produced in the late eighth century at Tallaght in Leinster, near Dublin, shows signs of strong influence by Roman practices.[74] Rubrics are few and the missal's prayers seem to refer to adults who, for instance, respond on their own behalf to the priest's questions. But two rubrics indicate that the liturgy was also performed with young children. One, in Irish, says, "Here salt is put into the mouth of the child," and a second, in Latin, says, "Let the hand of the boy (*puer*) be opened" in order to mark it with the sign of the cross.[75] The *Stowe Missal* has no reference to sponsors.

If references to the details of the baptismal liturgy in Celtic Christian sources from Britain and Ireland are scarce, references to a godparent complex do not exist. Even likely sources yield no evidence that British or Irish Christians had such a complex in their respective homelands in the sixth or seventh centuries. For example, Ludwig Bieler edited fifteen Irish penitential texts in Latin, composed between the fifth and eighth centuries, and

72. Margaret Pepperdene, "Baptism in the Early British and Irish Churches," *Irish Theological Quarterly* 22 (1955). Thomas, *Christianity in Roman Britain,* p. 209, argued that the Celts did anoint the neophytes on the forehead, but they did not reserve the ritual for a bishop, as did the Roman liturgy.

73. Bede, *HE,* 3.3, pp. 218–20; 3.5 and 3.6, pp. 226–30.

74. *Stowe Missal,* 2 vols., ed. G. F. Warner, HBS 31 and 32 (London, 1906–1915), on which see Jane Stevenson, "Introduction," pp. liii–liv. The baptismal liturgy of the Stowe Missal is translated in Whitaker, *Documents,* pp. 203–11.

75. *Stowe Missal, Ordo Baptismi,* in Warren, *Liturgy and Ritual,* pp. 210 and 217.

Daniel Binchy translated two penitential documents from Old Irish, perhaps composed in the eighth century. Some of the penitentials refer to infant baptism, to marriage, to marital prohibitions, and to many prohibited forms of sexual conduct. In them one might expect to find reference to the spiritual family created by sponsorship, but they contain no comment on sponsors or marriage among spiritual kin.[76]

The silence of British and Irish sources on the godparent complex may be explained in part by the relative isolation of the Celtic churches, whose liturgy and discipline took shape in the fifth and sixth centuries, after which the Germanic invasions impeded contact with theological and liturgical developments on the Continent. The Celts adopted baptismal practices before the godparent complex had developed on the Continent, and they seem to have sponsored infants but remained "archaic" with respect to spiritual kinship. Although arguments from silence are weak, it seems likely that Irish missionaries were an insignificant influence on godparenthood and coparenthood when compared with the Roman and Frankish missionaries.[77]

What the Missionaries Brought

What conclusions, however tentative, can be drawn about the introduction of sponsorship and spiritual kinship into Anglo-Saxon England? We do not know exactly the liturgical forms of baptism or the full contours of the godparent complex that came with various traditions of Christianity into Anglo-Saxon England during the seventh century. The Celtic contribution, if any, is simply unmeasurable because of a lack of sources; the main models sources do reveal to us are Roman and Frankish. We do know with certainty that in the baptismal liturgy, parents sponsored infants, but so did invited outsiders. We know that sponsorship had social consequences both in Rome and in Gaul—it brought participants together in godparent complexes with parent/child and coparental dimensions. In Italy there is evidence for a ban on sexual relations between godfather and goddaughter, but there is no evidence for such sexual prohibitions in Frankish Gaul. The silence of the Frankish sources might be misleading. If, as I believe, the Frankish custom was that the sponsor was a person of the same sex as the infant, a prohibition on marriage between godparent and god-

76. *The Irish Penitentials*, ed. and trans. Ludwig Bieler with Appendix by D. A. Binchy, Scriptores Latini Hiberniae 5 (Dublin, 1965).

77. Thomas Charles-Edwards, *Early Irish and Welsh Kinship* (Oxford, 1993), pp. 78–79, argued that the dominance of fosterage made baptismal kinship superfluous in Celtic societies.

child was unnecessary: the issue never arose in Frankish Gaul before the ninth century, when there is evidence that the custom changed. A prohibition on sexual relations between godparent and godchild was needed in Italy and the Byzantine world, where sponsors of the opposite sex from the baptizee are attested from the sixth century. Under Roman and Frankish influence, Anglo-Saxon Christianity practiced sponsorship that created a form of the godparent complex, one with features and emphases that must be more clearly described in subsequent chapters.

CHAPTER 3

Baptism and Sponsorship in the Anglo-Saxon Church before 800

Although there may have been significant variations in detail, the approximate contours of a solemn baptism with sponsorship in seventh-century Italy and Frankish Gaul have been established. The elaborate baptismal liturgy represented in the *Old Gelasian Sacramentary* and in *Ordo Romanus XI* was the product of generations of development, compilation, adaptation, and some misunderstanding. But even if the Roman and Frankish missionary bishops brought books containing versions of their respective baptismal liturgies, circumstances in Anglo-Saxon England forced major changes, because baptism and sponsorship could not take place in a vacuum.[1] Conditions in seventh-century Anglo-Saxon England, particularly the scarcity of clergy and churches, were not favorable for transplanting solemn baptism at Easter or Pentecost, as practiced on the Continent. In seventh-century Italy and Gaul, the population was almost entirely Christian, and in virtually every significant town and some insignificant ones, there was a bishop who could preside over solemn baptism. In such circumstances, the preparation of *competentes* or *electi,* even if they were predominantly infants, could be spread over several weeks, culminating in baptism at the times sanctioned by the canon law.

Even on the Continent, the changing sociology of Christianity upset the old ways, as a declining percentage of children and adults became Christians in the elaborate baptismal rituals. During the sixth and seventh centuries, Christianity penetrated the Frankish countryside, the rural *pagi*

1. I am indebted to the useful article by Sarah Foot, " 'By Water in the Spirit,' " which treated baptism in the seventh and eighth centuries.

where the *pagani* lived. This success eroded the observance of baptism in the bishop's church at Easter. The spiritual needs of rural people were increasingly met by founding rural churches, which were sometimes called baptismal churches (*ecclesiae baptismales*), to which the bishop gave the right to baptize, a right made concrete by possession of a baptismal font.[2] The baptismal churches were juridically superior to the private chapels and oratories scattered across the countryside. In them increasing numbers of infants were baptized, rather than in urban cathedrals where a bishop presided over elaborate ceremonies, often in a separate building, the baptistery. In the rural baptismal churches, there was a tendency to compress and simplify the rituals as well as to perform them soon after a child's birth, without observing the prescribed times of Easter or Pentecost.

Even in towns in Gaul, parents' neglect or refusal to bring their children to the protracted catechumenal services compromised the solemn liturgy. In the sixth century, Caesarius of Arles complained about parents who brought their infants for baptism at Easter with none of the preliminary anointings, exorcisms, or hand layings. He said the parents committed a grave sin, but he apparently baptized the infants.[3] An impressive gathering of nine metropolitans and fifty-five bishops at Mâcon in 585 attempted in vain to halt the erosion of the formal Easter baptism.

> We have learned from the report of some of our fellow bishops that Christians do not respect the prescribed day for baptism but baptize their sons on almost any day or martyr's feast, with the result that on Easter scarcely two or three children can be found who are to be reborn through water and the Holy Spirit. Therefore we command that henceforth no one be allowed to commit such abuses, with the exception of those people whom a serious illness or impending death compel to seek baptism for their sons. Therefore by the present admonitions we order that all, recalled from their errors or ignorance, come to church at the beginning of Lent (*a die quadragensimo*) with their infants, so that having received the imposition of hands on the fixed days and having been anointed with the fluid of holy oil, they may take part in the festival of the prescribed day and may be reborn by sacred baptism.[4]

In spite of such efforts, many infants in Gaul were baptized in rural churches soon after birth in ceremonies much less grand than those carried out in bishops' churches.

2. Michel Aubrun, *La paroisse en France des origines au xve siècle* (Paris, 1986), pp. 11–31.
3. Caesarius of Arles, *Sermo* 229, c. 6, in *Sancti Caesarii episcopi Arelatensis opera omnia,* ed. Germain Morin, *CCSL* 104 (Turnhout, 1953) 2: 910.
4. Council of Mâcon (585), c. 3, in *Concilia Galliae, A. 511–A. 695,* p. 240.

Missionary Baptism in the Seventh Century

The situation in England was even less favorable to implanting and maintaining the elaborate Lenten preparations for baptism at Easter. Whatever liturgical forms the missionaries brought to the Anglo-Saxons, they must often have been impossible to carry out. It was no simple matter in a missionary context to administer baptism in a liturgically correct way, if something similar to *Ordo Romanus XI* was taken as the norm. For a long time after the missionaries came, Anglo-Saxon England had few towns, few churches, and probably only one baptistery, built at Canterbury in the middle of the eighth century.[5] There were also few bishops—in 669 only one active bishop for all the Anglo-Saxon kingdoms, and in all of Anglo-Saxon history rarely more than twenty at one time.[6] Bishops had to delegate baptizing to priests and deacons, but the provision of a sufficient number of adequately trained clergy was also a slow process. Missionary baptism in England had features that distinguished it from baptism in contemporary Gaul and Italy. The need to baptize large numbers of adults created, temporarily, a situation quite unlike that in the long-Christianized areas of the Continent. Adult converts were instructed briefly, and their personal assent, however superficial, was elicited. Bishops, priests, and deacons baptized as opportunities presented themselves. The fixed times for baptism probably did not take root in Anglo-Saxon England, in spite of some efforts to order their observance.[7]

For much of the seventh century in Anglo-Saxon England, a bishop and his clerical *familia,* attached to a royal court, preached and baptized as opportunity permitted. Fledgling dioceses only slowly acquired the landed endowments needed to support local churches. Pastoral care in the early days was hampered by shortages of wealth and personnel and may have been more haphazard than the sources indicate, especially in isolated rural areas. After about A.D. 650, institutions similar in form and function to the Frankish baptismal churches began to be founded. Clerics lived in groups in a sort of church compound, called a "minster" (*monasterium*), which was the

5. Foot, " 'By Water in the Spirit,' " pp. 180–81.

6. Guy Lanoë, "Les évêques en Angleterre, 597–669," *Le Moyen Age* 89 (1983).

7. The legatine mission of 786 ordered the canonical times for baptism to be observed in c. 2, in George of Ostia to Pope Hadrian I, in *Alcuini sive Albini epistolae,* ed. Ernst Dümmler, *MGH Epistolae* 4 (Berlin, 1895), p. 21: "Secundo capitulo docuimus, ut baptismus secundum canonica statuta exerceatur et non alio tempore, nisi pro magna necessitate." Pierre-Marie Gy, "Du baptême pascal des petits enfants au baptême Quamprimum," in *Haut Moyen Age: Culture, éducation, et société: Etudes offertes à Pierre Riché* (La Garenne-Colombe, 1990), p. 357, expressed the view that the rule of Easter baptism was not introduced into Anglo-Saxon England or missionary Germany.

hard-to-define name for these Anglo-Saxon clerical communities. The minsters varied in the composition of their personnel—monks, secular clerics, or nuns—and in their activities. They probably also trained the clergy upon whom pastoral care depended, although the extent of the pastoral role of minsters has been debated. There is no disagreement that many minsters played a role in the pastoral care of their lay neighbors by sending out preachers into the countryside and by welcoming local people for religious ministrations, including baptism. At issue is whether other sorts of churches, which are poorly documented in the sources, also provided pastoral care.[8] Many Anglo-Saxons must have been baptized at minsters or by priests who were on a preaching trip from a minster. In such circumstances, the rituals of baptism were probably adapted to new conditions, which often meant compressing and truncating the traditional rituals.

Bede, who was writing in the first decades of the eighth century, is the prime source for the missionary phase of conversion. It is illuminating to see what his informants remembered about baptisms that took place decades or even a century earlier. Mass baptisms must have been common in the early days. Pope Gregory wrote to Patriarch Eulogius of Alexandria that at Christmas 597, "more than ten thousand Angles" had been baptized.[9] Even allowing for pious exaggeration, mass conversions were a reality. Bede's description of the work of Bishop Paulinus in Northumbria in the late 620s and early 630s gives a glimpse of the baptism of groups:

> So great is said to have been the fervour of the faith of the Northumbrians and their longing for the washing of salvation, that once when Paulinus came to the king and queen in their royal palace at Yeavering, he spent thirty-six days there occupied in the task of catechizing and baptizing. During these days, from morning till evening, he did nothing else but instruct the crowds who flocked to him from every village and district in the teaching of Christ. When they had received instruction, he washed them in the waters of regeneration in the river Glen, which was close at hand.[10]

The text does not say how much instruction any individual received, but it seems unlikely that rural families stayed for thirty-six days of instruc-

8. See especially the exchange between John Blair, "Debate: Ecclesiastical Organization and Pastoral Care in Anglo-Saxon England," *EME* 4 (1995), and Eric Cambridge and David Rollason, "Debate: The Pastoral Organization of the Anglo-Saxon Church: A Review of the 'Minster Hypothesis,' " ibid. On the minsters, see Sarah Foot, "Anglo-Saxon Minsters: A Review of Terminology," in *Pastoral Care,* ed. Blair and Sharpe, pp. 217–25, and John Blair, "Anglo-Saxon Minsters: A Topographical Review," in ibid.

9. Gregory I, *Registrum,* 8.29, p. 551.

10. Bede, *HE,* 2.14, pp. 188–89.

tion. Paulinus may have instructed and baptized successive groups over the course of thirty-six days, or perhaps the thirty-six days was an effort at a preparation similar in length to that at Lent. One of Bede's informants, Abbot Deda, told him that an old man recalled that "he had been baptized at midday by Bishop Paulinus in the presence of King Edwin, along with a whole crowd of people, in the River Trent."[11] The mass baptisms of the missionary period were quite different from formal Easter baptism in a church or baptistery built for the purpose. The instruction, given to Anglo-Saxon adults, was more haphazard and truncated, the fixed times were not observed, and the ceremonies were perhaps reduced to the renunciation of Satan and assent to the Creed, followed by baptism in whatever water was available.

At group baptisms in a missionary situation, sponsorship probably also differed from the pattern described in Continental liturgical documents and narrative sources. Roman and Frankish sponsoring practices presupposed an established Christian community in which there were reliable members, often parents, to stand as guarantors for the baptizees. But there was no Christian society in early Anglo-Saxon England when large numbers of adults were baptized in groups. As there were few adult Christians, sponsorship might have been abandoned at mass baptisms. Liturgical forms were conservative, however, and it is likely that sponsorship was carried out pro forma by clergy who acted as liturgical officers and not as personal patrons or spiritual kinsmen of the converts. Infants were readily baptized with their parents because infant baptism was already ingrained in the liturgy. The sources indicate that few people who had been baptized in a large group remembered who their sponsor had been. Apparently the bishop or priest who presided was more memorable, as in the case of the old man, cited above, who recalled that Bishop Paulinus baptized him. In another case, a boy remembered by name the priest who baptized him—improperly as it happened.[12]

Although they might strike the imagination of the modern reader of Bede, group baptisms are not the key to understanding the successes (and failures) of the missionaries. To stress them is to miss the central point about the way Christianity spread. Group baptisms were preceded and facilitated by the baptism, or at least the assent, of the local ruler. Between the sixth and tenth centuries, the most successful missionary strategy in the western church was to seek first the conversion of kings and social leaders. If the ruler and leading men converted, the native religion often collapsed

11. Ibid., 2.16, p. 192.
12. Ibid., 5.6, p. 468.

from the top, although some of its practices survived for a long time in the countryside. In some places, violence perpetrated by Christians and pagans accompanied the transition to the new religion, but in Anglo-Saxon England, there were no martyrs on either side.[13]

The political situation shaped the process of conversion. The seventh-century Anglo-Saxons were divided into seven unstable kingdoms, as well as subkingdoms and districts, varying in size from medium to small.[14] The strategy of conversion from the top made particular sense because the king's religious role was central in the native Germanic religions. As William Chaney put it in laying out the aims of his book, *The Cult of Kingship in Anglo-Saxon England,* "I shall attempt to investigate the often nebulous but nonetheless vital forces which illuminate the way in which the folk saw their king, as a sacral figure which held their tribal world together and related it to the cosmic forces in which that world was enmeshed. The ruler was himself a centre of the societal cult, and it is this cult of kingship in Anglo-Saxon England that is our subject."[15]

Pope Gregory I and the Roman missionaries initially concentrated their efforts on King Æthelberht of Kent, who had a Christian wife and contacts with the Franks. He was favorable to Christianity, although he might have invited or welcomed missionaries from Italy rather than Gaul so as to avoid subordination to the Merovingian kings.[16] An Anglo-Saxon king's decision to convert set in motion the conversion of his people and, if he was powerful enough, the conversion of neighboring kings. Such a strategy had the inherent problem that violent dynastic changes, which were frequent, or a pagan reaction could lead to the repudiation of Christianity. In several seventh-century Anglo-Saxon kingdoms, Christian rulers were succeeded by adherents of the old gods, sometimes led by royal sons supported by a pagan faction among the nobility.[17] During such periods, Christian clergy

13. Claire E. Stancliffe, "Kings and Conversion: Some Comparisons between the Roman Mission to England and Patrick's to Ireland," *FS* 14 (1980), 59–62. On the peaceful character of the conversion of the Anglo-Saxons, see Michael Richter, "Practical Aspects of the Conversion of the Anglo-Saxons," in *Irland und die Christenheit/Ireland and Christendom,* ed. Próinséas Ni Chatháin and Michael Richter (Stuttgart, 1987), p. 362. For an account of early medieval methods of conversion, see Jocelyn N. Hillgarth, "Modes of Evangelization of Western Europe in the Seventh Century," also in *Irland und die Christenheit.*

14. D. P. Kirby, *The Earliest English Kings* (London, 1991), pp. 1–29.

15. On the royal role in the conversion of Anglo-Saxons, see William A. Chaney, *The Cult of Kingship in Anglo-Saxon England: The Transition from Paganism to Christianity* (Berkeley and Los Angeles, 1970), pp. 156–73. The quotation is on p. 3.

16. Arnold Angenendt, "The Conversion of the Anglo-Saxons Considered against the Background of the Early Medieval Mission," in *Angli e Sassoni al di qua e al di là del mare, SSAM* 32 (Spoleto, 1986), pp. 778–81.

17. Ibid., pp. 749–54.

fled or were expelled (although never killed) and the work of conversion might be largely undone. Still, in a society where kings were religiously important and had the power to carry out a religious change if their leading supporters agreed, the strategy of conversion from the top usually set in motion the conversions of whole peoples, for whom mass baptisms were a major public acknowledgment of the change. Anglo-Saxon paganism did not simply collapse before the Christian advance, but within ninety years of the landing of Augustine, the South Saxons, the last holdout of official paganism, had yielded to Christianity, although the penetration of Christianity to the grass roots of society took much longer.[18]

Mass baptisms were not the only way that Christian initiation was carried out in seventh-century Anglo-Saxon England. Probably to impress on rulers the seriousness of their decision to convert, missionary bishops provided them and their families with something approximating the full episcopal liturgy of baptism.[19] Bede reported that when the still-pagan King Edwin's daughter was born on Easter 626, she was kept unbaptized until Pentecost, fifty days later, when she and eleven others were baptized.[20] When King Edwin himself decided to be baptized he became a catechumen and waited for baptism until one of the fixed times, Easter (12 April 627). While Bishop Paulinus was instructing Edwin during the catechumenate, the latter had a wooden church built for the occasion—no river or open-air baptism for him. When all was ready, "King Edwin [of Northumbria] with all the nobles of his race and a large number of the common people accepted the faith and the bath of holy rebirth." Conversion became a family affair for Edwin's kin. Bede went on to specify that Edwin's sons, Osfrith, Eadfrith, Æthelhun, and Uscfrea, and his daughter Æthelthryth were subsequently baptized, as well as his grandson Yffi, son of Osfrith.[21]

Bede's account of the conversion of the South Saxons by Bishop Wilfrid is a textbook case of the dynamics of conversion. In Bede's narrative, the political context surrounding the conversion is visible, though not stressed. Although a pagan, King Æthelwealh of the South Saxons had a Christian

18. Stancliffe, "Kings and Conversion," pp. 59–94; James Campbell, "Observations on the Conversion of England," *Ampleforth Journal* 78 (1973), and reprinted in idem, *Essays in Anglo-Saxon History* (London, 1986); Chaney, *Cult of Kingship*, p. 166.

19. Eleonore Varrentrapp, *Über den Zusammenhang von Taufe und kirchlichen Unterweisung in der christlichen Frühzeit Deutschlands* (Marburg, 1946), pp. 95–106.

20. Bede, *HE*, 2.9, pp. 166–67.

21. Ibid., 2.14, pp. 186–87. The *Vita sancti Gregorii*, c. 15, in *The Earliest Life of Gregory the Great by an Anonymous Monk of Whitby*, ed. and trans. Bertram Colgrave (Lawrence, Kan., 1968), pp. 96–98, related an incident that occurred while Edwin was a catechumen receiving instruction from Bishop Paulinus.

wife named Eafe. He also had a powerful neighboring king, Wulfhere of Mercia, who had become a Christian in unknown circumstances. During a royal parley with King Wulfhere in the Kingdom of Mercia, Æthelwealh was baptized by Bishop Wilfrid. We may presume that he was there for political reasons, but Bede said nothing of that. Bede also said nothing about a catechumenate for Æthelwealh, but Wilfrid may have omitted it to take advantage of an opportunity presented by political circumstances. Bede stressed that Æthelwealh was baptized in the presence of and with the encouragement of the Mercian king, who sponsored him. After Æthelwealh had been baptized, Bishop Wilfrid baptized other important people, and four priests subsequently baptized the lesser folk of the South Saxons.

> Æthelwealh, the king of that people, was baptized not too long before in the province of the Mercians, King Wulfhere was present and encouraging [him]. When he [Æthelwealh] had come out of the font, he was received by him [Wulfhere] in the position of a son; in a sign of that adoption he [Wulfhere] gave him two provinces, that is, the Isle of Wight and the district of the Meonware among the West Saxon people. [Thereafter, Bishop Wilfrid] with the king [Æthelwealh] permitting, nay rather very joyful, washed the first men of the region [of the South Saxons], ealdormen and gesiths in the very holy font, but the priests Eappa and Padda and Burghelm and Oiddi baptized the rest of the people either then or later.[22]

Bede and the *Anglo-Saxon Chronicle* named other kings who received a formal baptism with prominent sponsors—kings or bishops.[23]

Three points stand out. First, there was significant variation in how baptism was administered, ranging from elaborate preparation for kings and their families, culminating in solemn baptism at Easter or Pentecost, to a few days of preaching and exorcism for ordinary people followed by baptism in whatever water was available. The origin of particular baptismal rituals—Ireland, Italy, Gaul—may have contributed to the diversity. Second, in mass baptisms the bishop or priest who baptized was more likely to be

22. Bede, *HE,* 4.13, p. 372: "Erat autem rex gentis ipsius Aedilualch non multo ante baptizatus in prouincia Merciorum, praesente ac suggerente rege Uulfhere, a quo etiam egressus de fonte loco filii susceptus est; in cuius signum adoptionis duas illi prouincias donauit, Uectam uidelicet insulam et Meanuarorum prouinciam in gente Occidentalium Saxonum. Itaque episcopus concedente, immo multum gaudente rege primos prouinciae duces ac milites sacrosancto fonte abluebat; uerum presbyteri Eappa et Padda et Burghelm et Oiddi ceteram plebem uel tunc uel tempore sequente baptizabant."

23. Ibid., 3.7, p. 232: King Oswald sponsored King Cynegils; 4.13, p. 372: King Wulfhere sponsored King Æthelwealh; 3.22, pp. 280–82: King Ethelwald sponsored King Suidhelm; *ASC*(*A*), s.a. 639: Bishop Birinus baptized and sponsored Cuthred, son of Cwichelm.

remembered than the sponsor. Third, when a baptism was administered individually or in a small group, it was more likely that the sponsor was remembered. When the sources refer to individual royal baptisms, which had political as well as religious consequences, the sponsor was sometimes remembered even a generation or two later. When a powerful king sponsored another king, often at the dominant figure's court, he was expressing his political superiority, which Bede described once as a form of religious adoption.[24]

Baptism in the Anglo-Saxon Church after Archbishop Theodore

By the late seventh century, the missionary situation had begun to give way to a more settled ecclesiastical organization in the Anglo-Saxon kingdoms. The energetic Archbishop Theodore of Canterbury (669–690) created a church organization that included territorial dioceses, councils of bishops, and closer observance of canon law. A unified Anglo-Saxon church long preceded a unified Anglo-Saxon kingdom.[25] In 731 there were eleven bishops south of the Humber and four in Northumbria, all of them Anglo-Saxons.[26] In addition there were priests, deacons, and lesser clergy who served in minsters and perhaps even in village churches.[27] In the more settled situation of the eighth century and beyond, baptism and sponsorship came to resemble the Continental forms, especially because infants born to Christian Anglo-Saxons were the usual candidates. In spite of such organizational developments, resources were still inadequate to provide pastoral care everywhere. For instance, Bede's letter of 735 to Archbishop Egbert of York stressed the failure to minister to rural people in that large

24. Arnold Angenendt, *Kaiserherrschaft und Königstaufe: Kaiser, Könige, und Päpste als geistliche Patrone in der abendländischen Missionsgeschichte* (Berlin, 1984), esp. pp. 176–96; Stephen Fanning, "Bede, *Imperium*, and the Bretwaldas," *Speculum* 66 (1991), cast serious doubt on the existence of an institution of Bretwalda, but the fact remains that there were dominant kings, some of whom Bede lists in *HE*, 2.5, pp. 148–50.

25. On Theodore's achievements, see *Archbishop Theodore: Commemorative Studies on His Life and Influence*, ed. Michael Lapidge, CSAE 11 (Cambridge, 1995), esp. pp. 1–29, where Lapidge described Theodore's career.

26. Bede, *HE*, 5.23, pp. 558–61.

27. Alan Thacker, "Monks, Preaching, and Pastoral Care in Early Anglo-Saxon England," in Blair and Sharpe, *Pastoral Care*, pp. 137–52. Cambridge and Rollason, "Debate," pp. 88–97, argued that in addition to minsters, other churches provided pastoral care in the pre-Viking period, even though they are poorly recorded in the sources. Catherine Cubitt, *Anglo-Saxon Church Councils, c. 650–c. 850* (London and New York, 1995), pp. 116–18, cautiously argued that the "minster hypothesis" about the provision of pastoral care should be applied flexibly.

diocese. Sometime after 757, a monk reported a vision of hell in which infants mourned because Bishop Daniel of Winchester had not seen to their baptism.[28] But even in the more settled condition that prevailed after the episcopate of Theodore, baptism and sponsorship in the Anglo-Saxon church never became exactly like those on the Continent. They retained or developed some features that will be explored in subsequent chapters.

28. Bede, *Epistola ad Ecgbertum episcopum,* in *Venerabilis Baedae opera historica,* ed. Charles Plummer (Oxford, 1896), 2:405–23. See also Boniface, *Epistola* 114, 1:249: "simulque infantium numerosam multitudinem sub Danielo episcopo maxime sine baptismo morientium tristem et merentem aspexit."

CHAPTER 4

Godparenthood from the Catechumenate

The best-known occasion for sponsorship is baptism, but for centuries there were at least two others, confirmation, which followed baptism, and the catechumenate, which preceded it. The entry to the catechumenate in fifth-century Hippo may be taken as typical of the practice of late Roman Christianity. When an adult was interested in conversion, he came to the bishop's residence. In a session that lasted perhaps an hour or two, a catechist gave him a description of the Christian faith and of proper behavior. If he said he accepted that account, a brief ceremony made him a catechumen. The sign of Christ, the cross, was made on his forehead; hands were laid on him for exorcism, during which evil was breathed out of him (*exsufflatio*); and he received a taste of blessed salt and perhaps a bit of blessed bread of the sort given to Christians who did not receive communion at Mass.[1] Catechumens were regarded as Christians of a second-class sort: members of the community even though they were unbaptized. Because there was no fixed period of time after which catechumens had to give in their names for baptism, the catechumenate often took on a life of its own, preceding baptism by weeks, months, or years. By the fourth century, some people, especially men, remained catechumens until they settled down in a legitimate marriage, or until advancing age, illness, or personal conversion prompted them to wash away their sins in baptism. Some prominent fourth-century bishops were catechumens well into adulthood. Ambrose was a catechumen at thirty-

1. Van der Meer, *Augustine the Bishop*, pp. 353–54.

five, when he was elected bishop of Milan in 379, and Augustine had been a catechumen for about thirty-three years when he was baptized in 387.[2]

The success of Christianity, joined with the conviction that infants had to be baptized to free them from Adam's sin, undermined the practice of becoming a catechumen who then delayed baptism. By the sixth century, the adult who remained a catechumen for an extended period became rare, though probably not unknown. Conservative liturgies preserved the catechumenate as the first step in Christian initiation, but when most candidates for baptism were infants, there was a tendency to compress the catechumenate, baptism, and first communion together and, for reasons to be discussed later, to separate confirmation from them.[3]

The Catechumenate in Anglo-Saxon England

When Ælfric translated the *Passio sancti Eustacii* in about A.D. 1000, he ran through the stages of initiation for adults, which differed little from those for the initiation of children: "and he [the bishop] thereupon christened them all; and instructed them in the mysteries of the holy faith, and baptized them in the name of the Father, and of the Son, and of the Holy Ghost, and [re]named Placidas Eustachius, and his wife Theophistis, and his first son Agapetus, and the second Theophistus, and gave them the holy sacrament of Christ's body and blood."[4] Thus, at the beginning of initiation, the baptizer performed ceremonies the translator, Walter Skeat, rendered as "christened" but which in fact constituted the traditional practice of making them catechumens (*and he hi þa gecristnode*).

The catechumenate was an integral part of Christian initiation, and the missionaries introduced it into Anglo-Saxon England. Because the catechumenate was embedded in a liturgical ritual, the first place to search for it in Anglo-Saxon England is in liturgical texts. The harvest of evidence is modest. In spite of baptism's importance in the life of every Christian, no baptismal service survives from early Anglo-Saxon England. A few liturgical texts, some of them mere scraps, date from before the tenth century, but

2. Augustine, *Confessionum libri xiii,* 1.18, p. 10. On catechumens who delayed baptism for long periods, see Van der Meer, *Augustine the Bishop,* pp. 148–53, and Jean Danielou and Henri Marrou, *The First Six Hundred Years,* trans. Vincent Cronin (London, 1964), pp. 301–9.

3. J. D. C. Fisher, *Christian Initiation: Baptism in the Medieval West: A Study in the Disintegration of the Primitive Rite of Initiation* (London, 1965), esp. pp. 109–40.

4. Ælfric, *Passio sancti Eustacii,* in *Ælfric's Lives of Saints,* ed. and trans. Walter W. Skeat, EETS OS (rpr. London, 1966), 2:196–97, lines 93–98.

none contains a baptismal service.[5] From the tenth and eleventh centuries, about ten books, and some fragments, for the use of bishops, properly called "pontificals" but sometimes "missals" and "sacramentaries," survive.[6] But by the tenth century, priests, not bishops, ordinarily baptized. Consequently, only five extant Anglo-Saxon pontificals contain a baptismal service, the *Leofric Missal* (Bodleian MS 579), the *Missal of Robert of Jumièges* (Rouen, Bibliothèque municipale 274 [Y.6]), a copy of the Romano-Germanic Pontifical (CCCC 163), the Red Book of Darley (CCCC MS 422), and the *Winchcombe Sacramentary* (Orléans, Bibliothèque municipale 127 [105]).[7] Priests must have had a sort of manual—perhaps called a *handboc*—containing directions and prayers for their services, including baptism; but no Anglo-Saxon priests' manual has survived.[8]

The *Leofric Missal*, named for its donor, Bishop Leofric of Exeter (1050–1072), has a full baptismal service, although there is nothing particularly "Anglo-Saxon" about it. The baptismal ritual is in a portion of the manuscript copied in Lorraine in the tenth century.[9] The catechumenal

5. Foot, " 'By Water in the Spirit,' " pp. 171–92, reconstructed baptism in the seventh and eighth centuries primarily from references in sermons and other literary texts. Willis, "Early English Liturgy from Augustine to Alcuin," in *Further Essays* pp. 191–243, reviewed all liturgical forms between 597 and about 800, including the sparse information on baptism.

6. Richard W. Pfaff, "Massbooks: Sacramentaries and Missals," in *The Liturgical Books of Anglo-Saxon England*, ed. Richard W. Pfaff, *Old English Newsletter*, Subsidia 23 (1995), 9–34, described the ten surviving manuscript sacramentaries. See also Janet L. Nelson and Richard W. Pfaff, "Pontificals and Benedictionals," in ibid., and Helmut Gneuss, "Liturgical Books in Anglo-Saxon England and Their Old English Terminology," in *Learning and Literature in Anglo-Saxon England: Studies Presented to Peter Clemoes on the Occasion of His Sixty-fifth Birthday*, ed. Michael Lapidge and Helmut Gneuss (Cambridge, 1985), pp. 131–33. Published Anglo-Saxon pontificals that do not contain a baptismal service include (a) *The Pontifical of Egbert*, in *Two Anglo-Saxon Pontificals* (*The Egbert and Sidney Sussex Pontificals*), ed. H. M. J. Banting, HBS, 104 (London, 1989); (b) *The Sidney Sussex Pontifical*, in Banting, *Two Anglo-Saxon Pontificals;* (c) *Pontificale Lanaletense (Bibliothèque de la Ville de Rouen A. 27 Cat. 368): A Pontifical Formerly in Use at St. Germans, Cornwall*, ed. G. A. Doble, HBS 74 (London, 1936); (d) *Claudius Pontifical I*, in *The Claudius Pontificals (from Cotton Ms. Claudius A.iii in the British Museum)*, ed. by D. H. Turner, HBS 97 (Chichester, 1971); (e) *The Missal of New Minster, Winchester*, ed. D. H. Turner, HBS 93 (London, 1962); and (f) *The Missal of Saint Augustine's, Canterbury*, ed. Martin Rule (Cambridge, 1896).

7. The Anglo-Saxon pontificals that do have a baptismal service are (a) *The Missal of Robert of Jumièges*, ed. H. A. Wilson, HBS 11 (London, 1896); (b) *The Leofric Missal*, ed. F. E. Warren (Oxford, 1883); (c) Romano-Germanic Pontifical, CCCC MS 163, pp. 28–47; (d) The Red Book of Darley, CCCC MS 422, pp. 367–99; and (e) *The Winchcombe Sacramentary (Orléans, Bibliothèque municipale, 127 [105])*, ed. Anselme Davril, HBS 109 (London, 1995). On extant baptismal services, see Sarah Larratt Keefer, "Manuals," in Pfaff, *Liturgical Books*, pp. 101–2.

8. Gneuss, "Liturgical Books," pp. 134–35 on priests' manuals and pp. 131–33 on pontificals. Keefer, "Manuals," pp. 99–109, described the probable contents of priests' manuals on the basis of texts preserved in other sorts of liturgical books.

9. See Pfaff, "Massbooks," pp. 11–14, for a summary of scholarship on the *Leofric Missal's* complex history.

ceremony was composed of traditional elements of exorcism, making the sign of the cross, and giving salt, carried out with prayers and a few rubrics for each step.[10] First, the priest blew on the candidate (*exsufflatio*) as an exorcism to expel Satan. The *Ordo* included the prayer at the *exsufflatio:* "Expel all blindness of the heart from him or her or them" . . . "so that imbued by the sign of your wisdom, he, she or they may escape the foul odors of all forms of cupidity and, joyful in the sweet smell of your precepts, may he, she or they serve You in your church." Next, the priest signed the candidate with the cross, accompanied by a prayer that asked God to "mercifully hear our prayers and keep this or these *electi* of yours in the power of the cross, by whose impression we sign him, her or them." The priest then asked God to give a new birth to the *electi:* "God, Who are the creator of the human race, may You also be its reformer, be merciful to the adopted peoples, and assign to the new covenant the offspring of a new birth, so that they may rejoice that they are sons of the promise through grace, which they could not attain through nature." Finally, the priest exorcised salt and placed a bit of it in the child's mouth: "When this prayer has been completed, let the priest take some of the salt and place it in the mouth of the infant, saying. . . ." The candidates were now catechumens. In the *Leofric Missal,* there was no significant interval between the catechumenal ceremonies and baptism: immediately after an infant had become a catechumen, the priest blessed the font and baptized the candidate. The whole service might have been completed in about half an hour.[11]

The *Missal* of Robert of Jumièges, bishop of London (1044–1050) and archbishop of Canterbury (1050–1052), is a manuscript of the early eleventh century. Its *Ordo . . . ad caticuminum faciendum* also led directly to the blessing of the font and the baptism of the candidate. The *Winchcombe Sacramentary,* which also has a continuous service for initiating infants, poses a problem of interpretation. It was written in England between 975 and 1000 but perhaps for a foreign prelate and never used in England. Its relevance for the liturgy of Anglo-Saxon England is open to question.[12]

The Red Book of Darley, part of which is an eleventh-century miscellany of liturgical matter, provides significant evidence on initiation because its rubrics are in Old English. The rubrics are badly faded, but R. I. Page was able to decipher them.[13] Unfortunately, the first few lines of the

10. *Ordo super electos: Ad caticuminum faciendum,* in *Leofric Missal,* ed. Warren, pp. 235–36.
11. *Leofric Missal,* pp. 236–38.
12. *Missal of Robert of Jumièges,* pp. 93–100; *Winchcombe Sacramentary,* pp. 86–93. On doubts that the *Winchcombe Sacramentary* was used in England, see Pfaff, "Massbooks," pp. 14–15.
13. R. I. Page, "Old English Liturgical Rubrics in Corpus Christi College, Cambridge, MS 422," *Anglia* 96 (1978). On the Red Book of Darley, see Pfaff, "Massbooks," pp. 21–24.

first rubric are illegible, but Page was able to read the letters [. . . .]*nunge,* which might be the remains of the word *cristnunge,* the Old English term for the catechumenal ceremonies. Each Old English rubric was followed by a Latin prayer or prayers. At the beginning of the service, the child became a catechumen. The priest was instructed to blow three times on the child (. . . *ðonne blawe se preost .iii. on þæt cild and cweð[e]*); then he was instructed to make the sign of the cross with his thumb on the child's forehead (*Do nu rode tacn [m]id þinum þuman on ðæs cildes forhe[afod] and cweð*); then to make the same sign on the child's breast (*Do nu on ðam breostum rodetacn. and cweð*); then to place his hand on the child's head (*Do nu þi[n] hand uppan þæs cildes heafod and cweð*); then to bless the salt (*her is bletsung [t]o þam sealt[e]*); then to ask the child's name and to place salt in its mouth (*Axa nu þæs cildes naman and do of þisum gehalgodan sealte on þæs cildes muð*); then to mark again the child's head with the sign of the cross; and then to recite a series of collects or short prayers, certain of them over girls (*mædencild*), others over boys (*hise cild*), and some over either sex. Without any break, the priest then proceeded to recite the *Pater Noster* and the Creed, which signaled the beginning of the baptismal ritual proper.[14]

In the catechumenal ceremony, the candidate was anointed, usually on the head, chest, and back. Clergy were reminded of the distinctiveness of the catechumenal ceremonies because they were required to use a special consecrated oil. About 1000, Abbot Ælfric, who was learned in liturgy, wrote two letters to Archbishop Wulfstan, one in Latin and one in Old English, in which he treated the oil used in the catechumenal ceremonies. Ælfric distinguished three sorts of holy oil, which he insisted be kept in separate containers because they were for different uses. The three kinds, which priests obtained annually from their bishop at the Holy Thursday services, were *oleum sanctum (haliȝele), oleum chrismatis (crisma),* and *oleum infirmorum (seocera manna ele).* He reminded priests that only the *oleum sanctum* was used on catechumens: "With the holy oil you shall mark the heathen child on the chest and in the middle between the shoulders with the sign of the cross, before you baptize it in the baptismal water."[15]

14. Page, "Old English Liturgical Rubrics," pp. 150–52.

15. Ælfric, Second Old English Letter for Archbishop Wulfstan (Chrismabrief), c. 5, in *Die Hirtenbriefe Ælfrics in altenglischer und lateinischer Fassung,* ed. Bernhard Fehr, BAP 9 (Hamburg, 1914), p. 148: "Mid þam haliȝan ele ȝe scylan þa hæþenan cild mearcian on þam breoste and betwux þæm [ȝe]schuldru on middewearden mid rode tacne, ærþanþe ȝe hit fullian on þam fantwætere. "See also Ælfric's Latin Letter to Wulfstan, c. 5, in ibid., p. 58: "Cum oleo sancto debetis signare infantes in pectore and inter scapulos, antequam mittantur in fontem baptismatis."

Thus the Anglo-Saxon church preserved the catechumenate because a conservative liturgy demanded it, but for infants it was a status that lasted only a few minutes. The status of adult catechumen, between pagan and baptized, was also preserved in the liturgy, however, in something like suspended animation. In fact it came to life, at least temporarily, in Anglo-Saxon England to meet the special circumstances of a society in contact with numerous non-Christians.

The Vocabulary of the Catechumenate

Before the catechumenate in Anglo-Saxon England can be discussed, its vocabulary must be clarified. The Latin vocabulary was based on the Greek word *catechumenos,* which meant "one who is instructed." Not only did Latin texts from Anglo-Saxon England use the word *catecuminus,* but they were among the earliest to use a noun for the catechumenate itself. The early-eighth-century *Penitential* of Theodore recommended that there be a sponsor *in catecumeno,* implying *catecumenus* or *catecumenum* as the word's nominative form. This is an odd usage that would seem to designate the person, the catechumen (*catecumenus*), rather than the institution, the catechumenate. The lexicographers of the *Mittellateinisches Wörterbuch* corrected that citation from Theodore's *Penitential* to *catechumen*[*i*]*o.*[16] Their decision is confirmed by the *vita* of Pope Gregory I, written by an anonymous monk of Whitby between 704 and 714, which referred to King Edwin's time of preparation for baptism as the *catacumenium.*[17]

The Latin verb for carrying out the entry to the catechumenate was usually *cathecizare,* which originally meant "to instruct." Because infants could not really understand teaching or memorize prayers, the actual instruction was fossilized in the liturgy, and *cathecizare* came to mean the performance of the catechumenal rituals and exorcisms. Those who had been made catechumens and were ready for baptism, whatever their age, were sometimes called *catechizati* ("those who have been instructed").[18]

The Anglo-Saxon clergy had an Old English vocabulary for the catechumenate. In the tenth and eleventh centuries, the verbs *cristnian/gecristnian*

16. *Mittellateinisches Wörterbuch bis zum ausgehenden 13. Jahrhundert,* 2/3, col. 368. See also *A Dictionary of Medieval Latin from British Sources,* fascicule II:C, s.v. "catechumenium," ed. by R. E. Latham (Oxford, 1981), p. 299.

17. *Vita sancti Gregorii,* c. 15, p. 96: *peracto catacuminio.* In Italy, *catechumenium* apparently meant the space in a church set aside for the catechumens; see J. F. Niermeyer, *Mediae latinitatis lexicon minus* (Leiden, 1976), p. 157.

18. *Dictionary of Medieval Latin from British Sources,* fascicule II:C, s.v. "catechizare," p. 299.

designated entry to the catechumenate, and the noun *cristnung* named the ceremony itself.[19] A person who was a *catecumenus* or a *catechizatus* was designated by the Old English past participle *gecristnod*.[20]

The Old English terminology for the catechumenate has occasionally confused modern scholars because in Middle and Modern English it has come to mean something else. From the twelfth century onward, *cristnen* did not usually mean "to make a catechumen"; instead, it replaced the Old English verbs *fullian/fulwian* ("to baptize). By extension, *cristnen* could also mean "to name," as the word *christen* still does, because the infant was given a name when it became a catechumen.[21] In the high medieval baptismal service, the catechumenate continued to exist as the first ritual, but it was designated in Middle English by words different from the Old English ones. The Middle English verb for the making of a catechumen was *primseinen,* which is not attested in Old English. It was probably borrowed from the Old Norse and Old Icelandic term *prim-signa*.[22] The words *prim-signa* and its derivative *primseinen* presuppose Latin words such as *prima signatio* or *primum signum* ("first signing") or the verb *praesignare,* each of which emphasized that entry to the catechumenate was the first time that the pagan was marked with the sign of the cross. I have not found *prima signatio* or *primum signum* in Anglo-Saxon Latin. An eleventh-century text composed in England did, however, use a related word, *praesignaculum,* three times for entry to the catechumenate.

The *Vita sancti Rumwoldi,* composed in the late Anglo-Saxon period or soon after the Norman Conquest, is the life of a legendary seventh-century royal infant-saint, who lived only three days. Little Rumwold emerged from his mother's womb professing his faith in the Trinity and requesting baptism. He knew his baptismal ceremonies well and gave explicit instructions: "At the end of the hymn, the child asked to be made a catechumen by the priest Widerin, and to be held aloft by Eadwald for the preliminary

19. *Cristnian,* in Ælfric, *Vita s. Martini episcopi et confessoris,* line 522, in *Ælfric's Lives of Saints,* 2: 252; *gecristnian* in *Confessionale Pseudo-Egberti,* II.13b, in *Das altenglische Bussbuch (Sog. Confessionale Pseudo-Egberti): Ein Beitrag zu den kirchlichen Gesetzen der Angelsachsen,* ed. Robert Spindler (Leipzig, 1934), p. 180; *cristnung* in *Confessionale Pseudo-Egberti,* II.12a, p. 180.

20. See *A Microfiche Concordance to Old English,* comp. Richard L. Venezky and Antonette di Paolo Healey (Newark, Del., 1980), where versions of *catechumenus* and *catechizatus* appear under entries for *gecristnad, gecristnade, gecristnod, gecristnode* and *gecristnodes.*

21. *Middle English Dictionary,* p. 3:C (Ann Arbor, Mich. 1959), pp. 747–48, s.v. *cristnen* and *cristning.* On the replacement of *fulwian* ("to baptize") by *cristnen* and *baptizen,* see Hans Käsmann, *Studien zum kirchlichen Wortschatz des Mittelenglischen, 1100–1350* (Tübingen, 1961), pp. 202–3.

22. *Middle English Dictionary,* pp. 1302–3: "primseinen." On Old Norse *prim-signa,* see Richard Cleasby, *An Icelandic-English Dictionary,* subsequently enlarged by Gudbrand Vigfusson, 2d ed. with supple. William A. Craigie (Oxford, 1957); and Johan Fritzner, *Ordbog over det gamle norske Sprog,* ed. Didrik Seip and Trygve Knudsen (Oslo, 1954), 3:951–52.

rite of the faith (*ad praesignaculum fidei*) and to be named Rumwold."[23] Rumwold identified the priest Widerin as the person who *praesignauit* him.[24] Thus, the author of the *vita* called entry to the catechumenate the *praesignaculum*, a ceremony performed by a priest, at which the child received a name and—an important point for this book—with a sponsor who held (*tenere*) the child.

Most Old English sermons, penitentials, and other ecclesiastical documents were translated or adapted from Latin texts, some of which mentioned the catechumenate. Old English translators generally understood the distinction between the catechumenate and baptism. Martin of Tours (d. 397) was perhaps the most popular saint of the early Middle Ages and certainly the most popular in the Frankish kingdom.[25] Sulpicius Severus's *vita* of Martin of Tours, written in the early fifth century, was the fountain out of which flowed innumerable sermons, exempla, and miracle accounts. Like many males in the fourth century, Martin spent a period of time as a catechumen, in his case eight years. Sulpicius Severus understood contemporary practices and carefully distinguished between Martin the catechumen and Martin the baptized Christian; his text gave Old English translators and adaptors an opportunity to make that same distinction.[26]

In what must be a record, Martin's life was treated at least five times in Old English homilies and saints' lives.[27] Probably the earliest extant Old English sermon on Saint Martin is Blickling Homily 18, which survives in a late-tenth-century manuscript. It was composed for the saint's feast on 11

23. *Vita sancti Rumwoldi,* c. 3, in *Three Eleventh-Century Anglo-Latin Saints' Lives: Vita S. Birini, Vita et Miracula S. Kenelmi, and Vita S. Rumwoldi,* ed. Rosalind Love (Oxford, 1996), pp. 98–99: "Enimuero finito ymno rogat se infans catecuminum ab Widerino sacerdote fieri et ab Eadwaldo teneri ad praesignaculum fidei et Rumwoldum uocari"; see also c. 4, p. 98: "perfecto namque praesignaculo."

24. Ibid., c. 4, p. 100.

25. Sharon A. Farmer, *Communities of Saint Martin: Legend and Ritual in Medieval Tours* (Ithaca, N.Y., 1991).

26. Sulpicius Severus, *Vita sancti Martini,* 2.3, in *Vie de Saint Martin,* ed. Jacques Fontaine, (Paris, 1967), 1:254: "Nam cum esset annorum decem, inuitis parentibus ad ecclesiam confugit seque catechumenum fieri postulauit."

27. Marcia Dalbey, "The Good Shepherd and the Soldier of God: Old English Homilies on St. Martin of Tours," *Neuphilologische Mitteilungen* 85 (1984), pp 422. Homilies on Martin are (a) Blickling Homily 18, in *The Blickling Homilies,* ed. R. Morris, EETS OS 63 (London, 1876), pp. 210–27; (b) Vercelli Homily 18, in *The Vercelli Homilies and Related Texts,* ed. D. G. Scragg, EETS OS 300 (Oxford, 1992), pp. 289–309; (c) an unpublished (?) homily in MS Junius 86, ff. 62–81, described in N. R. Ker, *Catalogue of Manuscripts containing Anglo-Saxon* (Oxford, 1957), pp. 410–411, and collated with the Blickling version in A. S. Napier, "Old English Notes," *Modern Philology* 1 (1903–1904), 393; (d) Homily 34, in *Ælfric's Catholic Homilies: The Second Series: Text,* ed. Malcolm Godden, EETS SS 5 (London, 1979), pp. 288–97; and (e) Ælfric treated Martin in his *Lives of Saints,* 2:218–312.

November.[28] Sulpicius Severus reported that Martin's parents were pagans who opposed their son's conversion. The ten-year-old Martin defied them and became a catechumen. When the anonymous Anglo-Saxon preacher wanted to tell his hearers in their own language—Old English—what happened, he wrote: "When he was ten years old, and his parents put him to, and taught him, a temporal profession, then he fled to the church of God, and entreated to be cristened (*gecristnode*), that the first part of his endeavours and of his life might be turned toward belief and baptism."[29] Vercelli Homily 18 is another version of the same sermon, but is more explicit about the place of the catechumenate in Christian initiation: "And when he was ten years old, his parents then put him to a worldly profession and then he fled to God's church and entreated that he be christened there—*that is the beginning and the first part of holy baptism.*"[30] The Vercelli homilist had his theology right: the catechumenate was only "the beginning and first part of holy baptism," and as Napier pointed out, this comment had no corresponding passage in known Latin sources.[31] It was an explanation of the catechumenate for a contemporary hearer or reader.

Sulpicius Severus wrote that at age fifteen Martin was forced to become a Roman soldier, which the Blickling homily said was four years before his baptism and the Vercelli homily (following Sulpicius's *vita*) said was three years.[32] Both homilists stressed that even though Martin was not baptized, but only *gecristnod,* he led so good a life as a soldier that it was as if he were baptized.[33] Baptism remained, however, the decisive moment of escape from Satan's realm to that of Christ; it brought to completion the change that had only begun when Martin became a catechumen. Severus reported that Martin became a catechumen when he was ten years old and was baptized at about eighteen: hence his status as a catechumen lasted about eight years. The Vercelli homily repeated Severus's chronology, but the Blickling homily said Martin was twenty when he was baptized. Both homilists shared the same error with respect to Severus's account when they re-

28. Blickling Homily 18, pp. 210–27.

29. Ibid. pp. 210–11: "þa he wæs tyn wintre, & hine his yldran to woruld-folgaðe tyhton ond lærdan, ða fleah he to Godes ciricean, & bæd þæt hine mon gecristnode, þær æresta dæl his onginnes & lifes to geleafen & to fulwihte gecyrred."

30. Vercelli Homily 18, pp. 291–308, on p. 292: "þæt bið sio onginnes and se æresta dæl þære halgan fulwihte."

31. Cited in Paul Szarmach, *Vercelli Homilies IX–XXIII* (Toronto, 1981), p. 63, note to lines 15–16.

32. Blickling Homily 18, p. 231: "þa wæs feower gear ær his fulwihte." See also Vercelli Homily 18, p. 292, lines 22–23; Sulpicius, *Vita,* c. 2.6, 1:256: "triennium fere ante baptismum."

33. Blickling Homily 18, pp. 212–13; Vercelli Homily 18, p. 293, lines 28–35; cf. Sulpicius, *Vita,* 2.6, 1:256.

minded their hearers that at age eighteen he was baptized and "he was christened (*gecristnod*) three years previously, as I said before."[34]

Severus's *vita* recorded another incident in Martin's career which challenged translators to keep the linguistic distinction between a catechumen and a baptized Christian. After Martin had founded the monastery of Ligugé, a catechumen (Sulpicius's text said *quidam catechumenus*) came to him for instruction. While Martin was absent from the monastery, the man died unbaptized (*ungefullad*), which troubled the saint greatly. By Martin's prayers, the catechumen returned to life and was immediately baptized and lived for many years.[35] Both homilies called the catechumen *sum gecristnod man.*[36]

Abbot Ælfric treated Martin's life twice, once in his collection of saints' lives and once in a sermon. His saints' lives were probably composed for a relatively learned audience. In the *Vita sancti Martini,* he carefully distinguished the catechumenate from baptism, as Sulpicius and the two Anglo-Saxon preachers had done. He used a vocabulary similar to that of the Blickling and Vercelli homilies, including *gecristnod* three times, *cristnian* once, and *to cristnigenne* once. But in his sermon on Martin, Ælfric used other words, perhaps because the audience for his sermons consisted of unlearned lay people. Like the Blickling and Vercelli homilies, he wrote that Martin was *gecristnod* at the age of ten. But thereafter he abandoned the precise terminology and called Martin simply "unbaptized" (*ungefullod*), in places where Sulpicius had called him a *catechumenus* and where the other homilies had called him *gecristnod.* In his telling of the incident of the catechumen who died while Martin was absent, Ælfric called him a "heathen man" (*hæðen wer*) rather than a catechumen (*gecristnod*).[37] This simplification of terms may have been prompted by the audience. Although the more learned among the clergy and monks understood the place of the catechumenate, the unlearned clergy and laity perhaps assimilated it to the compact ritual they understood simply as *fulluht,* baptism.

Other historical and hagiographic references to catechumens confirm that translators, presumably learned men, understood what the catechumenate was and distinguished it from baptism. For instance, Bede recorded that some important people in the seventh century passed through the cat-

34. Blickling Homily 18, p. 215; Vercelli Homily 18, p. 296, line 84; cf. Sulpicius, *Vita,* 2.6, 1:256.

35. Sulpicius, *Vita,* 7.1–6, 1:266–68.

36. Blickling Homily 18, p. 217; Vercelli Homily 18, p. 296, line 97.

37. Ælfric, *Vita sancti Martini,* lines 23, 207, 1037 (*gecristnod*), line 523 (*cristnian*), line 1036 (*to cristnigenne*); Ælfric, *Depositio sancti Martini episcopi,* in *Catholic Homilies,* p. 288, line 10: *gecristnod;* p. 290, line 95: *hæðen wer.*

echumenate on their way to baptism.[38] When his *Ecclesiastical History* was translated into Old English in the late ninth century, the translator used forms of *cristnian/gecristnian* to render Bede's references to Anglo-Saxon catechumens.[39] For example, Bede (3:7) related in Latin how the West Saxon King Cynegils was converted by Bishop Birinus, who "taught God's word there and converted the king to Christ's faith, and catechized him and, after a time, washed him in the laver of baptism, with his people the West Saxons." The Old English translator rendered *rex ipse catechizatus* as *hine gecristnade.*[40] Bede's Latin account of the conversion of King Edwin of Northumbria (2.14) distinguished between things that the king did while a catechumen and those he did after he had been baptized. The Old English Bede wrote, "After being catechized, he had also assigned an episcopal residence to his teacher and bishop, Paulinus. As soon as he was baptized, he began under the bishop's direction to erect and complete a larger and loftier church of stone, around the church previously built and enclosing it."[41] The tenth-century *Confessionale Pseudo-Egberti* repeated a provision of Theodore's eighth-century *Penitential* which forbade the baptized (*gefullad*) to eat with or exchange the kiss of peace with catechumens (*gecristnodon*).[42] The *Confessionale* also used the noun *cristnung* to translate the Latin word *catechumino,* which designated the catechumenal ceremonies.[43] In two eleventh-century homilies on baptism, Archbishop Wulfstan used the word *cristnung* to designate the ceremonies that preceded baptism.[44] Learned Anglo-Saxon churchmen understood that the catechumenate was distinct from baptism, even though in their society the rituals were often combined in one ceremony.

38. Bede, *HE,* 2.14, p. 186: referring to King Edwin, "cum cathecizaretur atque ad percipiendum baptisma inbuetetur," *HE,* 3.7, p. 232: referring to King Cynegils, "Cum rex ipse cathecizatus."
39. Bede, *The Old English Version of Bede's Ecclesiastical History of the English People,* ed. and trans. Thomas Miller, EETS OS 95, 96, 110, 111 (London, 1890–1898; rpr. 1959–1963).
40. Ibid., 3:5, pp. 166–68.
41. Ibid., II, p. 138: "Siðþan he wæs gecristnad, swylce eac his lareowe & biscope Paulini biscopseðel forgeaf. Ond sona þæs þe he gefulwad wæs, he ongon mid þæs biscopes lare maran cirican & hyrran stænenne timbran & wyrcan ymb þa cirican utan, þe he ær worhte."
42. *Confessionale Pseudo-Egberti,* p. 180, Discipulus Umbrensium, *Canones Theodori,* 2.18.11, in *Die Canones Theodori Cantuariensis und ihre Überlieferungsformen,* ed. Paul W. Finsterwalder, (Weimar, 1929), p. 318; *Iudicia Theodori Greci et episcopi Saxonum,* c. 123, in ibid. p. 249; *Canones sancti Gregorii pape urbis Romae,* c. 129, in ibid., p. 265; *Iudicium de penitentia Theodori episcopi,* c. 67, in ibid., p. 275.
43. *Confessionale Pseudo-Egberti,* p. 180: "In cristnunga and on þam fulluhte an fæder mæg beon, gif hit nydþearf bið."
44. Wulfstan of York, Homily 8b, in *The Homilies of Wulfstan,* ed. Dorothy Bethurum (Oxford, 1957), p. 172: "On þære cristnunge þe man deð ær þam fulluhte is swiðe micel getacnunge." See also Homily 8c, line 69, p. 179.

Theologically, the *cristnung* was explained as an attack on Satan's hold over the unbeliever.[45] Every unbaptized person, even the child of a Christian family, was a *hæðen* ("pagan"), held in Satan's power.[46] Ælfric saw in the priest's christening of a child a spiritual miracle comparable to the physical miracles worked by the apostles.[47] Archbishop Wulfstan of York described the ceremonies of the *cristnung* in three sermons, one in Latin and two in Old English. In the second sermon, which Dorothy Bethurum designated 8b, the recipient was a child (*cild*). But in the final and most developed sermon, 8c, Wulfstan described the significance of the rituals for any recipient:

> Beloved men, there is great symbolism at the *cristnung* which one performs before baptism. When the priest *cristnað,* then he breathes on the man, just as is fitting, in the form of a cross. And then the devil is immediately very terrified by God's might and with the priest's exorcism the devil is put to flight from the human creature, who was previously ruined through Adam, and a dwelling place will be made in the man for the Holy Spirit. . . . And the salt which the priest gives to the man in the mouth, when he *cristnað,* that signifies divine wisdom. Just as the body then feels the pungency of the salt, so shall the soul understand the prudence of wisdom. And when the priest sings before him *Credo in Deum,* then he strengthens his faith and with the faith he adorns and decorates his house, that is, he prepares his heart to dwell in God. And when the priest touches the nose and ears of the man with his spittle, then he thus symbolizes with this that he shall receive divine holiness and discernment both through smell and hearing. And when the priest anoints his chest and shoulders with holy chrism, then he surrounds the man with God's shield on both sides, that the devil may not fix any of his poisonous weapons in him, neither in front nor in back, if he henceforth perseveres steadfastly in the right belief and follows God's law. And when this has been done completely, as befits the *cristnung,* then after all this it is [proper] to hasten eagerly with right belief to the baptismal font.[48]

There can be no doubt that the catechumen and the catechumenate were known to learned Anglo-Saxons, both through the liturgy and the

45. Henry Ansgar Kelly, *The Devil at Baptism: Ritual, Theology, and Drama* (Ithaca, N.Y., 1985), esp. pp. 201–321.

46. *Confessionale Pseudo-Egberti,* p. 179: "Se ðe ofslea his bearn haeðen, fæste X wintre æfter canones dome."

47. Ælfric, *Sermo in Ascensione Domini,* in *Sermones Catholici,* 1:304: "Þonne se preost cristnað þæt cild, þonne adræfð he þone deofol of ðam cilde."

48. Wulfstan of York, Homily 8c, pp. 176–79. The Latin version of the homily, 8a, is on pp. 169–71; the second homily, 8b, is on pp. 172–74.

Latin literary heritage that formed the basis for much of their literature. In Wulfstan's homily, there is an interesting liturgical point that highlights the changes since antiquity. Because the catechumenate and baptism in the tenth and eleventh centuries ran as one unbroken ceremony, Wulfstan and others like him had to decide where the one ended and the other began. In the homily quoted above, the *cristnung* was larger than its late Roman ancestor. Wulfstan's *cristnung* ran from the beginning of the service, when the priest blew on the child, up to the approach to the font itself. In ancient Christianity, many of those ceremonies would not have been part of the catechumenal service but of the baptismal one.

The Rebirth of the Catechumenate in the Germanic North

Anglo-Saxon liturgical texts, penitentials, sermons, and saints' lives, whether in Latin or Old English, were usually based on Latin texts written centuries earlier, when adult catechumens were a recognized group in Christian communities. But were there actually catechumens (other than the ten-minute infant catechumens) whom an Anglo-Saxon homilist and his audience might have known? Or was the catechumenate in Anglo-Saxon England nothing more than a fossilized liturgical detail preserved in ancient Latin texts copied and translated without reference to contemporary reality?

By the seventh century in Christianized societies on the Continent, the catechumenate was usually just the preliminary ritual to baptism. No child of a Christian family was supposed to linger in that state. But the appearance of pagan peoples, some of them quite dangerous, breathed life into the old institution in Anglo-Saxon England and also in the Scandinavian north.[49] The search for actual adult catechumens in Anglo-Saxon England must therefore be conducted in the two distinct periods when pagans and Christians confronted one another in considerable numbers: the seventh century and the ninth and tenth centuries. For almost the whole of their history, Anglo-Saxon Christians had contacts with pagans, at first among their own people and later among Scandinavian raiders, traders, and settlers. Christian relations with adult pagans were full of tension and ambiguity. Theologically, the unbaptized were in the devil's grip, unclean and a spiritual threat: they could not be full members of the social or political community, which was conceived as God's people. Ninth- and tenth-century sources stressed the paganism of the Vikings, whose oaths and

49. Åke Sandholm, *Primsigningsriten under nordisk Medeltid* (Åbo, Finland, 1965), pp. 23–47 (with a German summary, pp. 101–3) treated the use of the catechumenate among Vikings.

agreements were suspect because they did not share the same god.[50] And yet Anglo-Saxons needed to build ties with their pagan neighbors, whether fellow Anglo-Saxons or dangerous outsiders. Sometimes pagans also found it useful to eliminate, or at least lower, the religious barrier separating them from their Christian employers, trading partners, or neighbors.

There were adult catechumens in seventh-century Anglo-Saxon England. For instance, several texts connected with Theodore of Canterbury (669–690) forbade the baptized to eat with or exchange the kiss of peace with catechumens.[51] Bede also mentioned adult catechumens who were instructed for a time before baptism, as did the anonymous author of the *vita* of Gregory the Great.[52] But the missionaries intended to baptize their Anglo-Saxon converts quickly, and no adult was supposed to remain a catechumen for an indefinite time.

The missionaries could not always get their way, however. William Chaney emphasized the peril inherent in the conversion of an Anglo-Saxon king. The abandonment of the old gods might be a danger to the dynasty. A military defeat or a natural disaster might be interpreted as a failure of the new religion and provoke apostasy, as the plague of 664 did in the kingdom of the West Saxons. Arnold Angenendt noted that when some early Anglo-Saxon kings converted to Christianity, their sons were slower to do so.[53] Royal sons who remained pagan may have been an insurance policy for their family and their people should things go wrong under the new religion. Angenendt observed that in some seventh-century pagan reactions against Christianity, the unbaptized son(s) of a Christian king led the pagan faction.[54] I suggest, though I cannot prove it, that some of the unbaptized royal sons in the seventh century might have been catechumens, who had a foot in each religious world.[55]

Cædwalla of Wessex (685–688) is the best candidate for being a catechumen for an extended period of time.[56] At first sight, some aspects of his ca-

50. Alfred P. Smyth, *King Alfred the Great* (Oxford, 1995), pp. 83–84, stressed the significance of religious difference when Christians wrote about Vikings.

51. Discipulus Umbrensium, *Canones Theodori,* 2.4.11, p. 318: "Non licet baptizatis cum cateciminis manducare neque osculum pacis eis dare"; cf. *Iudicia Theodori,* c. 123, p. 249: "Non licet babtizatis cum caticuminis manducare communiter"; *Iudicium de penitentia,* c. 67, p. 275: "Catecumini autem non debent manducare cum baptizatis neque osculum dare eis." The prohibition probably goes back to Hippolytus, *Apostolic Tradition,* c. 18, p. 76, which forbade the exchange of the kiss because the catechumens' kiss was not yet "holy."

52. Bede, *HE,* 2.14, p. 186; *Vita sancti Gregorii,* c. 15, pp. 96–98.

53. Angenendt, *Kaiserherrschaft und Königstaufe* pp. 66–72; and "Conversion," pp. 749–54.

54. Angenendt, "Conversion," p. 754.

55. On the king's significance for the "luck" of his people and on royal apostasy, see Chaney, *Cult of Kingship* pp. 12–17 and 156–73.

56. See Kirby, *Earliest English Kings* pp. 119–22.

reer are puzzling. Eddius Stephanus reported that when Cædwalla was in exile he sought Bishop Wilfrid as a patron: "diligently seeking the friendship of our holy father, he promised with a vow that he [Cædwalla] would be an obedient son to him and that he [Wilfrid] would be a faithful father to him [Cædwalla] in teaching and aid. They faithfully carried out this pact which they initiated with God as their witness."[57] Thus the pagan royal exile became the adopted son and political ally of the bishop. Cædwalla subsequently seized control of Wessex and became a formidable military leader in southern England. According to Bede, Cædwalla vowed that when he captured the Isle of Wight he would exterminate the inhabitants and give one-fourth of the island and of the war booty to the Lord. Bishop Wilfrid, Cædwalla's "father," received the gifts that had been promised.[58]

What strikes me as unusual is that these things occurred while Cædwalla was unbaptized. Bede is explicit that Wilfrid's "obedient son" was "not yet reborn in Christ" (*quamuis necdum regeneratus, ut ferunt, in Christo*).[59] In fact Cædwalla was never baptized in England. In 688 he gave up his throne after reigning only two years, perhaps because he was ill, and went to Rome, where Pope Sergius baptized him and renamed him Peter on 10 April 689. He died in his white baptismal robes and was buried on 20 April in St. Peter's Church.[60] If Cædwalla was a pagan during his career in England, it is difficult to make sense of such things as his bond with Bishop Wilfrid, their mutual promises of faithful fatherhood and sonship, his bloody vow to offer booty to the Christian God, and his decision to seek baptism at Rome. I do not know of any comparable alliance in the early Middle Ages between a bishop and a pagan king. But if Cædwalla was a catechumen, who put off baptism for personal or political reasons, the accounts make better sense. Unfortunately, no text says that he was a catechumen. This must remain a hypothesis.

By the end of the seventh century, the missionary phase of Christianity was coming to a close: the Anglo-Saxons, divided among many kingdoms and subkingdoms, were officially Christian, and a church was organized. Christianity did not put an end to political instability. Kings continued to have many rivals, and royal depositions and murders continued. But the

57. Eddius Stephanus, *Vita Wilfridi episcopi Eboracensis,* c. 42, in *The Life of Bishop Wilfrid by Eddius Stephanus,* ed. and trans. Bertram Colgrave (Cambridge, 1927), pp. 84–85.

58. Bede, *HE,* 4.16, p. 382.

59. Ibid., 4.16, pp. 382–83.

60. Ibid., 5.7, pp. 468–73. Claire E. Stancliffe, "Kings Who Opted Out," in *Ideal and Reality in Frankish and Anglo-Saxon Society: Studies Presented to J. M. Wallace-Hadrill* (Oxford, 1983), discussed the remarkable number of seventh- and eighth-century Anglo-Saxon kings who became monks or went to Rome on lifelong pilgrimage.

political turmoil no longer involved pagan factions among the nobles or the people. The practice of keeping the royal heir unbaptized also ended. Within Christian Anglo-Saxon society, the speedy baptism of infants became the norm. For example, Felix reported that Guthlac, who was probably born in the 670s, was baptized on the eighth day after his birth.[61] In the 690s, King Ine of Wessex ordered that every child be baptized within thirty days of birth, under threat of a fine of thirty shillings.[62] As the speedy baptism of infants became the norm, it is unlikely that there were many adult Anglo-Saxon catechumens, although the dearth of sources in the 150 years between Bede and the *Anglo-Saxon Chronicle* make it unwise to be too positive.

The situation changed in later Anglo-Saxon England. Between 793 and 1066, Scandinavians raided, traded, and subsequently settled in Anglo-Saxon England (and in the Frankish kingdom as well).[63] The presence of numerous, aggressive pagans posed serious problems for the Christian Anglo-Saxons and the Franks, who fought, negotiated truces, made treaties, exchanged hostages, ceded territory, paid tribute, fled, and occasionally surrendered to the invaders. I believe that the renewal of the catechumenate was another effort, admittedly a secondary one, to find a modus vivendi between Christian and pagan, primarily in Anglo-Saxon England.

Contemporary writers emphasized the paganism of the Vikings, which made cooperation across religious lines difficult. It is true that conversion was no panacea, because Christian Vikings still might attack their fellow Christians. But social relations could be eased if the pagans became Christian. Einhard's comments on the end of the Franks' long, bitter wars of the later eighth century with the pagan Saxons, although not referring to Scandinavians, are relevant: "The war which lasted for so many years was ended with this condition proposed by the king [Charlemagne] and accepted by them [the Saxons] that, having cast aside the worship of demons and other native religious observances, they would receive the sacraments of the Christian faith and religion and united to the Franks, they would be made one people with them."[64] Charlemagne's policy of peace conditional on religious conversion was successful. Within a generation the Saxons had embraced Christianity and Saxony was an important part of the Frankish Empire and of Christendom.

61. Felix, *Vita sancti Guthlaci,* c. 10, in *Felix's Life of Saint Guthlac,* ed. and trans. Bertram Colgrave (Cambridge, 1956), pp. 76–77.
62. *The Laws of King Ine,* c. 2, in *EHD,* p. 399.
63. For a brief survey, see H. R. Loyn, *The Vikings in Britain* (London, 1977).
64. Einhard, *Vita Karoli Magni,* c. 7, in *Ausgewählte* 6 (Darmstadt) (1968), 174–76.

The religion of the northern Germanic peoples was not moribund.[65] A Viking's conversion to Christianity was a serious step; for it meant a break with his ancestors, his pagan kinsmen and neighbors, and the legal system intertwined with the worship of the traditional gods. The twelfth- and thirteenth-century writers of Icelandic sagas believed that their ninth- and tenth-century ancestors had been reluctant to convert.[66] Although it does not concern Vikings, the *vita* of Saint Wulfram of Sens, a late-eighth- or early-ninth-century text, is relevant because it offers an interpretation of a pagan Germanic reaction to the consequences of conversion. It reported that the Frisian leader Radbod was ready for baptism but drew back when Bishop Wulfram told him that the dead kings, princes, and nobles of his people were in hell and, were he baptized, he would not join them after death. Radbod is reported to have said that "he could not be without the companionship of his predecessors, the princes of the Frisians, and reside [instead] in that heavenly kingdom with a small number of the poor."[67]

In their northern homelands, Scandinavian kings and major chiefs were slow to accept Christianity, and until they did, it was unlikely that their warriors and ordinary people would do so. For a long period, Christianity was one element in the syncretistic mix of Scandinavian religions, introduced by warriors and traders returned from Christian lands.[68] Only in the late tenth and eleventh centuries did Christianity gain official acceptance in Scandinavia itself.[69] In Christian lands, however, some individual Scandinavian raiders and traders did accept baptism. In Anglo-Saxon England and in Francia, the Christian Viking was not an unusual figure in the ninth and tenth centuries.[70] Some Viking "converts" undoubtedly misunderstood the serious consequences attached to baptism, perhaps seeing it as little more than a rite they underwent in order to get along. Christians

65. On the strength of Viking religion in the ninth-century British Isles, including the practice of human sacrifice, see Alfred P. Smyth, *Scandinavian Kings in the British Isles, 850–880* (Oxford, 1977), pp. 189–94 and 221–23.
66. Paul Schach, "The Theme of the Reluctant Christian in the Icelandic Sagas," *Journal of English and Germanic Philology* 81 (1982).
67. Jonas, *Vita Uulframni episcopi Senonici*, c. 9, ed. Bruno Krusch and Wilhelm Levison, *MGH SRM* 5 (Hanover and Leipzig, 1910), p. 668.
68. Wolfgang Lange, *Studien zur christlichen Dichtung der Nordgermanen, 1000–1200* (Göttingen, 1958), pp. 17–23 and passim, on *die gemischte Glaube* ("mixed, i.e, syncretistic, belief") in tenth- and eleventh-century Norway and Iceland.
69. Lesley Abrams, "The Anglo-Saxons and the Christianization of Scandinavia," *ASE* 24 (1995); Peter Sawyer, "The Process of Scandinavian Christianization in the Tenth and Eleventh Centuries," in *The Christianization of Scandinavia*, ed. Birgit Sawyer, Peter Sawyer, and Ian Wood (Alingsas, Sweden, 1987); and Birgit Sawyer and Peter Sawyer, *Medieval Scandinavia: From Conversion to Reformation, circa 800–1500* (Minneapolis, 1993), pp. 100–128.
70. William G. Collingwood, "Christian Vikings," *Antiquity* 1 (1927).

hoped for a more profound change, and their eagerness to encourage baptism made them vulnerable to Viking behavior that they interpreted in retrospect as evidence of fraud or guile. In the late ninth century Notker Balbulus, a monk of St. Gall, complained that some *Nordmanni* had come annually around Easter to be rebaptized at the court of Louis the Pious in order to get baptismal gifts and baptismal clothes from their sponsors.[71]

Although some Vikings accepted baptism, others did not wish or dare to abandon the traditional gods fully, and yet they knew there were advantages in being Christians if they wanted to take mercenary service or conduct trade among Christians. They were open to a syncretistic participation in Christian and pagan beliefs and practices. The catechumenate offered a compromise between conversion and paganism for those who wanted to live in both religious worlds. In their desire for ways to tame the Vikings, Christian clergy and rulers must have suggested this strategy, because the pagan Vikings knew nothing about the catechumenate or other details of Christian liturgy and theology. This was a northern phenomenon. There was no revival of the catechumenate for adult pagans in Mediterranean Christianity or even, so far as I know, within the Frankish lands, where the practice with Vikings seems to have been baptism or nothing. In the late ninth and tenth centuries, Anglo-Saxon England pioneered in the revival of the catechumenate, which subsequently spread to Norway and Iceland through the activities of missionaries and through Christianized Vikings who returned home.

When a pagan Viking became a catechumen, in a ritual called "primesigning" in Old Norse, Christians could believe that he was no longer fully in Satan's control.[72] He was a Christian, although at the margins of the community. Cooperation was not guaranteed but more possible. From the Viking's own perspective, he had not fully abandoned his gods, and yet he could travel with safety in a Christian society, because he was a Christian of a sort and had a right to attend religious services and to interact peacefully with Christians.

An episode in *Egil's Saga,* composed about 1230, illustrates some of the social consequences of becoming a catechumen, at least as they were remembered or imagined by a thirteenth-century Christian Scandinavian. *Egil's Saga* reported that when the Anglo-Saxon King Athelstan (924–939)

71. Notker Balbulus, *Gesta Karoli,* c. 19, ed. Hans F. Haefele, *MGH SRG,* n.s. 12 (Berlin, 1959), and rpr. in *Ausgewählte* 7 (Darmstadt) (1969), 420–22.

72. On *primesigning* in Scandinavia, see Sandholm, *Primsigningsriten,* esp. pp. 23–47, and Lange, *Studien zur christlichen Dichtung,* pp. 179–81. Bernhard Kahle, "Die altnordische Sprache im Dienste des Christentums. Teil 1, Die Prosa," *Acta Germanica* 1 (1890), 364–67, treated the Old Norse vocabulary for baptism and sponsorship.

was seeking mercenaries, the pagan Vikings Thorulf and his brother Egil came from Flanders to England, where they entered Athelstan's service.

> England was Christian when these things took place, and had been so for a long time. King Athelstan was a good Christian: he was called Athelstan the Faithstrong. He requested Thórólf and his brother that they should have themselves primesigned [i.e., become catechumens], for this was a common custom of the time among traders and those who went on war-pay along with Christian men; for those who were primesigned held full communion with Christians and heathen too, yet kept to the faith which was most agreeable to them. Thórólf and Egil did this at the king's request; they both had themselves primesigned. They had three hundred men of theirs there who took the king's war-pay.[73]

Egil's Saga reported that these mercenaries saw in prime-signing a way to be acceptable both to Christians and to pagans, without much restraint on what they actually believed or did. A late-thirteenth-century source confirmed the views in *Egil's Saga.* In the *Norna-Gests Þáttr,* a stranger named "Guest" visited the court of King Olaf Tryggvason (c. 995–1000), where he was asked about his travels at other royal courts. After describing briefly life at a series of Scandinavian courts, he said, "I was also with King Hlödver [Louis] in the land of the Saxons, and it was there that I was prime-signed, because there I could not be otherwise, for Christianity was well observed there." Because "Guest" had been prime-signed, King Olaf permitted him to remain at court, although not for long if he continued to put off baptism.[74] *Egil's Saga* and the *Norna-Gests Þáttr* may reflect thirteenth-century views, but a Frankish source confirms their basic point that Scandinavian merchants, travelers, and mercenaries found it useful to enter the catechumenate. Rimbert, author of the *vita* of the missionary Anskar (801–865), wrote that in mid-ninth-century Denmark, "many willingly received the sign of the cross (*signaculum crucis*), in order to be made catechumens, as a consequence of which it was permitted to them to enter a church and to be present at services; but they put off the reception of

73. *Egil's Saga,* c. 50, trans. Gwyn Jones (Syracuse, N.Y., 1960), pp. 120–21; on Egil's two purported visits to England, see Gwyn Jones, "Egill Skallagrimsson in England," *Proceedings of the British Academy* (1952); on prime-signing in Old Norse sources, see Konrad Maurer, *Über altnordische Kirchenverfassung und Eherecht,* in *Vorlesungen über altnordische Rechtsgeschichte* (Leipzig, 1907; rpr. Osnabrück, 1966), 2:435–40; 447–49; and 569–73.

74. Excerpts from the *Nornagests þáttr,* c. 10, in *The Saga of the Völsungs,* trans. George K. Anderson (Newark, Del., 1982), p. 186. On the *Norna-gests Þáttr,* see Joseph Harris and Thomas D. Hill, "Gestr's 'Prime Sign': Source and Significance in *Norna-Gests Þáttr,*" *Arkiv för Nordisk Filologi* 104 (1989), 112–17.

baptism, judging that this would be good for themselves that they be baptized at the end of their life so that purified by the saving bath, pure and unsullied they might enter the doors of eternal life without delay."[75] Thus some ninth-century Danes, whose contemporaries and kinsmen might have been raiding in England, sought the halfway status of catechumens. Rimbert's explanation, that they waited to be purified by baptism on their deathbeds so as to go directly to heaven, is perhaps too theological; although it was one of the arguments used to delay baptism in the late Roman Empire. The Danes were probably seeking the benefits of Christianity without fully abandoning their traditional religion. An Old High German gloss on the word *cathecumenos* captured succinctly the catechumen's intermediate state: they were *halbgloubig,* "half believing."[76]

The *Grágás,* an Icelandic law code generally reflecting twelfth-century practices, also emphasized the liminal status of catechumens, whether adults or children. A pagan was to be buried in unconsecrated ground; a baptized Christian in good standing was to be buried in the church cemetery; but "if a child dies who has received the *primum signum* but not been baptized, it is to be buried out by the churchyard wall, where hallowed and unhallowed ground meet, and no burial service is to be sung over it."[77]

Thus the catechumenate for adults was revived in Anglo-Saxon England and subsequently spread in Norway and Iceland to provide a status within Christian society for Vikings who could not or would not be baptized. The reinvigorated catechumenate was tied to special historical circumstances: the presence of dangerous adult pagans who could not be induced or forced to accept baptism but who would accommodate Christians by accepting the "prime-signing."

When missionaries from England and Germany converted Scandinavia during the late tenth and eleventh centuries, many of the Continental patterns of Christian behavior were slowly adopted. The baptism of infants soon after birth became normal there, as everywhere in Christian lands. Entry to the catechumenate was reduced to a preliminary ritual of baptism, as it had become in most long-Christianized places.[78] The adult catechumen again became rare or vanished, although the infant catechumen persisted. In Anglo-Saxon England, the end of the Viking threat also led to the

75. Rimbert, *Vita Anskarii,* c. 24, ed. Georg Waitz, *MGH SRG* 55 (Hanover, 1884), p. 53.

76. *Die althochdeutschen Glossen,* ed. Elias von Steinmeyer and Eduard Sievers (Berlin, 1895), 3:413.

77. *Grágás,* c. 1, in *Laws of Early Iceland: Grágás: The Codex Regius of Grágás with Material from Other Manuscripts,* trans. Andrew Dennis, Peter Foote, and Richard Perkins (Winnepeg, 1980), p. 26.

78. Sandholm, *Primsigningsriten,* pp. 48–64; Maurer, *Über altnordische Kirchenverfassung,* pp. 386–96.

transformation of the catechumenate once more into the preliminary ritual of infant baptism.[79]

Sponsorship at the Catechumenate

The catechumenate existed in Anglo-Saxon England, usually as a brief, liturgical status that every baptizee passed through and, for a time, as a liminal status for some pagan adults. There was a sponsor at the catechumenate, whose role must now be examined. In the late seventh or eighth century, the *Penitential* and the *Iudicium de penitentia,* both attributed to Archbishop Theodore, had declared it customary that someone receive at the catechumenate, that is, be a sponsor: "In the catechumenate and baptism and confirmation there can be one father if it is necessary; nevertheless that is not the custom but rather individuals receive in the individual rituals."[80] For more than three centuries after the Theodoran texts were composed, there is no specific reference in Anglo-Saxon sources to sponsorship at the catechumenate. The eleventh-century Latin *Vita sancti Rumwoldi* attested that there was a sponsor at the catechumenate: "At the end of the hymn, the child asked to be made a catechumen by the priest Widerin, and to be held aloft by Eadwald for the preliminary rite of the faith (*ad praesignaculum fidei*) and to be named Rumwold."[81] Although a literary fiction, the *vita* does indicate that an eleventh-century author in England thought that a proper baptism began with the catechumenal rites, which he called *praesignaculum,* at which a sponsor held the child.[82]

An eleventh-century Continental source also recorded a sponsorship at the catechumenate. In his *vita* of the monastic reformer William of Volpiano (962–1031), Rodulfus Glaber reported that William was born inside a castle in Italy during a siege conducted by the Emperor Otto I. When Otto made peace with William's father, it was agreed that "the boy, whom his wife had brought forth to him during the siege of his castle, should be made a catechumen through the imperial hand. He [Otto I] willingly agreed . . . and with his own right hand he held the boy and gave him the

79. On the catechumenate at the baptism of Rumwold, see Love, *Three Eleventh-Century Anglo-Latin, Saints' Lives,* pp. 135–38. The baptismal rituals in *Winchcombe Sacramentary,* pp. 86–94, *Leofric Missal,* pp. 233–38, and *Missal of Robert of Jumièges,* pp. 93–100 ran without a break from the catechumenate to the first communion.

80. Discipulus Umbrensium, 2.4.8, *Canones Theodori,* p. 317; *Iudicium de penitentia,* c. 69, p. 275.

81. *Vita sancti Rumwoldi,* c. 3, pp. 98–99; see also c. 4, p. 98: "perfecto namque praesignaculo."

82. *Ibid.,* c. 3, pp. 98–99; p. clix: the oldest manuscript, CCCC 9, is dated to the third or fourth quarter of the eleventh century.

name William. Subsequently the queen, his wife, received the boy from the holy font of baptism."[83]

The *Vita Willelmi* and the *Vita Rumwoldi* offer some insight into the ceremony of making a catechumen in the tenth and eleventh centuries. Otto I sponsored the newborn William at the catechumenate, just as the priest Eadwald sponsored the newborn Rumwold—each held the child. In both *vitae,* entry to the catechumenate was the moment when a child was given a name. That is confirmed by Flodoard of Reims, writing about 966, who recorded in his annals under the year 945 that "Queen Gerberga bore a son at Laon, who was called Charles when he became a catechumen (*ad catezizandum*)."[84] Furthermore, in a society where liturgical gestures were important, the *vitae* indicate what an observer might have seen. Eadwald held Rumwold during the ceremony, and Otto I held William specifically in his right arm.[85] In both *vitae,* entry to the catechumenate was followed immediately by baptism. There was one difference: Eadwald sponsored Rumwold both at the catechumenate and at baptism, whereas the royal couple shared the task, Otto as catechumenal sponsor and Adelaide as baptismal sponsor. The baptism of William of Volpiano was perhaps exceptional in having two sponsors, although the opportunity to end warfare by having two important people sponsor may have been at work. The imagined baptism of Rumwold was probably closer to usual practice, where one person sponsored at both ceremonies; it reflected the reality that by the eleventh century the catechumenate flowed readily into baptism and one person often sponsored an infant at both rituals.

A tenth-century text seems to confirm that the move from catechumen to baptized person was continuous and that the same sponsor acted in both ritual moments. The *Confessionale Pseudo-Egberti* or *Scrift Boc* was a tenth-century adaptation/translation of an unknown form of Theodore's *Penitential.*[86] Theodore's *Penitential* and another text attributed to Theodore, the

83. Rodulfus Glaber, *Vita domni Willelmi abbatis,* c. 1, p. 257: "ut filium, quem ei uxor sua . . . peperat, catecuminum fieri per manum imperialem preciperet. Quod ille libentissime annuens, ut monitus fuerat, impleri mandavit ac propria puerum sustulit dextera eique nomen indidit Willelmum. Quem scilicet postmodum regina, coniux illius, ex sacro fonte suscepit baptismatis"; also in Bulst, "Rodulfus Glabers Vita domni Willelmi abbatis," p. 464.

84. Flodoard, *Annales de Flodoard,* s.a. 945, ed. Philippe Lauer, CTSEEH 39 (Paris, 1905), pp. 95–96.

85. On the importance of gestures, see Heinrich Fichtenau, *Living in the Tenth Century: Mentalities and Social Orders,* trans. Patrick J. Geary (Chicago, 1991), pp. 30–49. The *Ordo ad baptizandum infantes,* c. 38, in *Le Pontifical Romano-germanique du dixième siècle,* ed. Cyrille Vogel and Reinhard Elze, *ST* 227 (Vatican City, 1963), pp. 163–64, instructed sponsors at confirmation to hold an infant in the right arm and to have an older candidate place a foot on the sponsor's foot.

86. On the *Confessionale Pseudo-Egberti,* see Cyrille Vogel, *Les "Libri Paenitentiales,"* revised by Allen J. Frantzen (Turnhout, 1985), pp. 39–40, or Allen J. Frantzen, *The Literature of Penance in*

Iudicium de penitentia, had recommended a distinct sponsor at the ceremony for making a catechumen but grudgingly allowed the same person to sponsor at the catechumenate, at baptism, and at confirmation, "if it is necessary."[87] That was the situation in the eighth century; things were different in the tenth. The person who translated the Theodoran text in the tenth century adapted it to reflect contemporary practice. It is possible that the Anglo-Saxon translator had in front of him a Latin text in which changes had already been made, but if so, it does not survive.[88] The translator wrote: *In cristnunga and on ðam fulluhte an fæder mæg beon, gyf hit nydþearf bið* ("In making a catechumen and in baptism, there may be one father, if it is necessary").[89] Note how the Theodoran text was changed. First, it was truncated by the omission of the reference to a sponsor at confirmation. That was because, by the tenth century, confirmation had become a separate ceremony, indeed a separate sacrament. Second, the translator retained the link between the catechumenate (*cristnung*) and baptism (*fulluht*) because, in the tenth century, they were ordinarily performed on the same occasion, one after the other. Finally, the translator undermined Theodore's main point—that it was customary to have a separate sponsor at each ceremony. The translator (or his Latin original) probably omitted that assertion because in his day the custom was for one person to sponsor at both rituals, although the clause about "necessity" allowed for separate sponsors.

I have found no explicit text that states that in Anglo-Saxon England sponsorship at the catechumenate created spiritual kinship. In Norway and Iceland, however, sponsorship at prime-signing did create such kinship, with sexual and social consequences. Evidence from those regions is relevant because Norway was christianized in part through the efforts of Anglo-Saxon missionaries, who probably introduced their own ecclesiastical customs.[90] Two Norwegian law codes refer to marital prohibitions arising from sponsorship at the catechumenate.[91] The *Older Law of the Gu-*

Anglo-Saxon England (New Brunswick, N.J., 1983), pp. 132–38. Frantzen's book is translated with some revisions in *La littérature de la pénitence dans l'Angleterre anglo-saxonne,* trans. by Michel Lejeune (Fribourg, 1991).

87. Discipulus Umbrensium, *Canones Theodori,* 2.4.8, p. 317: "In catecumino et baptismate ct confirmatione unus potest esse pater si necesse est non est tamen consuetudo sed per singula singuli suscipiunt"; *Iudicium de penitentia,* c. 69, p. 275.

88. *Poenitentiale Pseudo-Egberti,* in *Die altenglische Version des Halitgar'schen Bussbuches (Sog. Poenitentiale Pseudo-Egberti*). ed. Joseph Raith, BAP 13 (Hamburg, 1933), pp. xxviii–xxx, on the unidentified version of Halitgar from which Old English translator worked.

89. *Confessionale Pseudo-Egberti,* 11.12a, p. 180.

90. Sawyer, "Process of Scandinavian Christianization," pp. 68–87, esp. p. 83 on Anglo-Saxon influence in Norway; and Abrams, "Anglo-Saxons," pp. 213–25 on Anglo-Saxon missionaries in Norway.

91. Maurer, *Über altnordische Kirchenverfassung,* 2: 435–36.

lathing, composed in the eleventh century in a region on the west coast of Norway, specified that there were "six persons of spiritual kinship from whom we shall abstain as we do from our own kinswomen." The first was the sponsor at the catechumenate: "[the one who] holds the child when it receives the sign of the cross (*undir primsignan*)."[92] The *Older Law of the Frostathing*, a twelfth-century compilation, also placed the sponsor at the catechumenate sexually off limits: "No man shall take to wife a woman to whom he stands in spiritual kinship. And we shall honor this kinship with respect to the father or the mother as to the child itself. The one who holds the child when it receives the sign of the cross (*undir primsigning*) is the first in spiritual kinship."[93]

The *Grágás*, an Icelandic law code recorded in the twelfth century, is explicit on some of the social consequences of sponsorship at the prime-signing. In court proceedings in Iceland, a litigant was allowed to challenge the presence on judicial panels of people whose kin ties might make them biased. A litigant could challenge the participation of people related to his opponent by blood, by marriage, and also by any of three forms of spiritual kinship: "And men related by three kinds of spiritual kinship have to withdraw from the court: if either of them stood sponsor for the other at prime-signing or at baptism or at confirmation."[94] The Norwegian and Icelandic sources indicate that sponsorship at the catechumenate created spiritual kinship that had sexual and other social consequences, but there is no evidence of that from Anglo-Saxon England.

The rise of infant baptism in late antiquity profoundly remade the catechumenate, leading to its decline as a separate religious status between pagan and baptized. The liturgical rituals to make infants catechumens persisted, but initiation became a single ceremony incorporating both the catechumenate and baptism, carried out on an infant in a brief time by a priest, usually in a rural baptismal church.[95] The catechumenate remained identifiable, in part because it came to be given at the church door, whereas baptism took place at the font, within the church.[96] In such circumstances,

92. *Gulathing, Older Law of the*, c. 26, in *Norges gamle love indtil 1387*, ed. R. Keyser and P.A. Munch (Christiania, 1846), 1:16 and trans. Laurence M. Larson, *The Earliest Norwegian Laws, Being the Gulathing Law and the Frostathing Law* (New York, 1935), p. 55.

93. *Frostathing, Older Law of the*, 3.8, in *Norges gamle love*, 1: 150, and Larson, *Earliest*, pp. 248–49.

94. *Grágás*, c. 35 pp. 60 and 61.

95. Gy, "Du baptême pascal," demonstrated that although older practices persisted sporadically, baptism of infants had, by the tenth century, become a relatively brief ceremony running without break from the catechumenate to the child's first communion.

96. See, e.g., *The Sarum Missal Edited from Three Early Manuscripts*, ed. J. Wickham Legg (Oxford, 1916), pp. 123–31, where a rubric notes that after the child is made a catechumen, "Et intro-

the sponsor at the catechumenate was usually the sponsor at baptism, who thus acted for the infant from the beginning to the end of the compressed baptismal ceremony.

But the liturgy kept the catechumenate and its form of sponsorship in suspended animation. As in the cases of William of Volpiano and of Rumwold, sponsorship at the catechumnate could be revived for important people or for especially solemn baptisms. It was also revived in England and in Scandinavia for dealing with Vikings who wanted a recognized standing in a Christian society but were unwilling to be baptized. The revival of the catechumenate for adults in the Germanic north was temporary. With the passing of Viking paganism, the catechumenate again became a preliminary to the baptism of infants.

In later canon law, sponsorship at the catechumenate remained a source of marital prohibitions until the Council of Trent.[97] Jews, whose (sometimes forced) conversion to Christianity was suspect, might be required to observe a period as catechumens before being baptized.[98] But in ordinary circumstances, sponsorship at the catechumenate was often absorbed into baptismal sponsorship, which will be treated in the next chapter.

---

mittat eum in ecclesiam" (p. 128); and *Manuale et Processionale ad usum insignis Ecclesiae Eboracensis,* ed. W. G. Henderson, (London, 1875), p. 5: "Imprimis deferatur infans ad valvas Ecclesiae."

97. Franz Laurin, "Die geistliche Verwandtschaft in ihrer geschichtlichen Entwicklung bis zum Rechte der Gegenwart," *AKKR* 15 (1866), 239–41 and 264. On debate among thirteenth-century canonists about the *compaternitas* arising from "holding" an infant at the *catechismus,* another term for the *catechumenium,* see Joseph Freisen, *Geschichte des kanonischen Eherechts bis zum Verfall der Glossenliteratur,* 2d ed. (Paderborn, 1893), pp. 534–36.

98. Gratian, *Decretum,* in *De consecratione* 4.92, in *Corpus iuris canonici,* ed. Emil Friedberg vol. 1, (1879; rpr. Graz, 1955), col. 1392, cited a canon from the council of Agde (506) which prescribed an eight-month catechumenate for Jews who were to be baptized.

CHAPTER 5

Godparenthood from Baptism

Of the three common forms of sponsorship—at the catechumenate, at baptism, and at confirmation—the second is most familiar to modern readers. Before the sixth century, parents ordinarily sponsored their own children at baptism, making sponsorship a domestic matter that did not draw in outsiders and had limited potential for social significance. By the middle of the eighth century, a remarkable change had occurred which needs to be stressed: Byzantine, Roman, and Frankish churches *forbade* parents to sponsor their own children. The reason for the prohibition lies in the development of spiritual kinship, which came to be regarded as so real as to prohibit sexual contact. In 530, Justinian was the first to command in a written text that sponsors not be sexual partners to those whom they sponsored.[1] As the significance of spiritual kinship grew, the conviction grew with it that no spiritual relatives could be sexual partners. This had an unintended consequence: by sponsoring one's own child, a man or woman became a coparent to his or her spouse and hence should not have sexual relations with him or her.[2] The sexual prohibitions arising out of sponsorship will be treated in chapter nine. What must be stressed here is that the exclusion of biological parents from the sponsorship of their own children opened baptismal sponsorship to significant social possibilities: every parent had to choose a sponsor for every child; the act of choosing provided parents with an opportunity

1. *Codex Iustinianus,* bk. 5, tit. 4, law 26, 2:197. On Justinian's prohibition, see Lynch, *Godparents,* pp. 224–31.
2. Lynch, *Godparents,* pp. 223–42.

to achieve social as well as religious purposes; every child gained a new parent; and every parent gained a coparent. The exclusion of parents from sponsoring was crucial to the creation of a socially significant godparent complex.

The Latin and Old English Vocabularies of Baptism

Because baptism was one of the two central religious rituals of the Christian church (the other was the Eucharist), the sources on baptism in medieval society in general and in Anglo-Saxon society in particular are rich.[3] The Latin vocabulary for baptism was borrowed from Greek, where the basic meaning of the verb *baptizein* was "to dip in water." The commonest Latin verb was *baptizare,* and the noun was *baptismus.*

Baptism must have been one of the earliest Christian concepts presented to the pagan Anglo-Saxons, and to make it comprehensible to them, the missionaries gave baptism a vernacular vocabulary. Old English words for baptism were not borrowed directly from Latin or Greek, as so many ecclesiastical terms were. Instead, native Old English words were adapted to a new use. The etymology of the words for baptism is not certain. The Old English words *fulwian* or *fullian* ("to baptize") were apparently derived from ***full-wihan,* "to consecrate fully."[4] The corresponding Old English nouns for baptism were *fulwiht* and *fulluht.* There is another set of Old English words for baptism. In the Rushworth Gospels, which are in the Mercian dialect, and a few other texts, translators used the verb *dyppan* or *depan,* literally "to immerse or dip," to translate forms of *baptizare.* The verb *dyppan* is related to a family of Germanic words for baptism, including Old Saxon *dopian,* Dutch *doopen,* and German *taufen.* But the predominant words for baptism in Old English were derived from *fulwian/fullian.*[5]

3. There is no study of baptism comparable to Joseph Jungmann's magisterial work on the Mass, *Missarum Solemnia,* 5th ed., 2 vols. (Vienna, 1962); on the evolving theology of baptism in the early Middle Ages, see Peter Cramer, *Baptism and Change in the Early Middle Ages, c. 200–c. 1150* (Cambridge, 1993). Sarah Foot provided a useful introduction to baptismal practice in early Anglo-Saxon England in " 'By Water in the Spirit.' " In spite of its age, Jules Corblet, *Histoire dogmatique, liturgique, et archéologique du sacrement de baptême,* 2 vols. (Paris, 1881), is still useful.
4. Ferdinand Holthausen, *Altenglisches Etymologisches Wörterbuch,* 2d ed. (Heidelberg, 1963), p. 118; Helmut Gneuss, *Lehnbildungen und Lehnbedeutungen im Altenglischen* (Berlin, 1955), p. 86.
5. *Rushworth Gospels,* in *The Four Gospels in Anglo-Saxon, Northumbrian, and Mercian Versions,* 4 vols., ed. W. W. Skeat (Cambridge, 1871–1887). See Bosworth-Toller, *An Anglo-Saxon Dictionary,* s.v. "dyppan," pp. 221–22, and supplement by Campbell, s.v. "dipan," p. 153, "gedipan," p. 313, and "gedyppan," p. 387; Gneuss, *Lehnbildungen,* p. 86, on *fulwian* and *depan.*

The Latin and Old English Vocabularies of Baptismal Sponsorship

The sponsorship that took place at baptism also had specialized Latin and Old English vocabularies. The origin of the Latin terms probably lies in what participants and spectators saw the sponsor do at a baptism. A rubric in the seventh-century *Ordo Romanus XI* provides an instructive verbal picture: "And those people who are going to receive (*suscepturi sunt*) them [the infants] are ready with towels in their hands and they take (*accipiunt*) them from the bishop or deacons who baptize them."[6] The sponsor's taking of the dripping-wet infant from the arms of the baptizing clergyman was a visually striking act and became the essential moment that shaped the vocabulary of baptismal sponsorship.

In Latin, the act of sponsoring was commonly expressed by verbs of "taking" or "receiving" (*excipere, suscipere*) from the baptismal font. For example, an episode in the life of the Merovingian Queen Balthild (died c. 680), who was Anglo-Saxon by birth, involved "a certain little girl, whom she had received from the font of holy baptism."[7] In his rule for nuns, Bishop Donatus of Besançon (627–658) provided that "no [nun] should presume to take in baptism the daughter of anyone, whether rich or poor."[8] When the infant Anglo-Saxon saint Rumwold was baptized, he was received by the priest Eadwald (*suscipitur ab Eadwaldo*).[9] The act of taking the child was so important that occasionally a sponsor was called simply a *susceptor,* "one who receives."

In Old English the most common expression for baptismal sponsorship was *onfon æt fulwihte,* which meant "to take or receive at baptism," a direct translation of the Latin *recipere/accipere/suscipere in baptismo.* The *Anglo-Saxon Chronicle* described King Oswald's sponsorship of King Cynegils by saying that "Oswald received him."[10] When it recorded Bishop Birinus's

6. *Ordo Romanus XI,* c. 98, in *Les ordines,* 2:446.

7. *Vita sanctae Balthildis, recensio B,* c. 14, ed. Bruno Krusch, *MGH SRM* 2 (Hanover, 1888), pp. 500–501: "quandam infantulam, quam ex fonte sacri baptismatis susceperat"; see also Caesarius of Arles, *Sermo* 71.2, *CCSL* 103, p. 300.

8. Donatus of Besançon, *Regula ad virgines,* c. 54, *PL* 87, col. 290: "Nulla cuiuslibet filiam in baptismo neque divitis neque pauperis praesumat excipere"; see also Caesarius of Arles, *Sermo* 130.5, *CCSL* 104, p. 537; Gregory, *HF,* 8.1, p. 370; Caesarius of Arles, *Regula monachorum,* c. 10, in *Sancti Caesarii episcopi Arelatensis opera omnia* ed. Germain Morin (Maredsous, Belgium, 1942), 2:150.

9. *Vita sancti Rumwoldi,* c. 6, p. 102.

10. *ASC(A)*, s.a. 635, p. 28: "Oswold his onfeng"; see also s.a. 661, p. 30: "forþon Wulfhere hine onfeng æt fulwihte," and s.a. 878, p. 51: "his cyning þær onfeng æt fulwihte."

sponsorship of Cuthred, it used the expressive phrase *onfon to suna,* which meant "to take as a son."[11] The eleventh-century Red Book of Darley (CCCC 422, pp. 367–99) contains both a full baptismal service that runs from entry to the catechumenate to the first communion immediately after baptism and a truncated service for an ill child. The prayers are in Latin, but the rubrics are in Old English. After the water in the baptismal font was consecrated, the priest asked the child's name on four separate occasions, and on each, the godfather (*se godfæder*) provided it. The godfathers (*Þa godfæderas*) or godfather renounced Satan on behalf of the child. After the godfather expressed belief for the child, the priest dipped it in the water three times, and then "the godfather lifts up that child out of the water" (*and brede se godfæder up þæt cild of ðam wætere*).[12]

The Vocabulary of the Spiritual Family Created by Sponsorship

After a baptism had taken place, each of the participants had a new status in a spiritual family. Latin and Old English word(s) or title(s) designated each person's place in that family.

The Baptizer

Christianity used many images based on family relationships—fatherhood, motherhood, brotherhood, sisterhood, adoption, and childhood. Paul, for example, had reminded the Corinthians that "you might have thousands of guardians in Christ, but not more than one father and it was I who begot you in Christ Jesus by preaching the Good News" (1 Cor. 4:14). He told the Galatians that they were adopted by God: "God sent his son, born of a woman, born subject to the law, to redeem the subjects of the law, so that we could receive adoption as sons" (Galatians 4:4–5). After the second century, every bishop could be called a "father" (*papa* in Greek) because, like Paul, he begot his flock spiritually through instruction.[13] Because the bishop was also the ordinary baptizer in his community, his fatherhood from baptizing reinforced his fatherhood from teaching. The *Didascalia,* composed in Syria about A.D. 250, exalted the office of bishop in several ways, including the bishop's fatherhood both as teacher and as bap-

11. *ASC*(*A*), s.a. 639, p. 28: "onfeng hine him to suna."
12. Page, "Old English Liturgical Rubrics," pp. 152–55.
13. Pierre de Labriolle, "Papa," *Archivum Latinitatis Medii Aevi* (*Bulletin du Cange*) 4 (1928).

tizer of his congregation: "But the levite and high priest is the bishop. He is minister of the word and mediator; but to you a teacher and, after God, your father, who begot you through the water."[14]

In Anglo-Saxon England also, a baptizer might be described as a father. The early-eighth-century *vita* of Pope Gregory I reported that when King Edwin was baptized in 627, Bishop Paulinus was his *pater in baptismo.*[15] Bertram Colgrave translated those words as "godfather at his baptism," which could be correct, although Charles W. Jones was more cautious in translating the words literally and ambiguously as "father in baptism."[16] I suggest that Jones was probably closer to the meaning. The words should be understood in the traditional context of the bishop as "father" to all whom he baptized. Neither a bishop nor any other cleric who baptized was automatically a godfather.

Old English was capable of expressing a precise distinction between the clergyman who performed a baptism and the godparent who sponsored at it. The cleric who baptized was the *fulluhtfæder* or *fulwihtfæder,* which is literally "baptism father." Two biblical examples were clear: John the Baptist was Christ's *fulwihtfæder,*[17] and the Apostle Peter was *fulluhtfæder* (and also godfather) to his disciple Mark.[18] A spurious charter of King Æthelwulf of Wessex (839–858), probably forged in the tenth century, referred to the seventh-century Bishop Birinus as the *fulluht fæder* of Cynegils, the first Christian king of the West Saxons, whose sponsor (*godfæder*) was King Oswald of Northumbria.[19] We may conclude that every cleric was a spiritual father to those he baptized, but he was not automatically the godfather. His spiritual fatherhood remained primarily religious with few social consequences—he was at the fringes of the many spiritual families his baptisms created.

A cleric who baptized could, however, *add* godfatherhood to his more vague spiritual fatherhood. That is, he could be both baptizer (*fulluhtfæder*) and sponsor (*godfæder*). He did so by baptizing and also performing the

14. *Didascalia* 2.26.4, in *Didascalia et Constitutiones Apostolorum,* ed. F. X. Funk (Paderborn, 1905), 1:86.
15. *Vita sancti Gregorii,* c. 14, p. 96.
16. Charles W. Jones, *Saints' Lives and Chronicles in Early England* (Ithaca, N.Y., 1947), p. 105.
17. *Homily XVII on St. Michael,* in *Blickling Homilies* (London, 1967), p. 205.
18. *Life of Saint Mark,* in *Ælfric's Lives of Saints,* 1:330: "Petrus wæs his god-fæder and hine gode gestrynde and he swa lange folgode his fulluhtfædere Petre."
19. Charter of King Æthelwulf for Winchester Cathedral, in *Cartularium Saxonicum,* 493 (S 325), ed. Walter de Gray Birch (London, 1887), 2:96. The account of Cynegisl's baptism is in Bede, *HE,* 3.7, p. 232, where Bishop Birinus baptized Cynegisl and King Oswald of Northumbria sponsored him. See also *ASC(A),* s.a. 635, p. 28. On the context in which the charter was forged, perhaps in the tenth century, see H. P. R. Finberg, *The Early Charters of Wessex* (Leicester, 1964), pp. 31 and 226–28.

duties of sponsorship, especially receiving the baptizee from the font. Gregory of Tours recorded six instances in which bishops both baptized and sponsored the sons of sixth-century Merovingian kings.[20] One involved the bishop of Tournai:

> After these things had happened, Samson, the younger son of King Chilperic, was seized by dysentery and fever and passed from earthly things. This boy was born when Chilperic was being besieged by his brother at Tournai. From a fear of death, the boy's mother [Fredegund] rejected him and wished him to die. But when, reprimanded by the king, she could not, she ordered him to be baptized. He was baptized and received by the bishop [of Tournai]. He died before he was five. (*Qui baptizatus et ab ipso episcopo susceptus, lustro uno nec pefuncto, defunctus est*).[21]

The *Anglo-Saxon Chronicle* also described such a combination of baptism and sponsorship: "Birinus baptized Cuthred in Dorchester and received him as his [god]son."[22] Early medieval people understood the difference between baptizer/father and sponsor/father. We should not confuse these two sorts of spiritual fathers created in baptism.

Godfather and Godmother

Although the baptizing cleric became a spiritual father in a vague sense, there was a person at a baptism who gained a more precise parenthood. At an early medieval baptism, for each baptizee there was one sponsor of the same sex, who was often called "spiritual father or mother" (*pater/mater spiritualis*), which were words ambiguous enough that for clarity they were sometimes qualified by words such as *de fonte* ("from the font") to distinguish them from other sorts of spiritual parents.[23] More precise terms for the godparents developed in the seventh century, when the male sponsor began to be called in Latin a *patrinus* and the female sponsor a *matrina.* Because the earliest recorded use of those terms is in the *Ordo Romanus XI,* which Antoine Chavasse dated between 650 and 700, the missionary Augustine and his immediate successors, who were active in England at least

20. Gregory, *HF,* 5.18, 5.22, 6.27, 9.4, 9.8, 9.10; for an analysis of these episcopal baptism/sponsorships of royal children, see Jussen, *Patenschaft,* pp. 177–213.
21. Gregory, *HF,* 5.22, pp. 229–30.
22. *ASC*(*A*), s.a. 639, p. 28: "Her Birinus fulwade Cuðræd on Dorcesceastre ⁊ onfeng hine him to suna."
23. *Vita beate Genovefae virginis,* c. 9, ed. Bruno Krusch, *MGH SRM* 3 (Hanover, 1896), p. 218: "mater spiritualis."

fifty years before the *Ordo* was composed, might not have used them.[24] Neither *patrinus* nor *matrina* is attested in sources from Frankish Gaul until the eighth century, when they became current as the liturgy was increasingly romanized.[25] Although I have not found *matrina* in a Latin text composed in Anglo-Saxon England, *patrinus* was known there in the tenth century. When the late-tenth-century chronicler Æthelweard recounted the death of the Danish Viking king Guthrum, whom King Alfred had sponsored at baptism in 878, he wrote that Alfred was the *patrinus* of Guthrum.[26]

The Old English vocabulary for godparents was not a straightforward borrowing of Latin terms. A literal Old English translation of *pater* or *mater spiritualis* might have been *gastlic(u) fæder/modor.* But those words were claimed for another meaning. They were used to designate abbots and abbesses in relation to their monks and nuns; or Holy Mother Church as the spiritual parent of her members.[27] To refer unambiguously to godparents, new words in Old English were coined, *godfæder* and *godmodor,* which probably meant "father/mother in God." In some documents, *god fæder* meant "God the Father," but that was always clear from the context and could not be confused with the baptismal godfather. The fact that when *god fæder* meant God the Father, it was often written as two words might also have stressed the distinction in meaning.[28] In a Latin–Old English glossary in MS Cotton Cleopatra A.III, the Latin word for godmothers, *matrenas,* was rendered *godmodra,*[29] and in MS Bodley 730, the word *paranimphus,* which in Greek meant the bridegroom's best man, was glossed as *godfeder* and further glossed in Old French with the word for godparent *i parren* (i.e., *parrain*).[30] Thus every baptism created a second father or mother for every baptizee, called in Old English a *godfæder* or a *godmodor.*

24. *Ordo Romanus XI,* c. 12, c. 17, c. 20, c. 23, c. 27, in *Les "ordines,"* 2:420–24; on the dating of *Ordo Romanus XI,* see Chavasse, *Le sacramentaire gélasien* pp. 166–71.

25. Lynch, "*Spiritale Vinculum,*" pp. 187–88.

26. Æthelweard, *Chronicon,* 4.3, in *The Chronicle of Æthelweard,* ed. and trans. Alistair Campbell (London, 1962), p. 47.

27. For abbots as *gastlican faderas* to their monks, see Ælfric, *Sermones,* 1:398, line 6. For an abbess as *gastlice modor* to a nun, see *Sermo in natale sanctorum martirum,* in Ælfric, *Catholic Homilies,* p. 316, lines 184 and 189; and for the church as spiritual mother (*gastlice moder*) of all the baptized, p. 6, lines 100–109.

28. See *Sermo in Cena Domini,* 13, in *Angelsächische Homilien und Heiligenleben,* ed. Bruno Assmann, BAP 3 (Kassel, 1889), p. 154, lines 59 and 77; p. 155, line 82, where Jesus' father is called "god fæder."

29. W. G. Stryker, "The Latin–Old English Glossary in Ms. Cotton Cleopatra A.III" (Ph.D. diss., Stanford University, 1951), cited under "godmodra" in *Microfiche Concordance,* p. 75.

30. Cited under "godfeder" in *Microfiche Concordance,* p. 67.

Godson, Goddaughter, Godchild

The person who had been sponsored became a spiritual child of the sponsor. In Latin, a godson was sometimes called a *filius spiritualis* and a goddaughter a *filia spiritualis*. According to Bili's late-ninth-century *Vita sancti Machuti,* a Breton abbot named Brendan sponsored Machutus and subsequently treated him "in the place of a spiritual son" (*loco filii spiritualis*). The Old English translator of the *vita* rendered those Latin words *for gastlicne sunu hæfde* ("he had [him] for a spiritual son"). There is some ambiguity in both the Latin and Old English. Because Abbot Brendan raised Machutus in a form of fosterage, the words might not refer to a godson but to a foster son. It has been suggested that in Celtic regions, where fosterage was strong, the statuses of godson and foster son sometimes merged.[31] In any case, the words *filius/filia spiritualis,* which might refer to several kinds of "spiritual" sons and daughters, were often superseded in the ninth century by more precise Latin technical terms for a godson and a goddaughter, *filiolus* or *filiola,* which literally meant "little son" or "little daughter," terms of affection with a long history.[32]

The use of *filiolus/filiola* for godchildren in Anglo-Saxon England is not attested. There are three interesting test cases. In the late ninth century, Bishop Asser used a lost version of the *Anglo-Saxon Chronicle* in his biography of King Alfred. When he translated the entry for 878, which culminated in the baptism of the Viking king Guthrum, he did not call Guthrum Alfred's *filiolus.* Instead he wrote that Alfred lifted him from the holy font and made him a *filium adoptionis,* "a son of adoption."[33] In the late tenth century, the learned ealdorman Æthelweard translated a now-lost version of the *Anglo-Saxon Chronicle* into Latin. In two instances where the *Chronicle* referred to godsons, we might expect to see *filiolus.* Instead, Æthelweard created circumlocutions. He translated *godsunu* once as *filius de baptismo* ("son from baptism"), and on another occasion he translated the account of the sponsorship of King Cuthred by Bishop Birinus in *ASC* 639 (*onfeng hine him to suna*) as *baptisticum filium sumpsit* ("he took a bap-

31. *Vita sancti Machuti,* in *The Old English Life of Machutus,* ed. David Yerkes (Toronto, 1984), pp. 4–5. François Kerlouegan, "Essai sur la mise en nourriture et l'éducation dans les pays celtiques d'après le témoinage des textes hagiographiques latins," *Etudes Celtiques* 12 (1968–1969), 120–21, argued for a convergence of foster sons and godsons in Celtic saints' lives. Charles-Edwards, *Early Irish,* pp. 78–82, argued that baptismal kinship had a hard time taking root in Ireland and Wales because of its rival, fosterage.

32. Lynch, "*Spiritale Vinculum,*" pp. 188–89. On the classical usage of *filiola* as a term of affection for a young girl, see "Filiola," in *Oxford Latin Dictionary,* ed. P. G. W. Glare (Oxford, 1982), p. 701.

33. Asser, *De rebus gestis Ælfredi,* in *Asser's Life of King Alfred Together with the Annals of Saint Neots, Erroneously Ascribed to Asser,* ed. William Henry Stevenson (Oxford, 1904), p. 47: "Quem Ælfred rex in filium adoptionis sibi suscipiens, de fonte sacro baptismatis elevavit."

tismal son").[34] The words *filiolus* and *filiola* are attested in England after the Norman Conquest. In the twelfth century, there were scattered efforts to make Anglo-Saxon law available in Latin to the new rulers of England, who generally knew no Old English. In the first book of the *Quadripartitus,* an early-twelfth-century legal scholar translated many Anglo-Saxon legal texts into Latin. In the translation of Ine's Law 76.1–3, the twelfth-century Latin vocabulary for godchildren asserted itself. The translator rendered the three occurrences of the word *godsunu* in Ine's Law 76 as *filiolus.*[35]

The Old English terms for godchildren, *godsunu* and *goddohter,* were neologisms rather than borrowings from Latin and they were commonly used. The *Chronicle* reported that two sons of the Viking chief Hæstan were *godsunu,* respectively, of King Alfred and of the ealdorman Æthelred of Mercia.[36] About 990, the noble woman Æthelgifu left a man, presumably a slave, to her *godsunu* Ætheric.[37] In his *Dialogues,* Pope Gregory I wrote about a man who received a young girl in baptism and subsequently molested her, but his Latin words to describe the goddaughter were vague.[38] In his Old English translation of the passage, Bishop Wærferth of Worcester clarified or modernized the vague *eandam filiam* as *his goddohter.*[39] In his will, Wulfric Spott left to his *goddeht*[*e*]*r* "the estate at Stretton and the brooch (*bulé*) which was her grandmother's."[40] In an Old English translation of the *Passion of Saint Margaret,* the heroine was tortured in a vat of boiling water, which became her baptismal font. In a passage not found in any extant Latin version of Margaret's life, a heavenly voice, presumably that of God, spoke to her saying, "I am your godfather and you are my goddaughter."[41] In 1 Peter 5:13, Peter referred to Mark as *filius meus.*

34. Æthelweard, *Chronicon,* 1.6 and 2.18, p. 19 and p. 24. On the lost version of the Anglo-Saxon Chronicle used by Æthelweard, see ibid., pp. xix–xxxi.

35. The *Quadripartitus* version of Ine's Law 76.1–3 in Ine, King of Wessex, *Institutiones,* in *Die Gesetze der Angelsächsen,* vol. 1, ed. Felix Liebermann. (1903; rpr. Aalen, 1960), 1:123. On the origin and nature of the *Quadripartitus,* see Patrick Wormald, " 'Quadripartitus,' " in *Law and Government in Medieval England and Normandy: Essays in Honour of Sir James Holt,* ed. George Garnett and John Hudson (Cambridge, 1994).

36. *ASC(A),* s.a. 893, p. 57.

37. Æthelgifu, *Will,* in *The Will of Æthelgifu* (S 1497), ed. Dorothy Whitelock and N. R. Ker (Oxford, 1968), p. 15.

38. Gregory, *Dialogus* 4.33, *SC* 265, p. 110: "Quidam curialis illic sacratissimo paschali sabbato iuuenculam cuiusdam filiam in baptismate suscepit. . . . Eandem filiam suam secum manere petiit, eamque nocte illa, quod dictu nefas est, perdidit."

39. Wærferth, *Bischofs Wærferth von Worcester Übersetzung der Dialoge Gregors des Grossen,* ed. Hans Hecht, BAP 5 (Leipzig, 1900), p. 308.

40. Wulfric Spott, *Will* (1002–1004) (S 1536), in *Anglo-Saxon Wills,* ed. and trans. Dorothy Whitelock (Cambridge, 1930), p. 50.

41. *Passio beatae Margaretae virginis et martyris,* c. 18, in *The Old English Lives of St. Margaret,* ed. Mary Clayton and Hugh Magennis (Cambridge, 1995), p. 168: "Ic eom þin godfæder and þu min goddohtor." This passage is from the Old English translation in MS CCCC 303.

Ælfric interpreted that to mean that Peter baptized and sponsored the evangelist, who was Peter's *godsunu*.[42] Thus, the words *godsunu* and *goddohter* were the normal terms in Old English for godson and goddaughter.

Archbishop Wulfstan (and perhaps one of his imitators) used another word for godchildren, *godbearn*, which combined the Old English words *god* and *child*. It could refer either to Christ, who was "God's son," or collectively to godchildren without reference to their sex. When it referred to Christ, the term *godbearn* was used primarily in poetry, and its meaning was clear from the context.[43] In one homily, Wulfstan exhorted each godfather to love and teach and correct the misdeeds of his *godbearn*.[44]

Spiritual Siblings

The spiritual family created by baptism had yet another dimension. In Byzantium and Lombard Italy, the children of the sponsor were regarded as the spiritual brothers and sisters of the sponsored child.[45] The Lombard king Liutprand issued a law in 723 which called the natural and spiritual children of the same person *germani spiritales*, literally "spiritual brothers," and forbade them to marry.[46] This relationship of "spiritual siblings" did not take root in the Frankish kingdom or in Anglo-Saxon England.[47] To be sure, Anglo-Saxons had "spiritual brothers (and sisters)" but they were fellow monks and nuns, or all of one's fellow Christians.[48] By Byzantine and Lombard standards, the Anglo-Saxons had a truncated spiritual family because the relationship of spiritual siblinghood (if such a word is permitted) did not exist or, to be precise, is not recorded in the sources.

42. Ælfric, *Letter to Sigeweard*, in *The Old English Version of the Heptateuch*, ed. S. J. Crawford (London, 1922; rpr. with additions by N. R. Ker, 1969), p. 53.

43. Hilding Bäck, *The Synonyms for 'Child,' 'Boy,' 'Girl' in Old English: An Etymological-Semasiological Investigation* (Lund, 1934), p. 32.

44. Wulfstan of York, *Homily* 10c, p. 209, lines 169–70: "Godfæder his godbearn lufie 7 lære 7 unrightes styre"; see also *Homily* 20 (Version 1), ibid., p. 258, line 72; *Homily* 20 (Version 2), ibid., p. 263, line 83; *Homily* 20 (Version 3), p. 270, line 78. *Homily* 58, line 5, in A. S. Napier, *Wulfstan*, Sammlung englischer Denkmäler 4 (Berlin, 1883, rpr. with app. by K. Ostheeren, 1967), p. 301. Homily 58 is probably not by Wulfstan but based on his sermons; see D. G. Scragg, "The Corpus of Vernacular Homilies and Prose Saints' Lives before Ælfric," *ASE* 8 (1979), 263.

45. *Ecloga* 2.2, p. 170, forbade a man to marry a woman whom his father had sponsored.

46. Liutprand, *Leges Liutprandi regis*, 34.5, p. 124.

47. Lynch, *Godparents*, p. 203.

48. Ælfric, Homily 35, in *Sermones Catholici*, p. 532, line 33: *gastlica broðer* of all the monks; Ker, *Catalogue of Manuscripts*, p. 317: the monks of Christ Church, Canterbury, received King Cnut into confraternity and called him *ure gastlica broðer for gode;* Ælfric, Homily 27, in *Sermones Catholici*, p. 398, line 6: monks forsake their worldly relatives for *gastlice gebroðru;* Homily 5, in *Twelfth-Century Homilies in MS. Bodley 343*, ed. A. O. Balfour, EETS OS 137 (London, 1909), p. 40, lines 12–14: because we all became God's children through baptism, we are all *gastlice ibroðrae*.

Anglo-Saxon Interpretations of Sponsorship

Sponsorship as Adoption

The traditional and dominant view of baptism in early medieval society was that of rebirth or second birth, which I treated earlier. Learned Anglo-Saxon bishops and monks shared that view, but that was not the only way they had to conceptualize the consequences of sponsorship. In a Germanic society where youngsters or adults were frequently "adopted," the notion that the baptized were adopted as God's children, which was expressed in Paul's writings (e.g., Rom. 8:15, 8:23, and 9:4; Gal. 4:5; Eph. 1:5), made cultural sense. In their pre-Christian and Christian phases, the Germanic peoples had several ways to "adopt," in order to create kinlike bonds where they were wanted but did not exist. A nonkinsman became a "child" of the adopter in symbolic acts, such as giving weapons, cutting hair, wrapping the adoptee in the adopter's cloak, or setting the adoptee on the adopter's knee.[49]

Like the Celts, the Anglo-Saxons practiced a kind of adoption called fosterage, in which youngsters were brought up in a different household than that of their parents.[50] Relationships created by fosterage were described in family terms, such as foster brother, foster father. Fritz Roeder analyzed the main features of fosterage in Anglo-Saxon Wessex, where the sources refer mostly to royal or aristocratic arrangements. He found that foster parents were usually close kinsmen or dependents of the natural parents. Some foster parents raised the child for "love," but others did so for a fee, called the *fostor-lean.* A child could be fostered from birth to marriage, and the man who married a fostered girl had to repay the *foster-lean* to her parents. As an adult, the fostered child might retain close bonds with the foster parents and foster siblings. Roeder suggested that the purpose of fosterage was to strengthen kinship bonds or to create new bonds for the sake of the child and its father, much like spiritual kinship, which might have been a rival practice.[51] Dorothy Whitelock cautioned against the assumption that fosterage was widespread among the Anglo-Saxons: "I know of no evidence that there was any general habit of letting them be fostered away from home, though youths of noble birth might be brought up at court."[52]

49. Pappenheim, "Über künstliche Verwandtschaft," ZSSRG, Germanistische Abteilung 29 (1908), 315–22; Karl A. Eckhardt, "Adoption," in *Studia Merovingica* (Aalen, 1975); Althoff, *Verwandte,* pp. 82–84.

50. On fosterage among the Irish, see Fergus Kelly, *A Guide to Early Irish Law* (Dublin, 1988), pp. 86–90; and Charles-Edwards, *Early Irish,* pp. 78–82.

51. Fritz Roeder, *Über die Erziehung der vornehmen angelsächsischen Jugend in fremden Häusern* (Halle, 1910).

52. Dorothy Whitelock, *The Beginnings of English Society* (Harmondsworth, 1974), p. 94.

Whatever the diffusion of fosterage, baptismal sponsorship was ubiquitous, and Anglo-Saxon Christians integrated it into their traditional practices, regarding it as another technique for adoption. In the early eighth century, Anglo-Saxons writing in Latin occasionally used the words *adoptare, adoptio,* and *adoptivus* to describe the consequences of sponsorship at baptism. I have not found this Latin usage so early elsewhere, although the idea may have Byzantine Greek parallels. One of the Greek verbs for adoption was *eispoieo.* The sixth-century Byzantine historian Procopius wrote that the great general Belisarius sponsored a Thracian boy and made him "an adopted child (*eispoieton paida*)" to him and his wife Antonina, "as is the law of Christians for making adoptions (*eispoiesthai*)."[53] The Old English phrase for baptismal sponsorship, "to take someone as a son" (*onfon to sunu*), expresses well the idea of adoption. It may be compared to the phrase *bearn onfon,* which could mean "to conceive a child" in a sexual sense.[54]

Bede was familiar with several ways to refer to a sponsorship; he used terms for "receiving," for "second birth," and for "adoption." When King Æthelwealh of Sussex emerged from the baptismal font, he was received by King Wulfhere of Mercia "in the place of a son," and Bede called the result of that sponsorship an *adoptio.*[55] He also reported that when Bishop Birinus baptized the West Saxon king Cynegils, "Oswald, the most holy and most victorious king of the Northumbrians was present, and he received him [Cynegils] as he came from the bath (*eumque de lavacro exeuntem suscepisse*). . . ; he accepted him as a son, who was earlier dedicated to God by the second birth [of baptism] (*ipsum prius secunda generatione Deo dedicatum sibi accepit in filium*)."[56] To judge from the language of this passage, Bede saw two consequences of baptism. King Cynegils was dedicated to God in a second birth and was adopted by his sponsor, Oswald.

Bede's view of sponsorship as an adoption was shared by his younger contemporary, the Anglo-Saxon missionary Boniface. The latter had raised a controversy in Frankish Gaul by permitting a man who had sponsored a boy to marry the boy's mother, after she became a widow. His Frankish critics said the two adults were coparents and should not marry. In about 735, Boniface wrote from Frankish Gaul to ask three Anglo-Saxon prelates

53. Procopius, *The Anecdota or Secret History,* 1.1., ed. and trans. H. B. Dewing (London and Cambridge, Mass., 1935), p. 10.

54. *Poenitentiale Theodori,* c. 201, in *Quellen und Forschungen zur Geschichte der teutschen Literatur und Sprache,* ed. F. J. Mone (Aachen and Leipzig, 1830), 1:526: "Wif seo ðe bearn onfeð and þæt acwelleð on hire innode, an gear fæste."

55. Bede, *HE,* 4.13, p. 372: "egressus de fonte loco filii susceptus est; in cuius signum adoptionis."

56. Ibid., bk. 3, c. 7, p. 232. See also *ASC(A),* s.a. 635, p. 28.

for advice. In his letters, he used the language of adoption to describe sponsorship. To Archbishop Nothelm of Canterbury, he reported that "a certain man, as many are accustomed, lifting the son of another man from the font of holy baptism adopted him as a son to himself" (*adoptavit sibi in filium*). To Bishop Pehthelm of Whithorn, describing the same incident, Boniface referred to the godchild as an "adoptive son in baptism" (*filium in baptismo adoptivum*).[57]

Thus some Anglo-Saxons did interpret sponsorship as adoption into the sponsor's family, a view that took on political significance when one king sponsored another. The royal godfather was asserting his dominance, and the royal godson was acknowledging the power of his overking; but the unequal relationship was sacralized and camouflaged by its appearance as a religiously sanctioned adoption.[58]

Sponsor as Legal Guarantor

In addition to rebirth and adoption, Anglo-Saxons could conceptualize baptismal sponsorship in a third way, which had nothing to do with kinship. By the tenth century, sponsorship was a six-hundred-year-old practice, which had functioned for more than three hundred years before Justinian formally associated it with spiritual kinship in 530. Some late-ancient and early-medieval texts talked about sponsorship as a contract. The secular Latin word *sacramentum* referred to an oath, such as that taken by soldiers enrolling in the imperial army. By the third century, Christians had applied the word *sacramentum* to baptism, because it could be regarded as a pact or contract with God.[59] For instance, in a sermon delivered about 390 to *competentes,* John Chrysostom addressed the sponsors (*anadechomenoi*) in his audience, reminding them that they were sureties for their godchildren in matters of the spirit.[60] The contractual view of sponsorship was summarized well in a sermon attributed to Eligius of Noyon (*fl.* 642–660). "Remember that then [i.e., at baptism] you made a pact (*pactum*) with God and you promised in that baptism to renounce the devil and all his works. At that time he who was able to do so answered these things himself

57. Boniface to Archbishop Nothelm of Canterbury, in Boniface, *Epistola* 33, pp. 57–58; Boniface to Bishop Pehthelm of Candida-Casa, in ibid., 32, p. 56.

58. Chaney, *Cult of Kingship,* pp. 168–72, argued that sponsorship replaced pagan fosterage as a way for Christian Anglo-Saxon kings to "adopt" other rulers. I think the main point is correct, although the practice of fosterage survived the introduction of Christianity.

59. Joseph Crehan, *Early Christian Baptism and the Creed: A Study in Ante-Nicene Theology* (London, 1950), pp. 96–110.

60. John Chrysostom, *Second Catechetical Sermon,* c. 15–16, in *Huit catéchèses baptismales inédites,* ed. Antoine Wenger, *SC* 50 (Paris, 1957), pp. 141–44.

and on his own behalf; [if] he was not able, a guarantor (*fideiussor*), that is to say, he who received him from the holy font, promised those things to God in his place. Think about the sort of pact you made with God."[61]

The contractual view of baptism led to consequences different for adults than for infants. Adults could personally make the contract with God; infants could not. In the contractual view, a sponsor was needed to compensate for an infant's weakness by guaranteeing the contract on its behalf. Tertullian's *De baptismo,* which was composed about 206, contains the earliest reference to a guarantor of the baptismal pact of an infant. Tertulian disapproved of infant baptism and wrote to discourage it. One of his arguments concerned the *sponsores,* those who made a promise on behalf of an infant. He asserted that they were in moral danger because circumstances might prevent them from carrying out the contract: "It follows that deferment of baptism is more profitable . . . especially so as regards children. For what need is there, if there really is no need, for even their sponsors (*sponsores*) to be brought into peril, seeing they [the sponsors] may possibly themselves fail of their promises by death, or be deceived by the subsequent development of an evil disposition [in the child]?"[62]

The word *sponsor* was a Roman legal term for a person who guaranteed the good faith of someone else, almost like a cosigner on a modern car loan.[63] Tertullian understood the role of the *sponsor* as that of guaranteeing the future behavior of the infant. He warned that if the *sponsor* died while the child was young or if the child developed "an evil disposition," the sponsor could not fulfill his promise. Tertullian's solution was to delay baptism until later in life, when the catechumen could make the contract on his own. His effort to discourage infant baptism failed, and infant baptism with its guarantor became normal.

It seems odd that the Latin word *sponsor* failed to take root in the medieval language of baptismal sponsorship, but in its place another word, *fideiussor,* was commonly used to identify the sponsor as the guarantor of a contract between the infant and God. Caesarius of Arles (502–542) was a key figure in disseminating the contractual view because his sermons were so widely known in the early Middle Ages.[64] He sometimes called bap-

61. Eligius of Noyon, *Predicacio sancti Eligii episcopi,* c. 4, ed. Bruno Krusch, *MGH SRM* 4 (Hanover and Leipzig, 1902), p. 751; Caesarius of Arles, *Sermo* 204.3, *CCSL* 104, p. 821, tells sponsors to be mindful that "se pro ipsis fideiussores aput deum extitisse"; Martin of Braga, *De correctione rusticorum,* c. 15, in *Martini episcopi bracariensis opera omnia,* ed. Claude Barlow (New Haven, 1950), p. 196.

62. *Tertullian's Homily on Baptism,* c. 18, ed. and trans. Ernest Evans (London, 1964), pp. 38–39.

63. "Sponsor," in *Oxford Latin Dictionary,* p. 1810.

64. Germain Morin edited Caesarius's writings, including the influential *Sermones,* in *Sancti Caesarii episcopi Arelatensis opera omnia.* On Caesarius, see William M. Daly, "Caesarius of Arles: A

tismal sponsors *fideiussores* ("swearers of faith"), which was also a Roman legal term for persons who gave a surety that something would be carried out by another person. In the contractual view of baptism, the *fideiussores* stood as surety that the baptized children would keep their side of the contract with God when they reached the age of responsibility. Unlike the word *sponsor, fideiussor* had a long life in medieval language about sponsorship.

Caesarius of Arles's Sermon 229, c. 6, was a key source for Anglo-Saxon knowledge of the sponsor as *fideiussor:* "Dearest brothers, know that you are *fideiussores* before God for those infants whom you received in baptism. Therefore try always to warn and castigate them that they may live chastely and justly and soberly. Before everything, reveal to them the Lord's Prayer and the Creed. Do not call them to good works by words alone, but also by examples."[65] Ker observed that Latin versions of this homily occur in two English pontificals and two English homilaries.[66] A vernacular homily, Brotanek 2, drew on Caesarius's Sermon 229 for its exhortation to godparents. "And also whatever men receive another at baptism or at the bishop's hand should know that they are their sureties with almighty God. And they should frequently teach and admonish that they have correct belief for God and that they live their lives rightly and cleanly. And before all other things that they reveal to them and teach the Creed and the Pater Noster."[67]

Some Anglo-Saxon preachers were perhaps drawn to the contract theory of sponsorship because they were aware that the spectacle of infants making "promises" posed practical and theological problems. In a sermon, Ælfric pointed to the example of the Canaanite woman (Matt. 15:21–28, Mark 7:24–30) who asked Jesus to heal her demoniac daughter. Jesus was at first reluctant, but her persistence and faith gained healing for her daughter.

Precursor of Medieval Christendom," *Traditio* 26 (1970); and William E. Klingshirn, *Caesarius of Arles: The Making of a Christian Community in Late Antique Gaul,* CSMLT, 4th ser. 22 (Cambridge, 1994).

65. Caesarius of Arles, *Sermo* 229, c. 6, in *CCSL* 104, p. 910: "Ipsos tamen infantes, fratres carissimi, quos in baptismo excepistis, scitote vos apud deum fideiussores esse illorum; et ideo semper eos ammonere et castigare contendite, ut caste et iuste et sobrie vivant. Ante omnia symbolum eis et orationem dominicam ostendite; nec eos verbis solum sed etiam exemplis ad bona opera provocate." Caesarius referred often to the sponsor as *fideiussor:* see Sermo 12.3, p. 60; Sermo 13.2, p. 64; Sermo 50.3, p. 217; Sermo 71.2, p. 288; and Sermo 204.3, p. 778. On Caesarius's influence on Old English literature, see Joseph Trahern, "Caesarius of Arles and Old English Literature: Some Contributions and a Recapitulation," *ASE* 5 (1976); Sermo 229 is discussed on pp. 117–18.

66. Ker, *Catalogue,* p. 438.

67. Rudolf Brotanek, *Texte und Untersuchungen zur altenglischen Literatur und Kirchengeschichte* (Halle, 1913), p. 25: "wite eac æʒhwylc þæra manna þe oþres onfehð æt fullwihte oððe æt bisceopes handa þæt hi sint hira boruhhanda wið ʒod ælmihtiʒne. and hi sceolun hi forþam ʒelomlice læran and myneʒian þæt hi rihtne ʒeleafan to gode hæbben. and þæt hi hira lif rihtlice and syferlice lybben. and toforan eallum oþrum þinʒum þæt hi him ʒesutelien and ʒetæcen credan and pater noster."

This biblical episode was a locus classicus for the defense of infant baptism and of sponsorship,[68] and Ælfric applied the text in just such a sense: "For the great belief of the mother the devil forsook the daughter. Thereby is given an example for our baptism, that the unspeaking child is healed at the baptism through the belief of the father and the mother, and of the responsible godfather, though the child be unaware."[69] In his sermon for Epiphany, Ælfric faced the problem of an infant's promises head on:

> Let us be mindful of what we promised to God at our baptism. Now wilt thou say, "What did I promise when I was a child, and could not speak?" We read in the old institutes, that holy teachers taught the true belief to those men who turned to christianity, and asked them, whether they would renounce the devil, and believe in God. They promised they would do so, and were then baptized in the holy font, with that promise. Unspeaking children they baptized through the belief of the father and of the mother, and the godfather was the child's sponsor and surety to God, that it should hold christianity according to God's teaching; for that sentence is very awful that Christ spake, That no unbaptized man shall come to eternal life. Now this law stands in God's church, that unspeaking children be baptized, and they shall be saved through the belief of other men, as through other men's sins they had been condemned; for it is doubtful whether it [the child] continue in life until it can answer the teacher with belief [Ælfric then cited again the example of the Canaanite woman whose daughter was freed from a demon by her mother's faith].[70]

Thus, the infant—defined as the child who could not yet speak—needed helpers to be baptized. His parents' belief substituted for his own, as the Canaanite woman's faith helped her daughter. But the child also needed a guarantee, provided by the sponsor, for the promises (*fulwiht hadas*) which she or he would not, for many years, understand.[71]

68. See Bede, *In Marci Evangelium expositio,* 7.29, p. 525: "Propter humilem matris fidelemque sermonem filiam deseruit daemonium. Ubi datur exemplum cathecizandi et baptizandi infantes quia videlicet per fidem et confessionem parentum in baptismo liberantur a diaboli paruuli qui necdum per se sapere uel aliquid agere boni possunt aut mali."

69. Ælfric, sermon in *Dominica II in Quadragesima,* in *Catholic Homilies,* pp. 70–71: "For þam micclum geleafan þære meder. forlet se deofol ða dohtor; Mid ðam is geseald bysen urum fulluhte. þæt ða unsprecendan cild beoð gehealdene on ðam fulluhte ðurh geleafan þæs fæder. and þære moder. and þæs foresprecendan godfæder. ðeah ðe þæt cild nyten sy."

70. Ælfric, *Sermo in Aepiphania Domini,* in ibid., pp. 26–27; the English trans. is from Ælfric, *Sermones Catholici,* 2:51.

71. *Blicking Homily* 10, p. 109: "is eallum mannum nedþearf & nytlic þæt hie heora fulwiht hadas wel gehealdan."

When late Old English texts referred to the sponsor as guarantor of the child's baptismal promises, three Old English nouns could be used, each of which also had a secular legal meaning. In legal usage, the noun *forespreca* designated an advocate, a defender, or a spokesperson. Archbishop Wulfstan favored the word *forespreca* when he wrote about sponsors. In one sermon he reminded his hearers of the Ten Commandments and the golden rule. He concluded: "And [we should hold] to all that which we promised when we received baptism or the things those who were our *forespecan* at the font bath [promised]."[72] In another sermon, Wulfstan was even more explicit: "Remember what we promised when we received baptism or those who were our *foresprecan* at baptism. That is, that we would always love God and believe in him and keep his commands and shun the devil and diligently avoid his evil teaching. This is promised for each of those who receive baptism. And although that child can not speak on account of youth when one baptizes it, his friend's promise (*forespræc*) profits just the same as if he himself spoke."[73] In his *Institutes of Polity*, Wulfstan repeated his encouragement to the faithful to remember what they promised when they received baptism or what was promised by "those who were our *foresprecan* at baptism."[74]

There were another two related words, *borh*, literally a "pledge," and *borhhand*, literally a "pledge by hand," which also designated baptismal sponsors in their role as guarantors. In Anglo-Saxon law, they referred to a person who gave security for someone else.[75] They were occasionally borrowed to designate baptismal sponsors. Ælfric, in his sermon for Epiphany, used both *forespreca* and *borh:* "the godfather was the child's advocate and surety with God that it should hold Christianity according to God's teaching."[76] An anonymous homily based on Sermon 229 of Caesarius of Arles reminded sponsors that they were the child's "surety with almighty God."[77]

72. Wulfstan of York, *Homily* 10c, p. 201, lines 34–38.

73. Ibid., pp. 226–27: "7 geðencan hwæt we behetan þa we fulluht underfengan, oðþon þa ðe æt fulluhte ure foresprecan wæran; þæt is, þæt we woldan a God lufian 7 on hine gelyfan 7 his bebodu healdan 7 deofol ascunian 7 his unlara georne forbugan. Þis man behæt for ælcne þæra þe fulluht underfehð; 7 ðeah þæt cild for geogoðe sprecan ne mage þonne hit man fullað, his freonda forespræc forstent him eal þæt ylce þe hit sylf spræce."

74. Wulfstan of York, *Institutes of Polity, Civil and Ecclesiastical*, c. 120, ed. Karl Jost (Bern, 1959), p. 158.

75. J. Laurence Laughlin, "The Anglo-Saxon Legal Procedure," in *Essays in Anglo-Saxon Law* (Boston, 1905), pp. 190–192 on *borh*.

76. Ælfric, *Sermo in Aepiphania Domini*, in *Catholic Homilies*, p. 26: "se godfæder wæs þæs cildes forspreca and borh wið God þæt hit heolde þone cristendom be Godes tæcunge."

77. Homily 2, in Brotanek, *Texte*, p. 25: "boruhhanda wið ȝod ælmihtiȝne," which translated *apud deum fideiussores* in Caesarius, *Sermo* 229, in *CCSL* 104, p. 910.

Historians correctly lament that much, indeed most, of the doings of daily life in the early Middle Ages are known to them very imperfectly—such things as marriage, gestures, diet, and the like. This is true of baptismal sponsorship as well. Although the sources are fragmentary, we can be certain that almost every child born in the relatively well organized church of Anglo-Saxon England was baptized with the help of a godparent. Sponsorship was understood in overlapping ways, as assistance at a rebirth, as the carrying out of an adoption, or as the guaranteeing of a solemn contract with God. We can be sure that most responsible men and women had both godchildren and coparents. Virtually everyone belonged to a spiritual family or families that placed claims on them and gave them rights. In general, those rights and claims could not be enforced at law and so have left few traces in the sources, which are so often legal. But they were real claims and rights, enforced by public opinion and by the moral authority of sacramental grace. Sponsorship at the catechumenate and baptism did not, however, exhaust the possibilities for creating spiritual kin. Confirmation provided a third occasion, which will be treated in the next chapter.

CHAPTER 6

Godparenthood from Confirmation

Confirmation was the third occasion that required a sponsor. There had not always been a separate confirmation rite. In the ancient liturgy, the anointing and laying on of hands, which were the core of later confirmation, had taken place within the baptismal liturgy, immediately after the candidate was baptized. The Roman liturgy was unusual in its requirement of two postbaptismal anointings. After neophytes emerged from the font, they were anointed first by a priest on the head, then by the bishop, who anointed each on the forehead in the sign of the cross with consecrated oil, called chrism. In an influential decretal letter of 416, Pope Innocent I had emphasized that priests could give the postbaptismal anointing on the head but were not to give the second anointing on the forehead, which was reserved for bishops, a unique feature of the Roman liturgy[1] In the *Ordo Romanus XI,* the bishop's confirmation is described thus:

> 99. . . . And the infants are brought before him and he gives to each a garment (*stola*), a hooded cape (*casula*), and a chrism-cloth (*crismale*), and ten coins (*siclos*), and they are dressed.
> 100. When they are dressed they are arranged in a circle in order, just as they were written down, and the bishop gives a prayer over them,

1. Robert Cabié, *La letter du pape Innocent Ier à Décentius de Gubbio, 19 Mars 416* (Louvain, 1973), p. 24, lines 60–65; see also Cabié's commentary on pp. 44–48. For an excellent account of the anointings at baptism in the early medieval western liturgies, see Leonel L. Mitchell, *Baptismal Anointing* (London, 1966; rpr. Notre Dame, Ind., 1978), pp. 80–190.

confirming them with the invocation of the seven-fold grace of the Holy Spirit.

101. When the prayer is finished, he makes a cross with his thumb and with chrism on the foreheads of each, thus saying: "In the name of the Father and of the Son and of the Holy Spirit. Peace be to you." And they respond "Amen."

102. There is to be great care that this not be neglected, because then [at the bishop's anointing] every legitimate baptism is confirmed with the name of Christianity.[2]

In the generally small urban Christian communities of the ancient world, bishops presided personally at baptisms on Easter and Pentecost, so the episcopal confirming of a baptism could be carried out at virtually every baptism. But if no bishop were present, there could be no *episcopal* confirmation. Liturgies other than the Roman had a single anointing, which the bishop would perform, if present, but which in his absence, the baptizing priest carried out.

Theological views and practical conditions led to a rise in the proportion of baptisms that ended without a bishop's confirmation. Priests and deacons were obliged to baptize persons in imminent danger of dying; for to die without baptism was a guarantee of damnation. In such circumstances, the postbaptismal anointing on the forehead had to be omitted. If the person should recover, the anointing was to be sought later. As Christianity spread into the countryside and as infant baptism became common, priests or deacons baptized most infants soon after birth in the "baptismal churches."[3] In areas that followed the Roman custom, whenever a priest baptized in the absence of a bishop, the second anointing, confirmation, was omitted. By the eighth century, confirmation was often separated in place and time from baptism and was regarded as a distinct sacrament wherever the Roman liturgy prevailed.[4]

The prescriptions of the Roman liturgy were not, however, the only way that baptisms were confirmed. Before the Roman liturgy became dominant in the west, the Gallican family of liturgies, which prevailed in one form or another in Gaul, Spain, Britain, the Celtic lands, and Northern Italy, confirmed baptisms in a different way: in a single postbaptismal anointing, which the baptizer, usually a priest, conferred on the baptizee with chrism obtained from his bishop. Thus, in the Gallican liturgy, the confirmation

2. *Ordo Romanus XI,* in *Les ordines,* 2:446.
3. Aubrun, *La paroisse,* pp. 11–31.
4. Fisher, *Christian Initiation,* pp. 120–40 and passim. *La Maison-Dieu* 54 (1958) devoted an issue to confirmation; see esp. pp. 5–78 on the vocabulary, development, and liturgy of confirmation.

of a baptism did not require the presence of a bishop, because his participation was mediated through the material used for the anointing[5] But as the liturgy in Gaul was "romanized" during the eighth century, the Roman practice of reserving confirmation to a bishop spread.[6]

Confirmation in Anglo-Saxon England

Anglo-Saxon England had been converted directly from Rome, and the Roman reservation of confirmation to a bishop probably prevailed there from the beginning.[7] Local conditions made actual episcopal confirmation of many baptism difficult, however. In Anglo-Saxon England, the practice of baptizing at Easter and Pentecost did not take root; instead, ecclesiastical law and royal legislation ordered that baptisms be carried out soon after birth. Some sources specified that the baptism take place within seven, nine, or thirty days after birth, or "as soon as possible."[8] Priests who were unwilling or unable (e.g., because of drunkenness or unauthorized absence) to baptize those presented to them, especially if the candidates were ill, were to be punished.[9] The administration of baptism soon after birth had profound implications for confirmation. Because there were few bishops in Anglo-Saxon England, baptisms in the mostly rural minsters must often

5. Arnold Angenendt, "Bonifatius und das Sacramentum initiationis: Zugleich ein Beitrag zur Geschichte der Firmung," RQCAKG 72 (1977), 142–50; Mitchell, *Baptismal Anointing,* pp. 112–31.

6. Cyrille Vogel, "Les échanges liturgiques entre Rome et les pays francs jusqu'à l'époque de Charlemagne," in *Le chiese nei regni dell'Europa occidentale e i loro rapporti con Roma sino all'800, SSAM* 7/1 (Spoleto, 1960). Angenendt, "Bonifatius," pp. 149–58.

7. Willis, "Early English Liturgy from Augustine to Alcuin," in *Further Essays in Early Roman Liturgy* (London, 1968), pp. 196–97.

8. (a) Baptize within thirty days: *Laws of King Ine,* c. 2, in *EHD,* p. 399; Sermon 24, in Napier, *Wulfstan,* p. 120; Sermon 58, ibid., p. 300; (b) baptize within nine days: *Northumbrian Priests' Law,* c. 10, in *Councils and Synods with Other Documents Relating to the English Church,* ed. Dorothy Whitelock, Martin Brett, and C. N. L. Brooke (Oxford, 1981), 1/1, p. 455; (c) baptize within seven days: Ælfric, *Latin Pastoral Letter* for Archbishop Wulfstan, c. 163, in *Die Hirtenbriefe,* p. 63, says that "infants should not be pagans beyond seven days"; *The Canons of Edgar* (1005x1008) c. 15, in *Councils and Synods,* 1/1, p. 319: baptize within seven days (literally "nights"). In one manuscript of the *Canons of Edgar,* baptism within thirty-seven days is specified, which is probably an error caused by combining xxx days with a gloss pointing out that vii was also traditional: see *Councils and Synods,* 1/1, p. 319, n. 2; (d) baptize as soon as possible: Ælfric, *First Old English Letter* for Archbishop Wulfstan, c. 177, in *Die Hirtenbriefe,* pp. 130–31. On the rise of baptism "as soon as possible,"see Pierre-Marie Gy, "Quamprimum: Note sur le baptême des enfants," *La Maison-Dieu* 32 (1952).

9. See, e.g., King Wihtred of Kent, *Laws,* 6, in *EHD,* p. 397; Sermon 24 in Napier, *Wulfstan,* p. 120; Sermon 58, ibid., p. 300.

have gone unconfirmed, the postbaptismal anointing by a bishop to be sought at a later time, if at all.

Parents were required to seek speedy baptism for their children, which was possible because so many clergy—bishops, priests, and deacons—could provide it. But there could be no requirement for parents to seek confirmation within a fixed period because bishops were scarce—there were never more than eighteen bishoprics in Anglo-Saxon England at any one time.[10] Instead of requiring confirmation within a fixed time after baptism, ecclesiastical and secular law in the tenth and eleventh centuries ordered a person baptized without confirmation to seek it when opportunity arose. The *Canons of Edgar* (1005x1007), composed by Wulfstan of York, warned parents that their children should not be left unconfirmed (*unbiscopad,* literally "unbishoped") too long, but they did not specify a fixed time within which confirmation had to be sought, as was done with baptism, because as a practical matter they could not.[11]

A bishop personally presiding at a baptism would confirm as a matter of course, but in the seventh and eighth centuries, Anglo-Saxon bishops had to confirm whenever an opportunity presented itself. Bede praised bishops who traveled around their large dioceses confirming the baptized and criticized those who neglected that duty.[12] Bishop Wilfrid of York traveled on horseback to carry out the duties of his episcopacy, which explicitly included confirming the people with the imposition of his hand.[13] Bishop Cuthbert of Lindesfarne stayed with baptized Christians in a remote area for two days, during which he preached the word of God, and "He blessed them, placing his hand over the heads of each and anointing them with the consecrated oil"—clearly confirmation.[14] A bishop would confirm in a church or oratory if one was available, but that was not necessary.

10. David Knowles, *The Monastic Order in England,* 2d ed. (Cambridge, 1963), pp. 697–700, listed the eighteen bishoprics in Anglo-Saxon England in the tenth and eleventh centuries. Bede, *HE,* 5.23, pp. 558–60, wrote that in 731 there were four bishops in Northumbria and eleven in the kingdoms south of the Humber.

11. *Canons of Edgar,* c. 15, in *Councils and Synods,* 1/1, p. 319.

12. Angenendt, "Bonifatius," p. 150, n. 86. Bede, *Vita sancti Cuthberti,* c. 29, in *Two Lives of Saint Cuthbert,* ed. Bertram Colgrave (Cambridge, 1940) p. 252, praised the saint's travels to confirm, and in his *Epistola ad Ecgbertum,* c. 7, p. 410, criticized the failure to confirm or teach rural people.

13. Eddius Stephanus, *Vita Wilfridi,* c. 18, p. 38: "Nam quadam die sancto Wilfritho episcopo equitanti et pergenti ad varia officia episcopatus sui, baptizandi utique et cum manus impositione confirmandi populos."

14. *Vita Cuthberti episcopi Lindisfarnensis,* cc. 4 and 5, in *Two Lives of Saint Cuthbert,* ed. and trans. Bertram Colgrave (Cambridge, 1940), p. 116:"Namque congregato populo de montanis, manum ponens super capita singulorum, liniens unctione consecrata benedixerat uerbum Dei predicans manserat ibi duos dies." Bede reported the same incident with more details in *Vita sancti Cuthberti,* c. xxxii, pp. 256–58.

Theodore's *Penitential* permitted a bishop to confirm even in an open field (*in campo*), that is, in rather rough circumstances.[15] When Bishop Wulfstan of Worcester confirmed at Gloucester in the late eleventh century, he apparently did so in a cemetery.[16]

Even in the late Anglo-Saxon period, when diocesan organization guaranteed the accessibility of baptism, confirmation retained its episodic nature. Bishops traveled with their chrism in order to confirm when asked or when opportunity presented. Wulfstan of Winchester, the biographer of Bishop Æthelwold of Winchester (963–984), related an incident about the cleric who had charge of the bishop's chrism. He put too little chrism in the container and then lost it on the road. When Æthelwold "had come to his destination, he celebrated mass, spoke the sweet words of his holy sermon, and then, as usual, ordered the oil for confirming the boys to be given to him. But the cleric who imagined that he was carrying the flask suddenly realized he had lost it." He retraced his steps and "found the flask of oil lying in the road full of oil, though shortly before it had not even been half full of liquid."[17] William of Malmesbury translated into Latin a lost Old English life of the last Anglo-Saxon bishop, Wulfstan of Worcester (1062–1095), which had been written by the bishop's chaplain, Colman. William stressed Wulfstan's unusual diligence in confirming:

> He never permitted himself to eat in the day until he had signed with the cross however many children were brought to him from all over. This he carried out from sunrise to sunset, not only in the days of winter but also in the summer sun. It is testified by good witnesses that he would confirm two thousand—often three or more—in a single day. And this not only when he was young . . . but even when grey hairs began to sprinkle his head like sparkling snow, and his frail and infirm body could scarcely keep up with the vigor of his spirit. Everyone was amazed when the eight or more clerics who carried the chrism in turns all succumbed to fatigue, while he carried on indefatigible.[18]

William also painted a vivid picture of the gathering of a crowd to await Bishop Wulfstan's confirmation:

15. Discipulus Umbrensium, *Canones Theodori,* 2.2.1, p. 313.
16. William of Malmesbury, *Vita Wulfstani,* c. 14, in *The Vita Wulfstani of William of Malmesbury,* ed. R. R. Darlington (London, 1928), p. 36, and trans. in Michael Swanton, *Three Lives of the Last Englishmen* (New York and London, 1984), p. 120.
17. Wulfstan of Winchester, *Vita Sancti Ethelwoldi,* c. 32, in *The Life of Saint Æthelwold,* ed. Michael Lapidge and Michael Winterbottom (Oxford, 1991), pp. 48–49.
18. William of Malmesbury, *Vita Wulfstani,* c. 14, p. 36, and trans. in *Three Lives,* p. 120.

Wulfstan was in the habit of doing this [confirming] while constantly fasting. Once at Gloucester he was entreated by the venerable Abbot Serlo to deviate from this. The customary masses having been said, he was about to go out to the children, when this abbot came asking him to honor the brethren's refectory with his presence that day. There were many reasons why he ought not to spurn the request. . . . Besides, in the meantime the crowd of children could be arranged in a row, so that he could go up and down them more easily. The bishop was persuaded by this and by the crowd of those eagerly pressing him. Meanwhile in the cemetery the common people were discussing many things among themselves.[19]

Because of the paucity of bishops and the rural character of settlement in England, the makeshift efforts of bishops must have been insufficient; indeed, in the eighth century, the provision of baptism itself was sometimes inadequate. An anonymous Anglo-Saxon monk who had a vision of hell saw "a sad and mourning multitude of children who had died without baptism under Bishop Daniel [of Winchester (705–745)]," who was blind but did not give up his office.[20] But the provision of confirmation was always more problematic than that of baptism. In a frank letter of 5 November 734, Bede criticized Archbishop Egbert of York for a series of shortcomings; including:

that many villages and hamlets of our people are situated in inaccessible mountains and dense woodlands, where there is never seen for many years at a time a bishop to exhibit any ministry or celestial grace; not one man of which, however, is immune from rendering dues to the bishop. *Nor is it only a bishop who is lacking in such places to confirm the baptized by the laying on of hands;* there is not even a teacher to teach the truth of the faith and the difference between good and evil conduct. [my italics][21]

Theodore's *Penitential* also expressed anxiety about the neglect of confirmation in early Anglo-Saxon England: "We do not believe that anyone is perfected in baptism without the confirmation of a bishop," but it added in the face of widespread neglect of confirmation, "nevertheless we do not despair."[22]

Not just Anglo-Saxons were concerned about the neglect of confirmation. A rubric in *Ordo Romanus XI* warned that "there is to be great care

19. Ibid., pp. 36–37 pp. 120–21.
20. Boniface, *Epistola* 115, in *S. Bonifatii et Lullii epistolae,* p. 249.
21. Bede, *Epistola ad Ecgbertum,* c. 7, p. 410, and trans. in *EHD* p. 802.
22. Discipulus Umbrensium, *Canones Theodori,* 2.4.5, p. 317.

that this not be neglected, because then [at the bishop's anointing] every legitimate baptism is confirmed with the name of Christianity."[23] The late-eighth-century Frankish *Ordo Romanus XV* provided directions for what must have been a common situation: "If they are able to have a bishop present, the baptized infants ought to be confirmed with chrism. But if on that day they can not find a bishop, as soon as they are able to find one, they ought to have this done without delay."[24] The reality was that many baptisms were never confirmed.

The reservation of confirmation to bishops was more than a liturgical detail: it had significant consequences for church organization. To make confirmation available, reformers, first in England and then in Francia, sought to increase the number of bishops by dividing large dioceses into smaller ones and by providing auxiliary bishops, sometimes called *chorepiscopi.* If dioceses were smaller and more numerous, bishops or their auxiliaries could confirm more, though probably not all, of their flock. Hanna Vollrath has argued that for the sake of pastoral care, including confirmation, Archbishop Theodore of Canterbury divided the vast diocese of York into smaller dioceses, which brought him into conflict with Bishop Wilfrid of York.[25] Bede recommended in his letter to Archbishop Egbert of York, whose diocese was still large a generation after Archbishop Theodore split it, that he consecrate "more bishops for our people. . . . For who, indeed, cannot see how much better it would be to divide such a great weight of ecclesiastical government among several, who could bear their share more easily, than to weigh down one [bishop] under a load which he cannot carry?"[26] Arnold Angenendt stressed that Archbishop Boniface and his supporters, drawing on their experience in England, encouraged Frankish bishops to make regular visits around their dioceses in order to confirm. Boniface also promoted the creation of new dioceses and the ordination of auxiliary bishops in the Frankish Kingdom to aid in the massive task of confirming.[27]

What did a confirmation in Anglo-Saxon England look like? The scanty information from the seventh and eighth centuries mentioned the laying on of hands and the use of chrism. Although a number of tenth- and eleventh-century Anglo-Saxon pontificals have a prayer for confirming

23. *Ordo Romanus XI,* c. 103, in *Les ordines,* 2:446.

24. *Ordo Romanus XV,* c. 119, in *Les ordines,* 3:120; Vogel, *Medieval Liturgy,* pp. 152–54, argued *Ordo Romanus XV* is the work of a Frankish monk writing a little before 787.

25. Hanna Vollrath, "Taufliturgie und Diözesaneinteilungen in der frühen angelsächsischen Kirche," in *Irland und Christenheit/Ireland and Christendom,* ed. Próinséas Ni Chatháin and Michael Richter (Stuttgart, 1987).

26. Bede, *Epistola ad Ecgbertum,* c. 9, p. 412 and trans. in *EHD,* pp. 803–4.

27. Angenendt, "Bonifatius," pp. 155–58.

children with the sign of the cross (*ad consignandos pueros*), only the *Sidney Sussex Pontifical* and the *Pontifical of Egbert* contain the full ritual.[28] The rubrics in the *Pontifical of Egbert* outline a tenth-century confirmation:

1) The Confirmation of men by a bishop, it ought to be said how he ought to confirm: "All-powerful Eternal God who has deigned. . . ." (*Confirmatio hominum ab episcopo Dicenda quomodo confirmare debet, "Omnipotens sempiterne deus qui dignatus es. . . ."*)
2) Here he ought to put chrism on the forehead of the man and say, "Receive the sign of the holy cross with the chrism of salvation in Christ Jesus to eternal life." (*Hic debet mittere crisma in fronte ipsius hominis et dicere: "Accipe signum sancte crucis chrismate salutis in christo iesu in uitam aeternam."*)
3) Afterward, he ought to recite this prayer: "May God the Father and the Son and the Holy Spirit confirm you. . . ." (*Postea hanc orationem recitare debet: "Confirmet te deus pater et filius et spiritus sanctus. . . ."*)
4) Then they ought to be bound [i.e., a cloth ought to be tied around the forehead of each confirmed person to cover the chrism]: "God who gave the Holy spirit to your apostles. . . ." (*Modo ligandi sunt: "Deus qui apostolis tuis sanctum dedisti spiritum. . . ."*)
5) The episcopal blessing follows: "May Almighty God bless you. He who created all things from nothing. . . ." (*Sequitur benedictio episcopalis: "Benedicat uos omnipotens deus, qui cuncta ex nichilo creauit. . . ."*)
6) Another blessing at the mass after confirmation: "Pour out, O Lord, we ask. . . ." (*Alia benedictio ad missam post confirmationem: "Effunde quaesumus domine. . . ."*)[29]

The prayers in the *Sidney Sussex Pontifical* are the same, but some of the rubrics differ. In particular, the confirmation is explicitly for children (*pueri*), and each youngster's name is said as he or she is confirmed:

1) Prayer for confirming boys (*Oratio ad pueros consignandos*)
2) Next let him make a cross on each, with holy chrism on their foreheads, with their own distinct names, thus saying: "I sign and confirm you with the sign of the holy cross. . . ." (*Deinde faciat crucem per singulos, de sancto crismate in frontibus eorum distinctis propriis nominibus ita dicendo: "Consigno et confirmo te signo sancte crucis. . . ."*)
3) Here they ought to be bound (*Hic ligandi sunt*)

28. *Sidney Sussex Pontifical* pp. 168–69; *Pontifical of Egbert,* pp. 14–15.
29. *Pontifical of Egbert,* pp. 14–15.

4) The blessing of the bishop over the boys (*Benedictio episcopi super pueros*)[30]

The conclusion of the confirmation episode, related above, in William of Malmesbury's life of Bishop Wulfstan of Worcester, gives a vivid picture of what a confirmation looked like in late-eleventh-century England. While Bishop Wulfstan was dining with the monks, the crowd awaiting confirmation became restless, and a young fellow parodied what laypeople must have seen when a bishop confirmed, that is, the anointing and binding up of the forehead, accompanied by a brief prayer:

> One young man among them, to whom the slipperiness of his age suggested words of impudence, then began to act up: "Why are you waiting for the bishop who is filling his belly with the monks? No, just do it. If anyone wants his child to be confirmed (*consignari*), let him come to me." And right then taking mud, anointing the forehead of the nearest child, he murmured obscene words. The insanity went on spreading, following up the foolish deed with a shout of this sort: "bind up that one's forehead, he's confirmed" (*frontem isti ligate: consignatus est*).[31]

Thus, in the late Anglo-Saxon period, confirmation ordinarily took place in groups. It was a brief ceremony at which the bishop made the sign of the cross in chrism with his thumb on the forehead of each person. The forehead was then bound up (*ligare*) with a cloth (*pannus crismalis*) to protect the consecrated substance for a period of days. Since the eighth century, the practice of speedy infant baptism, the postponement of the episcopal anointing after baptism, and the small number of bishops converged to create a separate sacrament, confirmation, which was always distinct from baptism in its minister and its sponsor and usually distinct in the time and location of its conferral.

The Vocabulary of Confirmation

Because confirmation emerged only slowly out of the integrated initiation process, its vocabulary was complex and is sometimes difficult to interpret. In some Latin texts, the sign of the cross was the feature of interest, and verbs such as *signare* or *consignare* were used, as in the episode of the

30. *Sidney Sussex Pontifical,* pp. 168–69.
31. William of Malmesbury, *Vita Wulfstani,* c. 14, p. 37.

young mocker. In other Latin texts, the consecrated oil (*chrisma*) was the feature of interest; from it, a verb, *chrismare,* was derived, and confirmation was called the *sacramentum chrismatis.*[32]

In fifth-century Gaul, the words *confirmare/confirmatio,* which meant to strengthen or complete a baptism, began to designate the postbaptismal anointing(s). For example, the Council of Riez (439) forbade an illicitly consecrated bishop to perform most episcopal functions but permitted him to continue to confirm the newly baptized (*confirmare neophytos*).[33] An anonymous compiler of sermons in fifth- or sixth-century Gaul, who has traditionally been called Eusebius of Emesa or Eusebius Gallicanus, contributed significantly to the victory of the words *confirmare/confirmatio.* Fr. Glorie, the editor of the homilies, hypothesized that their complier was Caesarius of Arles or one of his disciples.[34] The homilies in the collection had different authors. Homily 29, for delivery on Pentecost, was crucial in the history of the theology and vocabulary of confirmation. L. A. Van Buchem argued that its author was Faustus, bishop of Riez from 458 until his exile in 477.[35] The homily used as its rhetorical premise that some people in the congregation were puzzled why any further ritual was needed after baptism. The preacher posed for himself the question "What value has the ministry of the confirmer (*ministerium confirmantis*) to me after the mystery of baptism?"[36] Roman soldiers were often marked for the emperor's service by a brand, a tattoo, or by wearing a lead symbol on a chain. The preacher used that Roman military image to explain how confirmation completed baptism: "When the emperor receives someone in the number of his soldiers, he must not only put his mark on the one received but he must provide the warrior with suitable arms." The homilist drew the conclusion that baptism put God's "mark" on his soldiers, and confirmation "armed" them:[37] "Therefore the Holy Spirit, who descends over the waters of baptism in a salvation-bringing descent, gives fullness in the font for innocence; in confirmation he adds an increase in grace, because it [grace] is necessary for those who are going to live in this world to walk for an entire

32. Bernard Botte, "Le vocabulaire ancien de la confirmation," *La Maison-Dieu* 54 (1958); Fisher, *Christian Initiation,* pp. 141–48.

33. Council of Riez, c. 3, 4, and 5, in *Concilia Galliae, A. 314–A. 506,* ed. Charles Munier, *CCSL* 148 (Turnhout, 1963), p. 67. See L. A. Van Buchem, *L'homélie pseudoeusébienne de Pentecôte: L'origine de la confirmatio en Gaule Méridionale et l'interprétation de ce rite par Fauste de Riez* (Nijmegen, 1967), pp. 83–134.

34. Eusebius Gallicanus, *Collectio homiliarum,* ed. Fr. Glorie, *CCSL* 101 (Turnhout, 1970), pp. vii–xxi.

35. Van Buchem, *L'homélie pseudoeusébienne,* pp. 51–78.

36. Ibid., p. 40, lines 8–9: "Quid mihi prodest post mysterium baptismatis ministerium confirmantis?"

lifetime among invisible enemies and dangers. In baptism we are reborn to life; after baptism we are confirmed for the battle; in baptism we are washed, after baptism we are strengthened."[37] The homilist insisted that baptism alone was sufficient for those who died young but that those who had to live in the world needed the added assistance of confirmation: "Rebirth [in baptism] immediately saves those who are to be received into the peace of the holy world [i.e., those who die]; confirmation arms and instructs those who are preserved for the struggles and battles of this world."[38]

After confirmation emerged as a distinct rite reserved to the bishop, it needed not only a vocabulary but a theological explanation. Homily 29 was influential in creating a theology when it advanced the view that confirmation strengthened the Christian by conferring the Holy Spirit more fully than did baptism.[39] An important strain in the theology of confirmation held that this was so, that the bishop conferred specifically the sevenfold gifts of the Holy Spirit, as enumerated in Isaiah 11:2.[40]

The Pseudo-Eusebius's homily was reworked by the Pseudo-Isidorean forger in the ninth century as a letter of Pope Melchiades (311–314). It was taken into the canonical collection called *Collectio Anselmo dedicata* and probably from that source was taken into Gratian's *Decretum* (*De cons., dist.* v.1–2), which made virtually certain that the ordinary Latin noun for confirmation would be *confirmatio* and the verb would be *confirmare,* although other words, including *consignare,* were never entirely replaced.[41]

One might have expected that the Old English words for confirmation would be related to the literal translation of *confirmare,* which is *trymian/getrymian.* The word *untrymed* ("unstrengthened" or "unconfirmed") was used at least once to designate the absence of confirmation,[42] but the Old English words for confirming were based on the Latin verb *episcopare,* "to act like a bishop." Confirming was one of the few ritual acts that was reserved to a bishop and set him off from ordinary priests, who could do al-

37. Pp. 40–41, lines 10–19.

38. P. 41, lines 27–29: "Regeneratio per se saluat mox in pace beati saeculi recipiendos, confirmatio armat et instruit ad agones buius mundi et proelia reservandos"; the sermon is also Homily 29.2 in Eusebius Gallicanus, *Collectio homiliarum,* p. 338.

39. Van Buchem, *L'homélie pseudoeusébienne,* pp. 128–34.

40. Hippolytus, *Apostolic Tradition,* c. 21, pp. 86–90. On the separation of confirmation from the unified Christian initiation of the early period, see Fisher, *Christian Initiation* pp. 71–77.

41. Van Buchem, *L'homélie pseudoeusébienne,* pp. 206–17; Botte, "Le vocabulaire ancien," pp. 17–18.

42. *Confessionale Pseudo-Egberti,* p. 180: "Ne mot se oðrum onfon se ðe him bið unfullad oððe untrymed," which translates Theodore's *Penitential,* in Discipulus Umbrensian, 2.4.9, *Canones Theodori,* p. 317: "Non licet alium suscipere, qui non est baptizatus vel confirmatus."

most everything else a bishop could do, such as say mass, impose penance, and give blessings. In his letter to Bishop Wulfsige, Ælfric wrote, "There is nothing more between a mass-priest and a bishop except that the bishop is appointed to ordain priests and to confirm children (*to bisceopȝenne cild*) and to consecrate churches and to watch over God's law. For it would be too complicated if every mass-priest did thus."[43] Confirmation was the chief event that put a bishop face to face with his lay flock. The bishop stood before every Christian, called each by name, and placed chrism on his or her forehead in the form of a cross. Because confirming was a central duty of bishops, the Old English words *bisceopian* or *gebisceopian* (literally, "to bishop") had the precise meaning "to confirm."[44] The Old English noun for confirmation was *bisceopung,*[45] although it was sometimes called *bisceopes bletsung,* the bishop's blessing, presumably because only a bishop could confer it.[46]

Sponsorship at Confirmation

By the later seventh and eighth centuries, Anglo-Saxon and Frankish evidence indicates that confirmation had its own sponsor. Theodore's *Penitential* was the first source to assert that the participation of a separate "father" at confirmation was a custom (*consuetudo*): "In the catechumenate and baptism and confirmation there can be one father if it is necessary; nevertheless that is not the custom, but rather individuals receive in the individual rites."[47] A Frankish capitulary issued at Compiègne (757) treated sponsorship at confirmation as a fact needing no explanation when it forbade anyone to "hold a stepdaughter or stepson before the bishop for confirming."[48]

43. Ælfric, letter to Bishop Wulfsige, c. 43, in *Die Hirtenbriefe,* p. 43.

44. The fundamental article is Max Förster, "Die Bedeutung von AE Gebisceopian und ihre Sippe," *Anglia* 66 (1942).

45. *Ordo ad visitandum et unguendum infirmum,* c. 36, ed. Bernhard Fehr, in "Altenglische Ritualtexte für Krankenbesuch, heilige Ölung und Begräbnis," in *Texte und Forschungen zur englischen Kulturgeschichte: Festgabe für Felix Liebermann,* ed. by M. Förster and K. Wildhagen (Halle, 1921), pp. 54 (*bisceopunga*); Chrodegang of Metz, enlarged version of the *Regula canonicorum,* c. 42, in *The Old English Version, with the Latin Original, of the Enlarged Rule of Chrodegang,* ed. A. S. Napier (London, 1916), p. 50 (*butan bisceopunge* translates *absque confirmatione*); Ælfric, Sermon 22, in *Sermones Catholici* 1:328 (*bisceopunge*); Wulfstan of York, *Homily* 9, in p. 186, line 30 (*biscpunge*).

46. Sermon 2, in Brotanek, *Texte* p. 24, lines 4 and 10.

47. Discipulus Umbrensium, 2.2.8, *Canones Theodori,* p. 317.

48. *Capitulary of Compiègne,* c. 15, in *Capitularia regum Francorum,* ed. A. Boretius and V. Krause, *MGH Leges* 2 (Hanover, 1883), 1:38: "Si quis filiastrum aut filiastram ante episcopum ad confirmationem tenuerit, separetur ab uxore sua et alteram non accipiat. Similiter et femina alterum non accipiat."

There was a specific way of talking about sponsorship at confirmation which set it off from sponsorship at baptism. Baptismal sponsorship was described in words of "taking" or "receiving," whereas confirmation sponsorship was described by words of "holding" or "leading." Eighth-century Frankish sources said that the sponsor at confirmation "held someone before the bishop,"[49] "led someone to confirmation,"[50] or "held someone at the bishop's hand."[51] The *Romano-Germanic Pontifical,* produced at Mainz in the mid-tenth century, sheds light on the rituals behind the words chosen to describe confirmation. The rubric for confirmation said, "When they have been dressed [after being baptized naked], let them be arranged in order; and the infants are held in the right arms, but older persons place their foot on the foot of their godfather."[52] Thus the confirmation sponsor's visible action was to "lead" the candidate into the presence of the bishop, to hold an infant, or to stand behind an older child or adult with physical contact—specifically described as the foot of the candidate on the foot of the sponsor—when the bishop anointed the forehead.

Neither the Egbert or Sidney Sussex pontificals referred to sponsors, although other sources attest to their activity in Anglo-Saxon England.[53] In Old English, the sponsor was said "to receive someone at the bishop's hand" (*onfon æt bisceopes handa*).[54] In the early-tenth-century Fonthill letter, an important man, perhaps the Ealdorman Ordlaf, intervened with King Edward on behalf of Helmstan, whom he had received at the bishop's hand; that is, he identified Helmstan as his godson from confirmation.[55] If

49. Ibid., p. 38: "tenere ante episcopum"; Council of Chalons (813), c. 31, in *Concilia aevi Karolini,* p. 279: "tenere coram episcopum"; Theodulf of Orleans, *First Synodal Statue,* c. 22, ed. Peter Brommer, *MGH Capitula episcoporum* 1 (Hanover, 1984), p. 119: "coram episcopo ad confirmandum quemlibet teneat."

50. Council of Mainz (813), c. 55, in *Concilia aevi Karolini* p. 273: "ducere ad confirmationem."

51. Ghaerbald of Liège, *Second Diocesan Statute,* c. 17, ed. Peter Brommer, *MGH Capitula episcoporum* 1, p. 31: "tenere ad manum episcopi."

52. *Ordo ad baptizandum infantes,* c. 18, in *Le Pontifical Romano-germanique* pp. 163–64: "Induti vero ordinentur per ordinem et infantes quidem in brachiis dextris tenentur, maiores vero pedem ponunt super pedem patrini sui."

53. Asser, *De rebus gestis Ælfredi,* c. 80, pp. 66–67: Alfred received a Welsh king "ad manum episcopi in filium confirmationis"; *Canons of Edgar,* c. 22, in *Councils and Synods* 1/1, p. 322: a person who does not know the creed and Lord's Prayer is forbidden to receive at baptism, or *æt bisceopes handa.*

54. *ASC(C),* undated (943), p. 48: "he [King Edmund] onfeng Rægenoldes cyninges æt bisceopes handa"; *ASC(A),* s.a. 993, p. 79; "hine nam se cing syððan to bisceopes handa"; *ASC(C),* s.a. 994, p. 54: "and se cyning Æþelred his onfeng æt bisceopes handa"; Sermon 2, in Brotanek, *Texte,* p. 25: "onfehð . . . æt bisceopes handa"; Sermon 58, in Napier, *Wulfstan,* pp. 300 and 302: "onfon . . . æt bisceopes handum"; King Cnut, *I Laws,* 22.6, in *Councils and Synods* 1/1, p. 484.

55. The document is S 1445, on which see Simon Keynes, "The Fonthill Letter," *Words, Texts, and Manuscripts: Studies in Anglo-Saxon Culture Presented to Helmut Gneuss on the Occasion of His Sixty-fifth Birthday,* ed. Michael Korhammer (Cambridge, 1992), p. 66: "forþon ic his hæfde ær onfongen æt biscopes honda ær he ða undæde 'gedyde.'" The scholarly consensus holds that the

a person was both baptized and confirmed at the same time, there could be a single sponsor for the entire ritual, as Theodore's *Penitential* had reluctantly permitted. But when it became common for most people to be confirmed at some time after their baptism, it became more likely that there would be a separate sponsor.

As at baptism, sponsorship at confirmation created a spiritual relationship conceptualized as that of parent and child. In Latin, a godchild from confirmation could be designated in several ways, for instance *filius/filia ad confirmationem* or *filius/filia a chrismate.*[56] The Old English word for a godson from confirmation could not be confused with that of a godchild from baptism. It was a neologism, *bisceopsunu* ("bishop's son"), which is attested for the first time in Ine's law 76.3.[57] When that law was translated into Latin early in the twelfth-century *Quadripartitus,* the Old English word *biscepsunu* was rendered rather misleadingly as *episcopi filius* ("son of the bishop.") in three manuscripts and as *episcopi filiolus* ("godson of the bishop") in three others.[58] A much earlier Latin text, the eighth-century *vita* of Wilfrid of York (634–709), seems to offer the same equivalence of *bisceopsunu* and *filius episcopi.* Eddius Stephanus related that while Bishop Wilfrid was confirming during his travels, a mother presented to him her dead baby, who was unbaptized and unconfirmed. Wilfrid revived the child, baptized him, and probably confirmed him. The boy, named Eodwald, thereafter bore the nickname (*agnomen*) Filius-Episcopi (literally "son of the bishop"), which may be a Latin translation of *bisceopsunu.*[59] The tenth-century chronicler Æthelweard commented that in his own day, children sponsored at confirmation were called "sons" by those who received them under the bishop's hand.[60] Girls were certainly confirmed and one would expect a word like *bisceopsdohter* for a goddaughter from confirmation, but the corpus of Old English writings does not record the word.

Aldhelm and Aldfrith

Just as the Anglo-Saxons were precocious in their concern that confirmation not be neglected, so they were precocious about sponsorship at

---

author of the Fonthill letter was the Ealdorman Ordlaf, but Mark Boynton and Susan Reynolds, "The Author of the Fonthill Letter," *ASE* 25 (1996), tentatively suggested that the identification of the author with Ordlaf is not so secure as usually thought.

56. *Council of Mainz* (813), c. 55, *MGH Concilia* 2/1, p. 273; Æthelweard, *Chronicon,* 3.4, p. 32.

57. Ine, *Institutiones,* 1:122–23.

58. Ibid., p. 123, n. 24.

59. Eddius Stephanus, *Vita Wilfridi,* c. 18, pp. 38–40.

60. Æthelweard, *Chronicon,* 3.4, p. 32: "et filium a chrismate nominauit, ut modo sub manu episcopi solemus accipientes paruulos filios nominare."

confirmation. Theirs are the earliest references to sponsorship at confirmation. In two texts connected with Archbishop Theodore, a sponsor at confirmation is said to be customary.[61] But the earliest reference to an actual sponsorship at confirmation may be in a Latin letter written by the Anglo-Saxon Aldhelm, who died as bishop of Sherbourne in 709.[62] At a date between 685 and 695, he wrote a long letter—a treatise really—to King Aldfrith of Northumbria (685–704), whom he addressed as one who was "joined to me for some time by the bonds of spiritual clientship" (*mihique iam dudum spiritalis clientelae catenis conexo*).[63] He reminded the king that he had sponsored him in some ceremony that had taken place about twenty years earlier, when both were young (*tempore pubertatis nostrae*):

> I do not doubt . . . that the provident heart of your Wisdom may recall that twice-two revolutions of the *lustra* ago [i.e., twenty years ago] we made the unbreakable pledge of a binding agreement, and through the bond of spiritual association we established a comradeship of devoted charity. For a long time ago, in the era of our young manhood, when your talented Sagacity was equipped with the septiform munificence of spiritual gifts by the hand of a venerable bishop, I recall that I acquired the name of "father" and that you received the appellations of your adoptive station together with the privilege of heavenly grace.[64]

At least since Ehwald's edition of Aldhelm's works, this passage has been interpreted as a reference to Aldhelm's sponsorship of Aldfrith at baptism.[65] But the details of King Aldfrith's life argue against the delay of his baptism until *pubertas,* which was when Aldhelm said the ritual took place. Medieval words for the stages of life are difficult to pin down, and I hesitate to be overly precise as to what *pubertas* was. Michael Lapidge and James Rosier thought it was between the late teens and about age thirty-five.[66] If

61. Discipulus Umbrensium, *Canones Theodori,* 2.4.8, p. 317; *Iudicium de penitentia,* c. 69, p. 275.
62. Aldhelm, *Epistola ad Acircium,* in *Aldhelmi opera omnia,* ed. by Rudolph Ehwald, *MGH AA* 15 (Berlin, 1919), pp. 61–204; trans. partially in *Aldhelm: The Prose Works,* trans. Michael Lapidge and Michael Herren (Cambridge, 1979), pp. 34–47.
63. Aldhelm, *Epistola,* p. 61.
64. Lapidge and Herren, *Prose Works,* p. 34; Aldhelm, *Epistola,* pp. 61–62: "confido, quod provida sagacitatis vestrae praecordia reminiscantur, nos ante bis bina lustrorum volumina inextricabile conglutinati foederis pignus pepigisse et spiritali sodalitatis vinculo devotae caritatis contubernia copulasse. Nam pridem, tempore pubertatis nostrae, cum septiformi spiritalium charismatum munificentia vestra solers indolis sub manu venerandi pontificis ornaretur, paternum memini me nomen adeptum teque adoptivae dignitatis vocabula cum caelestis gratiae praerogativa sortitum."
65. Aldhelm, *Epistola,* p. 61, n. 1; see also Lapidge and Herren, *Prose Works,* pp. 12 and 32.
66. *Aldhelm: The Poetic Works,* trans. Michael Lapidge and James Rosier (Cambridge, 1985), pp. 11–12.

Aldhelm's letter is dated correctly (685x695), then the sponsorship took place twenty years earlier, between 665 and 675. If Aldhelm was born approximately 640 and Aldfrith was born approximately 650, then when the sponsoring ritual took place, the one was between twenty-five and thirty-five and the other between fifteen and twenty-five—each in his *pubertas,* I think.

Aldfrith was *nothus* ("illegitimate"), born of a union between the exiled Oswiu, who was later king of Northumbria (c. 642–c. 670), and a Christian Irish princess, Fin, Oswiu's concubine.[67] When King Oswiu died in 670, his son Egfrith (670–685) succeeded, and Aldfrith went—perhaps fled—to Iona, where he lived in exile for study among the Irish while his half-brother ruled Northumbria. Bede described him as "a man most learned in the scriptures" (*vir in scripturis doctissimus*).[68] With Christian parents and a long residence among the Christian Irish, it is likely that Aldfrith had been baptized as an infant and not in his *pubertas.*

But if Aldhelm was not referring to his baptismal sponsorship of Aldrith, of what was he reminding the king? I believe that the ceremony was confirmation. Aldhelm's reference to the time "when your talented Sagacity was equipped with the septiform munificence of spiritual gifts by the hand of a venerable bishop" evokes an episcopal confirmation, which was the occasion for a bishop to confer either the Holy Spirit or the seven gifts of the Spirit.[69] For instance, Ælfric wrote in a sermon for Pentecost that "bishops are of the same order [as the apostles] in God's church, and possess that ordinance in their confirming (*on heora biscepunge*), so that they set their hands over baptized men, and pray the Almighty Ruler to send to them the sevenfold gift of His Spirit, who lives and reigns forever without end."[70] Aldhelm's reference to the hand of the bishop (*sub manu venerandi pontificis*) also points to confirmation, at which the bishop placed his hand on or extended it over the candidates.[71]

There is no way to know for certain why Aldfrith's confirmation had been put off, if it had been. He was raised in a Celtic religious environment; his mother was an Irish Christian and his father Oswiu was a patron of Irish clergy and, until the Synod of Whitby (664), observed the Irish date for Easter.[72] If he had been baptized in Ireland or according to an Irish

67. Kirby, *Earliest English Kings,* pp. 142–47, sketched Aldfrith's career and suggested a date of birth about 650.

68. Bede, *HE,* 4.26, p. 430.

69. Jacques Lécuyer, "La confirmation chez les pères," *La Maison-Dieu* 54 (1958); Van Buchem, *L'homélie pseudoéusebienne,* pp. 130–32. *Ordo Romanus XI,* c. 100, in *Les ordines* 2:446, noted that the bishop confirmed the neophytes "cum invocatione septiformis gratiae spiritus sancti."

70. Ælfric, *In die sancto Pentecosten,* in *Sermones Catholici* 1:328.

71. Aldhelm, *Epistola,* p. 62.

72. Kirby, *Earliest English Kings,* pp. 143–44.

ritual, either of which is likely in view of his background, he might not have received the second, episcopal anointing, which was not part of the Gallican-type liturgy used in Ireland.[73]

Beginning with Augustine of Canterbury, Roman Christians found something to disapprove in the Celtic liturgy of baptism, but the sources do not say what it was.[74] The scholarly consensus seems to be that those accustomed to the Roman liturgy were troubled by the Celtic liturgy's omission of the bishop's anointing, that is, confirmation.[75] The Celtic liturgies were part of the widespread family of Gallican liturgies, which did not reserve a postbaptismal anointing for a bishop. Instead, the baptizing priest anointed the neophyte once after baptism with oil consecrated by a bishop, who was present through the material used in the anointing.[76] If Aldfrith had been baptized in a Celtic ritual, some in the Roman party might have thought that his baptism was incomplete and in need of episcopal confirmation. For instance, Theodore's *Penitential* said, "We do not believe that anyone is perfect in baptism without the confirmation of a bishop; nevertheless we do not despair."[77] At some point, whose context we can no longer recover, perhaps when Aldfrith adhered to the Roman party, the bishop's confirmation might have been added, with Aldhelm as sponsor.

If Aldhelm's letter does refer to confirmation, it is the earliest instance where we know the names of a sponsor and a godchild from confirmation. Furthermore, it proves that Theodore's *Penitential,* which gathered decisions roughly contemporary with Aldhelm's letter, was not merely theoretical when it recommended a "father" at confirmation. Furthermore, Aldhelm's use of the term *paternum nomen* ("paternal name") to describe his bond to Aldfrith and of the term *adoptiva dignitas* ("adoptive station") to describe Aldfrith's bond to him indicates that, by the seventh century, Anglo-Saxons regarded sponsorship at confirmation, just as they regarded that at baptism, as a kind of adoption.

There is another text from Northumbria which probably refers to a form of sponsorship, though it is not clear whether it took place at bap-

73. Fisher, *Christian Initiation,* pp. 78–80; Pepperdene, "Baptism" esp. pp. 117–21, who argued the Irish omitted the postbaptismal anointing entirely.

74. Bede, *HE,* 2.2, p. 139: one of three conditions Augustine tried to place on British bishops was "ut ministerium baptizandi quo Deo renascimur iuxta morem sanctae Romanae et apostolicae ecclesiae conpleatis."

75. Pepperdene, "Baptism," pp. 117–19, on omission of confirmation. Her view was accepted by Jane Stevenson, "Introduction," pp. liii–liv; Charles Thomas, *Christianity in Roman Britain* pp. 209 and 212–13; S. McKillop, "A Romano-British Baptismal Liturgy?" in *The Early Church in Western Britain and Ireland,* ed S. M. Pearce (Oxford, 1982).

76. Angenendt, "Bonifatius," pp. 159–63.

77. Discipulus umbrensium, *Canones Theodori,* 2.4.5, p. 317: "Nullum perfectum credimus in baptismo sine confirmatione episcopi non disperamus tamen."

tism, confirmation, or some other "adopting" ritual. Eddius Stephanus reported that when young Osred succeeded his father Aldfrith as king of Northumbria in 704, the boy was made an "adopted son to our holy bishop [Wilfrid]."[78] Osred was about eight years old and probably was already baptized. Perhaps, but only perhaps, this too was a sponsorship at confirmation.

The Delay of Confirmation

The possibility that the royal heir Osred was not confirmed until he was about eight years old points to a strategy for increasing the social usefulness of sponsorship at confirmation. Even though bishops were scarce in England, a king or aristocrat who wanted to do so could have had his child baptized and confirmed by a bishop, provided that the child was healthy and did not need emergency baptism. Many children of important families were probably confirmed as infants or as very young children. Some families, however, apparently kept a child unconfirmed intentionally. Spiritual kinsmen were a social asset, and a delayed confirmation could provide an opportunity to multiply their number.

The theology of baptism argued strongly against delay of that sacrament, whereas the theology of confirmation allowed for that strategy of holding a child unconfirmed to await a desirable sponsor. Theologically speaking, the delay of baptism was very risky because a child—or an adult—who died unbaptized was damned. Ælfric was reflecting a long tradition, reaching back at least to Augustine of Hippo, when he wrote, "You should not dangerously hold your child too long as a heathen, because he will have no entry to heaven if he dies heathen. In truth, on Judgment Day, they are no longer children but are as much men as they might have been if they grew to maturity at the customary interval. And the heathen child dwells always in hell and the baptized goes to heaven."[79] In contrast, a child who died soon after baptism was free of sin and guaranteed salvation.[80]

78. Eddius Stephanus, *Vita Wilfridi,* c. 59, p. 128: "sancto pontifici nostro filius adoptivus factus est."

79. Ælfric, *Dominica I Post Penecosten,* in *Homilies of Ælfric: A Supplementary Collection,* ed. John C. Pope, EETS OS 259 (London, 1967), 1:483–84.

80. *Poenitientiale Pseudo-Egberti,* in *Die altenglische Version des Halitgar'schen Bussbuches (Sog. Poenitentiale Pseudo-Egberti),* ed. Josef Raith, BAP 13 (Hamburg, 1933), p. 13, declared that the soul of a man who died after receiving the final anointing was a pure as that of a child who died immediately after baptism (*his sawl bið gelice clæne æfter his forsiðe ealswa þæt cild bið þe æfter fulwihte sona gewat*).

Even the ninth-century Frankish reformers, who tried to enforce the traditional fixed times for baptism, had to bow to the fearful consequences of dying unbaptized. The Frankish abbot and archbishop Hrabanus Maurus (d. 856) justified baptism at uncanonical times by arguing that such a baptism was better than allowing people to die unbaptized. In a letter to the archpriest Hathubrand written between 832 and 845, he criticized priests in rural and missionary areas who rigidly insisted on the observation of the fixed times for baptism, even for ill infants. Hrabanus emphasized the need for swift baptism for infants and adults, at least in rural or missionary areas:

> They even add that it is not permitted to any of the priests to baptize their infants except at Easter and at Pentecost, even though the infants are ill, unless the parents swear beforehand on the altar or on the relics of saints that the child who has been brought for baptism is not able to live longer. Since parents are unwilling to do this, because they do not know how long the infants will live, many of these infants die without having received the baptism of Christ. It is easy to see how absurd that is.
>
> Concerning the reception of baptism, it seems good to me that the newly converted people, who are under your authority but located among pagans, should not be held too strictly to observe the two legitimate times of Easter and Pentecost, but they should be baptized where opportunity demands and possibility permits. Because if they are in a city where there is a supply of clerics, they can easily observe the legitimate times, but those who live in the countryside far from priests and churches under the greatest danger of the pagans, [for them] I think it is better that they be baptized at times other than Easter and Pentecost than that they die without baptism and, held by the original sin, fall into endless death.[81]

Similar conditions prevailed in rural Anglo-Saxon England and led to the same consequence: speedy baptism without reference to the canon law's preference for Easter or Pentecost.

The consequences of delaying confirmation were quite different. Bishops, councils, penitentials, and rulers exhorted parents to seek confirmation for their children, but the theology represented in the Pseudo-Eusebian Homily 29 undermined such exhortations when it explicitly declared that baptism sufficed to save those who died young, and only those who had to struggle in the world as adults needed the strengthening given by

81. Hrabanus Maurus, *Epistola ad Hathubrandum*, in *Appendix ad Hrabanum epistolarum Fuldensium fragmenta ex octava nona et decima centuriis ecclesiasticae historiae, MGH Epistolae* 5 (Berlin, 1899), p. 522.

confirmation.[82] Because confirmation was not regarded as necessary for salvation in the way that baptism was, there was no serious danger to the child's afterlife if it should die unconfirmed. Theodore's *Penitential* had noted that even if children are not confirmed, "we do not despair," which he could not say about an unbaptized child.[83]

Some families probably did keep a child unconfirmed for use in creating an alliance of spiritual kinship. But there is another possible explanation for what might appear to be a delayed confirmation, namely, that a person who had already been confirmed was confirmed a second time because he or his family thought the benefits outweighed the sin. The *Confessionale Pseudo-Egberti* distinguished between unintentional and intentional repetition of confirmation when it imposed a fast of three winters on anyone who was reconfirmed out of ignorance but punished with a fast of six winters a conscious decision to be reconfirmed.[84]

The *Anglo-Saxon Chronicle* for 853 recorded a famous delayed confirmation. "King Æthelwulf [of Wessex] sent his son Alfred to Rome. The lord Leo [IV] was then pope of Rome, and he consecrated him king and stood sponsor to him at confirmation."[85] The *Chronicle*'s assertion that Pope Leo consecrated Alfred as king in 853 is probably not true. Æthelwulf could not have known that his youngest son would have a great future. The boy, who was only about four or five years old, had three older brothers and was unlikely ever to be king. From her analysis of the accounts of this incident, Janet Nelson concluded that Alfred, forty years after the events, interpreted his experience, whatever it actually was, as a royal anointing in order to gain contemporary political prestige: "If the motive behind the myth of the 853 anointing would have been Alfred's desire for a powerful spiritual and, moreover, papal sanction for his authority, the inspiration was provided by the memory of the infant Alfred's visit to Rome."[86] The *Chronicle* reported that King Æthelwulf himself visited Rome two years later, in 855, when Benedict III was pope; and Asser added that Alfred accompanied him.[87] Nelson dismissed the 853 visit as the product of a desire of the chronicler to have a Pope "Leo" consecrate

82. Homily 29, in Van Buchem, *L'homélie pseudoeusébienne,* p. 41, lines 26–27.

83. Discipulus Umbrensium, *Canones Theodori,* 2.4.5, p. 317: "Nullum perfectum credimus in baptismo sine confirmatione episcopi non desperamus tamen."

84. *Confessionale Pseudo-Egberti,* p. 194.

85. *ASC(A),* s.a. 853, p. 45: "þy ilcan geare sende Eþelwulf cyning Elfred his sunu to Rome. Þa wæs domne Leo papa on Rome ⁊ he hine to cyninge gehalgode ⁊ hine him to biscepsuna nam." *The Anglo-Saxon Chronicle,* trans. and ed. Dorothy Whitelock with David C. Douglas and Susie I. Tucker (New Brunswick, N.J., 1962), p. 43.

86. Janet Nelson, "The Problem of King Alfred's Royal Anointing," *Journal of Ecclesiastical History* 18 (1967), p. 161.

87. *ASC(A),* s.a. 855, p. 45; Asser, *De rebus gestis,* c. 10, p. 9.

young Alfred, just as Leo III had crowned Charlemagne in 800.[88] She suggested that Alfred came to Rome just once, in 855, when King Æthelwulf visited Pope Benedict III. In his revisionist work, Alfred P. Smyth concluded that the 853 entry in the *Chronicle* was simply untrue, a fabrication made or allowed by Alfred to enhance his prestige.[89]

In spite of the recent consensus that Alfred's "royal" consecration at Rome did not take place, the possibility of his *confirmation* at Rome is another matter. If, as Smyth believed, Alfred never went to Rome, then the confirmation could not have taken place. But if, as Nelson argued, he went in 855 with his father but subsequently misinterpreted or misrepresented what happened as the pope's "royal anointing," then he might actually have been confirmed. Whether or not Alfred was confirmed at Rome, the entry of 853 is still significant for this book because the *Chronicle* and the sources derived from it throw light on the delay at confirmation for religious and political purposes.

If Alfred was in fact confirmed at Rome, he had almost certainly been baptized as an infant, both because of the dire consequences of dying in original sin and because infant baptism was customary in the ninth century. It was probably not accidental that he was kept unconfirmed until age four or six, depending on the year of the trip to Rome. The few lines in the *Chronicle* must not hide the fact that a trip to Rome was a major undertaking and required considerable planning. If King Æthelwulf had wished it, his son could have been confirmed by an Anglo-Saxon bishop, but he might have kept his son unconfirmed to fulfill a plan of creating a direct bond with the pope, just as Charlemagne had done in 781 when Pope Hadrian sponsored his son Carloman, whose name was changed to Pepin at the baptism.[90] As a consequence of the papal confirmation, Alfred was Pope Leo's godson in confirmation (*biscep sunu*). About forty years after the confirmation, Bishop Asser, who was working from some version of the *Chronicle,* wrote in Latin that the pope took Alfred as a son of adoption (*in filium adoptionis*) when he confirmed him.[91] About 140 years after the events in Rome, the chronicler Æthelweard called Alfred the pope's son from the chrism (*filium a chrismate*).[92]

88. Nelson, "Problem," p. 162.

89. Smyth, *King Alfred,* pp. 12–17: "In the absence of other supporting evidence we can never be sure that Alfred ever went to Rome or met a pope there," p. 17.

90. J. M. Wallace-Hadrill, "The Franks and the English in the Ninth Century: Some Common Historical Interests," in *Early Medieval History* (New York, 1976), stressed the flood of Frankish influences during the reign of Alfred.

91. Asser, *De rebus gestis,* p. 7.

92. Æthelweard, *Chronicon,* 3.4, p. 32.

Of course King Æthelwulf also became Pope Leo's *compater,* just as Charlemagne had been Pope Hadrian's.[93] In fact the chief contemporary purpose of Alfred's confirmation was probably the creation of the bond between King Æthelwulf and the pope. Little Alfred might simply have been the unconfirmed child—a tool—to create the alliance. The royal-papal coparenthood was not mentioned in any source, however. That silence might be explained by the interval between the sponsorship and its recording in the *Chronicle.* When the A-Version of the *Chronicle* was composed in about 892, King Æthelwulf was dead more than thirty years and his coparenthood to the pope may no longer have seemed significant. It was Alfred's supposed royal anointing and spiritual sonship to a pope which received stress, probably for its contemporary political value.

There were Carolingian precedents for delaying confirmation—and even baptism—for the sake of creating a useful spiritual relationship. When Charlemagne and Pope Hadrian created their spiritual kinship, young Carloman/Pepin had been kept unbaptized until about age seven. In the subsequent correspondence between Hadrian and Charlemagne, Carolman/Pepin is rarely mentioned. The relationship of the adults was stressed: Pope Hadrian and Charlemagne always addressed one another in their letters as *compater spiritalis.*[94] There are Continental examples from the later tenth and early eleventh centuries of powerful families keeping children unconfirmed so as to have a child at the ready to use in the creation of an alliance. In 996, the emperor Otto III sponsored at confirmation the young son of Peter II Orseolo, doge of Venice, and changed the boy's name to Otto. In 1004, the emperor Henry II sponsored at confirmation another son of Doge Peter and renamed him Henry.[95] Thus the spiritual kinship created by sponsorship at confirmation supplemented and expanded that created at baptism.

Sponsorship at confirmation held a significance between that at the catechumenate and that at baptism. It was more important than sponsorship at the catechumenate because confirmation was eventually recognized as a sacrament in its own right. But it was never so important as that at baptism, a sacrament regarded as necessay for salvation. Sponsorship at baptism was always the model on which other forms of sponsorship were

93. Angenendt, "Das geistliche Bündnis der Päpste," pp. 70–90.

94. *Annales mosellani,* s.a. 781, ed. J. M. Lappenberg, *MGH Scriptores* 16 (Hanover, 1859), p. 497; *Annales regni Francorum,* s.a. 781, 40. See the twenty-eight letters in the *Codex Carolinus,* pp. 594–632, in which Hadrian addressed Charlemagne as *spiritalis compater.*

95. John the Deacon, *Chronicon venetum et gradense,* in *Cronache veneziane antichissime,* ed. Giovanni Monticolo, Fonti per la storia d'Italia 9 (Rome, 1890), pp. 151–52 and 167.

based. In Anglo-Saxon England, sponsorship at confirmation provided the opportunity to create more spiritual parents and spiritual children and new bonds of patronage and support. But even three official occasions for sponsorship were sometimes not enough. In the next chapter I shall examine other strategies for acquiring spiritual kin.

CHAPTER 7

The Proliferation of Sponsors

Since the seventh century, the liturgy sanctioned three occasions for sponsorship. One of them, the *catechumenium/cristnung,* had a flowering during the Viking period but withered in late Anglo-Saxon history as the rites for making a catechumen became mere preliminaries to the baptismal ritual. *Baptismus/fulluht* and *confirmatio/bisceopung* remained important occasions for sponsorship among the Anglo-Saxons, as they did everywhere in the western church.

In some areas of western Christendom, two or three occasions for sponsorship were not enough. Because spiritual kinsmen were socially useful as patrons for the young and allies for their parents, there was a tendency to seek more of them, a process that has continued into modern times, especially in Latin America. Hugo Nutini and Betty Bell described a luxuriant proliferation of spiritual kinship in Tlaxcala, Mexico, during the 1960s, where there were thirty-one ways to create *compadrazgo,* the Spanish word for coparenthood, some of them sacramental, some of them religious, and some secular.[1] Historically, there have been two techniques for gaining more spiritual kinsmen. Either the number of sponsors at a ceremony was increased, or new sponsoring ceremonies were created. Each was pursued in the western church.

The Multiplication of Sponsors

Ancient and early medieval canon law said nothing about the number of sponsors. Custom seems to have governed the matter, and to judge from

1. Nutini and Bell, *Ritual Kinship,* 1:50–194.

recorded cases, it prescribed only one sponsor, of the same sex as the person being sponsored. Texts claiming the authority of Theodore of Canterbury were the first to raise the issue of the number of sponsors. The *Penitential* of the "Northumbrian Disciple" and the *Iudicium de penitentia Theodori episcopi* are the earliest known that specified that there be one sponsor for each ceremony.[2] The point was not, however, to forbid multiple sponsors at each ceremony but to encourage the presence of a separate sponsor at each one. In other words, the Theodoran texts were not opposing a tendency to multiply sponsors but, rather, a tendency to reduce the number of sponsors by having the same sponsor for all three ceremonies.

It was in the Frankish kingdom in the later ninth century, under the pressure to gain more spiritual kin, that the custom of having only one sponsor at baptism began to break down. A council at Metz in 893 found it necessary to decree that "in no way should two or more receive a child from the font of baptism, but only one, since in a path of this sort a place is given to the devil and the reverence of so great a ministry is cheapened. For [just as there are] one God [and] one baptism, there ought to be one father or mother of the infant who receives from the font."[3] In the long run, efforts to preserve the custom of one sponsor at baptism were not successful in the face of an insistent demand for more spiritual kin. In the high and late Middle Ages, the number of baptismal sponsors grew.[4] Between the twelfth century and the Council of Trent, numerous councils and episcopal statutes tried to hold the line at three sponsors, two of the same sex as the child and one of the opposite sex.[5] For the rich and powerful, even that number was breached: the presence of a dozen or more sponsors is occasionally recorded in high medieval texts.[6]

Things were different in Anglo-Saxon England, where there is no evidence for the multiplication of sponsors at any ceremony. The Anglo-Saxons were content with the traditional pattern of one same-sex sponsor

2. Discipulus Umbrensium, *Canones Theodori,* 4.2.8, p. 317; *Iudicium de penitentia Theodori episcopi,* 7.69, p. 275.

3. Council of Metz (893), c. 6, Mansi 18, col. 79 D–E: "et infantem nequaquam duo vel plures, sed unus a fonte baptismatis suscipiat, quia in hujuscemodi secta diabolo datur locus, et tanti ministerii reverentia vilescit. Nam unus Deus, unum baptisma, unus, qui a fonte suscipit, debet esse pater vel mater infantis."

4. On the proliferation of sponsors, which began in the ninth century, see Lynch, *Godparents,* pp. 208–10.

5. For legislation on numbers of sponsors in the high and late Middle Ages, see Franz Gillmann, "Das Ehehindernis der gegenseitigen geistlichen Verwandschaft der Paten?" *AKKR* 86 (1906), 697–98, n. 4.

6. Berthold von Regensburg, *Sermon III,* in *Vollständige Ausgabe seiner Predigten,* ed. Franz Pfeiffer (Vienna, 1862), 1:31: the thirteenth-century friar complained that some people had twelve, nine, seven, or five sponsors.

at each ceremony. The Norman conquest opened England to the Continental custom of having three sponsors, two of the same sex as the child and one of the opposite sex, which became the norm in England, as it was elsewhere, for the remainder of the Middle Ages.[7]

The Multiplication of Ceremonies

The second way to gain more spiritual kin was to create new occasions for sponsorship. In the seventh century, that strategy had produced sponsorship at the catechumenate and confirmation, both of which were observed early and with special interest in Anglo-Saxon England. But in some places the tendency to multiply sponsoring occasions pushed further. An apocryphal letter of Pope Deusdedit to Bishop Gordianus, which survives in at least two tenth-century manuscripts and was included in Burchard of Worms's *Decretum* (composed 1008x1012), encouraged the extension of spiritual kinship and, by implication, sponsorship to seven ceremonies within the process of initiation. "You know that just as there are seven gifts of the Holy Spirit, so there are seven gifts of baptism, from the first taste of holy salt and the entrance to the church to the confirmation of the Holy Spirit through chrism. From the first gift of the Holy Spirit to the seventh, no Christian ought to take his comother in marriage."[8] Deusdedit's letter assumed that at each of the seven ceremonies, someone sponsored the child and became coparent to its parents, with the usual consequences that there should be no sexual contact. Gratian included Deusdedit's letter in *Decretum,* C. 30, q. 1, c. 1, but canonists and theologians did not accept the seven ceremonies surrounding initiation as occasions to create spiritual kin, although they did recognize the usual three. Nevertheless, the letter of Deusdedit expressed a tendency to expand sponsoring occasions, which some clergy and laypeople embraced at the fringes of official theology. As we shall see, in parts of Norway, five or six sponsoring occasions were carved out of the rituals for creating new Christians.

At least one new occasion for creating spiritual kinship appeared on the Continent in the ninth or tenth century, the *compaternitas sancti Johannis* ("cofatherhood of Saint John"), which survived into modern times in Italy,

7. Legatine Council at York (1195), c. 5, in *Councils and Synods* 1/2, pp. 1048–49: "Statuimus ne in baptismate plures quam tres suscipiant puerum de sacro fonte, masculum duo mares et una mulier, feminam unus mas et due femine."

8. Burchard of Worms, *Decretum,* 17.44, *PL* 140, col. 928. On the letter of Deusdedit, see Hartmut Hoffman and Rudolf Pokorny, *Das Dekret des Bischofs Burchard von Worms. Textstufen, Frühe Verbreitung, Vorlagen, MGH Hilfsmittel* 12 (Munich, 1991), p. 158, n. 129.

Sicily, and Sardinia. The coparenthood was named for John the Baptist, who baptized Jesus in the Jordan and was the quintessential model of one who baptized. The details varied significantly across time and space, but in essence the ceremony was a way for people to become coparents to one another, in spite of the fact that they had no unbaptized or unconfirmed child available. The ceremony generally took place on 23 June, the Vigil of the Feast of John the Baptist. Although the *compaternitas sancti Johannis* is mentioned often in texts from the tenth century to modern times, I have searched without success for a medieval description of what specific rituals created it. With some hesitation, I offer a synodal canon from Sardinia in 1566, which gives a hint of how people might have become *compatres* without a child:

> Many are accustomed [to do this] in our diocese, which we have heard is done in other dioceses of Sardinia, at night on the vigil of the blessed John the Baptist. Two at a time they hold a reed drawn over a bonfire with bread stuffed into it. When they have kissed the reed and one another, they embrace one another and greet one another as cofathers and they call one another "cofathers of the flowers." They observe this superstition so obstinately that they persuade themselves that when they have created a bond or coparenthood from this most filthy rite, they are prevented from contracting a marriage.[9]

I do not know how medieval Frenchmen or Italians made themselves into cofathers of Saint John, but they did do it. And to judge from rich early modern evidence, they could have done it in many different ways.[10]

At least one Anglo-Saxon became aware of the coparenthood of Saint John when he translated the "Letter from Heaven," an ancient and tenacious apocryphal text that purports to have been written by Christ and sent from heaven. In it Christ warned his people to observe a strict Sunday rest and other ecclesiastical requirements, such as tithing.[11] From the sixth century until modern times, the letter has often been rewritten to adapt it to

9. Synod of Alès and Terralba (1566), cited in Clito Corrain and Pierluigi Zampini, *Documenti etnografici e folkloristici nei sinodi diocesani italiani* (Bologna, 1970), pp. 299–300; see also Lynch, *Godparents,* pp. 216–18.

10. On the *compérage de saint Jean* since the fifteenth century, see Fine, *Parrains, marraines,* pp. 139–54.

11. On the "Letter from Heaven," which is sometimes called the *carta dominica* or the "Sunday Letter," see Michel Van Esbroeck, "La lettre sur le dimanche, descendu du ciel," *Analecta Bollandiana* 107 (1989); and Robert Priebsch, *The Letter from Heaven on the Observance of Sunday* (Oxford, 1936). There is a good bibliography in B. Schnell, "Himmelsbrief," *Verfasserlexicon,* zweite Auflegung 4 (1982).

new circumstances and to expand its commands and prohibitions. As coparenthood grew in importance, the failure to respect its demand for friendship and love seemed a great sin. Some revisers of the "Letter from Heaven" tried to increase respect for coparenthood by adding an exhortation from Christ.[12]

Latin versions of the "Letter" were translated or adapted in Old English at least seven times.[13] One Old English version was destroyed in the Cotton fire of 1731, and we do not know if it said anything about spiritual kinship.[14] Three versions published by Napier (Homilies 43, 44, and 57) do not refer to godparents.[15] The version edited by Napier from CCCC 162 is also silent on godparents.[16] But in two other versions, Christ commanded respect for coparents, and in one of them he specifically commanded respect for what the translator called the *godsibbrædenne,* coparenthood, of Saint John.

The Homily in CCCC 140

Robert Priebsch edited the homily from CCCC 140 in which Christ demanded respect for *godsybbas.*[17] When Priebsch edited it in 1899, he believed that a fourteenth-century manuscript (Vienna, Nationalbibliothek, lat. 1355, fols. 89–90v), contained a close copy of the Latin text on which it was based.[18] In 1936, Priebsch changed his view and agreed with Hippolyte

12. The following are some of Latin versions of the "Letter from Heaven" which mention respect for *compatres:* (a) Mattsee, Austria, MS 49, fols. 182r–84r: "vos facitis compatres et non tractis eos ut decet"; (b) Toulouse, MS 208, fols. 101–4, ed. Ernest-M. Rivière, "La lettre du Christ tombée du ciel," *Revue des Questions Historiques* 79 (1906), 603: "Vos autem non estis fratres, sed inimici, et vos facitis compatres, et tamen eos non tenetis, sicuti decet;" (c) Vienna, Nationalbibliothek 1355, discussed later.

13. Clare A. Lees, "The 'Sunday Letter' and the 'Sunday Lists,' " *ASE* 14 (1985), 129–36, untangled the complex web of Latin texts and Old English translations. See also Karl Jost, *Wulfstanstudien* (Bern, 1950), pp. 221–36, who concluded that Wulfstan composed none of the extant versions. The seven translations/adaptations are: (a) Pseudo-Wulfstan Homilies 43–45 and 57, in Napier, *Wulfstan,* pp. 205–15, 215–26, 226–32, and 291–99; (b) Napier also edited an anonymous homily from CCCC 162, pp. 44–52, in "Contributions to Old English Literature 1: An Old English Homily on the Observance of Sunday," in *An English Miscellany Presented to Dr. Furnivall in Honour of His Seventy-Fifth Birthday* (Oxford, 1901), pp. 357–62; (c) Robert Priebsch edited a version from CCCC 140, fols. 71–72v, in "The Chief Sources of Some Anglo-Saxon Homilies," *Otia Merseiana* 1 (1899), 135–38; (d) on p. 129, Priebsch mentioned a now-destroyed version in Cotton Otho B 10.

14. Ker, *Catalogue of Manuscripts* art. 178, p. 229, based on a description of the manuscript by Humphrey Wanley before the fire of 1731.

15. See above, n. 13a.

16. Napier, "Contributions."

17. Priebsch, "Chief Sources," p. 137.

18. On the manuscript, see Lees, " 'Sunday Letter,' " pp. 131–32.

Delahaye, who argued that Paris, BN MS lat. 12270, fols. 31v–32v, a twelfth-century manuscript from Corbie, contained a close copy of the source for the homily in CCCC 140.[19] In BN MS lat. 12270, Christians were warned: "Know that on account of your tithes which you have defrauded and on account of inappropriate tasks which you have done on Sundays and on account of the faith which you do not observe among friends and neighbors and coparents (*conpatres*) and all the faithful of Christ—on account of those things I shall delete your names from the book of life, if you do not emend through penance and do not receive confession."[20] The Old English homily in CCCC 140 translated this passage with only slight changes, and *conpatres* was rendered as *godsybbas.*[21]

Napier Homily 45

One Old English homiletic version of the "Letter from Heaven" specifically mentioned the coparenthood of Saint John. In Napier Homily 45, Christ warned about misdeeds that would bring on His wrath.[22] Priebsch identified the Latin source for this version as something close to the text in a fourteenth-century manuscript, Vienna, Nationalbibliothek, lat. 1355, fols. 89–90v, which threatened to send heavy stones upon Christians "if you have not emended and if you do not do penance and if you do not observe the holy Lord's day and the coparenthood of Saint John (*compatratam de sancto Johanne*) and if you do not pay tithes."[23] The translator of Napier Homily 45 rendered the words *compatratam de sancto Johanne,* as *þa godsibbrædenne, þe ge habbað for gode and for Sce Iohannes dæle begetene* ("the coparenthood which you have undertaken for the sake of God and of saint

19. Priebsch, *Letter from Heaven,* p. 10. The version of the letter in BN 12270 was edited by Hippolyte Delahaye, "Note sur la légende de la lettre du Christ tombée du ciel," *Bulletins de l'Académie Royale de Belgique,* Classe des Lettres (1899), and reprinted in his *Mélanges d'hagiographie grecque et latine* (Brussels, 1966). The text in BN 12270 is edited in the reprint on pp. 156–59.
20. Delahaye, "Note" (1966), p. 158: "Et scitote quia propter decimas vestras quas fraudastis et propter labores importunos quos fecistis in dominicis diebus et propter fidem quam non observastis inter amicos et vicinos et conpatres et omnes fideles Christi, propterea delebo nomina vestra de libro vite, si per penitentiam non emendaveritis et confessionem receperitis."
21. Priebsch, "Chief Sources," p. 137: "Witað, la yrmingas, þæt for eowre teoðunge þe ge me ætbrudon and for eower untimlican geswince þe ge dydon on sunnan dagum and on þam halgum freolsdagum, and for eower untrywleaste þe ge ne heoldon ongean eowre frynd þæt synd eower neheboras and godsybbas and ealle geleaffulle: ic adylgie eower naman of þære liflican bec gif ge purh dædbote nellað gebetan."
22. Napier, *Wulfstan,* pp. 226–32. The homily, titled *Sermo angelorum nomina,* survives in CCCC 419–421, pp. 73–95.
23. Priebsch, "Chief Sources," p. 131: "si non emendaveritis et si poenitentiam non egeritis et sanctum diem dominicum et compatratam de sancto Johanne non observaveritis et decimas non reddideritis."

John").[24] Priebsch was not sure what the *compatratam de sancto Johanne* was, perhaps because *compatrata* is an unusual though not unknown substitute for *compaternitas.* The Old English translator probably knew what it was, however, although his rendering of the words is closer to paraphrase than to exact translation. His words did enable Priebsch to guess that the *compatrata de sancto Johanne* had something to do with sponsorial obligation and the sacrament of baptism.[25] This use of the word *godsibbrædenne* to translate *compatrata* is important because it gives us the Old English word for coparenthood. This is the only attested use of the word in Old English, but it might have been more widely used because the word *godsibrede* became the standard term for coparenthood in Middle English.[26]

Can we conclude that the Anglo-Saxons sought to increase their spiritual kin by adopting the coparenthood of Saint John? A single translated sermon does not prove that Anglo-Saxons practiced it, though it might be significant that whereas the Latin version of the letter in Vienna, Nationalbibliothek 1355, mentioned the *compatratam de sancto Johanne* five times, the Old English homilist edited out all but one reference to the *compatrata/godsibrædenne* of Saint John, perhaps because repetition about an institution his society did not know seemed superfluous. Aside from Napier Homily 45, there is no evidence that the coparenthood of Saint John functioned in Anglo-Saxon society. Although the coparenthood of Saint John needs a thorough historical study, I doubt that it existed as an institution in Anglo-Saxon England.

The *Crismlysing*

If the coparenthood of Saint John did not exist in Anglo-Saxon England, then it would seem that from Theodore's *Penitential* to the Norman Conquest, Anglo-Saxons were content with three occasions for sponsorship—two of them lively (baptism and confirmation) and one (the catechumenate) increasingly vestigial except where Vikings were concerned. But Anglo-Saxon sources refer to another occasion for sponsorship, called the *crismlysing,* which meant the "loosing of the chrism(cloth)."

Like other forms of sponsorship, the *crismlysing* was rooted in the liturgy of initiation. From antiquity, the newly baptized spent a week dressed in white garments, called the week *in albis,* to symbolize their purification in

24. Napier, *Wulfstan,* p. 226–32, the quoted text on p. 228.
25. Priebsch, "Chief Sources," p. 131, n. 7.
26. "Godsibrede," in *Middle English Dictionary,* p. 217.

baptism. During that week, the neophytes and their parents (and in some places their sponsors) were expected to attend mass daily. Seven days after baptism, on the *Dominica in albis* or Low Sunday, the white clothes were ceremonially removed. The Anglo-Saxons observed the week *in albis* from early times, although it is possible that the full set of white robes worn by neophytes in antiquity was reduced to a white veil or head covering. Four Theodoran texts referred to a baptismal veil (*velamen*) in order to make a point about entry to monastic life. A monk's profession of vows was often regarded as a second baptism, which, like the first, washed away sins.[27] Theodore's *Penitential* recommended that newly professed monks cover their heads with their cowls for seven days, after which the abbot ritually uncovered them. It cited as an analogy the practice of dressing the newly baptized in a *velamen,* which was removed by a priest on the seventh day after the baptism.[28]

In an age of high mortality and deathbed conversions, the person who died in baptismal clothes was a familiar figure. Bede recorded that King Cædwalla, who was baptized at Rome in 689, was buried ten days after baptism still wearing his white robes (*in adhuc albis positus*).[29] In an early ninth-century text, the monk Merhtheof had an otherworldly vision in which he was guided by his own children, who had died soon after baptism and who had appeared to him in their baptismal robes (*albis indutos*).[30]

The Old English vocabulary to describe the wearing of the white baptismal robes was varied. As every baptizee was anointed on the head at least once after baptism, some translations stressed the presence of the chrism, which accompanied the garment. Whereas Bede had written that Cædwalla died "still placed in the white [robes]," the ninth-century translator of Bede's history wrote that Cædwalla died "wearing the chrism robe" (*under crisman*).[31] A gloss to Aldhelm's prose version of *De laude virginitatis* explained that *in albis* ("in white robes") meant *under crismum,* "under chrism."[32] The *Anglo-Saxon Chronicle* (E-Version), s.a. 688, noted that

27. Philipp Oppenheim, "Mönchsweihen und Taufritus," in *Miscellanea liturgica in honorem L. Cuniberti Mohlberg* (Rome, 1948–9), pp. 259–82.

28. Discipulus Umbrensium, *Canones Theodori,* 2.3.3, p. 315: "In monachi vero ordinatione abbas debet missam agere et III orationes super caput eius complere et VII dies velet caput suum coculla sua et septima die abbas tollat velamen sicut in baptismo presbiter solet velamen infantum auffere; ita et abbas debet monacho quia secundum baptismum est iuxta iudicium patrum in quo omnia peccata dimittuntur sicut in baptismo." The text is repeated in three other Theodoran texts: (a) *Iudicia Theodori Greci,* c. 2, p. 239; (b) *Canones sancti Gregorii,* c. 3, p. 253; and (c) *Iudicium de penitentia,* c. 3, p. 271.

29. Bede, *HE,* 5.7, p. 470.

30. Æthelwulf, *De abbatibus,* c. 11, ed. Alistair Campbell (Oxford, 1967), pp. 27–32.

31. Bede, *Old English Version,* 5.7, EETS OS 96 (London, 1891), p. 404.

32. A. S. Napier, *Old English Glosses* (Oxford, 1900), p. 57.

Cædwalla died *under Cristes claðum* ("in Christ's clothes").[33] In his translation of the *Passion of Saints Alexander, Eventius, and Theodolus,* Ælfric recounted the conversion of some prisoners. The Latin version said that the neophytes "were dressed in new and white clothes because the Christian religion demands this" (*et vestibus candidis novisque vestiti, quia hoc exigit religio Christiana*). Ælfric quoted Quirinius as saying, "and I dressed them all with all-white garments" (*ic hi ealle gescrydde mid eall-hwitum reaf*).[34] In a sermon on baptism Wulfstan referred to the *hwite hrægel* ("white garment") in which a baptized person was clothed, which he interpreted as a sign of the splendor the baptized has received through God's grace. In the same sermon he referred to the *crismale* placed on the head of the newly baptized, which he interpreted as symbolizing the crown that he would have in heaven if he held his Christianity properly and persisted in correct belief.[35] The baptismal service in the Red Book of Darley (CCCC 422), which has rubrics in Old English, ordered that the priest make the sign of the cross with oil on a cloth (*crisman*), which apparently had never been used for another child, and then place it upon the newly baptized child's head.[36]

When confirmation was given with or apart from baptism, its recipients also wore a special vestment for a time. Out of reverence for the chrism the bishop placed on each confirmand's forehead, a white band of cloth was tied around the spot to protect it. When a young man parodied confirmation in the eleventh century, he put mud on children's foreheads and some of the onlookers shouted, "Bind his forehead; he has been confirmed" (*frontem isti ligate; consignatus est*).[37] The *Ordo Romanus XI* called the binding cloth a *crismale.*[38] Other Latin terms included *pannus crismalis* ("the chrism cloth"), *pannus chrismatis* ("the cloth of the chrism"), and *vestis chrismalis* ("the chrism garment").[39] The *Pontifical of Egbert* and the *Sidney*

33. *ASC(E),* s.a. 688, p. 65.

34. Ælfric, Sermon *for V Non. Maii Sanctorum Alexandri, Eventii, et Theodoli,* in *Homilies of Ælfric,* 2:744, line 172.

35. Wulfstan of York, *Homily* 8c, pp. 179–80: "And þæt hwite hrægel ðe man mid þæne mann befehð þonne he gefullod bið, þæt getacnað þæne gastlican wlite þe se man ðurh Godes gife habban sceal; . . . And mid þam crismale þe man him onufan þæt heafod deð man tacnað þæne cristenan cynehelm þe he on heofonum ah gyt he þanonforð his cristendom mid rihte gehealdeð and on rihtan geleafan rihtlice þurhwunað." See also *Homily* 8a, p. 171: "Vestimenta candida et inreprehensibilia sunt spirituales uirtutes animae. Perunguitur et caput sacro crismate et mistico tegitur velamine, ut intellegat se diadema regni et sacerdotii dignitatem portare," and also *Homily* 8b, p. 173, lines 47–55, on the white garment (*hwyte hrægel*), anointing with chrism (*mid ðam crism smyrelse*), and the *crism claðe.*

36. Page, "Old English Liturgical Rubrics," p. 155: "Nime man her [þis]ne crisman ðe næfre ær[. .]e æt nanum cylde and do nu rodetacn mid ele þæron and sette uppon þæs cildes heafod."

37. William of Malmesbury, *Vita Wulfstani,* c. 14, p. 37.

38. *Ordo Romanus XI,* c. 100, in *Les ordines,* 2:446.

39. Dudo of St. Quentin, *De moribus et actis primorum Normanniae ducum,* 2.31, ed. Jules Lair (Caen, 1865), p. 171: on the eighth day after his baptism, Rollo "vestibus chrismalibus et bap-

Sussex Pontifical included a prayer (*modo ligandi sunt*) for the ceremony of binding the foreheads of the newly confirmed.[40] Some time after confirmation, perhaps three days, the chrism cloth was removed and the spot of chrism on the forehead was washed. There must have been some doubt about what to do with the chrism cloth. Two texts associated with Theodore said that it could be reused, but in thirteenth- and fourteenth-century England it was either reworked into liturgical cloths or burned.[41] If confirmation was given immediately after baptism, the neophyte might wear both garments for a week, as Dudo of St. Quentin reported that Rollo did;[42] but if either sacrament was given without the other, then only the appropriate white cloth would be worn.

In eleventh- and twelfth-century Norway, a sponsor assisted at the ceremony for removing the white baptismal robes.[43] For Anglo-Saxon England, a formal ceremony to remove the white baptismal garments is not attested, although they were certainly removed, possibly a week after the baptism. The removal of the chrism cloth from the forehead is attested, however. Because this occurred some days after confirmation, the bishop had probably gone elsewhere. A sponsor finished the ritual by removing the chrism band and washing away the holy substance. Perhaps this was the person who had sponsored at confirmation, but it could have been someone else in order to multiply spiritual kin.

Three interdependent texts describe the only recorded episode of Anglo-Saxon *crismlysing*. After a military defeat in 878, the Danish King Guthrum agreed to become a Christian. He was baptized and probably confirmed at Athelney. The *Chronicle* reported that King Alfred sponsored him at baptism and that the two spent twelve days together. The *Chronicle* continued:

---

tismalibus exutus"; Robert Grosseteste, *Epistola* 52, ed. Henry Luard, Rolls Series 25 (London, 1861), p. 156: "Panni etiam chrismales in usus seculares non convertantur."

40. *Pontifical of Egbert,* pp. 14–15. In spite of an attribution to Archbishop Egbert of York (732–766), this pontifical is not an eighth-century text, but rather a mid-tenth-century book. The confirmation *ordo* in the Sidney Sussex Pontifical has the same rubric and prayer for binding the foreheads of the newly confirmed, ibid., p. 168. In neither pontifical is there liturgical provision for the unbinding, probably because the bishop was not present when that rite took place.

41. Discipulus Umbrensium, *Canones Theodori,* 2.4.7, p. 317: "pannus crismatis iterum super alium baptizatum imponi non est absurdum"; and *Iudicium de penitentia,* c. 70, p. 275: "De crisme panno modico iterum licet mittere super alterum baptizatum." On high medieval uses for chrism cloths, see Grosseteste, *Epistola* 52, p. 156: "Panni etiam chrismales in usus seculares non convertantur"; see also Council of Ripon (1289), c. 30, in *Memorials of the Church of S.S. Peter and Wilfrid, Ripon,* Surtees Society 74 (Durham, 1882), p. 73: make them into *manutergia* or surplices; and Archbishop Walter Reynolds, Synod of Oxford (1322), cited in Frederick Charles MacDonald, *A History of Confirmation* (London, 1938), p. 131: burn the chrism fillets.

42. Dudo of St. Quentin, *De moribus,* 2.31 (Caen); p. 171: on the eighth day after his baptism, Rollo "vestibus chrismalibus et baptismalibus exutus."

43. *Gulathing, Older Law of the,* c. 26, 1:16, and trans. Larson, *Earliest Norwegian Laws,* p. 55; and *Frostathing, Older Law of the,* 3.8, 1:150, and trans. ibid., pp. 248–49.

"and the unbinding of the chrism (*crismlysing*) took place at Wedmore."[44] There is no fuller explanation, probably because the reader or hearer was presumed to understand what the *crismlysing* was. Every confirmed person had gone through it. When Bishop Asser drew on the *Chronicle* to describe the same event, he wrote that "the loosing of his chrism (*cuius chrismatis solutio*) was on the eighth day in the royal villa which is called Wedmore."[45] That is, Guthrum wore the white confirmation band, and probably white baptismal robes for a week, and it or they were ceremonially removed at Wedmore. When the chronicler Æthelweard retold this episode in Latin about a century and a half later, he added a significant detail: "After that [baptismal] bath, Ealdorman Æthelnoth washed him [presumably he washed off the chrism from Guthrum's forehead] in the place Wedmore."[46] Æthelweard's use of the name of the sponsor, Æthelnoth, argues that he had a source lost to us, perhaps the lost version of the *Chronicle* he was using.[47] I interpret this passage to mean that the chronicler Æthelweard thought that Æthelnoth, the ealdorman of Somerset, was Guthrum's sponsor in the ceremonial unbinding of the cloth and washing off of the chrism, just as Alfred had been his sponsor at baptism. Æthelnoth perhaps had also been the sponsor at confirmation and was completing his liturgical duties by removing the chrism cloth and washing the anointed forehead of Guthrum. The political advantage of two sponsorships with different sponsors is evident. Two important Anglo-Saxon leaders, King Alfred and Ealdorman Æthelnoth, created spiritual kinship with a defeated but still dangerous Viking foe, Guthrum. Alfred sought such a double bond in 893 when he and Æthelred, the ealdorman of Mercia, each sponsored a son of the Viking Hæsten.[48]

No other Anglo-Saxon text mentions the *crismlysing*, but eleventh- and twelfth-century Norwegian sources may throw light on what occurred at Wedmore in 878. Norwegian evidence is relevant because the English missionaries active in the conversion of Norway during the eleventh century brought Anglo-Saxon ecclesiastical practices with them.[49] The Old Norse

44. *ASC(A)*, s.a. 878, p. 51: "his crismlising was æt Weþmor."

45. Asser, *De rebus gestis Ælfredi*, p. 47: "Cuius chrismatis solutio octavo die in villa regia, quae dicitur Wædmor, fuit."

46. Æthelweard, *Chronicon*, 4.3, p. 43: "rex eorum scilicet suscipit baptismatis fontem, quem superstes de lauacro sumit rex Ælfred in Alnea insula paludensi. Dux pariter Æthelnoth abluit post lavacrum eundem in loco Vuedmor, illicque ei præbuit rex Ælfred honores magnifice."

47. On Æthelweard's version of the *ASC*, see ibid., Campbell, pp. xxi–xxxvi.

48. *ASC(A)*, s.a. 893, p. 57.

49. Abrams, "Anglo-Saxons," pp. 213–24, presented a cautious assessment of the activity of Anglo-Saxon missionaries in late-tenth- and eleventh-century Norway; see also Peter Sawyer, "Process of Scandinavian Christianization."

vocabulary of spiritual kinship, for example, reveals Anglo-Saxon influence:[50]

Modern English	Old English	Old Norse
godfather	godfæder	guðfaðir
godmother	godmodor	guðmoðir
godson	godsunu	guðsonur
goddaughter	goddohtor	guðdottir
spiritual kinship	godsibbræden	guðsifjar

Two Norwegian law codes mention sponsorship at a ceremony equivalent to the *crismlysing*. In the *Older Law of the Frostathing*, parts of which go back to the eleventh century, there is a chapter that treats the effects of sponsorship on marriage. The law began by affirming that spiritual kinship created a marital impediment: "No man shall take to wife a woman to whom he stands in spiritual kinship. And we shall honor this kinship with respect to the father or the mother as to the child itself." For the scope of the marital impediment to be stated clearly, the law enumerated the sources of spiritual kinship. The text contained an interesting list of five occasions for sponsorship which, at least in its tendency to proliferation, harks back to the spirit of the apocryphal letter of Pope Deusdedit. I have divided the text into clauses for ease of analysis:

1. Sponsorship at the catechumenate: "The one who holds the child when it receives the sign of the cross is the first in spiritual kinship."
2. Sponsorship at baptism: "The one who brings the child to baptism is the second."
3. Sponsorship at the removal of the white baptismal garment: "The one who removes the white robe is the third."
4. Sponsorship at confirmation: "The one who leads [the child] to the bishop at confirmation is the fourth."

A fifth form of sponsorship seems to be that which Æthelnoth performed at Wedmore for Guthrum:

5. Sponsorship at the removal of the chrism cloth: "*The one who loosens the chrism-band about the forehead (loyser dregil af enni) is the fifth.* All these [sponsors] are of equal rank in spiritual kinship."[51]

50. Maurer, *Über altnordische Kirchenverfassung und Eherecht,* in *Vorlesungen,* 2:434–69, remains a reliable treatment of sponsorship and spiritual kinship in Norway and Iceland; see pp. 434–35 on the introduction of Old English vocabulary into Old Norse.

51. *Frostathing, Older Law of the,* 3.8, 1:150 and trans. Larson, *Earliest Norwegian Laws,* pp. 248–49.

A second Norwegian law code, *The Older Law of the Gulathing*, probably a twelfth-century compilation, contained the same five provisions, although it added a sixth form of sponsorship, which created a bond only between the woman who had given birth and the women who accompanied her at her ritual purification, the so-called churching.

> There are six persons of spiritual kinship from whom we shall abstain as we do from our kinswomen.
>
> 1) Now the first [is the one who] holds the child when it receives the sign of the cross (*hallda barne undir primsignan*);
> 2) the second [the one who] receives [the child when the priest lifts it] out of the water (*taka ór vatne*);
> 3) the third [the one who] removes the white robe (*fora ór hvíta váðom*);
> 4) the fourth [the one who] leads the child to the bishop (*hallda undir biscops hond*) [at confirmation];
> 5) the fifth [the one who] loosens the chrism band (*leysa fermidregil*);
> 6) the sixth [the one who] leads the mother into the church (*leiða kono í kirkiu*). In the last case the kinship concerns . . . the woman [only] but in the other five cases the spiritual kinship must be respected both as regards the father, the mother, and the child.[52]

Both law codes specified that separate sponsors removed the white baptismal robe (*hvita vaðom*) and the chrism band (*fermidregil* or *dregil*). Because other Norwegian laws did not contain these provisions and they were not mentioned in official canon law, Konrad Maurer concluded that these sponsoring rituals were local practices in the regions where the laws of the Frostathing and the Gulathing prevailed.[53] But the episode of Guthrum's *crismlysing* indicates that the removal of the chrism band by a sponsor was also known in ninth-century Anglo-Saxon England, from which it spread to Scandinavia with Anglo-Saxon missionaries.

The Anglo-Saxons were generally conservative in their handling of sponsorship. They did not multiply the number of sponsors at any ceremony. The lone reference to the *godsibbrædenne* of Saint John does not justify the conclusion that it existed in Anglo-Saxon England. But they had been pioneers in the creation of sponsorship at the catechumenate and at confirmation. They also probably created a fourth occasion for sponsorship at the *crismlysing*, which they appear to have disseminated to at least parts of Norway.

52. *Gulathing, Older Law of the*, c. 26, 1:16 and trans. ibid., p. 55. The translation is modified.
53. Maurer, *Vorlesungen*, 2:448.

CHAPTER 8

Coparenthood in Anglo-Saxon England

The words godfather/godmother and godson/goddaughter are meaningful in English because the godparent-godchild bond still exists among Christian groups practicing infant baptism. But in many societies sponsorship also created that other kind of relationship, coparenthood, a horizontal bond between the child's parents on the one hand and the sponsor on the other. In English-speaking communities, when parents ask relatives or friends to sponsor their child, rarely do they think that they have created a new and significant bond of coparenthood among the adults. Even scholars occasionally lump all spiritual kin into the category of godparents. The distinction between coparent and godparent was clear and important, however, to medieval people, including Anglo-Saxons.

Like godparenthood, coparenthood was rooted in the view that at baptism the recipient experienced a second, spiritual birth. When parents were forbidden to sponsor their own child, they were obliged to invite someone for the honor, to whom they granted a share in their parenthood. This sharing in the child often initiated an ongoing relationship among the adults or strengthened preexisting bonds. To express this notion of sharing in the birth(s), early medieval peoples coined new words, attested first in Latin and subsequently in the vernaculars. By the sixth century, Christians in Italy and Frankish Gaul called the relationship between the natural parents and the spiritual parent *compaternitas* or *conpatratio* ("cofatherhood") and, more rarely, *commaternitas* or *conmatratio* ("comotherhood").[1] There

1. Diocesan synod of Autun (between 561 and 605), c. 25, in *Concilia Galliae, A. 511–A. 695*, p. 268: monks forbidden to have *comatres; Canones Agustudinenses* (between 663 and 675), c. 5, in

were other rarely used Latin words for coparenthood, such as *compatrata, comparatum,* and *compateratum.*[2] All such words were built on the Latin elements *cum* ("with") and *pater* or *mater* ("father or mother"). Because coparenthood was a reciprocal relationship of more or less equal adults, it became customary for coparents to address one another with words coined for the new institution, *compatres* ("cofathers") for men and *commatres* ("comothers") for women. The status was socially sanctioned, and sources frequently identified people as coparents to one another.

The institution of coparenthood has survived, sometimes vestigially, in European Catholicism. Consequently, many European languages still have terms for coparents and coparenthood, which are quite distinct from those for godparenthood. In French, *compère/commère/compérage* stand in contrast to *parrain/marraine/parrainage;* in Italian, *compare/comare* stand in contrast to *padrino/madrina;* in German, *Gevatter/Gevatterin/Gevatterschaft* stand in contrast to *Pate/Patin/Patenschaft.* The situation is different in English, which no longer has living words for coparents or for coparenthood. Until the eighteenth century, however, English coparents called one another and were called "gossip" (*godsibbe* = kin in God), and the relationship among coparents was called *gossipred.*[3]

The Nature of Coparenthood

Early medieval Germanic societies had a range of practices by which outsiders became kinsmen or by which distant kinsmen were drawn closer together. Some practices, loosely classified as adoptions, created bonds modeled on those of a parent to a child, including fosterage, the giving of

---

ibid., p. 319: monks forbidden to have *compatres;* Bertram of Le Mans, *Testamentum* (27 March 616), p. 133: Bertram left a bequest to his *dulcissime compater,* named Ghiso. An early use of *commatratio* is in texts connected with Benedict of Aniane's reform council for monks at Aachen in 816; see *Actuum praeliminarium Synodi primi Aquisgranensis commentationes sive Statuta Murbacensia,* ed. Josef Semmler, in *Corpus consuetudinum monasticarum, Initia consuetudinis Benedictinae,* ed. Kassius Hallinger (Siegburg, 1963), p. 488: "De conpatratione et conmatratione omnino caveatur."

2. For *compatrata,* see Priebsch, "Chief Sources," p. 131, line 36, p. 321, line 55, and p. 133, lines 88 and 92. For *comparatum* and *compateratum,* see Bertram of Le Mans, *Testamentum* (27 March 616) p. 133; and Germain Morin, "Textes inédits relatifs au Symbole et à la vie chrétienne," *RB* 22 (1905), p. 517, who edited a sermon from a twelfth-century manuscript: "Comparato sancto Iohanni bene debetis colere, quia fidem et caritatem sanctam accepistis inter uos; et qui ipsam fidem et caritatem corruperit, malum peccatum facit." The *Instituta Cnuti,* 7.1, in *Gesetze der Angelsachsen,* ed. Felix Liebermann (Halle, 1903; rpr. Aalen, 1960), 1:291, translated *his gefæderan* as *compatra sua.*

3. *Middle English Dictionary,* s.v. "god-sib(be)" and "godsibrede"; *Oxford English Dictionary,* 2d ed. J. A. Simpson and E. S. C. Weiner, vol. 6 (Oxford, 1989), s.v. "gossip" and "gossipred."

weapons to a young man, the first cutting of an adolescent's beard, and of course baptismal sponsorship. Others practices created bonds modeled on sibling relationships, which included blood brotherhood, oath brotherhood (*Schwurfreundschaft*), and coparenthood.[4] The ninth-century author of the *Life of Saint Bertin* described coparenthood as "a praiseworthy ritual among Christians which is dedicated to joining together bonds of brotherly love."[5] It is no fluke that coparental love is described not as "paternal" but as "brotherly." Just as godparenthood was an idealized version of the parent-child bond, coparenthood was an idealized version of the bond that united siblings.

Coparenthood could produce quicker social consequences than godparenthood. Before godparenthood could become socially effective, it required an interval of years to allow the infant to become old enough to participate. The participants in coparenthood were adults who could immediately observe mutual respect and exchange mutual assistance. Parents must often have chosen a particular person to sponsor their child in order to become that person's coparent, as when the fictional saint Rumwold was ready to be baptized, "his parents said to one another: 'Let us send for the neighboring kings and rulers, so that they can receive our dearest son from the holy water of baptism.' " In this case, little Rumwold refused high-born sponsors in order to imitate Jesus' humility—in reality such a refusal must have been very rare.[6] An Old English text, perhaps by Ælfric, lamented the materialistic side of this search for rich and powerful sponsors:

> We ask and command you men in God's name that you act more wisely and more carefully about your heathen children than you have acted before this, so that so many souls not be lost to God as happens now among you. Now we ask you in God's name that you have your children baptized as soon as they are born, because you do not have his [the child's] life for a certainty even as far as the next day and that does great harm to your child if through your negligence you take from him the joy of the heavenly kingdom and he be sent to the abyss of hell forever with all the devils. You might do penance with God for this negligence, but it never happens that the child will come into the kingdom of heaven. Now some man will say that he will gain for

4. Althoff, *Verwandte,* pp. 82–84; Pappenheim, "Über künstliche Verwandtschaft"; Wolfgang Fritze, "Die fränkische Schwurfreundschaft der Merowingerzeit: Ihr Wesen und ihre politische Funktion," ZSSRG, Germanistische Abteilung 71 (1954). Ludwig Buisson,. "Formen normannischer Staatsbildung, bis 11. Jahrhundert," in *Studien zum mittelalterlichen Lehenswesen,* Vorträge und Forschungen 5 (Lindau and Konstanz, 1960), surveyed forms of kinship.

5. *Vita Bertini,* c. 19, p. 765: "et compater fuit secundum laudabilem ritum, inter christianos ad coniungenda fraternae caritatis foedera."

6. *Vita sancti Rumwoldi,* c. 4, pp. 98–101.

himself a good friend with his child and waits for this sometimes too long. For the holy gospel says to us that God's wrath remains against the heathen. It is better for the heathen child that it take a beggar [as a sponsor] than that it not have eternal joy and have eternal punishments.[7]

In addition to its immediate social usefulness, coparenthood differed significantly from godparenthood in another respect: it did not receive ecclesiastical encouragement nor a function in pastoral practice. Since at least the sixth century, bishops and theologians actively promoted godparenthood, which was woven into the traditional liturgies to accommodate infants and was useful for their subsequent religious instruction and moral nurture. Numerous pastoral texts exhorted godparents to teach their godchildren the Creed and the Lord's Prayer, and sometimes also the elements of good moral behavior.[8] In contrast, no early medieval liturgical text legitimated coparenthood by referring to it. No early medieval sermon or conciliar canon made a positive theological comment about coparenthood or gave it a pastoral role comparable to that of teaching godchildren. After the seventh century, coparenthood was occasionally mentioned in sermons and canons, but only as an impediment to marriage or as a secular distraction for monks and nuns. When the Lombard laws and Frankish capitularies mentioned coparenthood in the eighth and ninth centuries, they also treated it only as an impediment to marriage.[9]

A very different picture, however, emerges from narrative sources such as chronicles, saints' lives, and letters, which make clear that coparenthood had a role in Frankish society quite independent of the church's approval and much greater than that of impeding marriages. What do the Frankish sources say that coparenthood did? It could make an outsider a friend (*amicus*).[10] It could create alliances between adults. When King Carloman had a son in 770, Pope Stephen III took the initiative to ask to sponsor the boy at either baptism or confirmation so that "the grace of the holy spirit, that is, the state of coparenthood, might come about between us."[11]

This contrast between grudging ecclesiastical recognition and obvious social importance may be explained by the fact that coparenthood was not

7. *De infantibus,* A. S. Napier, "Ein altenglisches Leben des heiligen Chad," *Anglia* 10 (1888), 154. Napier edited the *De infantibus* from MS Junius 24, p. 379. On the attribution of *De infantibus* to Ælfric, see John C. Pope in *Homilies of Ælfric,* 1:55–56.

8. Lynch, *Godparents,* pp. 305–32. On the godparents' duty to teach their godchildren, see below, Chapter 10.

9. Lynch, *Godparents,* pp. 234–57.

10. Donatus of Metz, *Vita Trudonis confessoris Hasbaniensis,* c. 19, ed. Wilhelm Levison, *MGH SRM* 6 (Hanover, 1913), p. 290.

11. Pope Stephen III to King Carloman, in *Codex Carolinus,* 47, p. 565: "ut spiritus sancti gratia, scilicet compaternitatis affectio, inter nos eveniat."

a creation of the church. It was rooted in a "popular" interpretation of sponsorship, which pushed theological ideas further than the bishops were willing to go. Parents and sponsors were taught that they shared in making the infant a full human being, the natural parents giving it physical life and the sponsors giving it spiritual life. It is not surprising that after baptism the participants saw one another in a positive light, regarded one another as kinsmen, literally "coparents" to the child, and acted benevolently toward one another, as kinsmen ought to act. Bishops and lawgivers did not encourage that view, but eventually they accepted the situation and regarded coparents as kinsmen, and they drew the narrow conclusion that like any kinship, coparenthood created an impediment to marriage. They could not control the functioning of coparenthood in society, and they did not try. They accepted the social fact (many bishops were themselves coparents), but they did not give it a place in the pastoral mission of the church, and they did not give it an explicit theology.

Coparenthood and Confirmation

Not every form of sponsorship produced the same sort of coparenthood. Sponsorship at baptism was primary. After the mid-eighth century, Frankish sources treated sponsorship at confirmation as creating coparenthood. I know of no early medieval source that says that sponsorship at the catechumenate created coparenthood, although some high medieval canonists believed it did.[12] Under Byzantine influence, Pope Gregory II's Roman Council of 721 declared that coparenthood from baptism was a marital impediment, a new view in the west, which was echoed in Frankish texts composed in the subsequent generation.[13] Byzantine law could not directly influence western views of the consequences of sponsorship at confirmation because the Byzantine liturgy never recognized a sacrament of confirmation separate from baptism. But if coparents from baptism could not marry one another, then by an argument from analogy the Franks were confronted with the possibility that coparents from confirmation could not marry either. For the first time of which I am aware, King Pepin's Capitulary of Compiègne (757) applied to coparents from confirmation the marital prohibition that bound coparents from baptism: they could not marry one another or, if married, had to separate: "If anyone has held a stepdaughter or stepson before the bishop for confirmation, let him be separated from his wife and may he not take another wife. Likewise a woman

12. Freisen, *Geschichte des kanonischen Eherechts,* pp. 534–36.
13. Roman Council (721), c. 4, Mansi 12, col. 263. See Lynch, *Godparents,* pp. 242–57.

[who has sponsored her stepchild at confirmation] may not take another husband."[14] The capitulary was aimed at a person who sponsored at confirmation his or her spouse's child from a previous marriage (i.e., a stepchild) and thus became the spouse's coparent. Persons who became kin through God's grace, whether in baptism or in confirmation, could not subsequently be linked by sexual activity: grace and sex were incompatible. The wider implication of the capitulary is clear: sponsorship at confirmation created coparenthood with the power to prevent marriage.

Just as godparenthood from confirmation was less important than godparenthood from baptism, so coparenthood from confirmation had less social significance than that from baptism. Chronicles, letters, saints' lives, and other sources that reflect actual practice often mentioned coparenthood from baptism but rarely referred to coparenthood from confirmation. There is one significant exception to the relative silence: legal texts frequently treated coparenthood from confirmation because it created a marital impediment. In what follows, unless otherwise stated, coparenthood from both forms of sponsorship is being treated as the same.

Opposition to Spiritual Kinship

One way to gauge an institution's social importance is to study its critics. In the sixth century, some monastic legislators and bishops in southern Gaul and Italy forbade monks and nuns to be sponsors. Some singled out the burdens of godparenthood as the reason for the ban, but others stressed that coparenthood in particular was incompatible with the monastic life because it created ties to secular adults and had worldly consequences.[15] Bishop Caesarius of Arles was the first to forbid nuns and monks to sponsor infants. In his *Rule for Nuns,* he explained that "she who has rejected her freedom to have children ought not to wish for nor to possess the freedom belonging to others, so that she may without hindrance concentrate unceasingly on God."[16] He also forbade monks to sponsor, but without

14. *Capitulary of Compiègne,* c. 15, in *Capitularia regum Francorum,* 1:38: "Si quis filiastrum aut filiastram ante episcopum ad confirmationem tenuerit, separetur ab uxore sua et alteram non accipiat. Similiter et femina alterum non accipiat."

15. Joseph H. Lynch, "Baptismal Sponsorship and Monks and Nuns, 500–1000," *American Benedictine Review* 31 (1980).

16. Caesarius of Arles, *Statuta sanctarum virginum,* c. 11, in *Sancti Caesarii Arelatensis episcopi Regula sanctarum virginum aliaque opuscula ad sanctimoniales directa,* ed. Germain Morin, Florilegium patristicum 34 (Berlin, 1933), p. 7. There is an English translation by Mary Caritas McCarthy, *The Rule for Nuns of St. Caesarius of Arles: A Translation with a Critical Introduction* (Washington, D.C., 1960). Caesarius also forbade monks to sponsor: Caesarius, *Regula monachorum,* c. 10, (1942), 2:150.

expressing a rationale.[17] He evidently reasoned or knew from experience that when a nun (or a monk) sponsored, she "had" a child, with whom close relations could distract her from her religious calling. Godparenthood was therefore inappropriate for a nun or a monk. Caesarius forbade nuns to be godmothers and monks to be godfathers, but did not mention coparents. That silence is consistent with the content of his extensive body of sermons, in which godparental obligations loomed large and coparenthood was absent. It is possible that coparenthood did not yet exist in early sixth-century Arles or that Caesarius did not acknowledge it because it was not a church practice.

Other monastic rules and conciliar canons, inspired directly or indirectly by Caesarius, also banned sponsorship by monks and nuns.[18] Some of them forbade religious to create either coparenthood or godparenthood. But from the later sixth century, the prohibitions singled out coparenthood as the reason why a religious should not sponsor a child. A monastic rule probably composed by Ferreolus, bishop of Uzès (died 581), pointed to the monks' coparental bond with the child's parents as the reason not to sponsor: ". . . nor is it proper for a monk in any place to take from the holy bath the sons of anyone whatsoever: lest, as is accustomed to happen, he be linked to the parents of that child bit by bit with an improper or shameful friendship (*illicita . . . vel turpi familiaritate*)."[19] Ferreolus described coparenthood as leading to an *illicita* or even *turpis familiaritas* for a monk, presumably because it could draw him into concern for worldly matters and secular friendships. Two Gallican councils of the seventh century also forbade monks to sponsor and, in each case, forbade them to become coparents.[20] The main Gallican canonical collection of the seventh and eighth centuries, the *Collectio vetus gallica,* incorporated a canon of the Council of Autun (c. 670), which forbade monks to have *conpatres.*[21]

Pope Gregory I, who had been a monk, also disapproved of monks having coparents. In August of 594 he criticized an otherwise unknown abbot,

17. Caesarius, *Regula monachorum,* c. 10, (1942), 2:150: "filium de baptismum nullus excipiat."
18. Aurelian, *Regula ad monachos,* c. 10, *PL* 68, col. 390, and *Regula ad virgines,* c. 16, *PL* 68, col. 402; *Regula Tarnantensis,* c. 3, in Fernando Villegas, "La 'Regula Monasterii Tarnantensis': Texte, sources, et tradition," *RB* 84 (1974), 19–20; Donatus of Besançon, *Regula ad virgines,* c. 54, *PL* 87, col. 290.
19. Ferreolus of Uzès, *Regula,* c. 15, *PL* 66, col. 965: "neque monachi ullo loco de lavacro sancto filios cuiuslibet excipere: ne parentibus illius, ut fieri solet, illicita paulatim vel turpe familiaritate jungatur. Quod si quis praesumpserit, ut transgressor regulae corrigatur."
20. Synod of Auxerre (561–605), c. 25, in *Concilia Galliae, A. 511–A. 695,* p. 268: "Non licet abbati filios de baptismo habere nec monachus commatres habere"; Canons of Bishop Leudgarius of Autun (663–680), c. 5, in ibid., p. 319: "Ut conpatres nullus eorum audeat habere."
21. *Collectio vetus gallica,* 46.10, in *Kirchenrecht und Reform im Frankenreich: Die Collectio Vetus Gallica, die älteste systematische Kanonessammlung des fränkischen Gallien,* ed. Hubert Mordeck (Berlin and New York, 1975), p. 532.

Valentinus, because he allowed his monks to make comothers (*commatres*) for themselves.

> It has been reported to us that women come up into your monastery indiscriminately and, what is even worse, your monks make women their comothers and as a consequence have dangerous familiarity with them. Therefore, lest on account of this the enemy of the human race deceive them [the monks] with his craftiness—may it not happen!—we warn you through this precept that henceforth you not permit women to come up into your monastery for any reason and that your monks not make comothers for themselves. For if this comes to our attention again in any way, know that you must undergo a very severe punishment so that by the nature of your correction others may undoubtedly be corrected.[22]

It is important to be clear that disapproval of sponsorship applied only to ascetics who had abandoned the world and for whom godparenthood and especially coparenthood might demand a return to secular affairs and friendships. Not all ascetics agreed; for some did sponsor children. Indeed, Arnold Angenendt argued that in Frankish Gaul an ascetic, "a man of God" (*vir dei*), was especially favored both as a baptizer and as a sponsor because his holiness added something to the rituals.[23] Outside the strict ascetic circles of southern Gaul and Italy, early medieval laypeople, secular clergy, monks, and nuns often became godparents and at the same time coparents.

In spite of such ascetic disapproval, coparenthood became a preferred form of "created" kinship in Frankish, Italian, and Byzantine societies.[24] For two generations, coparenthood was a basic factor in papal-Carolingian relations: Charlemagne's father Pepin was cofather to two popes. We do not know the sponsoring occasion that created Pepin's coparenthood with Pope Stephen II (752–757), but that with Paul I (757–767) was created in 758 when the pope sponsored by proxy Pepin's daughter Gisela.[25] Pope Stephen III (768–772) actively sought coparenthood when he asked Charlemagne's brother Carloman to allow him to sponsor his newborn son Pepin, but the plan came to nothing when Carloman died in 771.[26] Mod-

22. Gregory I to Abbot Valentinus, 4.40, in Gregory I, *Epistolae,* 1:261: "Pervenit ad nos, eo quod in monasterio tuo passim mulieres ascendant, et quod adhuc gravius, monachos tuos mulieres sibi commatres facere, et ex hoc incautam cum eis communionem habere. Ne ergo hac occasione humani generis inimicus sua eos quod absit calliditate decipiat, ideoque huius te praecepti serie commonemus, ut neque mulieres in monasterio tuo deinceps qualibet occasione permittas ascendere, neque monachos tuos sibi commatres facere."

23. Angenendt, "Bonifatius," pp. 163–69.

24. Lynch, *Godparents,* pp. 192–201; on Byzantine *synteknoi* (coparents), see Macrides, "Byzantine Godfather," pp. 149–56.

25. Angendendt, "Das geistliche Bündis," pp. 40–63.

26. Ibid., p. 64. The request was made in *Codex Carolinus,* 47, pp. 565–66.

ern historians have studied most closely the coparental relationship created in 781 when Pope Hadrian I sponsored a son of Charlemagne. After the sponsorship, pope and king always addressed one another in letters as *compater spiritalis.*[27] It would be wrong to think that these relationships, because well-documented, were unusual. Popes and Carolingian kings were doing what multitudes in their own societies did, sponsoring children at least in part to create a coparental bond of trust and mutual help among adults.[28]

Coparenthood among the Anglo-Saxons

The texts cited thus far on coparenthood were composed either in Gaul or the papal territories between the sixth and ninth centuries. That is no accident. If Anglo-Saxon Christians of the seventh and eighth centuries practiced coparenthood, that could not be proved from the sources. In that early period, godparenthood was the dominant, perhaps the only, element in the Anglo-Saxon version of the godparent complex. In view of the importance of coparenthood in contemporary Continental Christianity, it is surprising that no source originating in Anglo-Saxon England before the last decade of the ninth century referred to it. Between the late ninth and eleventh centuries, Anglo-Saxon sources did refer to coparenthood, perhaps because the institution then took root among the Anglo-Saxons, much later than on the Continent; or perhaps the sources are richer.

Latin Terms

The Latin terms for cofather and comother appear in at least two texts from Anglo-Saxon England. The first text is a charter of Bishop Oswald of Worcester, dated 966, which identified Eadric, the recipient of a grant of land, as the bishop's *compater.*[29] Oswald had no children, so he must have sponsored Eadric's child. The second text is a canonical collection. Robin Aronstam, who edited the *Excerptiones Pseudo-Egberti,* argued that Hucarius of St. Germans in Cornwall probably compiled it in about 1005 and that it was subsequently used by Ælfric in his letters to Archbishop Wulfs-

27. Angenendt, "Das geistliche Bündnis," pp. 70–90. After May/June 781, Charlemagne and Hadrian addressed one another as *compatres.* Charlemagne's letters to Hadrian are published in the *Codex Carolinus,* pp. 594–632 passim. In a letter of early 791, Hadrian addressed Charlemagne as "Domino excellentissimo filio nostroque spiritali compatri Carolo" in *MGH Epistolae* 5 (Berlin, 1899), p. 6.

28. On Frankish *compaternitas,* see Lynch, *Godparents,* pp. 192–201.

29. Charter of Bishop Oswald to Eadric, in *Cartularium Saxonicum,* 1182 (S 1310) (1893), 3:445.

tan. She concluded that the *Excerptiones* was the chief eleventh-century handbook of canon law for Anglo-Saxon bishops.[30] Recently James Cross and Andrew Hamer reexamined the issue of authorship and concluded that someone in the circle of Archbishop Wulfstan, perhaps Ælfric or Wulfstan himself, created the short recension of the *Excerptiones.* In any case, the *Excerptiones* is an early eleventh-century collection of canonical material with links to Ælfric and Wulfstan.[31] Two canons in the *Excerptiones* mentioned sexual activity with a comother (*comater spiritalis*). In the first, marriage with a comother was included in a list of forbidden unions: "If any man takes as wife a nun or a spiritual comother or the wife of a brother or a niece or a stepmother or a cousin or a woman from his own kin group or whom his kinsman had known [sexually], let him be anathema."[32]

But "marriage" with a *comater* was not the only sexual bond that attracted the canonist's disapproval. The *Excerptiones* also forbade fornication with a comother. "If a layman stains himself with a servant of God, or with a spiritual comother, or with a relative or by chance with a woman with whom he had sexual intercourse before, first let him be anathematized, afterward let him do penance for seven years, three in bread and water. Likewise let the woman do penance, since the Christian religion condemns fornication in either sex for the same reason."[33]

Old English Terms

Cumpæder and *Cummædre*

Old English also had words for coparents, which are attested in later Anglo-Saxon documents. Sometimes the Latin words are evident behind the Old English, as when *compater* became *cumpæder* and *commater* became *cummædre.* The earliest Anglo-Saxon reference to coparenthood is in the *Chronicle,* s.a. 893, which identified the ealdorman Æthelred of Mercia as the *cumpæder* or *cumpæðer* of the Viking Hæstan, whose son he had sponsored.[34] An eleventh-century bidding prayer from York instructed the

30. Robin Aronstam, "Recovering Hucarius: A Historiographical Study in Early English Canon Law," *Bulletin of Medieval Canon Law* 5 (1975); and "The Latin Canonical Tradition in Late Anglo-Saxon England: The *Excerptiones Egberti*" (Ph.D diss., Columbia University, 1974), pp. 7–45.

31. James E. Cross and Andrew Hamer, "Ælfric's *Letters* and the *Excerptiones Ecgberhti,*" in *Alfred the Wise: Studies in Honour of Janet Bately on the Occasion of Her Sixty-fifth Birthday,* ed. Jane Roberts and Janet L. Nelson with Malcolm Godden (Cambridge, 1997). The authors promise an edition of the unprinted short recension.

32. *Excerptiones Egberti,* c. 115, in Aronstam, "Latin Canonical Tradition," pp. 99–100: "Si quis monacham vel commatrem spiritalem vel fratris uxorem, vel neptem, vel novercam, vel consobrinam, vel de propria cognatione, vel quam cognatus habuit, duxerit uxorem, anathema sit."

33. Ibid., c. 118, p. 102: "Laicus maculans se cum ancilla Dei, vel cum spiritali commatre."

34. *ASC(A),* s.a. 893, p. 57: "þone ilcan ende þe Æþred his cumpæder healdan sceolde." *ASC(C),* s.a. 894, p. 38, also used *cumpæder;* and *ASC(D),* s.a. 894, p. 32, used *cumpæðer.*

faithful to pray for a series of people, including their *godsybbas* and their *cumæðran.* The *Dictionary of Old English* translated *cumæðran* in this text as "godmother," although it probably should be "comothers" in parallel with *godsybbas,* which, as I shall show, meant "cofathers."[35] Translators also grappled with the Latin words *compater/commater.* Pope Gregory II's council of 721 had decreed: "If anyone has taken a spiritual comother in marriage, let him be anathema. And all [the bishops] responded three times, 'let him be anathema.' "[36] The influential canons of 721 were often copied and even translated into Old English.[37] The translation in Bodleian MS Laud 482, fols. 20–21, rendered the words *commatrem spiritalem* as *gastlican cumædran.*[38] In Brussels MS 8558–63, fol. 146, the reading is *gastlican cumendran,* which might be a scribal error, although the *Dictionary of Old English* appears to accept the form *cumendran.*[39]

Gefædera and *Gefædere*

On other occasions, Old English translators rendered *compater* and *commater* as *gefædera* and *gefædere,* clearly related to Old High German *givatara* and modern German *gevatter* and *gevatterin.*[40] For example, in a will composed between 968 and 971, the ealdorman Ælfheah granted an estate to Ælfthryth, King Edgar's wife, whom he called his *gefæðeran.* According to Napier and Stevenson, the word puzzled John Kemble, who translated it "cousin"; they wrote that "it usually means 'godmother.' This cannot well be the meaning here." The problem is solved when one recognizes that it is a word for comother. The relationship of coparent was reciprocal, so either Ælfheah had sponsored one of Ælfthryth's children or she had sponsored

35. Bidding Prayer, in W. H. Stevenson, "Yorkshire Surveys and Other Documents of the Eleventh Century in the York Gospels," *EHR* 27 (1912), p. 11: "Wutan we gebiddan for ure godsybbas and for ure cumæðran, and for ure gildan and gildsweostra." For a definition of *cumæðran* as "godmothers," see the *Dictionary of Old English,* ed. Angus Cameron, Antonette Di Paolo Healey et al. s.v. "cum-mædre."

36. Roman Council (721), c. 4, Mansi 12, col. 263: "Si quis commatrem spiritalem duxerit in conjugium, anathema sit. Et responderunt omnes tertio: Anathema sit."

37. Gregory II, *Old English Version of the Council of 721,* ed. Joseph Raith from Bodleian MS Laud 482, fols. 20–21, and Brussels 8558–63, fol. 146, in *Die altenglische Version des Halitgar'schen Bussbuches (Sog Poenitentiale Pseudo-Ecgberti*), BAP 13 (Hamburg, 1933), p. 72.

38. Ibid.: "gif hwa his gastlican cumædran hæbbe him on (ge)sinscipe, si he amansumad; ⁊ him andwyrdon ealle þa bisceopas þriwa ⁊ cwædon: 'si [he] amansumod.' "

39. On the possible scribal error in Brussels 8558–63, see Otto B. Schlutter, "Weitere Beiträge zur altenglischen Wortforschung," *Anglia* 37 (1913), 52–53, who, however, confused the role of godmother with that of comother. The *Dictionary of Old English* s.v. "cum-mædre," cited the variant reading without comment.

40. Reiner Hildebrandt, "Germania Romana im deutschen Wortatlas, 2, Die Bezeichnungen der Patenschaft," in *Deutscher Wortschatz: Lexikologische Studien Ludwig Erich Schmitt zum 80 Geburtstag von seinen Marburger Schülern* ed. H. H. Munske, P. von Polenz, O. Reichmann, and R. Hildebrandt (Berlin, 1988), pp. 672–74, on the word *(Ge)vatter.*

one of his.[41] The word *gefædera* was also used in a vernacular reference to a well-known incident in Pope Gregory I's life. Gregory of Tours wrote that Pope Gregory had sponsored a son of the Byzantine emperor Maurice.[42] That information became part of the lore about Gregory, often repeated. When Ælfric reported the sponsorship in Old English, he noted that Pope Gregory I had been the *gefædera* of Maurice, a word that laid stress on coparenthood, an emphasis not in Gregory of Tours's brief reference, which had reported Pope Gregory's reception of the child from the font, namely, the simple sponsorship.[43]

At least four other eleventh-century texts also used the term *gefædere*, "comother," in listings of forbidden marriages. I included them here for the light they throw on the language of coparenthood; I will discuss them again in Chapter 9 as evidence for the sexual taboos surrounding spiritual kinship. The first text is the *Poenitentiale Pseudo-Egberti,* one of the three surviving Old English penitential handbooks, which declared: "If any man marries his close relative or his comother (*gefæderan*) or his stepmother, let him be anathema from all Christian men."[44] Joseph Raith, the editor of the *Poenitentiale,* could not find in Halitgar's *Penitential* an exact Latin source for this text. It is possible the translator had a version of Halitgar which is not extant or has not been identified. But, as Allen Frantzen noted, the Old English translator adapted Halitgars's text in many places and might have done so here to suit English circumstances.[45]

The three other eleventh-century texts that used *gefædere* for comother are clearly interrelated, probably because Archbishop Wulfstan of York had a role in the composition of each. Between 1008 and his death in 1023, Archbishop Wulfstan was instrumental in drafting the laws of King Æthelred, which in turn influenced the first law code of King Cnut.[46] The three texts forbade any man to marry a nun, his comother, or a divorced

41. The Will of the Ealdorman Ælfheah (S 1485), in Dorothy Whitelock, *Anglo-Saxon Wills* (Cambridge, 1930), pp. 22–23; for a discussion of the meaning of *gefaeðeran,* see A. S. Napier and William H. Stevenson, *The Crawford Collection of Early Charters and Documents Now in the Bodleian Library,* Anecdota Oxoniensia, Medieval and Modern, Series, 7 (Oxford, 1895), p. 84.

42. Gregory, *HF,* 10.1, p. 478: "Unde factum est, ut epistulam ad imperatorem Mauricium dirigeret, cuius filium ex lavacro sancto susciperet."

43. Ælfric, *Sermon on St. Gregory,* in *Ælfric's Catholic Homiliest,* p. 75, line 98.

44. *Poenitentiale Pseudo-Egberti,* pp. 25–26: "Gif hwylce man wifige on his nehstan magan oþþe on his gefæderan oþþe on his steopmoder, beo he amansumad fram eallum cristenum mannum."

45. On the *Poenitentiale,* see Allen J. Frantzen, *La littérature de la pénitence,* rev. ed., trans. Michel Lejeune (Fribourg, 1991), pp. 125–30. On the great variation in versions of Halitgar's *Penitential,* see Raymund Kottje, *Die Bussbücher Halitgars von Cambrai und des Hrabanus Maurus* (Berlin, 1980), pp. 13–111.

46. Whitelock's articles in which she demonstrated Wulfstan's influence on the composition of early-eleventh-century law codes are conveniently gathered in her *History, Law, and Literature in 10th–11th Century England* (London, 1980).

woman. The first is in the law code issued by Æthelred (VI Æthelred "ad Eanham," 16 May 1008x13 May 1011), which declared that "no Christian man may marry any consecrated nun, his comother, or any woman who has been abandoned [by her husband]."[47] In King Cnut's first set of laws (25 December 1027x1034), the same three categories of women were put off limits, although in a different order of presentation: "Nor is any Christian man ever to marry his comother, or a consecrated nun or a woman abandoned by her husband."[48]

The third text, Napier Homily 50, composed in Wulfstan's literary style, repeated the prohibitions in the order in which they appeared in I Cnut 7.1: "And we teach and pray . . . that no Christian man marry in his own kin within the sixth degree of relationship, or with the widow of his kinsman who was so closely related, nor with his wife's near relative whom he himself had [intercourse with] before nor with his comother, nor with a hallowed nun; nor should any Christian man ever marry a woman abandoned by her husband."[49] Karl Jost argued that a later compiler used Wulfstan's materials to put Napier Homily 50 together. Dorothy Bethurum argued that Wulfstan composed the document, which she did not classify as a sermon.[50] In either case, Napier Homily 50 used Wulfstan's words and ideas, including his ban on marriage with one's *gefædere,* comother. Thus, in the eleventh century, Wulfstan was accustomed to call a comother a *gefædere,* and we may assume that a male coparent was a *gefædera.*

The activity of post-Conquest translators supports the point that *gefædere* meant "comother." Cnut's laws were rendered into Latin three times: in the *Quadripartitus,* translated about 1110x1120, the *Instituta Cnuti,* made about 1110 in Mercia, and the *Consiliatio Cnuti,* made about 1110 in southeast England. Felix Liebermann published Cnut's Old English text and the three Latin texts in parallel columns.[51] The words *his gefæderan* in I Cnut 7.1 were rendered in three ways. The translator of the *Instituta Cnuti*

47. Æthelred, *Laws "ad Eanham,"* 6.12.1, in *Die Gesetze der Angelsachsen,* ed. Felix Liebermann (Halle, 1903) 1:250: "Ne on gehalgodre ænige nunnan, ne on his gefæderan, ne on ælætan ænig Cristen man ne gewifige æfre"; also edited in *Councils and Synods,* 1/1, p. 350, n. e. On Wulfstan's role in their composition, see *Councils and Synods,* 1/1, pp. 340–41.

48. I Cnut 7.1 (25 Dec. 1020x1022), in *Councils and Synods,* 1/1, p. 474: "Ne on his gefæderan, ne on gehalgodre nunnan, ne on ælætan ænig cristen mann æfre gewifige."

49. Homily 50, in Napier, *Wulfstan,* p. 271: "And we læreþ and biddað . . . þæt ænig cristen man bynnan syx manna sibfæce æfre ne wifige on his agenum cynne ne on his mæges lafe, þe swa neahsib wære, ne on þæs wifes nydmagan, þe he sylf ær hæfde, ne on his gefæderan; ne on gehalgodre nunnan ne on ælætan ænig cristen man ne gewifige æfre."

50. Jost, *Wulfstanstudien,* pp. 249–61, argued that Napier 50 was a careful mosaic of sentences from Wulfstan's work, probably delivered before the king and nobles sometime in the decades after Wulfstan's death in 1023. Dorothy Bethurum (*Wulfstan, Homilies of,* pp. 39–41), argued that it was a set of notes Wulfstan put together late in his career, unoriginal and showing signs of haste.

51. *Instituta Cnuti,* 1:278–371.

used *compatrata sua,* a rare word which clearly means comother; the translator of the *Consiliatio Cnuti* rendered it *commatrem suam,* the usual term for comother. The translator of the *Quadripartitus* made a more interesting choice. Since at least the ninth century, Continental canonical texts almost automatically linked together a ban on marriage with one's comother and with one's goddaughter. As I argued earlier, Anglo-Saxons practiced same-sex sponsorship; that is, males sponsored males and females sponsored females. Consequently Anglo-Saxon bishops and kings had no occasion to forbid marriage between godparent and godchild. The Norman conquerors brought the practice of cross-sex sponsorship as well as the Continental canon law that forbade godparents to marry their godchildren. The translator of the *Quaripartitus* "modernized" the text in front of him by rendering *gefædere* as *commatrem uel filiolam,* that is, comother or goddaughter, which was the canon law familiar to him.[52]

Godsibb

There was yet a third way to refer to a coparent, as a *godsibb.* I know of only one occasion when an Old English translator confronted the word *compaternitas.* He used the word *godsibbræden* to translate it, which combined *godsibb* and *ræden* ("the condition of").[53] Although the word *godsibbræden* appeared only once in surviving Old English texts, *godsibrede* became the ordinary term for coparenthood in Middle English and survived in dialectal usage until the nineteenth century.[54] The translator of the word *compaternitas* rendered the element *compater* as *godsibb,* which is thus another Old English word for "cofather." Some scholars have not translated *godsibb* that way, however, and I need to demonstrate the point more fully.

Every dictionary compiler and translator knows *godsibb* is a word related to sponsorship, but its interpretation demands a precise understanding of the forms of spiritual kinship. Bosworth-Toller defined *god-sibb* simply as "a sponsor."[55] In the *Supplements* to Bosworth-Toller, the definition was refined: "One who has become spiritually related to another (a baptized child or its parents) by acting as sponsor at baptism."[56] Thus the standard dictionary interpreted *god-sibb* as a word for both godparent and coparent, that is, for any spiritual kinsman. I believe that the meaning of the word is more precise than that: it means "coparent."

52. Ibid., 1:290–91.

53. Homily 45, in Napier, *Wulfstan,* p. 228: "þa godsibbrædenne, þe ge habbað for gode and for Sce Johannis dæle begetene."

54. *Middle English Dictionary,* s.v. "godsib-rede," p. 206; for later usage, see *Oxford English Dictionary,* 6:701.

55. Bosworth, *Anglo-Saxon Dictionary,* p. 484.

56. Ibid., *Supplements,* p. 480.

Godsibb appears six times in surviving Old English texts.[57] Modern translations are vague or incorrect. Wulfstan used the word *godsibbas* in the three versions of his *Sermo Lupi,* where he lamented, in Dorothy Whitelock's translation, that "too many sponsors (*godsybbas*) and godchildren (*godbearn*) have killed one another far and wide throughout this land."[58] The *Northumbrian Priests' Law,* which Wulfstan might have composed, forbade a man to marry his *godsibbe,* which both Liebermann and Hans Tenhaken translated as "Taufverwandte" (baptismal relative) and *Councils and Synods* rendered as "anyone spiritually related to him."[59] The meaning is again taken to be any spiritual kinsman from sponsorship. A bidding prayer was an invitation, sometimes in the vernacular, for the congregation to pray for particular people and particular intentions. In such a prayer copied on folio 153v of the York Gospels, the congregation was asked to pray for "our *godsybbas* and *cumæðran,*" which Stevenson translated as "sponsors and godfathers."[60] His translation is certainly incorrect as to the meaning of *cumæðran,* which should be "comothers" and, I believe, also incorrect on *godsybbas,* which I think is "cofathers." The *Anglo-Saxon Chronicle* (*E-Version*), s.a 1093, mentioned the murder of a man identified as the *godsib* of King Malcolm of Scotland.[61] In each of these instances, I think the proper translation for *godsybbas* is "cofather" or "comother" or "coparent."

The surest way to know what *godsibb* meant is to find it in translations whose original Latin texts can be identified. We are fortunate to have two Old English uses of *godsibb* for which a Latin text close to the original is extant. The first is the version of the "Letter from Heaven" (Napier 45) whose translator rendered *compaternitas* as *godsibbrædenn,* clearly taking *compater* and *godsibb* as equivalent. The second is another version of the "Letter from Heaven" with *conpatres* translated as *godsybbas.*[62] These seem to me to be conclusive. When we turn back to the examples of *godsibb* given above, the translation "cofather" or "comother" seems as or more likely than "godfather" or "godmother." In the context of lamenting about

57. *The Microfiche Concordance* found the forms *godsib* (once), *godsibbas* (four times), *godsibbe* (once), and *godsybbas* (once).

58. Bethurum edited the three versions of the *Sermo Lupi* (Homily 20a, b, and c) in *Homilies,* pp. 255–75. Although the versions differ in some respects, each says "And godsibbas ⁊ godbearn to fela man forspilde wide geond þas ðeode." (p. 258, lines 72–73; p. 263, lines 83–84; p. 270, lines 78–79). Dorothy Whitelock's translation is in *EHD,* p. 931.

59. *Die Gesetze,* 1:384; *Das northumbrische Priestergesetz,* ed. Hans P. Tenhaken (Dusseldorf, 1979), p. 47; *Councils and Synods,* 1/1, p. 465.

60. William H. Stevenson, "Yorkshire Surveys and Other Documents of the Eleventh Century in the York Gospels," *EHR* 27 (1912) 9–10.

61. *ASC*(*E*), s.a. 1093, p. 228: "Hine sloh Moræl of Bebbaburh. se wæs þæs eorles stiward. and Melcolmes cynges godsib."

62. Priebsch, "Chief Sources," p. 137.

contemporary treachery and violations of social order, Wulfstan chose as examples the killing of the two distinct forms of spiritual kin, cofathers (*godsybbas*) and godchildren (*godbearn*). He seems to be taking the viewpoint of the person who does the killing, who slays either his own coparent or his own godchild. The bidding prayer called on the congregation to pray for their male and female coparents, just as it called on them to pray for their guild brothers (*gildan*) and guild sisters (*gildsweostra*).[63] The *Northumbrian Priests' Law* forbade marriage with someone it called a *godsibbe,* in parallel with the contemporary laws of Æthelred and Cnut, which however used the word *gefædere,* which certainly means comother. The translation of the two versions of the "Letter from Heaven" has not been localized, but the other instances of *godsibb* suggest that it is a northern word, associated with York and with Wulfstan.

Subsequent chapters will treat the functioning of coparenthood in Anglo-Saxon society, but some conclusions are possible now about the history of the institution. In the first two centuries of Anglo-Saxon Christianity, coparenthood was insignificant, perhaps even unknown. It emerged in the sources and perhaps in society during the ninth century and was thereafter a way to bind adults in a siblinglike relationship, quite distinct from the parent/child bond of godparenthood. Every baptism transformed the child's parents and sponsor into coparents to one another. Occasionally the sources reveal coparenthood's social aspect, as when Bishop Oswald identified the recipient of a lease as his cofather or when Ælfheah mentioned his royal comother in a will. But coparenthood was recorded most often in Anglo-Saxon sources of the eleventh century as an impediment to marriage. Archbishop Wulfstan, who did so much to bring Carolingian ideas to his countrymen, seems to have been important in adding the marital impediment to Anglo-Saxon canon and royal law, but the institution of coparenthood had a significance beyond its consequences for marriage.

63. W. H. Stevenson, "Yorkshire Surveys," p. 11: "Wutan we gebiddan for ure godsybbas and for ure cumæðran, and for ure gildan and gildsweostra."

CHAPTER 9

Spiritual Kinship and Sexual Prohibitions

Sponsorships that united could also divide. Earlier chapters have mentioned in passing the sexual/marital consequences of spiritual kinship, but now they must be analyzed more fully. The reader will have to bear with me, because to reach the Anglo-Saxons requires a circuitous route. But the complexity of the route is, in itself, significant.

Judaism, Christianity, and Islam, shaped by the stern God of the Old Testament, have traditionally been concerned with marriage, kinship, and sexual behavior among their adherents. Early medieval Christians took a keen interest in marriage law, particularly in preventing marriages: drawing in part on the Old Testament, they created a remarkable system of impediments. According to David Herlihy, when the medieval Christian prohibitions on marriage between persons related by blood, by marriage, or by spiritual kinship reached their fullest development in the twelfth century, they were the most elaborate of any known society.[1] But the focus and intensity of that concern with sex and marriage has varied across time. In the later Roman Empire, for instance, the Christian bishops were much concerned with divorce, which was relatively easy to obtain under Roman law; whereas bishops in early medieval Gaul were concerned with incest, per-

1. David Herlihy, "Making Sense of Incest: Women and the Marriage Rules of the Early Middle Ages," in *Law, Custom, and the Social Fabric in Medieval Europe: Essays in Honor of Bryce Lyon,* ed. Bernard S. Bachrach and David Nicholas (Kalamazoo, Mich. 1990), pp. 1–4. See also Mayke de Jong, "To the Limits of Kinship: Anti-Incest Legislation in the Early Medieval West 500–900," in *From Sappho to De Sade: Moments in the History of Sexuality,* ed. Jan Bremmer (London, 1989), pp. 36–59. For a detailed survey of early medieval views of sexuality, see James A. Brundage, *Law, Sex, and Christian Society in Medieval Europe* (Chicago, 1987), pp. 77–175.

haps because for economic reasons contemporary practices favored marriage with close kin.[2] To prevent what they regarded as incest, the bishops of Gaul enacted for their contemporaries the marital prohibitions that had been laid out in the eighteenth chapter of Leviticus, and subsequently extended them.[3] This concern with incest is key to understanding the development of sexual prohibitions based on sponsorship. In societies where the spiritual family has been taken seriously, it is usually enveloped in some forms of sexual prohibition to avoid incest.[4]

The Spiritual Family and Incest

It was in sixth-century Byzantium that a significant shift in Christian marriage practice occurred, when Byzantine churchmen and rulers began to regard the spiritual kinship created by baptismal sponsorship as real kinship. In A.D. 530, the emperor Justinian issued a legal text that influenced directly or indirectly all subsequent legislation about sexual prohibitions based on sponsorship. The emperor was presented with the case of a man who married his goddaughter, which bothered somebody enough to bring a legal action. In a letter to the Praetorian Prefect Julian, the emperor wrote that "any woman should be forbidden to marry a man who received her from most holy baptism . . . since nothing else can bring about paternal affection and a just prohibition of marriage as a relationship of that sort by which their souls are joined through God's mediation."[5] Justinian recognized in the parent/child relationship created by sponsorship a religious kinship that precluded any form of sexual contact. That view was not confined to the law. In his *Secret History,* the Byzantine historian Procopius (c. 500–c. 565) told a malicious story about the general Belisarius and his wife Antonina. The kernel of the story was that Antonina fell in love with Theodosius, a godson of herself and Belisarius, and had intercourse with him. Procopius's account assumed a proper way for godparent and godchild to behave. They were expected to have a parental love ("Antonina

2. On preference for the marriage of close kin, see Goody, *Development,* pp. 34–47.
3. Lynch, *Godparents,* pp. 219–23; Paul Mikat, *Die Inzestgesetzgebung der merowingisch-fränkischen Konzilien, 511–626/27* (Paderborn, 1994).
4. Lynch, *Godparents,* pp. 219–57.
5. *Codex Iustinianus,* bk. 5, title 4, law 26, p. 197: "Ea videlicet persona omnimodo ad nuptias venire prohibenda, quam aliquis . . . a sacrosancto suscepit baptismate, cum nihil aliud sic inducere potest paternam adfectionem et iustam nuptiarum prohibitionem, quam huiusmodi nexus, per quem deo mediante animae eorum copulatae sunt." English translation in *The Civil Law including the Twelve Tables, the Institutes of Gaius, the Rules of Ulpian. . . ,* trans., S. P. Scott (Cincinnati, 1932), 13:154.

loved Theodosius, as she naturally would, as being her son through the sacred word"), but they broke a taboo when that love became sexual. Procopius wrote that in her carnal love for Theodosius, Antonina abandoned "fear and respect for everything both divine and human."[6]

In the eventful century and a half after Justinian issued the *Corpus iuris civilis,* Byzantine society changed considerably but without a corresponding revision of the law to take account of the new situation. In 691/92, Justinian II (685–695; 705–711) summoned a major council, known as the Quinisext or the Council in Trullo, whose 102 decisions were virtually a new codification of the canon law. Canon 53 broke new ground when it extended Justinian I's ban: it forbade coparents to marry one another. "Since a spiritual bond is greater than a joining of bodies, and since we have learned that in some places some men who receive infants from the holy and saving baptism subsequently contract marriage with the infants' mothers who have become widows, we decree that henceforth nothing of that sort be done. However if after this present canon they are observed doing this, first they should give up this illegal marriage and then be subjected to the punishments of fornicators."[7]

The expansion of marital prohibitions based on spiritual kinship did not stop with Justinian II. The *Ecloga,* a law code issued by the emperors Leo III and Constantine V between 726 and 741, repeated the ban on marriage between godparent and godchild, and between coparents. But it added a new category, spiritual siblings, who were the natural and spiritual children of the same person:

> 2.2. Marriage is forbidden to those who are bound together by holy and salvation-bringing baptism, that is to say, the marriage of the sponsor (*anadoxos*) and his goddaughter and her mother [is forbidden], and also the marriage of son of the sponsor with the goddaughter or her mother [is forbidden]. . . .
>
> 17.25. Whoever "marries" or without marriage has carnal relations with a woman who became his comother (*sunteknos*) through holy and salvation-bringing baptism, after they have been separated from one another, such an evil-doer shall be subject to the punishment for adultery, i.e., both he and she shall have their noses cut off.

6. Procopius, *Anecdota or Secret History,* 1.1, pp. 10–13.

7. Trullo (Council in), c. 53, p. 51. On Canon 53, see Constantin G. Pitsakis, "Le droit matrimonial dans les canons du concile in Trullo," *Annuarium Historiae Conciliorum* 24 (1992), 178–80; and on Canon 53's influence on subsequent Byzantine legislation, see Spyros N. Troianos, "Die Wirkungsgeschichte des Trullanum (Quinisextum) in der byzantinischen Gesetzgebung," ibid., pp. 95–100.

17.26. If a man does such a thing and the comother is married, then in addition to the cutting off of their noses, each shall be vigorously beaten.[8]

In addition, in another version of the *Ecloga,* the priest became "father" to the person he baptized, and as a consequence, his children were forbidden to marry that person because they were spiritual siblings.[9]

Initially, Byzantine rulers and churchmen were more concerned than their counterparts in the Latin west about the sexual consequences of spiritual kinship, but that began to change in the eighth century. Although the Latin Christian west and Byzantine Christian east were drifting apart in the early Middle Ages for reasons of language, politics, and theology, Byzantine religious practices continued to influence the west. During the eighth century, the Byzantine efforts to prevent the marriage of spiritual kin entered Italy and then Frankish Gaul. Much is lost in our knowledge of the channels by which the sexual prohibitions spread from Byzantium. Sources written in Italy and Gaul over a period of about twenty-five years (721–747) do allow a glimpse of the east-to-west transmission of the sexual taboos, with the papacy as the main intermediary.

The emperor Justinian II, patron of the Council in Trullo, wanted papal ratification of its canons in order to gain ecumenical status for his council. Pope Sergius (687–701) refused to accept the council because some canons were critical of Roman practices on matters such as fasting, the marriage of lower clergy, and the position of the patriarch of Constantinople relative to the bishop of Rome.[10] Because Byzantine emperors governed the city of Rome, it would have been difficult for Sergius to resist the imperial will for long. Justinian II was deposed in 695, however, so the potential crisis over the conciliar canons passed. When Justinian regained the throne in 705, he opened negotiations with Pope John VII (705–707) and then with his successor Constantine I (708–715). The details of the discussions are lost, but in 711, Justinian and Constantine were reconciled at Nicaea in Asia Minor, where the emperor apparently agreed that the pope could reject unacceptable canons and ratify the others. Many of the decisions of the Council in Trullo were thus accepted by the papacy.[11]

8. *Ecloga,* 2.2, p. 170, and 17.25 and 17.26, p. 232.
9. *Ecloga,* 2.3, trans. Edwin H. Freshfield, *A Manual of Roman Law: The Ecloga Published by the Emperors Leo III and Constantine V of Isauria* (Cambridge, 1926), p. 73.
10. On the Council in Trullo, see Judith Herrin, *The Formation of Christendom* (Princeton, N.J., 1987), pp. 284–88; Constance Head, *Justinian II of Byzantium* (Madison, Wis., 1972), pp. 72–79; and V. Laurent, "L'oeuvre canonique du concile *in Trullo,* 691–692, source primaire du droit de l'église orientale," *Revue des Etudes Byzantines* 23 (1965), 32–33.
11. Herrin, *Formation,* p. 288; Head, *Justinian II,* pp. 132–36. Laurent, "L'oeuvre canonique," p. 34.

The papal negotiators accepted Canon 53 forbidding the marriage of coparents. In a Roman council of 721, Pope Gregory II, who as a deacon had been a leading negotiator at the meeting between Justinian II and Pope Constantine, introduced the prohibition on marriage between coparents into western canon law for the first time, although in a more succinct form than Canon 53 of the Council in Trullo: "If anyone marries a spiritual comother, let him be anathema. And all responded three times: let him be anathema."[12] Gregory II took more than a passing interest in the prohibition. At his urging, King Liutprand (712–744), the greatest royal legislator among the Lombards, introduced into Lombard law in 723 a ban on marriage between persons related by godparenthood, coparenthood, or spiritual siblinghood. "We likewise decree that no one may presume to take to wife his comother nor a daughter whom he lifted from the holy font; nor may his son presume to take as wife the daughter of the man who received him from the font, because they are known to be spiritual siblings (*spiritalis germani*)."[13] Thus, by the mid-720s papal and Lombard Italy had accepted the Byzantine view of the broad marital consequences of sponsorship: no one could marry his or her spiritual relative, whether godparent, godchild, coparent, or spiritual sibling. Pope Gregory's successors, Zachary and Stephen II, continued to propagate the ban on the marriage of coparents, in northern Italy and also in Frankish Gaul.[14]

The Byzantine-papal legislation did not pass without modification into Gaul, however, because conditions differed there. In Byzantium and Italy, a male could sponsor a female or vice versa: hence the prohibition on marriage between godparent and godchild. In eighth-century Frankish Gaul, the sponsor was of the same sex as the child, making the ban on marriage between godparent and godchild unnecessary. Likewise, the ban on marriage of spiritual siblings had little impact in Gaul, because the notion of spiritual siblinghood did not travel well across the Alps. Evidence for its

12. Roman Council (721), c. 4, Mansi 12, col. 263: "Si quis commatrem spiritalem duxerit in conjugium, anathema sit. Et responderunt omnes tertio: anathema sit." For an Old English translation of these canons, see Gregory II, *Old English Version,* pp. 71–73.

13. Liutprand, *Leges Liutprandi regis,* c. 34, 124: "ut nullus presumat cummatrem suam uxorem ducere, sed nec filiam, quam de sacro fonte levavit; neque filius eius presumat filiam illius uxorem ducere, qui eum de fonte suscepit, quia spiritalis germani esse noscuntur." Katherine F. Drew, *The Lombard Laws* (Philadelphia, 1973), p. 161, has an error in translating the provision on spiritual siblings. See also Lynch, *Godparents,* pp. 238–40.

14. Zachary's Roman Council (743), c. 5, Mansi 12, col. 383; Zachary, letter to Bishop Theodore of Pavia, p. 710; Stephen II's *responsa* to the monks of Bretigny (Jaffé 2315), c. 4, Mansi 12, col. 559: "ut nullus habeat cummatrem suam spiritalem, tam de fonte sacra, quam de confirmatione, neque sibi clam in neutra parte conjugio sociatam. Quod si conjuncti fuerint, separentur."

recognition in the kingdom of the Franks is very slim, and evidence that it prohibited marriages does not exist.[15]

But coparenthood was a common way to link adults in Frankish society, and the Byzantine-papal ban on marriage between coparents took root. The first evidence for the prohibition in Gaul comes from the late 720s and 730s and has an Anglo-Saxon aspect. At about age thirty-five, the Anglo-Saxon monk Wynfrith, better known as Boniface (680–754), left his monastic community at Nursling to work among the Germanic peoples who lived east of the Rhine. He became a leading religious figure, both a dynamic missionary and a church reformer. In the course of his long career on the Continent (716–754), both popes and Frankish rulers supported him. After Pepin the Short became the Frankish mayor of the palace in 741, Boniface entered a new phase of his career when he was invited to participate in the reform of the Frankish church.[16]

Boniface's letters are an indispensable source for the history of the eighth century.[17] In about 735, when Boniface had lived on the Continent for almost twenty years, he became embroiled in a controversy because he had permitted marriage between persons who were coparents to one another. He wrote to three Anglo-Saxon prelates—Archbishop Nothelm of Canterbury (735–739), Bishop Pehthelm of Whithorn (c. 730–735), and an abbot named Duddo—to ask for their advice and support. His letter to Nothelm contained an account of the matter.

> I desire to hear your advice about one sin that has occurred, which I committed unknowingly in permitting a marriage to a certain man. It happened in this way. A certain man, as many are accustomed, by lifting the son of another man from the font of holy baptism adopted the boy to himself as a son. Afterward he married the boy's mother, whose husband had died. This is something the Romans call a sin and a sin worthy of death, so that in such cases they order divorces to be made. And they affirm that where Christian emperors reign the crime of such a marriage must be punished by a capital sentence or expiated by perpetual pilgrimage. . . . If you should find this marriage to be counted as so great a sin in the decrees of the Catholic fathers

15. The eighth-century *Vita Lupi episcopi Senonensis,* c. 8, ed. Bruno Krusch, *MGH SRM* 4 (Hanover and Leipzig, 1902), p. 181: Fulcarius is *amicus* to Lupus "quia Betto pater ipsius de sacris eum susceperat fontibus."

16. The bibliography on Boniface and the Anglo-Saxon missionaries is extensive; for an introduction, see *The Greatest Englishman: Essays on St. Boniface and the Church at Crediton,* ed. Timothy Reuter (Exeter, 1980). Theodor Schieffer, *Winfrid-Bonifatius und die christliche Grundlegung Europas* (Freiburg, 1954; rpr. Darmstadt, 1972, with updated bibliography), is fundamental. See also Wilhelm Levison, *England and the Continent in the Eighth Century* (Oxford, 1946).

17. Boniface, *Epistolae.*

> or in the canons or even in holy writ, you should take care to point it out to me, so that in understanding I may know whose authority is in that judgment. For I can not understand at all why in one place spiritual kinship (*spiritalis propinquitas*) may be so great a sin in the matter of marital intercourse, when in the holy baptism of Christ we are all proved to be sons and daughters of the church and brothers and sisters [of one another].[18]

Boniface identified his critics as "Romans," which may refer to papal clerics or to a Frankish party defending its views by reference to papal law. The background to Boniface's offense that so annoyed his "Roman" critics lay in the evolving nature of spiritual kinship. For a century and a half, coparenthood had been a traditional practice of Frankish society, but *without a sexual taboo.* It was during Boniface's missionary career that the sexual prohibition began to spread north of the Alps under the urging of the popes, who in their turn had been influenced by developments at Byzantium, especially Canon 53 of the Council in Trullo. Boniface's reference to his critics' argument that "where Christian emperors reign the crime of such a marriage must be punished by a capital sentence or expiated by perpetual pilgrimage" indicates that they might have been citing against him the Council in Trullo or the *Ecloga* of emperors Leo and Constantine or a related Byzantine legal text.[19]

Boniface's rejection of the prohibition on marriage between coparents sheds light not only on the situation in Frankish Gaul but also on that in Anglo-Saxon England, where he had been educated in the last quarter of the seventh century. During his long missionary career, he was in constant communication with Anglo-Saxon clerics, nuns, and kings through letters and messengers. He knew a great deal about the state of religion in his homeland, even though he did not set foot in it during the last forty-five years of his life. His letters make clear that he was not familiar with the prohibition of marriage between coparents and was hostile toward it. In his letter to Bishop Pehthelm, he expressed his exasperation. ". . . up to now I knew nothing about this kind of sin—if it is truly a sin—nor was I aware that the fathers had enumerated it in the ancient canons or in the decrees of the popes, or that the apostles had enumerated it in a list of sins. Conse-

18. Iden, *Epistula* 33, pp. 57–58.

19. *Ecloga,* 17.25, p. 232, ordered that coparents who married have their noses cut off, and if they fornicated without attempting to marry, they should also be severely beaten; Dieter Simon, "Zur Ehegesetzsgebung der Isaurier," in *Fontes minores,* vol. 1, Forschungen zur byzantinischen Rechtsgeschichte 1 (Frankfurt am Main, 1976), pp. 21–30, edited a *Novella* of the emperors Leo III and Constantine V, issued between 31 March 726 and 30 March 727, which forbade the marriage of coparents and imposed severe physical and financial penalities on offenders, including perpetual exile for those who sought to marry again after being separated from their spouse/coparent.

quently, if you should find anything anywhere in ecclesiastical writings, take care to point it out to us and let us know your view of the matter."[20]

Boniface was astute in asking his correspondents to search out the *religious* authority that might justify such a marital ban. He probably knew that there were no venerable ecclesiastical texts on the subject: it was not scriptural; it was unknown to the patristic writers; and it appeared in none of the authoritative early medieval canonical collections. The ban was a Byzantine innovation, confirmed in a papal council only about fifteen years earlier. Boniface did not mention the papal council of 721, although his critics may have been citing it against him. His letter to Nothelm drew attention instead to his critics' citation of Byzantine law, which he may not have regarded as binding.

A source contemporary with Boniface voiced the views of his critics. In about 727 an anonymous Neustrian monk, perhaps connected with the monastery of Saint Denis near Paris or with that of Saint Médard at Soissons, composed the *Liber historiae Francorum.*[21] The author of the *Liber* related a tale about the Merovingian king Chilperic (561–584) and his wives or concubines, Audovera and Fredegund. The story, which has no parallel elsewhere in the sources of Merovingian history, is marked by anachronisms and errors and is probably not true. It may have arisen to explain why one female companion of Chilperic replaced the other. It does, however, shed light on the views of Boniface's critics.

The *Liber* stated that Queen Audovera gave birth to a daughter while her husband, Chilperic, was on campaign against the Saxons. Fredegund advised her to have the child baptized immediately. At the ceremony, the female sponsor—called in the text a *matrona,* which could be a corruption of *matrina,* although Krusch's edition signals no such variant in the manuscripts—was absent. On Fredegund's advice, Audovera received her own child from the baptismal font. When Chilperic returned, Fredegund greeted him with these words. "Thanks be to God because our lord king received victory over his enemies and because a daughter has been born to you. My lord king, with whom will you sleep tonight, since my lady queen is your comother (*conmater*) from your daughter Childesinda?"[22] Chilperic responded that he would sleep with Fredegund, as he could no longer sleep

20. Boniface, *Epistola* 32, p. 56.

21. On the anonymous author, see Richard Gerberding, *The Rise of the Carolingians and the Liber historiae Francorum* (Oxford, 1987), pp. 46–72. *Liber historiae Francorum* in English trans. Bernard Bachrach (Lawrence, Kans., 1973).

22. *Liber historiae Francorum,* c. 31, pp. 292–93: "Deo gratias, quia dominus noster rex victoriam recepit de adversariis suis, nataque est tibi filia. Cum qua dominus meus rex dormiet hac nocte, quia domina mea regina conmater tua est de filia tua Childesinda?"

with Audovera. His meeting with the latter was angry: "You have done an unspeakable thing (*nefanda res*) through your stupidity. Now you are no longer able to be my wife." In the tale, Chilperic forced Audovera and her daughter to become nuns, exiled the unnamed bishop who had performed the baptism and had permitted the illicit sponsorship, and accepted Fredegund as his queen.

Thus, by the late 720s, the author of the *Liber historiae Francorum* accepted as common knowledge in need of no defense that coparenthood was incompatible with sexual intercourse: if one member of a couple sponsored their common child, the couple could no longer have sexual intercourse. This was the position advocated only recently by a Byzantine council (692), a papal council (721), and Lombard law (723) but which Boniface vigorously resisted in 730s. His old-fashioned view clashed with the modern opinion, which was defended by reference to what was done at Rome and Byzantium. His expressions of indignation, incomprehension, and disapproval indicate that the prohibition of marriage between coparents had only recently been introduced in Gaul. More important for this book, he did not know of it from his thirty-five years in Anglo-Saxon England.

Boniface does not seem to have given up his opposition. He presided over five reform councils for the Frankish church between 742 and 747, which attacked adultery, incest, marriage with nuns, and other marital irregularities but never endorsed the ban on marriage between coparents.[23] But even while he was still alive, Boniface lost his argument in the Frankish church. Pepin, the mayor of the palace, sent an inquiry on many topics to Pope Zachary, who had forbidden the marriage of coparents in two texts that survive.[24] Pepin's letter, which does not survive, included a question about the marriage of coparents because that was an issue of contention. Zachary's long response, dated 5 January 747, replied directly to Boniface's objections, without using the great missionary's name: "Nor may anyone with a foolish boldness take as wife [his] spiritual comother or daughter. For that is unspeakable and a deadly sin before God and his angels. It is so serious that it was condemned by none of the holy fathers and decisions of the holy synods or even in imperial laws; but, fearing the terrible judgment of God, they were reluctant to render an opinion."[25]

23. Boniface's councils are (a) the *Concilium Germanicum* (742), (b) the *Concilium Liftinense* (1 March 743), (c) the *Concilium Suessionense* (2 March 744), (d) the *Concilium* at an unspecified place (745), and (e) the *Concilium in Francia habitum* (747), edited in *Concilia aevi Karolini,* pp. 1–36 and 45–50. On these councils, see Wilfried Hartmann, *Die Synoden der Karolingerzeit im Frankenreich und in Italien* (Paderborn, 1989), pp. 47–63.

24. See above, n. 14.

25. Pope Zachary to Pippin (Jaffé 2278), c. 22, in *Codex Carolinus,* p. 485; Lynch, *Godparents,* pp. 248–51.

Without relying on Byzantine law (in fact he says quite erroneously that the imperial laws did not condemn such marriages), Zachary strongly endorsed the ban on the marriage of coparents. He explained away Boniface's point that no ancient authority condemned such marriages by insisting that it was so unclean that the fathers, councils, and emperors were ashamed even to record the words. When Pepin became king of the Franks in 751, his capitularies began the long western tradition of legislating against the marriage of coparents.[26]

Spiritual Kinship and Marriage in Anglo-Saxon England

From the Sixth to the Late Tenth Centuries

With the historical background set, we finally reach Anglo-Saxon England. The sexual mores of the pre-Christian Anglo-Saxons are not well recorded, but they were different from, and yielded only slowly to, Christianity's rather different norms.[27] Even after conversion to Christianity, some Anglo-Saxons resisted significant changes in such fundamental sexual institutions as marriage between close kin, remarriage after repudiation of a spouse, polygamy, and concubinage.[28] From the beginning of christianization, Anglo-Saxon marriage customs bothered foreign bishops and native purists such as Bede and Alcuin. They repeatedly criticized divorce, concubinage, marriage within the prohibited degrees of blood and affinal kinship, and the uniquely Christian sin of marriage with nuns or consecrated virgins. The first Roman missionary, Augustine of Canterbury, may have compiled a sermon from an earlier source in which he laid out the Christian marital prohibitions, based largely on Leviticus 18.[29] It was blunt about forms of incest and sexual immorality, but as might be expected from its early date, it made no reference to spiritual kinship. In laws issued about 695, King Wihtred of Kent forbade his people to form illicit marriages, although he did not specify what made them illicit.[30]

26. Capitulary of King Pepin (751–755), c. 1, *MGH Capitularia* 1, p. 31: no marriage with *commater* or with *matrina spiritualis de fonte et confirmatione episcopi;* Capitulary of Compiègne (757), c. 1, ibid., p. 38: no marriage between coparents from confirmation.

27. Whitelock, *Beginnings of English Society,* pp. 149–52; Rosalind Hill, "Marriage in Seventh Century England," in *Saints, Scholars, and Heroes: Studies in Medieval Culture in Honour of Charles W. Jones* (Collegeville, Minn., 1979): ". . . marriages were of full surprising contradictions."

28. Ross, "Concubinage," is a succinct, useful account of ecclesiastical efforts to curtail traditional sexual patterns, especially what churchmen regarded as concubinage.

29. *Allocutio sacerdotum de coniugiis inlicitis ad plebem,* ed. in L. Machielsen, "Fragments patristiques non-identifiés du ms. Vat. Pal. 577," *Sacris Erudiri* 12 (1961), 533–35.

30. Wihtred, *Laws,* 3, 4; 4.1, 5; and 5.1, 6, in *EHD* pp. 396–98.

Native and foreign clergy continued to criticize the Anglo-Saxons for their marital irregularities, although some references are not specific enough to give us an idea of what lay behind such words as "illicit" or "incestuous." The papal legates of 786 forbade kings to be chosen from among those royal sons "who were born from adultery or incest." They also forbade the sons of nuns and prostitutes, which might have been a clerical term of opprobrium for concubines, to inherit from their fathers.[31] In a long, critical letter to King Æthelbald of Mercia, Boniface and seven other bishops in the Frankish kingdom lamented that the king had never contracted "a legitimate marriage" but instead indulged his sexual appetites with many women, including nuns and consecrated virgins.[32] Also from the safety of Francia, Alcuin criticized King Eardwulf of Northumbria for dismissing his wife and taking a concubine.[33] In 873/74, Pope John VIII wrote to King Burgred of Mercia about reports that some of his subjects were making marriages with nuns and with close kin. In 877/78, Pope John wrote to Archbishop Æthelred of Canterbury to encourage him to forbid divorces and marriages within the forbidden degrees of kinship.[34] About 890, Archbishop Fulk of Reims wrote to Archbishop Plegmund of Canterbury to encourage him "to cut off and extirpate the incestuous heats of lasciviousness" among the Anglo-Saxons.[35] In his *Constitutiones* (942x946), Archbishop Oda of Canterbury forbade illicit or incestuous marriages with nuns, close kin, or other illicit persons.[36] Archbishop Oswald of York (d. 992) reported a case of polyandry: two brothers with one woman as sexual partner.[37] Ælfric and others complained that some of the clergy married in defiance of the canon law.[38] The summary of a letter from Archbishop Fulk of Reims to King Alfred is typical:

> To Alfred, a king across the sea he [Archbishop Fulk] sent friendly letters, thanking him that he had appointed a man [Archbishop Plegmund] so good and devout and suitable according to the rules of the Church as bishop in

31. Legate George of Ostia to Pope Hadrian I, c. 12 and c. 16, in *Alcuini sive Albini epistulae,* ed. Ernst Dümmler, *MGH Epistolae* 4 (Berlin, 1895), pp. 23–24 and 25. Ross, "Concubinage," p. 27, interpreted the word *meretrix* in Canon 16, which ordinarily means prostitute, as a clerical attack on concubines.
32. Boniface, *Epistola* 73, pp. 148–51.
33. Alcuin to the Mercian Ealdorman Osbert (797), in *EHD,* pp. 855–56.
34. Pope John VIII to Burgred, king of the Mercians, in *Councils and Synods,* 1/1, pp. 1–2; Pope John VIII to Archbishop Æthelred of Canterbury, ibid., p. 5.
35. Fulk to Plegmund (about 890), in *EHD,* p. 887.
36. Oda, Archbishop of Canterbury, *Constitutiones,* c. 7, in *Councils and Synods,* 1/1, pp. 72–73.
37. *Archbishop Oswald's Memorandum on the Estates of the See of York* (975–992), in *EHD,* p. 565.
38. Herbert Thurston, "Clerical Celibacy in the Anglo-Saxon Church," *Month* 542 (1909).

> the city called Canterbury. For he had heard that he was concerned to cut down with the sword of the word that most perverse opinion, arisen from pagan errors, until then surviving among the people. This opinion seemed to permit bishops and priests to have women living near them, and anyone, who wished, to approach kinswomen of his own stock, and, moreover, to defile women consecrated to God, and, although married, to have at the same time a concubine.[39]

Although our knowledge of pre-Christian Anglo-Saxon marital customs is hazy, one conclusion seems to emerge from this litany of criticism. Even after christianization, many Anglo-Saxons conducted their sexual and marital lives according to norms not of the canon law.[40]

It is significant that none of the critics between the seventh and late tenth centuries mentioned the prohibition on sexual intercourse with spiritual kin. At least in part, local conditions explain such silence. North of the Alps, spiritual siblinghood was not generally recognized, and one would not expect a marriage prohibition. The failure to mention the prohibition of marriage between godparent and godchild, a ban that went back to Justinian, is at first surprising. The explanation lies in the fact that Anglo-Saxons practiced same-sex sponsorship. The Northumbrian disciple of Theodore gathered three unique texts on sponsorship in *Penitential* 2.4. Canon 10 stated that "it is permitted for a man to receive a woman in baptism; and likewise to a woman to receive a man."[41] What question might have prompted Theodore (or some one else) to make this decision? We may surmise that at some point, Archbishop Theodore was asked whether same-sex sponsorship was obligatory. Theodore was familiar with cross-sex sponsorship, which was certainly a Byzantine and Roman practice. Recall that Justinian's law was based on the problem posed by a man who had sponsored a girl and subsequently wished to marry her and that Pope Gregory's *Dialogues* recounted the punishment of a man who had sexually vio-

39. A summary of Fulk's letter to Alfred survives in Flodoard, *Historia Remensis ecclesiae,* ed. J. Heller and G. Waitz, *MGH Scriptores* 13 (Hanover, 1881), p. 566; for the Latin, see *Councils and Synods,* 1/1, pp. 12–13; and trans. in *EHD,* p. 887.

40. Hans Hattenhauer, "Observantia christianitatis: St. Dunstan und das Eherecht," in *Vom mittelalterlichen Recht zur neuzeitlichen Rechtswissenschaft* (Paderborn, 1994), placed the difficulties of interpreting and enforcing Anglo-Saxon marriage law in a wider European context. For an introduction to the ways Anglo-Saxons carried out marriages, see Harold D. Hazeltine, "Geschichte der Eheschliessung nach angelsächsischen Recht," in *Festgabe für Dr. Bernhard Hübler . . . zum 70. Geburtstag am 25. Mai 1905* (Berlin, 1905); and Andreas Fischer, *Engagement, Wedding, and Marriage in Old English* (Heidelberg, 1986).

41. Discipulus Umbrensium, 2.4.10, *Canones Theodori,* p. 317: "Viro autem licet feminam suscipere in baptismo similiter et feminae virum licet." Also in *Canones sancti Gregorii pape urbis Romae,* c. 180, p. 269.

lated his goddaughter. Theodore had responded that cross-sex sponsorship was permissible: a male could sponsor a female and vice versa. His opinion did not, however, change the Anglo-Saxon custom of same-sex sponsorship, which explains why Anglo-Saxon texts never prohibited marriage between godparent and godchild: as long as males sponsored males and females sponsored females, there was no possibility of marriage between godparent and godchild.

Before the eleventh century, the critics of Anglo-Saxon sexual and marital practices also said nothing about the marriage of coparents. Perhaps such marriages were included implicitly in vague references to incestuous or illicit unions. But it is more likely that the Anglo-Saxon church did not observe such a prohibition. Boniface's testimony is convincing for the seventh and early eighth centuries. When he wrote to the Anglo-Saxon prelates, he seems to have expected them to use their erudition to strengthen his case against the ban on the marriage of coparents—unfortunately no response from the prelates survives. His negative reaction to the prohibition illuminates the situation in Wessex in his youth and early manhood, where such marital impediments were unknown, and they may have remained so for generations. Sources originating in Anglo-Saxon England between the seventh and the early eleventh centuries are silent on *any* sexual consequences arising out of sponsorship.

The silence of other sources strengthens the argument that seventh- and eighth-century Anglo-Saxons did not recognize a godparent complex with sexual consequences. At least two of the texts attributed to Theodore of Canterbury, the *Penitential* and the *Iudicia Theodori,* were probably compiled during Boniface's missionary career.[42] In them, sexual misconduct loomed very large, as it did in the entire tradition of penitential handbooks.[43] Yet, in spite of their concern with marriage and sexuality, the Theodoran texts have no reference to any form of spiritual kinship as an impediment to marriage.

A third piece of evidence also throws light on the early situation. Bede recounted how King Oswald of Northumbria sponsored King Cynegils of Wessex. Oswald subsequently strengthened their alliance by marrying Cynegils's daughter, who was thus the daughter of his godson. Bede praised

42. Thomas Charles-Edwards, "The Penitential of Theodore and the *Iudicia Theodori,*" in *Archbishop Theodore: Commemorative Studies on His Life and Influence,* ed. Michael Lapidge (Cambridge, 1995), pp. 141–45, argued that the *Iudicia* may have been composed earlier than the *Penitential.*

43. See, e.g., *Iudicia Theodori,* c. 42, p. 243 (menstruating women not to enter church or take communion); c. 56, p. 244 (married couples to abstain sexually during holy seasons); c. 94, p. 246 (baptism by a fornicating priest to be repeated); also Pierre J. Payer, *Sex and the Penitentials: The Development of a Sexual Code, 550–1150* (Toronto, 1984).

both the baptism and the marriage.[44] In contemporary Byzantium, the *Procheiron* explicitly forbade a man to marry the daughter of a woman whom he had sponsored.[45]

It is not surprising that early Anglo-Saxons did not recognize a prohibition that was introduced into Frankish Gaul only a generation after Theodore's death, late in Bede's lifetime, and when Boniface was in his fifties. The dearth of sources from 750 to 890 prevents any firm conclusions about the situation then. One thing is certain: there is no evidence of Anglo-Saxon prohibition of marriage between coparents until the eleventh century—quite a difference from Frankish Gaul, Italy, and Byzantium, where the ban on the marriage of all spiritual kin (godparents/godchildren, coparents, and spiritual siblings) spread rapidly after the mid-eighth century.

In the Late Tenth and Eleventh Centuries

After the serious disruptions caused by the Vikings in the ninth and tenth centuries, the Anglo-Saxon church began to rebuild during the Benedictine Revival, which seems to have begun in the 940s. The Frankish church and its successors on the Continent provided models and even personnel to help carry out reform. Because the marital prohibitions were a central feature of the Frankish godparent complex, it was inevitable that they would enter Anglo-Saxon England with successive importations of Frankish documents. Tenth- and eleventh-century Old English translations, laws, and sermons provide evidence that a ban on the marriage of coparents had reached England.

Translations represented an early stage in the assimilation of Frankish models. Not surprisingly, the first evidence for a prohibition of marriage between coparents in Anglo-Saxon England comes from translations of canonical and penitential texts. Pope Gregory II's Roman council of 721, which was the first in the west to ban the marriage of coparents, had treated all sorts of forbidden marriages succinctly. It was a very useful summary of marriage law and widely disseminated. An Old English translation of the canons, extant in two eleventh-century manuscripts, ordered that "if anyone has his spiritual comother in marriage, let him be anathema."[46] The *Poenitentiale Pseudo-Egberti,* a tenth-century text based in part on the

44. Bede, *HE,* 3.7, p. 232.

45. *Ecloga,* 2.3, in Freshfield, *Manual,* p. 73. Karl Eduard Zachariä von Lingenthal, *Geschichte des griechisch-römischen Rechts,* 3d ed. (Berlin, 1893; rpr. Aalen, 1955), p. 70.

46. Gregory II, *Old English Version,* pp. 71–73: "gif hwa his gastlican cumædran hæbbe him on (ge)sinscipe, si he amansumod."

Latin penitential of Halitgar of Cambrai, forbade any man to marry his *gefædere.*[47] The *Excerptiones Egberti,* an eleventh-century canonical collection with links to both Ælfric and Wulfstan, forbade marriage or fornication with one's comother.[48]

The translation of a text from Latin into Old English is one indication that some Anglo-Saxon regarded the Latin original or some part of it as important. But not every detail in a translated text can be assumed to have been put into practice; for such a text may indicate little or nothing about what was actually done in the region where the translation was made. Eleventh-century translated texts do take on more significance because, by then, "original" texts composed in England were beginning to treat the marriage of coparents.

Archbishop Wulfstan of York (active 996–1023) was the central figure in the active dissemination of the prohibition on marriage between coparents. Dorothy Bethurum wrote of him "The archbishop's aim was . . . to Romanize and modernize his church, to cure its insularity and to reform its practices by the best models he could find."[49] Proper marriage law, including the ban on the marriage of coparents, was part of that "Roman and modern" church. Wulfstan was adviser to King Æthelred II and to King Cnut. His ghost writing has been detected behind several eleventh-century law codes, including "The Laws of Edward and Guthrum," *The Canons of Edgar,* Æthelred's legislation after 1008, and Cnut's legislation.[50] One of the law codes influenced by Wulfstan was issued at Enham by King Æthelred between 16 May 1008 and 13 May 1011. It survives in three versions, two composed in Old English (V Æthelred and VI Æthelred) and one in a Latin paraphrase based on VI Æthelred. Wulfstan was identified in the Latin version as the compiler.[51]

47. *Poenitentiale Pseudo-Egberti,* p. 25. On Halitgar's penitential, see Kottje, *Die Bussbücher Halitgars von Cambrai.*

48. *Excerptiones Egberti,* c. 115 and c. 118, pp. 100 and 102.

49. Wulfstan, *Homilies,* p. 86.

50. Dorothy Whitelock, "Wulfstan and the So-Called Laws of Edward and Guthrum," *EHR* 56 (1941); "Wulfstan and the Laws of Cnut," *EHR* 63 (1948) and "Wulfstan's Authorship of Cnut's Laws," *EHR* 70 (1970). In the "Introduction" to her edition of the *Sermo Lupi ad Anglos* (London, 1939; rev. ed., Exeter, 1976), pp. 23–28, Whitelock surveyed the remarkable number of legal texts certainly or probably composed by Wulfstan. On Wulfstan's authorship of the *Canons of Edgar,* see *Councils and Synods,* 1/1, pp. 313–15. Whitelock's articles on Wulfstan are reprinted in her *History, Law, and Literature.*

51. V Æthelred and the Latin version of VI Æthelred are in *Councils and Synods,* 1/1, pp. 344–73. Where the Old English version of VI Æthelred differs from V Æthelred, the variations were printed in the footnotes to V Æthelred in *Councils and Synods,* 1/1, pp. 344–62 and in full in *Gesetze,* 1:247–58.

There has been a great deal of debate about the relationships among the three versions of the legislation at Enham.[52] All three forbade illicit marriages, but V Æthelred and the Latin version spoke in generalities.[53] VI Æthelred is much more detailed about what constituted an illicit marriage. As was often true in legislation, the law took up the case of a man who married a woman to whom he ought not to have sexual access, but one can safely assume that the law also bound women in analogous situations. He was forbidden to marry anyone related to him within the sixth degree of kinship or the widow of anyone who was related to him in that degree; or a near relative of his deceased wife, or a nun, or a woman deserted by her husband. He was not to have more than one wife at a time.[54] Each of these prohibitions can be found in earlier documents written about Anglo-Saxon England or composed in Anglo-Saxon England—for several centuries they were the staple criticisms of native and foreign critics of Anglo-Saxon marriage practices. VI Æthelred also contains something new, the earliest datable text composed in Anglo-Saxon England to ban marriage between coparents. It forbid any man to marry his comother (*gefædere*).[55] Kenneth Sisam argued that Wulfstan produced VI Æthelred for parish priests in the Danelaw, who were close to laymen's transgressions in marital arrangements and needed detailed guidance. Patrick Wormald argued that Wulfstan felt free to elaborate, in written form, laws which were oral and fluid and that the peculiar features of VI Æthelred "are therefore best explained . . . as developments of Wulfstan's own ideas."[56]

Wulfstan also influenced—probably drafted—the first laws issued by King Cnut, between 25 December 1020 and 25 December 1022, which repeated almost word for word the provisions of VI Æthelred, including the ban on marriage with one's *gefædere*.[57]

Wulfstan's archbishopric of York was impoverished and disorderly because of long Danish occupation. In an effort to restore ecclesiastical discipline, he is thought to have issued the text known as the *Northumbrian*

52. On the complex relationship among these texts, see *Councils and Synods,* 1/1, pp. 338–43; and Patrick Wormald, "Æthelred the Lawmaker," in *Ethelred the Unready: Papers from the Millenary Conference,* ed. David Hill, *British Archaeological Reports,* British ser., 3 (1978).

53. V Æthelred, c. 10, in *Councils and Synods,* 1/1, p. 350: "æghwylc Cristen man eac unriht hæmed georne forbuge ⁊ godcunde lage rihtlice healde"; Latin version of VI Æthelred, c. 11, ibid., p. 367: "Conubia inlicita cunctis generaliter interdicimus Christianis; sed legi divine cum Dei timore ubique adstringantur."

54. *Councils and Synods,* 1/1, p. 350, n. e.

55. VI Æthelred, c. 12.1, in *Councils and Synods,* 1/1, p. 350, n. e: "Ne on gehalgodre ænigre nunnan, ne on his gefæderan, ne on ælætan ænig Cristen man ne gewifige æfre."

56. Kenneth Sisam, *Studies in the History of Old English Literature* (Oxford, 1953), pp. 278–87; Wormald, "Æthelred the Lawmaker," pp. 54–57, quotation on p. 55.

57. I Cnut 7.1, in *Councils and Synods,* 1/1, p. 474.

Priests' Law, which has instructions for priests (cc. 1–45) and for the laity (cc. 46–67).[58] The part of the law directed to laypeople forbade anyone to marry his *godsibbe,* which, as I argued earlier, was a word for coparent.[59]

Two Old English homilies associated with Wulfstan treated the marital prohibitions in the same order and in almost the same words as they had been treated in I Cnut 7. Napier Homily 59, which both Jost and Bethurum accepted as a composition of Wulfstan, exhorted Christian men not to marry their close kin, or their late wife's close kin, or their *gefædere,* or a nun, or a woman who has been abandoned by her husband.[60] Napier Homily 50 also forbade the same marriages in the same order and in virtually the same words. Jost declared it the work of a compiler, but Bethurum defended it as a genuine composition of Wulfstan, though hasty and unoriginal.[61] Finally, if Cross and Hamer are right that the *Excerptiones Egberti* were complied in Wulfstan's circle, then its prohibitions on marriage and fornication between coparents are linked to Wulfstan as well.[62]

By 750, on the great arc of Christian lands from Paris through Rome to Constantinople, sexual contact between spiritual kin was regarded as an abomination. That was not true in Anglo-Saxon England, where marriage remained essentially a secular matter, the business of families. Ecclesiastical efforts to influence the way Anglo-Saxons married were only sporadically successful. Only after the Conquest did marriage become a matter commonly governed by church courts and canon law.[63] Furthermore, in the Anglo-Saxon godparent complex, godparenthood overshadowed coparenthood, and godparenthood entailed no marital prohibitions because of same-sex sponsorship. In particular, the sexual taboos concerning coparents are not recorded in England until the eleventh century. It is quite striking

58. *Councils and Synods,* 1/1, pp. 450–451.

59. *The Northumbrian Priests' Law,* c. 61.1, in *Councils and Synods,* 1/1, p. 465: "ne nan man on his godsibbe ne wifige." Law 61.1 is also in Tenhaken, *Das Nordhumbrische Priestergesetz,* p. 47; and in *Gesetze,* 1:384.

60. Homily 59, in Napier, *Wulfstan,* p. 308: "and we lærað and biddað and on godes naman beodað, þæt ænig cristen man binnan syx manna sibbfæce æfre ne wifige on his agenum cynne ne on his mæges lafe, þe swa neahsibb wære, ne on his wifes nydmagan, Þe he sylf ær ahte, *ne on his gefæderan* ne on gehalgodre nunnan; ne on ælætan ænig cristen man ne gewifige æfre ne na ma wife, þonne an, hæbbe." On the historiography of the authorship of Napier 59, see Klaus Ostheeren, "Bibliographischer Anhang," in Napier, *Wulfstan,* pp. 363–64. Jost, *Wulfstanstudien,* pp. 86–94, argued for its authenticity. Bethurum wrote, in Wulfstan, *Homilies,* pp. 38–39, that "it is . . . only a combination of passages from Polity and the laws and I think it may have been Wulfstan's own summary of statements of Christian duty."

61. Homily 50, in Napier, *Wulfstan,* p. 271. On the authorship, see Ostheeren, "Bibliographischer Anhang," pp. 357–58; Jost, *Wulfstanstudien,* pp. 249–61; and Bethurum, in Wulfstan, *Homilies,* pp. 39–41.

62. Cross and Hamer, "Ælfric's *Letters* and the *Excerptiones Ecgberhti,*" pp. 12–13.

63. Fischer, *Engagement,* pp. 18–24.

that Archbishop Wulfstan was involved in the composition of almost every text forbidding the marriage of coparents and that the legal and homiletic texts associated with Wulfstan were hortatory without expressed penalties. I conclude tentatively that the effort to impose sexual taboos on coparenthood was Wulfstan's campaign, which might not have had much resonance among his contemporaries. The Anglo-Saxon godparent complex differed markedly from Continental versions in its late and restrained concern about the sexual conduct of spiritual kin.

CHAPTER 10

The Religious Duties of Godparents

If sponsorship had been only a liturgical detail, it would not be worth more than a cursory study. But it was in fact the occasion to create important religious and social relationships, which have endured in Orthodox and Latin Christianity from the sixth century to the present. Spiritual kin probably regarded all their obligations as part of a unity, but for conceptual clarity, I shall distinguish the "religious" from the "social," leaving the latter for the next chapter.

Catechumenal sponsors helped the adult convert or infant to begin the transition from Satan's power to that of Christ. Baptismal sponsors assisted in baptismal rebirth, especially for infants, whom they carried and received from the font and on whose behalf they renounced Satan and assented to the Creed. Confirmation sponsors "held the person before the bishop's hand" so that he or she would be strengthened by the seven gifts of the Holy Spirit. After each ceremony, the godparents could have an enduring personal bond with their godchildren, although that did not always happen. Factors such as the premature death of one party or the physical distance between them must often have prevented the transformation of a liturgical bond into a personal one. But a personal bond was the ideal outcome of a sponsorship and it was often realized in practice.

In the Frankish kingdom during the ninth century the baptismal liturgy was thoroughly revised, probably to remove the incoherence introduced by infant baptism and generations of liturgical compiling.[1] The revised liturgy made the sponsor the central lay actor in baptism. In all the actions per-

1. Lynch, *Godparents,* pp. 285–304.

formed and words uttered on behalf of the child, the sponsor replaced parents and clergy, who had been active in the rituals represented in such texts as the seventh-century *Ordo Romanus XI*. The Frankish reformers also laid renewed stress on the religious role of the sponsor in the years after the baptism. Early medieval churchmen, especially Caesarius of Arles, had given godparents the duty of teaching their godchildren the basics of the faith to which they had assented on their behalf. Caesarius addressed the sponsors in his congregation thus.

> Remember the Creed and the Lord's Prayer yourself, and teach them to your children. I do not know with what boldness a man says he is a Christian, if he refuses to learn the few lines of the Creed and the Lord's Prayer. Remember that you stood as surety before God for the sons you received in baptism, so always reprove and rebuke those whom you adopted at the font just as you do those who were born of you, so that they may live chastely, justly, and soberly. You yourself should live in such a way that, if your children want to imitate you, they will not burn with you in the fire but together with you obtain eternal rewards.[2]

In another sermon he warned sponsors: "Dearest brethren, be aware that you are guarantors before God for those infants whom you took in baptism. Therefore always strive to warn and correct them so that they may live chastely and soberly. Before everything else, show them the Creed and the Lord's Prayer; don't summon them to good deeds by words alone but also by examples."[3]

But in the seventh and eighth centuries, that duty to teach had been neglected or forgotten. The ninth-century Frankish reformers, who looked to the past for their inspiration, placed renewed insistence on the duty of godparents to carry out basic religious instruction, which necessarily took place years after the infant's baptism. Frankish councils, capitularies, sermons, and penitential manuals told godparents repeatedly that they were responsible, along with natural parents, for the basic religious education of their godchildren, which in practice meant teaching them the Creed and the Pater Noster.[4]

2. Caesarius of Arles, *Sermo* 13.2, *CCSL* 103, p. 64. See also Eligius of Noyon, *Predicacio,* cc. 2, 5, 6, pp. 751–53; and Pirminius, *Dicta abbatis Pirminii de singulis libris canonicis scarapsus,* c. 32, in *Der heilige Pirmin und sein Pastoralbüchlein,* ed. G. Jecker and trans. into German by Ursmar Engelmann (Sigmaringen, 1976), p. 76.
3. Caesarius, *Sermo* 229.6, *CCSL* 104, p. 910. This sermon was known in Anglo-Saxon England; see Trahern, "Caesarius of Arles," pp. 117–8.
4. Lynch, *Godparents,* pp. 303–32.

The prominence of the Creed and the Pater Noster in Christian life was very ancient. During the fourth and fifth centuries, those who were actively preparing for baptism, the *competentes,* were told for the first time the exact words of the Creed, and sometimes those of the Pater Noster, in a ceremony called the *traditio* ("the handing over"). After they had memorized the prayer(s), they were required to recite the Creed or both prayers from memory on a Sunday late in Lent, in a ceremony called the *redditio* ("the giving back").[5] When infants predominated at baptism, these ceremonies could have disappeared, but in so conservative a practice as liturgy, that was unacceptable. For instance, the *Ordo Romanus XI* retained the rituals by having an acolyte perform the *traditio* of the Creed and a priest receive from him the *redditio.*[6]

The Frankish reformers breathed new life into the ancient tradition, stressing the need for every layperson to know the Creed, which told Christians what to believe, and the Pater Noster, which told them what to ask from God. Those prayers were central to the pastoral efforts of the Frankish church and were explained in numerous sermons and tracts.[7] They became a nodal point of interaction between laypeople and their priests. Laypeople might be required to recite the prayers before confession or communion. They were encouraged to recite the prayers on their deathbeds, perhaps as a precondition for Christian burial. The prayers even entered christianized folklore, as a way to displace pagan incantations: they were recited when gathering medicinal herbs or when setting out on a journey.[8] Most people, baptized very young, could not learn the Creed and Pa-

5. E. J. Yarnold, "Initiation: The Fourth and Fifth Centuries," in *The Study of Liturgy,* rev. ed. Cheslyn Jones, Geoffrey Wainwright, Edward Yarnold, and Paul Bradshaw (New York, 1992), pp. 133–34.

6. *Ordo Romanus XI,* c. 62 (*traditio* of the creed) and c. 82 and c. 86 (*redditio* of the creed) in *Les ordines* 2:434 and 443. A priest performed the *traditio* and explanation of the Lord's Prayer, c. 69 (ibid., pp. 437–40); there was no *redditio* of the Lord's Prayer in *Ordo Romanus XI.*

7. We shall know much more about Carolingian commentaries on the creed and the Lord's Prayer when Susan Keefe of Duke University has published her studies of both topics.

8. Regino of Prüm, *Libri duo de synodalibus causis et disciplinis ecclesiasticis,* 1.275, ed. F. G. A. Wasserschleben (Leipzig, 1840), p. 128: recite the two prayers at Lenten confession and before communion; *Vita Hucberti episcopi Traiectensis,* c. 14, ed. Wilhelm Levison, *MGH SRM* 6 (Hanover, 1913), p. 491: Bishop Hucbert recited *Credo* and *Pater Noster* on his deathbed; *Homilia de sacrilegiis,* 8.27, in *Eine Augustin fälschlich beilegte Homilia de sacrilegiis,* ed. C. P. Caspari (Christiania, 1886), p. 16, recommended the sign of the cross and recitation of creed and Lord's Prayer as substitutes for pagan forms of augury before beginning a journey. See also Ælfric, *On Auguries,* in *Ælfric's Lives of Saints,* 2:370, who also recommended the singing of the *pater noster* and *credo* by one who was setting out on a journey. *Lacnunga,* paragraph 183, in *Anglo-Saxon Magic and Medicine,* ed. J. H. G. Grattan and C. Singer (London, 1952), pp. 196–97, gave instructions for a cure that included a virgin singing the *credo* and the *pater noster* over a cup of spring water. R. A. Banks, "A Study of the Old English Versions of the Lord's Prayer, the Creeds, the Gloria, and Some Prayers Found in British Museum Ms. Cotton Galba A. XIV, Together

ter Noster. Parents and godparents were encouraged to teach the prayers to their children when they reached an appropriate age, so that they would have personal knowledge of the prayers "given" to them as infants.

Godparents had to know the prayers in order to teach them, but in the pre-Carolingian period there had been no test of that knowledge. The Frankish reformers took an important step when they made memorization of the Creed and the Pater Noster a requirement to sponsor at baptism and confirmation. A remarkable document, which survives in a compilation associated with Bishop Ghaerbald of Liège (785/87–809), demonstrates that the requirement was not just theoretical. Sometime between 802 and 806, Emperor Charlemagne was present at Liège for baptism *in die apparitionis Domini,* probably Epiphany. Much to the consternation of participants, he demanded that those who wanted to sponsor recite in his presence the Apostles' Creed and the Pater Noster. Those who could not—and apparently there were many—were turned away until they remedied their deficiency. Charlemagne subsequently sent a stern letter on the episode to Bishop Ghaerbald, who in turn sent a pastoral letter to the clergy of his diocese, ordering them to require the recitation of the prayers before allowing anyone to sponsor.[9]

Many Frankish capitularies, bishops' statutes, and conciliar canons required every sponsor to recite the Creed and the Pater Noster to the baptizing bishop or priest as a condition of sponsoring.[10] In his synodal book, composed about 906, Regino of Prüm summarized more than a century of Frankish legislation on the centrality of the Creed and the Pater Noster and their direct link to sponsorship.

> That every priest teach or cause to be taught to all his parishioners the Creed and the Lord's Prayer. And when they come to confession during Lent, he should have these prayers recited from memory by each person; nor should he give holy communion to anyone before that person knows how to say these [prayers] by heart, because without a knowledge of them, no one can be saved. In one [the Creed] the Christian faith and belief is contained; in the other [the Lord's Prayer] is expressed that which we ought to pray for and seek from God. The Lord demonstrated that no one can be saved with-

---

with a New Examination of the Place of the Liturgy in the Literature of Anglo-Saxon Magic and Medicine" (Ph.D., University of London, 1968), pp. 384–410, surveyed magical/medical uses of creeds and the *pater noster* among the Anglo-Saxons.

9. Ghaerbald of Liège, *Die Kapitulariensammlung Bischof Ghaerbalds von Lüttich,* ed. Wilhelm A. Eckhardt, Germanenrechte, Neue Folge, Deutschrechtliches Archiv 5 (Göttingen, 1955), pp. 113–14. Ghaerbald's letter to his flock is printed in *Die Kapitulariensammlung,* pp. 106–12. The episode is treated in Lynch, *Godparents,* pp. 322–26.

10. Lynch, *Godparents,* pp. 285–332.

> out faith, when he said "He who shall have believed and is baptized will be saved" [Mark 16:16]. But no one can believe what he does not know and has not heard. For Paul says "How will they believe him, whom they have not heard?" [Rom. 10:14] Faith [held] only in the heart is not sufficient, unless it is also expressed in words, as the same Apostle is witness. "In the heart," he says, "it is believed to justice, by the mouth confession is made for salvation." [Rom. 10:10] Because these [prayers] are very brief, there is no person of such thickness of intelligence or feebleness of intellect, and there is no one so lazy and barbaric, that he can not learn these and say them in common [i.e., vernacular] words. The [prayers] are so great that he who is fully able to grasp their meaning may believe that it is enough for him to gain unending salvation.

Regino was faithful to Frankish developments when he required that in addition to reciting the prayers before they could sponsor, godparents also had a specific duty to teach them to their godchildren when the latter reached an appropriate age: "That too must be observed, that no one may receive an infant in baptism from the holy font before he recites that same Creed and Lord's Prayer before the priest; and the priest should announce to all godfathers that they are obligated to their godchildren to teach these prayers when they come to the age of reason."[11]

Regino did not mention sponsors at confirmation, who were sometimes required to know the prayers but never told to teach their godchildren, which was the special task of baptismal godparents. Bishop Haito of Basel (802–823) wanted priests to remind godparents of their enduring responsibility for the religious instruction of their godchildren, in order to fulfill the pact they had made at baptism:

> Let the priests announce to the people that they are guarantors for the spiritual sons and daughters whom they received in baptism, and they are the ones who promised faith and on their behalf when they renounced the devil, to whom they [the infants] were enslaved before. And therefore let them have them in their safe-keeping until they are adults and until they have explained and handed on to them the promise of their faith and renunciation. And that which they [sponsors] promised for them [the godchildren], they should demand from them fully.[12]

11. Regino of Prüm, *Libri duo,* 1.275, pp. 128–29. Regino identified this as canon 20 of an otherwise unknown Council of Reims.
12. Haito of Basel, *Capitula,* c. 25, ed. Peter Brommer, *MGH Capitula episcoporum* 1 (Hanover, 1984), p. 219. See also *Admonitio synodalis,* c. 79, in "Une 'Admonitio synodalis' de l'époque carolingienne: Etude critique et édition," ed. Robert Amiet, *Mediaeval Studies* 26 (1964), p. 64: "Pa-

The Creed and the Lord's Prayer in Anglo-Saxon England

The traditional stress on the Apostles' Creed and the Lord's Prayer as basic knowledge for all lay people is attested in Anglo-Saxon England from at least the early eighth century. In a letter written 5 November 734, Bede admonished Archbishop Egbert of York:

> . . . I think that you ought before everything else to see to it with all urgency that you endeavor to impress deeply on the memory of all under your rule the Catholic faith which is contained in the Apostles' Creed and the Lord's Prayer, which the text of the holy gospel teaches us. Indeed it is most certain that all who have studied the Latin language have also learnt these well; but make the ignorant people—that is, those who are acquainted with no language but their own—say them in their own language and repeat them assiduously. This ought to be done, not only in the case of laymen, that is, those still leading a secular life, but also of those clerics and monks who are ignorant of the Latin language. . . . On this account I have myself often given to many ignorant priests both of these, the Creed and the Lord's Prayer, translated into the English language.[13]

Bede did not refer to sponsors in this text, probably because the demand that sponsors personally memorize the prayers and then teach them to their godchildren had not yet reached Anglo-Saxon England from the continent. But within twenty years of Bede's death, the situation had begun to change.

The Council of Clofesho (747)

In 747, at an unidentified place called Clofesho, Archbishop Cuthbert of Canterbury met with twelve bishops, many priests and lesser clergy, as well as King Æthelbald of Mercia (716–757), and other laypeople.[14] Pope

trini filiolis suis simbolum et orationem dominicam insinuent, aut insinuari faciant"; Boniface, [pseudo-], *Sermo XV,* c. 4, *PL* 89, col. 870: "Orationem dominicam et Symbolum tenete, et filiis vestris et filiolis vestris, quorum in baptismo fidejussores exstitisse." See also the vernacular *Exhortatio ad plebem Christianam,* in *Denkmäler deutscher Poesie und Prosa aus dem VIII–XII Jahrhundert,* vol. 1, ed. K. Müllenhoff and W. Scherer (Berlin, 1892); Ghaerbald of Liège, *Second Diocesan Statute,* c. 3, p. 26: "Ut, si patrini vel matrinae, qui infantes de fonte suscipiunt sive masculos sive feminas, si ipsum symbolum et orationem dominicam sciunt, et filios et filias suas spiritales, quos et quas de fonte susceperunt, pleniter instructos habeant de fide, de qua pro eis fideiussores exstiterint."

13. Bede, *Epistola ad Ecgbertum,* c. 5, 1:408–9, and trans. in *EHD,* p. 801.

14. I am indebted to the thorough treatment of the Council of Clofesho in Cubitt, *Anglo-Saxon Church Councils* pp. 99–152. See also Catherine Cubitt, "Pastoral Care and Conciliar Canons:

Zachary (741–752) had requested the meeting. To open the proceedings, Zachary's letter (Jaffé-Wattenbach 2279) was read aloud in Latin and rendered into the vernacular. The letter does not survive, but the account of the council noted that it filled two pages (*kartae*). This account reported that the pope ordered Anglo-Saxons of different statuses and professions to do certain unspecified things, presumably observe the canons he sent. All who remained in their "pertinacious wickedness" were threatened with anathema.[15]

The Council of Clofesho promulgated thirty canons, which Catherine Cubitt has described as "the single most important and detailed source on pastoral care in England before the tenth and eleventh centuries."[16] The council attempted to impose order and organize pastoral care in a church that had emerged no more than two generations earlier from a missionary situation.[17] The canons echo reformist ideas being promoted by Archbishop Boniface and others in Frankish Gaul and Rome, but they are not a mere copy of any surviving Roman or Frankish canons.[18] In fact, nothing so sophisticated survives from the Frankish church until Charlemagne issued the *Admonitio generalis* (789) more than forty years later.[19] Cubitt argued convincingly that the canons of Clofesho were formulated at least in part to meet actual conditions in the Anglo-Saxon church south of the Humber River.[20]

Canon 10 specified what priests should know. It ordered that, like all Christians, they should know the words of the Creed and the Lord's Prayer. In addition, their occupation as clergy required knowledge of the words of the mass, baptism, and other ecclesiastical offices. They should also know how to explain in the vernacular, presumably to the laity and the clergy who knew no Latin, both the meaning of the Latin words and their spiritual significance.

Canon 11 continued the listing of priests' duties, with a stress on what they should teach the laity, and singled out the importance of the Creed and

---

The Provisions of the 747 Council of Clofesho," in *Pastoral Care before the Parish*, ed. John Blair and Richard Sharpe (Leicester, 1992); and Hanna Vollrath, *Die Synoden Englands bis 1066* (Paderborn, 1985), pp. 141–61.

15. Council of Clofesho *Prooemium*, in *Councils and Ecclesiastical Documents Relating to Great Britain and Ireland*, ed. Arthur Haddan and William Stubbs (Oxford, 1878), 3:362–63.

16. Cubitt, "Pastoral Care," p. 194.

17. Cubitt, *Anglo-Saxon Church Councils*, pp. 113–22.

18. On Boniface's influence on the canons, see the careful analysis in ibid., pp. 102–10.

19. On the *Admonitio generalis*, see Rosamond McKitterick, *The Frankish Church and the Carolingian Reforms*, 789–895 (London, 1977), pp. 1–44. The *Admonitio generalis* is edited in *Capitularia regum Francorum*, 1: pp. 52–62.

20. Cubitt, *Anglo-Saxon Church Councils*, pp. 110–13.

the role of baptismal sponsors: "May the priests also diligently teach them the Creed so that they may know what to believe, what they ought to hope for. *Let them* [the priests] *hand over the creed to infants or to those who wish to receive them in baptism, and may they teach them to say the renunciation of the devil's pomps, auguries and divinations, and after these things may they carefully instruct them to profess the proper professions* [of faith]" (my italics).[21]

This canon's formulation is unusual in that it did not mention the Lord's Prayer, which was, however, mentioned in Canon 10 as required of both clergy and laity. But Canon 11 embodied both the traditional view, that laypeople ought to know the Creed, and also the relatively new view, that sponsors were particularly obliged to know it. The canon instructed the priests to teach the Creed to the infants or, more realistically, to those who wished to receive the children in baptism. It also instructed them to teach the infants or the sponsors to renounce the devil's pomps, auguries, and divinations and to profess the faith, perhaps in the form of the Creed.

The core of the sponsor's verbal participation in baptism was the renunciation of Satan and the profession of faith. But unlike later Frankish and Anglo-Saxon texts, Canon 11 did not require sponsors to teach the Creed to their godchildren at a later date. The simplest explanation for the provisions of Canon 11 may be that there could be no proper baptism unless the sponsor for an infant was able to recite the renunciation of Satan and the profession of faith at the proper moments in the ceremony. Hence the priest had to teach the sponsors those words, perhaps on the very day of the baptism. The subsequent teaching of godchildren by godparents was not yet proposed.

Canon 10 of Clofesho instructed priests to be able to explain important prayers in the vernacular. Although Canon 11 does not say so, I assume that the words of the baptismal renunciations and professions could be taught in the vernacular to people who did not know Latin. Bede wrote to Archbishop Egbert that he gave vernacular translations of the Creed and Lord's Prayer to ignorant priests. Although no early Old English version of the baptismal renunciation and profession of faith survives, there are late-eighth- or ninth-century translations of the baptismal vows in the Saxon and Frankish languages, and some Frankish bishops explicitly allowed laypeople to memorize the basic prayers in the vernacular.[22] In the late

21. Council of Clovesho, c. 11, in *Councils and Ecclesiastical Documents,* 3:366: "symbolum quoque eis diligenter insinuant, ut intelligant quid credere, quid sperare debeant, infantibusque illud vel eis, qui eos in Baptismate suscipere voluerint, tradant, abrenuntiationemque doceant diabolicis pompis atque augoris, divinationibusque dicere, et post hacc legitimas professiones profiteri solerter instruant."

22. J. Knight Bostock, *A Handbook on Old High German Literature,* 2d ed. K. C. King and D. R. McLintock (Oxford, 1976), pp. 109–10. On explicit references to memorization in the vernacular,

tenth or early eleventh century, Ælfric paraphrased in Old English the words of the baptismal ceremony for his adult hearers who, when they had been baptized years before, labored under the double burden of being infants in a ceremony conducted in Latin.[23]

The Council of Clofesho predated the Carolingian reform of the baptismal liturgy. Canons 10 and 11 do not embody the tight connection between knowledge of the two prayers and the right to be a sponsor, which Charlemagne would stress to Ghaerbald of Liège about sixty years later. But the canons were responding to the same problems that troubled the Frankish reformers: the desire that all Christians know the Creed and the Lord's Prayer and the special responsibility of sponsors to know them in order to participate in the liturgy of baptism.

The Legatine Councils of 786

Zachary's letter of 746/47 was in the tradition of his predecessors, who wrote occasionally to Anglo-Saxon prelates and kings. It was rare, however, for papal representatives to come to England. Since the arrival of Augustine and his companions in the late sixth and early seventh centuries, the only known papal representatives were Archbishop Theodore and Abbot Hadrian, who arrived in 669, and John the Archcantor, who attended the council of Hæthfeld in 679.[24] But in 786, Pope Hadrian I (772–795) dispatched to England Bishop Theophylact of Todi and Bishop George of Ostia, who had also been bishop of Amiens since 768. A Frankish abbot named Wigbod, whom Charlemagne sent, accompanied them. Alcuin joined them in England. Although the legates represented Pope Hadrian, three of the participants in the proceedings—Bishop George, Abbot Wigbod, and Alcuin—were closely connected to the Carolingian court and were familiar with the issues of Frankish reform. Alcuin was in fact a leading architect of the Carolingian reforms.[25] The legates summoned two councils, which issued canons presenting a more "modern" description of sponsors' duties than that of the Council of Clofesho.[26]

---

see Herard of Tours, *Capitula*, c. 55, *PL* 121, col. 768: "Ut nemo a sacro fonte aliquem suscipiat, nisi orationem dominicam et symbolum juxta linguam suam et intellectum teneat"; Haito of Basel, *Capitula*, c. 2, p. 210: all should learn the prayers "tam latine quam barbarice, ut, quod ore profitentur, corde credatur et intellegatur." See also Boniface, [Pseudo-] *Capitula*, c. 27, *PL* 89, cols. 822–23.

23. Ælfric, *Sermo in Aepiphania Domini*, in *Ælfric's Catholic Homilies*, pp. 26–27.

24. Cubitt, *Anglo-Saxon Church Councils*, pp. 39–40.

25. On George, Theophylact, and Wigbod, see ibid. pp. 153–56.

26. On the legatine councils of 786, see ibid. pp. 153–90; also Frank M. Stenton, *Anglo-Saxon England*, 3d ed. (Oxford, 1971), pp. 215–17, and Vollrath, *Die Synoden Englands*, pp. 162–76.

Bishop George's report to Pope Hadrian survives. He wrote that he and Theophylact were the first papal envoys to the Anglo-Saxons since the time of Augustine, more than 180 years earlier.[27] The legates' mission was "to root out weeds from the field planted by Pope Gregory through the mouth of the holy Augustine" and to reinforce the unity of the Anglo-Saxon church with the Roman church. The legates brought letters from Pope Hadrian and *saluberrima statuta,* which were perhaps a canonical collection. In a council attended by the dominant Anglo-Saxon king, Offa of Mercia (757–796), and King Cynewulf of the West Saxons (757–786), the pope's letters were read aloud. They urged the kings to abandon unspecified vices, which the kings promised to do. After this meeting, the legates separated. Theophylact went to the Mercian kingdom and "the parts of Britain," probably the Welsh region. George went to Northumbria, accompanied by the Frankish abbot Wigbod.

George reported to Hadrian that in the course of his consultations in Northumbria, he learned of "not insignificant vices which had to be corrected."[28] At his request, King Ælfwald of Northumbria (779–788) summoned a council at which twenty canons were formulated, ten directed to the clergy and ten to the laity. Alcuin was present at the Northumbrian council, and Cubitt argued in detail that "ideological, stylistic and textual links" between the writings of Alcuin and the legatine canons suggest that Alcuin played a part in their formulation.[29] George and Alcuin then went south to a council in Mercia, where they presented the same canons for approval. George reported that at the Mercian council the canons were read in Latin and English (*theodisce*—the earliest use of that term for the Germanic languages). King Offa, his nobles, and the bishops accepted the canons, and each expressed his approval with an oath in the hands of the legate, who was a proxy for the pope, and by signing the document containing the canons.[30]

George included in his report to Hadrian the canons that had been enacted in the two councils. Canon 2 quite traditionally required every layperson to know the Creed and the Lord's Prayer, but in addition it tied such knowledge closely to baptismal sponsorship. It required those who wanted to sponsor to know the prayers and to teach them to their godchil-

27. George, Bishop of Ostia, to Pope Hadrian I, p. 21; the text is also in *Councils and Ecclesiastical Documents,* 3:448–49.

28. George to Hadrian, p. 21.

29. Cubitt, *Anglo-Saxon Church Councils,* pp. 164–84.

30. George to Hadrian, p. 28. Patrick Wormald, "In Search of Offa's 'Law-Code,'" in *People and Places in Northern Europe: Essays in Honour of Peter Hayes Sawyer,* ed. Ian Wood and Niels Lund (Woodbridge, England, 1991), pp. 25–45, argued that the canons of the Mercian council might be the "law code of Offa" to which King Alfred referred in the prologue to his laws.

dren. To justify the sponsor's duty to teach, Canon 2 invoked the contractual view of baptism, in which the sponsors acted as guarantors for the pact with God made on behalf of the infants. The sponsor's subsequent teaching helped him or her to fulfill that contract:

> In the second chapter, we taught that baptism should be carried out according to the canonical statutes, and not at another time unless for a major necessity. [We taught] that all people should know the Creed and the Lord's Prayer. [We taught] that those who receive little children from the holy font and respond for those not speaking—whether it is the renunciation of Satan, of his works, and pomps, or the expression of belief—should know that they are the guarantors (*fideiussores*) to the Lord for the little children because of the promise they made. [We taught] that when the children come to the perfection of age, those [who received and promised for them] should teach them the previously mentioned Lord's Prayer and Creed, because unless they do it, it will be strictly demanded from them, because a promise was made to God on behalf of those who did not speak. We ordered the whole of the people to keep this in memory.[31]

In the context of eighth-century reforms, this is the earliest comprehensive statement of the sponsor's obligations to keep his promise for the child by subsequently teaching the prayers that made up the content of the contract to which the sponsor had agreed on the child's behalf.

Hanna Vollrath argued that the two legatine councils of 786 were to a large degree an exercise of papal power: the legates proposed canons they brought with them, which kings and bishops simply accepted. In her view, the canons tell us almost nothing about conditions in England because the legates saw every peculiarity in the Anglo-Saxon church as a problem. Catherine Cubitt argued convincingly to the contrary that the canons should be understood in the Northumbrian context in which they were formulated as well as in the Mercian context in which they were subsequently adopted.[32] As was true of virtually every church council, some of the legatine canons were general in nature or reiterated universal features of

31. George to Hadrian, p. 21: "Secundo capitulo docuimus, ut baptismus secundum canonica statuta exerceatur et non alio tempore, nisi pro magna necessitate, et ut omnes generaliter symbolum et orationem dominicam sciant. Et illi, qui parvulos de sacro fonte suscipiunt et pro non loquentibus respondent abrenuntiationem satanae et operum ac pomparum eius seu fidei credulitatem, sciant se fideiussores ipsorum esse ad Deum pro ipsa sponsione, ut dum ad perfectionem aetatis venerint, doceant ipsos predictam dominicam orationem et symbolum, quia nisi fecerint, districte ab eis exigetur, quod pro non loquentibus Deo promittitur. Ideo generaliter omni vulgo precipimus hoc memorie commandari."

32. Vollrath, *Die Synoden Englands,* p. 175; Cubitt, *Anglo-Saxon Church Councils,* pp. 185–87.

the canon law. Bishop George wrote, however, that before the canons were formulated, he held discussions in Northumbria and heard about significant local problems. He emphasized that in Mercia the canons were explained orally to the king, bishops, and notable secular and ecclesiastical persons.[33] Several of the canons seem quite specific to the Anglo-Saxon situation. For instance, the Anglo-Saxons had a penchant for violence within and between royal houses. Canon 12 forbade the killing of kings, which might be ironic or prophetic in light of the fact that King Cynewulf, who met with the legates when they arrived, was killed in the same year, 786.[34] Canon 16 forbade the children of prostitutes—perhaps in fact concubines[35]—to receive hereditary rights, and the children of nuns were declared illegitimate, both of which were unusual provisions, perhaps unprecedented. Canon 19 forbade the wearing of pagan clothing and such pagan practices as the mutilation of horses by cropping their ears, tails, and noses; the eating of horsemeat; and the use of *sortes,* which was the casting of lots to decide litigation or to foretell the future.[36] Canon 2 on the knowledge and duties of sponsors may also represent an attempt to correct actual situations. It has some links to Canon 11 of the council of Clofesho, thirty-nine years earlier, but also reflects Frankish concerns expressed in roughly contemporary councils and other Continental texts.[37]

Because of papal and Frankish initiatives, the Anglo-Saxon church in the later eighth century was introduced to the new configuration of two traditional practices. Baptismal sponsors were required to memorize the Creed and the Lord's Prayer as a precondition for sponsoring, and they were warned to teach the prayers to their godchildren when the latter were old enough to understand.

In the late tenth and eleventh centuries, another wave of Frankish influence was reflected in Anglo-Saxon law codes and sermons that disseminated the developed Carolingian view of the religious duties of sponsors. Abbot Ælfric emphasized the cooperation of the sponsor and parents in expressing a child's belief and acting as his or her guarantor at baptism. His division of duties between parents and a godparent is an archaic feature of Anglo-Saxon baptismal practice:

33. George to Hadrian, p. 21: "Sed audientibus nobis relatum est, quod reliqua vicia non minima necessaria erant ad corrigendum. . . . Scripsimus namque capitulare de singulis rebus et per ordinem cuncta disserentes auribus illorum protulimus."
34. *ASC(A)*, s.a. 755 (recte 757), pp. 36–38.
35. Ross, "Concubinage in Anglo-Saxon England," pp. 27–28.
36. Canon 19, in *Alcuini sive Albini epistolae,* p. 27.
37. Cubitt, *Anglo-Saxon Church Councils,* pp. 159–60. Lynch, *Godparents,* pp. 305–19, treated eighth-century Frankish efforts to promote knowledge of the creed and the Lord's Prayer.

> Let us be mindful what we promised to God at our baptism. Now you say, "What did I promise, when I was a child and could not speak?" We read in the old accounts that the holy teachers taught the true belief to the men who converted to Christianity and they asked them whether they would renounce the devil and believe in God. They promised that they would do so and were then baptized in the holy font, with that promise. They baptized the unspeaking child through the belief of the father and the mother, and the godfather was the child's guarantor and security with God (*þa unsprecendan cild hi fullodon ðurh geleafan þæs fæder, and ðære meder. and se godfæder wæs þæs cildes forspreca. and borh wið god*) that the child would hold Christianity according to God's teaching, [they did so] because the saying which Christ said is so fearful, that no unbaptized person shall come to the eternal life. Now this ordinance stands in God's church, that one baptizes unspeaking children and they shall be saved through the belief of other men just as they were damned through the sin of other men. Because there is doubt whether the child will survive until it may answer the teacher with belief. . . . The mass-priest asks the child and says, "Do you renounce the devil?" Then the godfather answers in the words of the child and says, "I renounce the devil." Then he asks again, "Do you renounce all his works?" He says, "I do renounce." He asks a third time, "Do you renounce all his pomps?" He says, "I renounce." Then he has renounced in these three sentences the devil and all sins. Then he [the mass-priest] asks again, "Do you believe in the holy Trinity and true Unity?" He answers, "I believe." The servant of God inquires then again, "Do you believe that we shall all rise with our bodies on doomsday to meet Christ and that then everyone will receive recompense of all his deeds, such as he ever merited while living?" He answers, "I believe." And the priest baptizes the child with this belief. The child grows and goes forth and knows nothing of this belief. For that reason there is now a great need for everyone that he learn from his teacher how he must hold his Christianity with true belief, and how he may reject the devil and hell pains and gain the eternal life and eternal happiness with God.[38]

In some sermons that are anonymous or of doubtful attribution, the same themes were repeated. Everyone should know the Creed and Pater Noster; those who refused to learn them were unfit to sponsor, to receive communion, or to be buried in consecrated ground.[39] The godparents

38. Ælfric, *Sermo in Aepiphania,* in *Ælfric's Catholic Homilies,* pp. 26–27.

39. Napier Homily 58, in Napier, *Wulfstan,* p. 302: one who is unwilling to learn the prayers "ne he nah mid rihte æniges mannes æt fulluhte to onfenne ne æt bisceopes handum . . . ne he rihtlice ne bið husles wurðe . . . ne furðon clænes legeres æfter his forðsiðe." See also Napier Homily 59, ibid., p. 307.

must teach the prayers as part of their duty to instruct and guide their godchild.[40] One homilist encouraged his audience to teach early: "and as soon as the child can speak, teach him at once before all other things his Pater Noster and Creed, and that he know how to bless himself properly."[41]

Archbishop Wulfstan was especially interested in the matter, to which he returned often in sermons, tracts, and laws, in which he laid out the legal and moral obligation for the sponsor to know and to teach the Creed and Pater Noster. In one sermon, he encouraged his hearers to "remember what we promised when we received baptism or those who were our guarantors (*foresprecan*) at baptism. That is, that we would always love God and believe in Him and keep his commands and shun the devil and avoid his evil teaching. One promises this for each of those who receives baptism. Although the child may not speak on account of youth when one baptizes it, his friends (*freonda*) offer a promise for him just as if he himself should speak."[42] He went on to explain to his audience the content of the promises they or their sponsors made, under the headings of *credo* ("I believe") and *abrenuntio* ("I renounce"). In another sermon, he encouraged the godfather to love and teach and to restrain his godchild from sin. He also warned adults to remember the Pater Noster and the Creed and to teach their children with correct belief.[43] In his *Institutes of Polity,* he forbade anyone who did not know the prayers to receive another person at baptism or at confirmation, until he learned them.[44] In a third homily, he waxed eloquent on the centrality of the Creed and Lord's Prayer:

> But let us understand what those two words mean, *abrenuntio* and *credo,* which one is accustomed [to use] at the baptismal service. *Abrenuntio,* that is in English, I renounce always henceforth the devil's company. *Credo,* that is in English, I believe in God Almighty who created and made all things. We

40. Napier Homily 24, in *ibid.,* p. 121, a manuscript variant printed in apparatus: the person who received the child should "tæcen him pater noster and credan." See also Brotanek Homily 2, in Brotanek, *Texte und Untersuchungen,* p. 25: "and toforan eallum oðrum ðingum ðæt hi him geswutelian and getæcen credan and pater noster. forðamðe nan man ne mæg beon rihtlice geleaffull butun he ðæt cunne. forðamðe he sceal on ðam credan his rihtan geleafan gode andettan and on ðam paternostre him æt gode are biddan ægðer ðyses lifes, ge ec ðæs toweardan."

41. Napier Homily 58, in Napier, *Wulfstan,* p. 301: "and swa raðe, swa ðæt cild mage sprecan, tæce man him sona eallra ðinga ærest his paternr and his credan, and ðæt hit cunne hit sylf bletsjan rihtlice."

42. Wulfstan, *Homily* 13, pp. 226–27.

43. Wulfstan, *Homily 10c,* p. 209: "Godfæder his godbearn lufie and lære and unrihtes styre. Pater noster and credan mymerian ða yldran and tæcen heora gingran mid rihtan geleafan."

44. Wulfstan, *Institutes of Polity,* c. 22, p. 186: "forðam he ne bið wel cristen, ðe ðæt geleornian nele, ne he nah mid rihte oðres mannes to onfonne æt fulluhte ne æt biscopes handa, se ðe ðæt ne cann, ær he hit geleornige."

ought not to be false about these, but let us do what is necessary for us, fulfill them eagerly. And although the child be so young that it cannot speak when it is baptized, his friends offer a promise for him entirely as if the child itself speaks. Unless, when it is of age, the child carries out all that was promised to God for him in his youth, he may perish on his final day, if he neglected God's law, because he had the age and the understanding that he might observe God's law. Therefore parents among the Christian people have a great need to beget their youngsters for God and to wean them from the devil. Consequently everything which they permit of sin to their children, all that will be contrary to that which they promised to God when they obtained baptism for them. They must suffer stiff punishment according to God's judgment unless they atone for that which they could have done. Every Christian man has great need that he always have right belief in God and that he learn the understanding of his baptism and always rightly hold that and eagerly encourage his children to the same. And as soon as the child can say anything, teach him immediately before everything else the Lord's Prayer and creed: then it must always henceforth go better for him. And also I pray and command in God's name, if any Christian man who is of age is so neglectful that he does not know them, may he learn them eagerly, and it should not cause shame to any man because of his age, but do what is necessary for him, help himself, because he is not a good Christian who is unwilling to learn them. He who does not know them does not have any right to receive any man at baptism or at the bishop's hand, until he learns them, nor is he rightly worthy of the Eucharist or of burial in consecrated ground, he who while alive is unwilling to learn them, at least in English, unless he is able to do so in Latin.[45]

The Vernacular Creed and Lord's Prayer

The overwhelming majority of laypeople in early medieval Europe were nonliterate both in Latin and in their native tongue; as Bede noted, even some clergy and monks were illiterate in Latin. If such people were really to know the Creed and the Lord's Prayer, vernacular translations had to be made, as Wulfstan suggested in the homily quoted above. The Anglo-Saxons were pioneers in the effort to make religious knowledge accessible to the people in their own language. From early in its history, the Anglo-Saxon church used the vernacular language to convey religious and legal materials. One need only think of the shepherd Cædmon's biblical poems,

45. Wulfstan, *Homily* 8c (*Sermo de baptismate*) pp. 181–83.

the thousands of surviving lines of Old English religious poetry, Bede's translations of the Creed and Lord's Prayer and his translation of the opening chapters of the Gospel of John, left unfinished when he died, and the seventh-century vernacular law codes of Æthelberht, Ine, and Wihtred.

The Frankish church reformers, perhaps influenced by the eighth-century Anglo-Saxon missionaries, also occasionally used the people's languages to achieve their goal of wide dissemination of knowledge of the prayers. This was especially true in Germanic regions, where Latin prayers must have been incomprehensible to the illiterate Germanic laity.[46] At the Council of Tours (813), the bishops encouraged the translation of sermons into the vernacular: "Let each take care to translate these homilies clearly into the vulgar Roman or Germanic tongue so that everyone may understand more readily what is said in them."[47] Only scattered fragments of the Continental translators' efforts survive, but they are illuminating. There are eighth- and ninth-century translations, into various Continental Germanic dialects, of the Lord's Prayer, the Apostles' Creed, the Athanasian Creed, the baptismal vows themselves, and even one sermon on godparents.[48]

The Viking invasions and the accompanying disruption of church life in the ninth century apparently cut short Anglo-Saxon efforts to use the vernacular in religious teaching. In so far as the evidence shows, the translating seems to have stopped between the 830s and 890s, as did the copying of manuscripts in Latin and Old English.[49] During the political and religious recovery that began in the last decade of the ninth century, Anglo-Saxon churchmen restored ecclesiastical life in good part by turning for models to texts of Continental origin. Although many texts remained in Latin, Anglo-Saxons also revived the native tradition of teaching in the vernacular. During the tenth and eleventh centuries, known and anonymous Anglo-Saxon clerics drew on Continental Latin sources to

46. Werner Betz, "Karl der Grosse und die Lingua Theodisca," in *Karl der Grosse: Lebenswerk und Nachleben,* vol. 2, *Das geistige Leben,* ed. Bernhard Bischoff (Düsseldorf, 1965), emphasized the role of Charlemagne in the initial effort to translate the creed, Lord's Prayer, and other religious texts into Germanic languages. Francesco del Bono, "La letteratura catechetica di lingua tedesca," in *La conversione al cristianesimo nell'Europa dell'alto medioevo* (Spoleto, 1967), argued, however, that the extant vernacular religious texts are from the later ninth century and were often the result of local initiatives. McKitterick, *Frankish Church,* pp. 184–205, also stressed local initiatives.

47. Council of Tours (813), c. 17, in *Concilia aevi Karolini,* p. 288.

48. Bostock, *Handbook,* pp. 108–112.

49. David Dumville, "Liturgical Books from Late Anglo-Saxon England: A Review of Some Historical Problems," in *Liturgy and the Ecclesiastical History of Late Anglo-Saxon England* (Woodbridge, England, 1992), pp. 98–101.

produce a significant body of Old English sermons, saints' lives, and other ecclesiastical texts.[50]

The Anglo-Saxons were in fact more ambitious and sophisticated in their uses of the vernacular than their Continental contemporaries. In addition to elementary texts such as the Lord's Prayer and the Creed, important religious and historical works were translated from Latin into Old English. Translations attributed to King Alfred include Pope Gregory's *Pastoral Care,* Boethius's *Consolation of Philosophy,* and Augustine's *Soliloquies* and perhaps an incomplete translation of the psalter. Others translated as well. Bishop Wærferth of Worcester translated Pope Gregory's *Dialogues.* An unidentified person began the *Anglo-Saxon Chronicle* in the 890s. An unknown late-ninth-century scholar paraphrased Orosius's *Seven Books of History against the Pagans.* Another unknown scholar translated Bede's *History.*[51]

Anglo-Saxon laws, canons, and sermons picked up three basic themes from Frankish sources: the centrality of the Creed and the Lord's Prayer as the basic religious knowledge to be demanded of laypeople, the special obligation of sponsors at both baptism and confirmation to know the prayers, and the duty of baptismal sponsors to teach them to their godchildren. Bishop Theodulf of Orleans's *First Synodal Statute,* composed between 798 and 813, is especially significant for the introduction of the Frankish view of the godparents' religious duties. The Latin text of the statute was widely known in late Anglo-Saxon England, and there were at least two translations into Old English. The Old English translation of Chapter 22 is not a slavish rendering of the Latin version, but it makes the main points:

> All faithful men are to be warned in general, from the least to the greatest, that each man learn the Lord's Prayer and the Creed. They ought to be told that on those two texts the basis of the whole Christian faith rests. Unless a person can sing the two texts and believes just as it says therein and prays with them often, he can not be a good Christian. For it was laid down long ago that no one who does not know the Creed and Lord's prayer—that he must neither receive any man at the bishop's hand nor at baptism, nor must one baptize nor confirm him—unless he is not old enough to learn the aforementioned texts already.[52]

50. Milton McC. Gatch, *Preaching and Theology in Anglo-Saxon England: Ælfric and Wulfstan* (Toronto, 1977), pp. 25–59; Kathleen Greenfield, "Changing Emphases" Scragg, "Corpus of Vernacular Homilies."

51. On the translations of the later ninth century, see Stanley B. Greenfield and Daniel G. Calder, *A New Critical History of Old English Literature* (New York, 1986), pp. 38–67.

52. Theodulf of Orléans, *First Synodal Statute,* c. 22, p. 119. The Old English translations of Chapter 22 are edited in Hans Sauer, *Theodulfi Capitula in England* (Munich, 1978), p. 333:

Thus Theodulf forbade anyone to sponsor at baptism or confirmation who did not know the Creed and Lord's Prayer. He also forbade the ignorant to be baptized or confirmed, although as an unavoidable concession to infant baptism, he exempted from the ban those too young to memorize the prayers.

Ælfric may have used Theodulf's Chapter 22 in his pastoral letters. Wulfstan certainly used it on numerous occasions: in three of his sermons, in his *Canons of Edgar,* and in the laws of Æthelred II, which he helped to draft.[53] Indeed Wulfstan was a central figure in the introduction or reintroduction of a direct link between sponsorship and the key prayers, just as he was in the introduction of the ban on marriage between coparents. He composed the so-called *Canons of Edgar,* which Roger Fowler, the editor of the *Canons,* described as "a kind of *Pastoral Letter* addressed to the secular clergy, outlining their status, their standards of morality, and their responsibilities toward their flocks."[54] The canons, based on Carolingian models, followed Theodulf's Chapter 22 in presenting a clear statement of the centrality of the Creed and the Lord's Prayer and their connection with sponsorship at baptism and confirmation:

> 15. And it is right that every priest . . . announce everywhere in his parish that each child is to be baptized within seven days, and that no one is to remain too long unconfirmed (*unbiscopad*).
> 17. And it is right that every Christian man zealously accustom his children to Christianity, and teach them the paternoster and creed.
> 22. And it is right that every man learn so that he knows paternoster and creed, according as he wishes to be buried in a consecrated grave or to be entitled to the sacrament [of the Eucharist]; for he who will not learn it is not truly Christian, nor ought he by rights to stand sponsor to another man at baptism or at confirmation, until he learn it.[55]

"Eall[e ge]leafulle men synt to myngienne gemænlice, from ðon læston oð ðone mæsten, þætte ælc mon geleornige pater noster ond credon; ond him is to cyðenne ond to bodienne ðæt on ðissum twam cwydum is se staðol ealles cristenes geleafan, ond buton hwa ðas twege[n] cwydas asingan mæge, ond swa gelyfe swa ðæron sægð, ond hyne mid oft gebidde, ne mæg he beon wel cristen. Hit wæs gefyrn gesett þæt nan þara manna þe ne cuðe credan ond pater noster, þæt ne ne moste naþer ne æt biscopes handa ne æt fulwihte nanum men onfoon, ne hine mon furðon fulluhte ne moste ne biscopian—buton he þa ylde næfde þæt he þonne gyt þa ærgenemnedan cwydas geleornian ne mihte." Sauer's edition is based on an eleventh-century manuscript from Exeter, CCCC 201, 179–272.

53. Sauer, *Theodulfi Capitula,* pp. 281–87.

54. Roger Fowler, *Wulfstan's Canons of Edgar,* EETS 05 266 (London, 1972), p. xlvii (see under *Canons of Edgar*).

55. *Canons of Edgar,* 1/1, pp. 319, 321, 322. On the influence of Theodulf's *capitula* in late Anglo-Saxon England, see Fowler, *Wulfstan's Canons,* pp. xxxvi–xxxix and 28–30; see also Abbot Ælfric

In addition to teaching the Creed and Lord's Prayer, a few Old English sources also recommended that the godparent carry out the more sophisticated task of shaping the godchild morally. An anonymous sermon reminded sponsors of this duty: "Those who receive a child should know that they bring it to correct belief and to good behavior and to useful deeds and always thereafter guide it to that which pleases God and is useful to himself. Then they are really what they are called, godfathers, if they beget their godchild to God."[56]

The requirement that everyone know the two prayers has left its mark in the sources. The Lord's Prayer and various creeds were translated, paraphrased, glossed, and preached about in late Anglo-Saxon England.[57] For example, Ælfric translated the Pater Noster, the Apostles' Creed (*se læssa creda*), the Nicene-Constantinopolitan Creed (*se Mæssa creda*), and other brief prayers "for laymen who know not Latin."[58] Wulfstan also translated and preached on the Lord's Prayer and Apostles' Creed for the use of laymen who could not understand Latin.[59] The commonest form of the creed was the Apostles' Creed, which was used at baptism. After the Benedictine reform of the tenth century, the Athanasian Creed and the Nicene-Constantinopolitan Creed entered the monastic liturgy and were also occasionally translated, paraphrased, glossed, and treated in sermons.[60] It is

---

to Bishop Wulfsige, c. 62, in *Die Hirtenbriefe Ælfrics,* p. 15; and Wulfstan of York, *Institutes of Polity,* c. 17 and 22, pp. 185 and 186.

56. Napier Sermon 24, in Napier, *Wulfstan,* pp. 120–21: "and witan þa, ðe cildes onfon, þaet heo hit on rihtan geleafan gebringan and on godan þeawan and on þearflican dædan and â forð on hit wisjan to ðam, Þe gode licige and his sylfes ðearf sy; þonne beoð heo rihtlice ealswa hy genamode beoð, godfæderas, gif hy heora godbearn gode gestrynaþ."

57. Banks, "Study of the Old English Versions," surveyed the manuscript evidence for translations of the Lord's Prayer (pp. 19–46), of the Apostles' Creed (pp. 94–109), of the Nicene Creed (pp. 110–15), and of the Athanasian Creed (pp. 116–75). Dorothy Bethurum, in Wulfstan, *Homilies,* pp. 299–302, surveyed briefly the evidence for Old English translation of the creed and Lord's Prayer.

58. Ælfric, *Her is Geleafa,* in *Sermones Catholici,* pp. 596–600. Ælfric, *De penitentia,* ibid., pp. 602–9, paraphrased and interwove several creeds. He explained the Apostles' Creed in *De fide catholica,* ibid., pp. 274–91. In *De dominica oratione,* ibid., pp. 258–74, he explained the Pater Noster clause by clause.

59. Wulfstan, *Homilies* 7 and 7*a,* pp. 156–171, paraphrased and explained the Apostles' Creed and the Pater Noster.

60. E. V. K. Dobbie, *The Anglo-Saxon Minor Poems,* (New York, 1942), pp. 70–74 and 77–78, edited two poetic versions of the Lord's Prayer. See also F. G. A. M. Aarts, "The Pater Noster in Medieval English Literature," *Papers on Language and Literature* 5 (1969), who treated Old English versions on pp. 3–6; see also Albert Cook, "The Evolution of the Lord's Prayer in English," *American Journal of Philology* 12 (1891), and "New Texts of the Lord's Prayer and Hymns," *Modern Language Notes* 7 (1892). For a brief survey of Old English translations of the Apostles', Athanasian, and Nicene-Constantinopolitan Creeds, see Max Förster, "Die altenglischen Bekenntnisformeln," *ES* 75 (1942–43). There is an Old English version of the Apostles' Creed in Dobbie, *Anglo-Saxon Minor Poems,* pp. 78–80. On the Athanasian Creed, see Ferdinand Holthausen,

worth noting, however, that there was probably no standard translation of either the Our Father or the Creed. Laypeople presumably memorized the fixed Latin version or varying vernacular ones.[61]

At least from the eighth century, the Anglo-Saxon church tried to impose the ancient tradition that all Christians should memorize and understand the Creed and the Lord's Prayer. In the Council of Clofesho (747) and the legatine councils (786), the linking of knowledge of the prayers with baptismal sponsorship began, but because of the subsequent drying up of sources, we cannot know whether it continued in the ninth century. In the tenth and eleventh centuries, especially under the influence of Archbishop Wulfstan, the "modern" Frankish views on the duties of sponsors were introduced into the sermons and legislation of the Anglo-Saxon church. Potential sponsors at baptism and at confirmation were required to know the Creed and the Lord's Prayer. After they had sponsored, they had a well-defined religious obligation to teach their godchildren the prayers that were the core of religious knowledge for all laypeople.

It is worth noting that neither Frankish nor Anglo-Saxon sources recommended any religious duties for coparents, which fits with the fact that coparenthood received little official ecclesiastical approval. Coparenthood was a significant social institution with negligible religious consequences of a formal sort. But spiritual kinship also had consequences beyond the world of liturgy and religious instruction, which will be treated in the next chapter.

"Eine ae Interlinearversion des athanasischen Glaubensbekenntnisse," *ES* 75 (1942–43), 6–8. There is a version of the Nicene-Constantinopolitan Creed in Samuel J. Crawford, "The Worcester Marks and Glosses of the Old English Manuscripts in the Bodleian Together with the Worcester Version of the Nicene Creed," *Anglia* 52 (1928), 5.

61. Banks, "Study of the Old English Versions," p. 22.

CHAPTER 11

The Social Bonds between Godparents and Godchildren

In addition to their religious duties, sponsors often had enduring social bonds with their godchildren and their godchildren's parents. By the ninth century, godparent complexes were so deeply rooted in Christian societies as to be taken for granted and, like so much of ordinary life, were recorded only sporadically in written documents. The personal, day-to-day aspects of the early medieval godparent complexes must therefore be pieced together from sparse evidence. Anglo-Saxon sources provide some information about the social relations among spiritual kinsmen, although many topics about which we would like to know are shrouded in silence. The richer contemporary Frankish sources can be used cautiously to illuminate the meaning of some of the scattered Anglo-Saxon evidence, just as they were used earlier to illuminate the religious duties of godparents.

Godparent and Godchild

The Social Bonds of Godparent to Godchild

The godparental bond was modeled on the natural bond of parent and child. Like that relationship, it was unequal, with the godparent superior to the godchild in age, dignity, and responsibility. It was expected to be a nurturing relationship. In the 840s, the Frankish aristocratic woman Dhuoda reminded her son that his godfather, who was deceased, would have been his *nutritor* (teacher/adviser/mentor) and *amator* (cherisher) in all things, had he lived.[1]

There were differences between natural and spiritual kinship which gave the latter a sort of moral superiority. Even though natural kinship was important and frequently idealized, it was the source of much litigation and violence, primarily over property. In contrast, spiritual kinship was not tied to property and was not a legal matter to be argued about in courts. It was rooted in sacramental grace and its influence was moral, which did not make it less real. Ideally, it was an altruistic relationship, which set it apart from natural kinship, which was never far from struggles over inheritance and, for the upper classes, power.

The assimilation of godchildren to natural children could never be complete. Godchildren could not expect to inherit from godparents. Indeed godparents were not legally obliged to give anything to their godchildren. Generosity was expected of godparents, however, and the bond of godparent to godchild was generally marked by gifts. One important occasion for gift giving was baptism itself, whose gift was identified in some places in tenth-century France with a special word, *filiolatum* or *filioladium,* from *filiolus/a,* "godson/goddaughter."[2] When Louis the Pious sponsored the Danish royal pretender Heriold in 826, he gave him the county of Rüstringen as a place of refuge. By the eleventh century, Adhemar of Chabannes interpreted that gift as Louis's *filiolatum* to his godson.[3]

Although the word *filiolatum* is not found in Anglo-Saxon sources, there is evidence for such baptismal gifts. One possible baptismal gift appears almost at the dawn of the christianization of the Anglo-Saxons. The significance of the silver spoons excavated at Sutton Hoo, which were inscribed with the words *Saulos* and *Paulos,* has been hotly debated. Angela Evans summarized the debate thus.

> Alongside the bowls lay two spoons of a well-known late classical type. These are a mould pair and are identical except for the names that are inscribed in Greek on their handles. . . . The inscriptions on their handles have provoked a mass of conflicting interpretation. One clearly reads "Paulos" in a well organised inscription competently executed with a half-circular

1. Dhuoda, *Manuel pour mon fils,* c. 15, ed. Pierre Riché and French trans. Bernard de Vregille and Claude Mondésert, *SC* 225 (Paris, 1975), p. 320: "Nutritor etenim atque amator tuus fuerat in cunctis, si ei licuisset."

2. Jean Richard, "La donation en filleulage dans le droit bourguignon," *Mémoires de la Société pour l'Histoire du Droit et des Institutions des Anciens Pays Bourguignons, Comtois et Romands* 16 (1954).

3. *Annales regni Francorum,* s.a. 826, (1968), 144; Adhemar of Chabannes, *Chronicon,* 3.11, ed. Jules Chavanon, CTSEEH 30 (Paris, 1897), p. 126.

> punch. The other, executed by a different hand in a similar but careless manner, reads "Saulos." On the strength of the inscriptions, the spoons have been interpreted as a direct Christian statement referring to the conversion of St. Paul on the road to Damascus. This Christian link has been used as an indication that the man buried in the grave is Raedwald, king of the East Angles (d. 624/5), who was briefly converted to Christianity but soon reverted to paganism and subsequently maintained altars to his pagan deities alongside a Christian altar. . . . It has also been argued that the Saulos inscription is an illiterate attempt to copy the name Paulos, suggesting that both spoons are intended to read Paulos, weakening the reference to Paul's conversion. It has moreover been pointed out that the technique used to cut the inscriptions is the same as that used to cut inscriptions on coins. . . . This could well have happened on the initial S of the Saulos spoon. However, if the spoons were originally inscribed as a deliberately Christian statement, it should perhaps be asked whether in an East Anglia that was only on the very brink of conversion in the early seventh century, there was anyone, priest or king, who could interpret the Greek lettering on the spoons or whether the spoons had come into East Anglia, perhaps with the rest of the silver, simply as a gift and that their inscriptions were of no great consequence to the people who ultimately buried them. Their significance as a possible symbol of Christianity should not be overstated.[4]

In spite of such hesitations, Evans concluded in her earlier careful description of the spoons that they were a baptismal gift, probably to King Rædwald, "made at the instigation of the patron, no doubt an ecclesiastic keen on stressing the importance of adult conversions."[5]

It is impossible to say with certainty that the Sutton Hoo spoons were baptismal gifts, but they might have been reminders to someone, perhaps to King Rædwald (if that is who was buried in the mound) of his transition, like Saul/Paul, from unbelief to belief through baptism. Apparently there are no other extant Paulos/Saulos spoons, but there is early medieval evidence for gifts at baptism to remind recipients of their rebirth. Bishop Zeno of Verona (362–375) reported that baptizees received a coin (a *denar-*

4. Angela Care Evans, *The Sutton Hoo Ship Burial* (London, 1986), pp. 60–63. For a sample of the debate, see D. A. Sherlock, "Saul, Paul, and the Silver Spoons from Sutton Hoo," *Speculum* 47 (1972), who thinks that the most likely use for the spoons was as "christening presents following conversion or baptism"; and Robert Kaske, "The Silver Spoons of Sutton Hoo," *Speculum* 42 (1967), who argued, on the basis of the crude lettering of the "Saulos" inscription, that it might have been the effort of a native craftsman, unfamiliar with Greek, to copy the word *Paulos.*

5. Angela Care Evans, "Late Roman and Byzantine Silver, Hanging-Bowls, Drinking Vessels, Cauldrons and Other Containers, Textiles, the Lyre, Pottery Bottle, and Other Items," in *The Sutton Hoo Ship-Burial,* ed. Rupert Bruce-Mitford (London, 1983), 3:140.

ius) with an image of the Trinity on it.[6] The *Ordo Romanus XI* reported that the bishop gave each baptizee a *stola*, a *casula*, a *crismale*, and *decem siclos*, which were coins of small value.[7] These gifts seem to have been given by the baptizing clergyman rather than by the sponsor, but some Anglo-Saxon sources point clearly to a baptismal gift from the sponsor. When King Wulfhere of Mercia sponsored King Æthelwealh of Sussex, "as a token of his adoption Wulfhere gave him two provinces."[8] An early eleventh-century will in Old English mentioned a gift of land which a man had received from his godfather, although it did not say when the gift was given.[9]

Godparents also gave gifts after baptism. Three of the approximately forty surviving wills in Old English refer to a total of four instances of gift giving by godparents.[10] In a will of 968/971, the ealdorman Ælfheah identified Queen Ælfthryth, the second wife of King Edgar, as his co-mother (*gefæðere*) and left substantial gifts to her two sons, at least one of whom might have been his godson, perhaps the future king Æthelred II: "And to Ælfthryth the King's wife, his *gefædere*, he grants the estate at Schirburn (?) just as it stands; and to the elder Ætheling, the King's son and her's, thirty mancuses of gold and a sword; and to the younger an estate at Walkhampstead."[11] In about 990, the noble woman Æthelgifu left a slave to her godson Ætheric, who incidentally might have had the same name as her husband, who could well have been Ætheric's sponsor.[12] The most informative will is that of Wulfric Spott, made about 1002/4, who granted to his "goddaughter (*goddeht*[*e*]*r*), [who was the daughter] of Morkar and Ealdgyth, the estate at Stretton and the brooch (*bule*) which was her grandmother's."[13] In the same will, Wulfric gave his biological daughter a life interest in two estates, with the condition that after her death they were to go to Burton Abbey. He noted that the estates originally came to him as a gift from his godfather (*mines godfæder gyfu*). Perhaps Wulfric had received the gift at baptism, but whenever he got it, it was certainly a gift from a godfather to a godchild.[14] Thus Wulfric Spott's will

6. Zeno of Verona, *Tractatus,* 1.23 and 2.6, in *Zenonis Veroniensis Tractatus,* ed. Bengst Löfstedt, in *CCSL* 22 (Turnhout, 1971), pp. 70 and 169. On baptismal gifts, see Helga Schwarz, *Das Taufgeld: Ein Beitrag zur historischen Entwicklung der Taufbräuche* (Graz, 1950), who argued that the coin was given by the baptizer rather than by the sponsor.

7. *Ordo Romanus XI,* c. 99, in *Les ordines romani,* 2:446.

8. Bede, *HE,* 4.13, pp. 372–73: "In cuius signum adoptionis duas illi prouincias donauit."

9. Wulfric Spott, *Will of* (S 1536), p. 48.

10. On Old English wills, see Sheehan, *Will in Medieval England,* pp. 21–23, esp. n. 11. Most of the Old English wills are edited in Whitelock, *Anglo-Saxon Wills.*

11. Ælfheah, *Will of* (S 1485), in Whitelock, *Anglo-Saxon Wills,* p. 22. The translation is Whitelock's.

12. Æthelgifu, *Will of* (S 1497), pp. 15 and 25–26.

13. Wulfric Spott, *Will of* (S 1536), p. 50.

14. Ibid., p. 48.

showed baptismal gift giving across three generations: he had received a gift of land from his godfather and had, in his turn, left to his own goddaughter a piece of jewelry and a gift of land—not his godfather's land, which was intended for Burton Abbey. *Domesday Book* also contains a reference to a gift from a godfather to a godson. Edward the Confessor gave lands in Oxfordshire to the Abbey of Westminster, to "Saint Peter of Westminster and to his godson Baldwin (*Balduino filiolo suo*)," who was probably a monk at Westminster.[15]

Sometimes gift giving at baptism, perhaps coupled with sponsorship, was on a wider scale. Queen Emma (died 1052), the Norman wife of King Æthelred and then of King Cnut, gave gifts at baptism to orphans as a form of charity and perhaps for favorable propaganda. The *Encomium Emmae* reported that when she went into exile in Flanders in 1037, "the widows mourned with the orphans, whom she had freely enriched when they were taken from the holy baptismal font. Therefore I do not know with what praises to exalt her, who never failed to be immediately present with those being reborn in Christ."[16] Nor was Queen Emma the only Christian ruler to give baptismal gifts on a large scale. Her contemporary, the Byzantine emperor Michael IV (1034–1042), "baptized," which I think meant sponsored, newborns and gave them gifts in hopes of gaining a cure from what might have been epilepsy.[17] It is not clear whether Queen Emma or Emperor Michael personally sponsored the infants to whom they gave gifts, but their actions do illustrate the tie between baptism and gift giving.

Godparents gave not only gifts but also and perhaps primarily patronage and protection. They were *nutritores* and *amatores,* as Dhuoda had reminded her son. In an Old English letter addressed to King Edward the Elder (899–925), the author, probably the ealdorman Ordlaf, explained how he had obtained possession of five hides of land at a place called Fonthill.[18] The complicated case dragged on for years, but what is significant in this context is that Ordlaf identified himself as the confirmation sponsor of the main party to the case. This is a summary of the relevant points of the letter. A certain Helmstan committed theft and as a consequence might have been legally unable to swear an oath. Æthelm Higa used the opportunity to claim Helmstan's five hides of land at Fonthill. Helmstan asked Ordlaf, an

15. *Domesday Book,* 1, 154 b 1, cited in Frank Barlow, *Edward the Confessor* (Berkeley and Los Angeles, 1970), p. 191, n. 2.

16. *Encomium Emmae reginae,* ed. Alistair Campbell (London, 1949), pp. 50–51.

17. John Skylitzes, *Synopsis historiarum,* c. 18, ed. by Johannes Thurn (Berlin, 1973), p. 405.

18. The "Fonthill Letter" is S 1445. I am endebted to the detailed analysis of the letter by Keynes, "Fonthill Letter." See also Mechtild Gretsch, "The Language of the 'Fonthill Letter,'" *ASE* 23 (1994). Boynton and Reynolds, "Author of the Fonthill Letter," questioned the identification of the letter's author with Ordlaf, but whoever wrote the letter, he was a godfather from confirmation intervening on behalf of his godson.

ealdorman and his godfather, to intercede with King Alfred "because," as Ordlaf noted, "I had received him [Helmstan] formerly at the bishop's hand before he committed the misdeed (*forðon ic his hæfde ær onfongen æt biscopes honda ær he ða undæde gedyde*)."[19] Ordlaf agreed to speak to King Alfred on behalf of his godson. The intercession was successful: Alfred allowed Helmstan to confirm his title deeds with an oath against the claim of Æthelm Higa. But that was not the end. In the course of the long dispute, which continued into the reign of King Edward, the godfather from confirmation served as one of several mediators between the parties. Ordlaf made an agreement with his godson that if he was successful in aiding him, he would be given the five hides and would allow Helmstan to use them for life: "He asked me to help him, and said that he would rather give [the land to me] than that the oath should fail or it ever [. . .] Then I said that I would help him to obtain justice, but never to any wrong, on condition that he granted it to me; and he gave me a pledge to that." When Helmstan successfully completed his oath, "he then gave me the title-deed just as he had pledged to do, as soon as the oath was given; and I promised him that he might use the land as long as he lived, if he would keep himself out of disgrace."[20] Within two years, Helmstan committed the crime of cattle stealing, for which he was outlawed. His godfather Ordlaf was with King Edward at Chippenham and intervened yet again for his godson. The king released Helmstan from outlawry and gave him an estate on which to live. The writer of the letter asked King Edward to confirm his possession of the five hides Helmstan had given him, which he apparently did. In this case, a powerful godfather was a source of legal support and patronage with two kings.

Violence was ever present in early Germanic societies, and godfathers sometimes protected their godsons from it or avenged them after the fact. An entry in the *Anglo-Saxon Chronicle* apparently referred to the protection of a godchild by a godparent, although the text is not entirely clear. The *Chronicle*'s entries for the sixth, seventh, and eighth centuries are generally brief and dry, recording such things as battles and the deaths of bishops and kings. The entry for 757, which is erroneously dated to 755 in all versions of the *Chronicle,* stands out for its length and detail. Stenton wrote that "it seems to be the earliest known piece of English narrative prose."[21] A tale of the tension between loyalty to one's kin and loyalty to one's lord, it is a drama of betrayal, feud and revenge, in which some modern com-

19. Keynes, "Fonthill Letter," p. 66.
20. Ibid. p. 75.
21. Stenton, *Anglo-Saxon England,* p. 209, n. 3.

mentators have seen the summary of an Anglo-Saxon "saga," similar to the twelfth- and thirteenth-century sagas in Old Norse.[22]

The *Chronicle* recorded the accession of King Cynewulf of Wessex in 755 (actually 757) and then related the events that surrounded his death twenty-nine years later. In 757, Cynewulf deposed King Sigeberht of Wessex, who was subsequently murdered. Late in his reign, Cynewulf tried to drive out his rival, the ætheling Cyneheard, who was King Sigheberht's brother. Cyneheard, however, surprised Cynewulf at his mistress's house with only a few bodyguards and killed him. The ealdorman Osric led the slain king's thanes to avenge the murder. The ætheling Cyneheard was trapped in the place where he had slain King Cynewulf. The *ASC* continued:

> And then the atheling [Cyneheard] offered them money and land on their own terms, if they would allow him the kingdom, and told them that kinsmen of theirs, who would not desert him, were with him. Then they [Osric and his men] replied that no kinsman was dearer to them than their lord [King Cynewulf], and they would never serve his slayer; and they offered their kinsmen that they might go away unharmed. Their kinsmen said that the same offer had been made to their comrades who had been with the king [Cynewulf]. Moreover they said that they would pay no regard to it, "any more than did your comrades who were slain with the king." And they proceeded to fight around the gates until they broke their way in, and killed the atheling [Cyneheard] and the men who were with him, all except one, who was the ealdorman's [Osric] godson (*godsunu*). And he saved his life, though he was often wounded.[23]

Ealdorman Osric's godson could have been spared by chance or by the wish of his godfather—the text does not explicitly say—but he was the only person not killed.

22. Stephen D. White, "Kingship and Lordship in Early Medieval England: The Story of Cynewulf and Cyneheard," *Viator* 20 (1989); Karen Ferro, "The King in the Doorway: The Anglo-Saxon Chronicle, A.D. 755," in *Kings and Kingship,* ed. Joel Rosenthal (Binghamton, N.Y., 1986); R. W. McTurk, " 'Cynewulf and Cyneheard' and the Icelandic Sagas," *Leeds Studies in English,* new ser. 12 (1981); Paul J. Hopper, "Some Observations on the Typology of Focus and Aspect in Narrative Language," *Studies in Language* 3 (1979); James H. Wilson, "Cynewulf and Cyneheard: The Falls of Princes," *Papers on Language and Literature* 13 (1977); Ruth Waterhouse, "The Theme and Structure of 755 Anglo-Saxon Chronicle," *Neuphilologische Mitteilungen* 70 (1969); Francis J. Battaglia, "Anglo-Saxon Chronicle for 755: The Missing Evidence for a Traditional Reading," *Publications of the Modern Language Association* 81 (1966); Tom H. Towers, "Thematic Unity in the Story of Cynewulf and Cyneheard," *Journal of English and Germanic Philology* 62 (1963); Charles Moorman, "The Anglo-Saxon Chronicle for 755," *Notes and Queries* 199 (1954); C. L. Wrenn, "A Saga of the Anglo-Saxons," *History* 25 (1940); and Francis P. Magoun, "Cynewulf, Cyneheard, and Osric," *Anglia* 57 (1933).

23. *ASC(A)*, s.a. 755 [recte 757], pp. 36–38; *Anglo-Saxon Chronicle,* trans. Whitelock, pp. 30–31.

It may be significant that the decision to include this episode in the *Chronicle* was made in the 890s, more than a century after the events. It reflects the interests and concerns of the reign of Alfred, although Alfred himself was probably not the patron of the *Chronicle*.[24] Alfred certainly wanted to encourage loyalty to himself as king against the competing claims of loyalty to kinsmen or to lesser lords. He declared in his laws that every man should be loyal to his lord and, above him, to the king.[25] King Alfred also understood the usefulness of sponsorship to turn adversaries into spiritual relatives and, if conditions were right, political allies. He used baptismal sponsorship in 878 to make the Viking king Guthrum his godson and again in 893 to make a son of the Viking chief Hæsten his godson and Hæsten his cofather. In the *Chronicle's* account of the conflict in 755 (757) between the demands of loyalty to one's relatives and to one's lord/king, a godson was singled out as the only survivor of the massacre of the regicides. Janet Nelson pointed out that the nominal element *Os-* was that of King Alfred's maternal line. Perhaps the story of Osric and his godson was known through Alfred's maternal kin. The unusually elaborate account for 755 (757) gave a balanced *exemplum* of loyalty to a king and mercy to a spiritual son, each of which took precedence over the claims of blood kinsmen. Seen in this way, it may be no accident that the *Anglo-Saxon Chronicle* chose this episode for unusually ample treatment.[26]

A third vernacular text throws an unexpected light on the social significance of the godparent/godchild relationship in Anglo-Saxon Wessex. King Ine of Wessex (689–726) issued a set of vernacular laws, or *dooms*, which in its present form consists of seventy-six chapters.[27] The last provisions in Ine's code are unparalleled in the history of the integration of godparenthood into Anglo-Saxon society, indeed into any Germanic legal system. Law 76 incorporated the godparental relationships created by baptism and by confirmation into the native system of feud and compensation in Wessex.[28] In customary law, a killing would ordinarily be settled and a feud

24. *EHD*, 1:121–24.

25. See *Laws of Alfred*, on loyalty to lords, Introduction 49.7, Law 1.1, 4.2, Law 42.5, Law 42.6; on loyalty to the king, Law 4, in *EHD* 1:408–16.

26. Janet Nelson, "Reconstructing a Royal Family: Reflections on Alfred, from Asser, Chapter 2," in *People and Places in Northern Europe: Essays in Honour of Peter Hayes Sawyer*, ed. Ian Wood and Niels Lund (Woodbridge, England, 1991), pp. 58–59.

27. Felix Liebermann, "Über die Gesetze Ines von Wessex," in *Mélanges d'histoire offerts à M. Charles Bémont* (Paris, 1913).

28. On the general topic of wergelds, see Heinrich Brunner, "Sippe und Wergeld nach niederdeutschen Rechten," ZSSRG, Germanistische Abteilung 3 (1882), where Anglo-Saxon wergilds were treated on pp. 14–18; Frederic Seebohm, *Tribal Custom in Anglo-Saxon Law* (London, 1902), esp. pp. 370–495; and Bertha Philpotts, *Kindred and Clan* (Cambridge, 1913), pp. 205–44.

averted by paying compensation to the dead man's relatives. Law 76 ordered that compensation for killing a godson be paid to a godfather and that compensation for killing a godfather be paid to a godson. It mentioned spiritual kin from baptism and confirmation but not from the catechumenate or *crismlysing*. The law runs as follows:

> 76. If anyone kills the godson (*godsunu*) or godfather (*godfæder*) of another, the compensation (*mægbot*) for the [spiritual] relationship is to be the same [amount] as the compensation (*manbot*) to the lord; the compensation (*bot*) is to increase in proportion to the wergeld, just as the compensation for his man does which has to be paid to the lord.[29]

These entitlements were thus in addition to other compensation owed for a slaying.

Ine's laws privileged the godson of a king, such as the eleventh-century monk Baldwin who was Edward the Confessor's godson. In compensation for a royal godson's slaying, the king received a wergeld equal to that owed to the slain man's kin.

> 76.1. If, however, it is the king's godson (*kyninges godsunu*), his wergild is to be paid to the king the same as to the kindred.
> 76.2. If, however, he was resisting him who slew him, then the compensation to the godfather (*godfæder*) is remitted, in the same way as the fine to the lord is [in such circumstances].[30]

Law 76 also recognized the godparental relationship created at confirmation but tariffed it at half that of baptismal kinship. If a godson from confirmation (*biscepsunu*) was slain, half the normal compensation was due to his godfather, but the law did not say that compensation was due if a godfather from confirmation was killed:

> 76.3. If it is a spiritual son at confirmation (*biscepsunu*), the compensation is to be half as much.[31]

29. Ine, *Institutiones* 76, 1:122–23: "Gif hwa oðres godsunu slea oððe his godfæder, sie sio mægbot 7 sio manbot gelic; weaxe sio bot be ðam were, swa ilce swa sio manbot deð þe þam hlaforde sceal." Translation from *EHD,* p. 407.
30. Ibid., p. 122: "Gif hit þonne kyninges godsunu sie, bete be his were þam cyninge swa ilce swa þære mægþe," and "Gif he þonne on þone geonbyrde þe hine slog, þonne ætfealle sio bot þæm godfæder swa ilce swa þæt wite þam hlaforde deð."
31. Ibid.: "Gif his biscepsunu sie, sie be healfum þam."

There are several points to note about this law. The vocabulary is precise. The words *godfæder* and *godsunu* referred only to godfather and godson from baptismal sponsorship. A distinct word, *biscepsunu,* was used to designate a godson from confirmation sponsorship. The greater importance of spiritual kinship created by baptismal sponsorship was emphasized by the fact that godfathers from confirmation received one-half the compensation that godparents and godchildren from baptism received. Law 76 did not mention a spiritual relationship created by sponsorship at the catechumenate, nor did it mention compensation for the killing of coparents.

Law 76 has neither precedent nor analogy nor even faint echo in the surviving Germanic laws, which are generally silent on spiritual kinship. Only Law 34.V of the Lombard King Liutprand, issued in 723, treated kinship from baptismal sponsorship. But it incorporated into Lombard law only the marital impediments spiritual kinship created.[32] Ine's Law 76 was unique in its concern for the wergild of spiritual kin.

I have serious doubts about dating Ine's Law 76 to the late seventh century. Felix Liebermann suggested that it was a later addition to Ine's *dooms,* partly on the grounds that it appeared at the very end of the laws: ecclesiastical provisions tended to be added at the beginning or the end of essentially secular laws, as is the case with Ine's code.[33] It is not even certain that Ine's laws were issued as a single enactment at one time and place. As Richardson and Sayles observed, "To take the surviving texts of early Kentish and West Saxon legislation for what they purport to be—a single legislative act on a particular occasion—would be highly incautious. . . . There are many proved examples in later centuries of the conflation of texts to serve as a warning to those who handle these imperfect renderings of legislation of an earlier age."[34] They noted, for instance, that Laws 55 to 69 in Ine's code differ in style from those in the first two-thirds, being briefer and more obscure. Law 76's vernacular vocabulary of spiritual kinship, which is precocious for the late seventh century, indeed suspiciously so, increases doubt about its seventh-century origin. If Law 76 is an authentic text of the seventh century, it is isolated and unusual.

Can another approximate date for Law 76 be suggested? Ine's *dooms* do not survive in an independent manuscript tradition: they are linked to King Alfred's law code, issued in the late ninth century. In the prologue to

32. Liutprand, *Leges Liutprandi regis,* 34.V, p. 124. On the background to Liutprand's legislation, see Lynch, *Godparents,* pp. 238–40.
33. Liebermann, "Über die Gesetze," pp. 23–24.
34. Richardson and Sayles, *Law and Legislation,* p. 15.

his laws, Alfred declared that he had based them on those of his royal predecessors, Æthelberht of Kent,[35] Offa of Mercia,[36] and Ine of Wessex. The laws of King Ine survive because King Alfred appended them, and only them, to his own code. The oldest surviving copy of Alfred's laws is in CCCC MS 173, a tenth-century manuscript, which has the appendix of Ine's *dooms*.[37] Thus the earliest extant copy of Ine's laws was written more than three hundred years after their supposed promulgation.

The extent to which Alfred might have revised and culled Ine's laws cannot now be assessed.[38] In his prologue, Alfred wrote: "Then I, King Alfred, collected these [laws] together and ordered to be written many of them which our forefathers observed, those which I liked; and many of those which I did not like I rejected with the advice of my councillors and ordered them to be differently observed."[39] Dorothy Whitelock commented, "He [Alfred] tells us that he rejected many of the observances of his forefathers which he did not like, and for all we know some of these may have been omitted from the copy of Ine's code appended to his own."[40] Alfred did not say, however, that he interpolated his views into his predecessors' laws—only that he rejected some. What is at issue is not an omission from Ine's *dooms* but the possibility that Law 76 was added to it. I suggest that Law 76 was added to the end of Ine's code before Alfred obtained it. That hypothesis can not be proved, but the law's position at the very end of the code and its precocious vernacular vocabulary of spiritual kinship point to an origin later than the seventh century, perhaps in the ninth century. It is probably significant that, putting aside Ine's Law 76, the first instance of the word *biscepsunu* appeared in the *Chronicle* (*A*), s.a. 853, which contained the account of Alfred's confirmation.[41]

Regardless of when Law 76 was composed, the basic point remains that it integrated godparental kinship into the native system of compensation before or during Alfred's reign: godparents and godchildren from baptism and from confirmation were real relatives for whose slaying compensation was owed. To be a godchild or a godparent was to have some protection or promise of vengeance, at least in the Kingdom of Wessex.

35. Æthelberht, *Dooms,* in *Die Gesetze der Angelsachsen,* ed. Felix Liebermann (Halle, 1903; rpr. Aalen, 1960), 1:3–8.
36. Wormald, "Offa's 'Law-Code,'" argued that Alfred might have been referring to the extensive legatine canons of 786, issued with Offa's support, as "Offa's laws."
37. Ker described the manuscript in *Catalogue of Manuscripts,* pp. 57–59.
38. Dorothy Whitelock, in *EHD,* pp. 357–62.
39. *The Laws of Alfred,* Introduction 49.9, in *EHD,* pp. 408–9.
40. *EHD* p. 358.
41. *ASC*(*A*), s.a. 853, p. 45.

We may conclude that in addition to their religious duties, godparents provided their godchildren with practical support, the extent of which must not be exaggerated. Blood kin, affinal kin, neighbors, and other groups were the very stuff of the social support for most people. But godfathers—and we presume godmothers, although the sources are silent—aided and protected their spiritual children. The Anglo-Saxon sources stressed protection against violence or litigation, but it must have been true that godparents nourished and loved their godchildren in more pacific ways.

The search for rich and powerful sponsors was not without contemporary critics. A brief text called *De infantibus,* which Ælfric might have written, criticized parents who delayed the baptism to get a rich sponsor for their child. The text said that the parents wanted to get friends through the child (*Nu cw sum man. Þæt he wile cepan him godra freonda. mid his cilde*). The author insisted that in view of the dire consequences of death without baptism, the child was better off with a poor man (*an ælmes man*) as a sponsor than to die "heathen" while waiting for a rich one.[42] The eleventh-century author of the *vita* of Saint Rumwold also criticized, at least implicitly, the search for rich and powerful sponsors. To imitate Christ's humility, Rumwold, the newborn saint, resisted his parents' worldly ambition in the choice of sponsors:

> This rite [the catechumenate] being completed, the parents said to one another: "Let us send for the neighboring kings and rulers, so that they can receive our dearest son from the holy water of baptism." When he heard this, the blessed Rumwold summoned his parents and said to them: "It is not right for me, a servant of God, to be received from the rebirth of holy baptism into the hands of the proud and rich of this world, but I must imitate the example of God. He, having humbled Himself for our sake, by taking on human flesh, and having been conceived in the cherishing womb of a virgin, did not choose to be baptized in the waters of the Jordan by the powerful men of a fallen age, but by the forerunner of his nativity [John the Baptist]. . . . Hence, therefore, I require to be baptized by the priest Widerin, who anointed me, and to be received by Eadwald, because in their hands, through the power and mystery of God, I desire to be made a Christian.[43]

Such pious exhortations ran against the common reality. Wise parents sought for their child and for themselves the most useful sponsor to whom they had access.

42. *De infantibus,* p. 154.
43. *Vita sancti Rumwoldi,* c. 4, pp. 98–101.

The Social Bonds of Godchild to Godparent

Historically, the relationship between godparent and godchild has been asymmetric. The godparent was an adult who owed more to the godchild than vice versa. But the godchild was not without duties. So far as I know, the Anglo-Saxon sources do not refer to duties owed by a godchild to a godparent. To judge from godparental relations in the Frankish world, however, the godchild owed deference and honor to his or her spiritual parent and, in the most successful bondings, love. Dhuoda, for example, asked her son to pray personally, give alms, and offer masses for his godfather, Theodoric, who died when the boy was about five years old and left him a considerable inheritance.[44]

The duty of the godchild to the godparent came into focus when a godchild failed to uphold her or his end of the relationship. Such a betrayal was a disturbance of moral order worth mentioning as an evil exemplum. In his famous *Sermo Lupi,* Wulfstan lamented the moral corruption of his own time, to which he attributed the defeats of his people by the Danes. One sign of that moral corruption was the breakdown of the traditional bonds of kinship: "Now too often a kinsman does not protect a kinsman any more than a stranger, neither a father his son, nor sometimes a son his own father, nor one brother another." In the context of criticizing the decline of loyalty and the rise of treachery among kin, he added that "too many cofathers and godchildren have killed one another far and wide throughout this people."[45]

In some saints' lives there was a topos about the godson who betrayed his godfather. In the legendary *vita* of King Dagobert III, written according to Bruno Krusch between 840 and the twelfth century, a greedy godson killed the king in order to search for a treasure Dagobert had seen in a dream. The godson was punished by damnation.[46] In Adso's *vita* of Bercharius (d. 685/696), written about 990, the saint disciplined one of his monks who was also his godson. In retaliation, the monk/godson (a "spiritual son" from two perspectives) tried unsuccessfully to murder his sleeping godfather.[47] For Dudo of Saint Quentin, the Viking Hæsten was the embodiment of treachery, and he told a tale in which Hæsten killed at least one and perhaps two of his godfathers![48]

44. Dhuoda, *Manuel,* cc. 15–17, pp. 320–24.
45. Wulfstan, *Homily* 20, p. 263, lines 69–71 and 83–84. The translation adapted from Whitelock in *EHD,* p. 931.
46. *Vita Dagoberti III regis Francorum,* c. 12, ed. Bruno Krusch, *MGH SRM* 2 (Hanover, 1888), pp. 518–20.
47. Adso of Montier-en-Der, *Vita sancti Berchari,* chap. 26, *Acta sanctorum,* October, 7/2, p. 1017.
48. Dudo of Saint Quentin, *De moribus* 2, cc. 5–7 (Caen), pp. 132–35.

The theme of the bad godson was taken up in the *vita* of Archbishop Ælfheah of Canterbury, which was written after the Norman Conquest but treated events in Anglo-Saxon history. Ælfheah was Archbishop of Canterbury from 1006 to 1012, when Danish invaders were ravaging the kingdom of Æthelred II. Some Danish warriors were Christian, others were converted during their stay in England, and still others remained pagan. The conversion of individuals did not, however, pacify the invaders as a group. In 1011, a mixed group of Christian and pagan Danes seized Canterbury, captured the archbishop, and held him prisoner for months. When he refused to seek ransom from his people, they brutally murdered him. Archbishop Ælfheah's martyrdom, as it came to be regarded, was recorded in the C-Version of the *Anglo-Saxon Chronicle,* sub anno 1012:

> Then on the Saturday the army became greatly incensed against the bishop because he would not promise them any money, but forbade that anything should be paid for him. They were also very drunk, for wine from the south had been brought there. They seized the bishop, and brought him to their assembly on the eve of the Sunday of the octave of Easter, which was 19 April, and shamefully put him to death there: they pelted him with bones and with ox-heads, and one of them struck him on the head with the back of an axe, that he sank down with the blow, and his holy blood fell on the ground, and so he sent his holy soul to God's kingdom.[49]

The killing of an archbishop was shocking, and within a few years of the events, Thietmar of Merseburg recorded substantially the same story, told to him by an informant named Sewald.[50] In neither early account was there reference to a godson.

In 1023, Ælfheah's body was translated from London to Canterbury.[51] In succeeding decades, the brief account of his martyrdom in the *Anglo-Saxon Chronicle* must have come to be regarded as inadequate. In the 1080s, Osbern of Canterbury wrote a life of the archbishop in which the theme of the bad godson appeared, but with a twist. Osbern reported that Ælfheah's godson did a wicked thing, but for a good reason: he called it "an impious piety" (*impia pietas*). According to Osbern's *vita,* Archbishop Ælfheah had converted some Danish warriors, at least one of whom he sponsored at baptism. When the captive Ælfheah refused to pay the Danes ransom, he

49. *ASC(C)*, s.a. 1011 and 1012, pp. 61–62; *Anglo-Saxon Chronicle,* trans. Whitelock, pp. 91–92.
50. Thietmar of Merseburg, *Chronicon,* 7, cc. 42–43, ed. Robert Holtzmann and reprinted with German trans. by Werner Trillmich in *Ausgewählte* 9 (Berlin) (1957), 398–400; English translation in *EHD,* pp. 349–50.
51. *ASC(C, D, E)*, s.a. 1023, in *Anglo-Saxon Chronicle,* trans. Whitelock, pp. 99–100.

was brutally tortured. The baptismal godson saw his plight and carried out a mercy killing: "A certain man ran up, whom he [Ælfheah] had received from the holy font. When he saw the man [Ælfheah] near to death suffering longer, he was moved by an impious piety and stuck an axe into his head. He [Ælfheah], immediately resting in eternal peace, sent his victorious spirit to heaven in triumph."[52] John of Worcester's chronicle, which was formerly attributed to Florence of Worcester, was dependent on Osbern's *vita* but added two details: the killer's name was Thrum, and he was a godson not from baptism but from a confirmation that Ælfheah had carried out the day before, while he was in captivity.[53]

The story of Ælfheah's death, as told by Osbern and John of Worcester, is an extreme, perhaps even mythical, reflection of the bond of godchild to godparent. The violation of that bond heightened the drama of the archbishop's death, and the *impia pietas* that motivated the killer added an element of moral ambiguity. But the respect and compassion a godchild owed to a godparent were real.

Social Bonds between Coparents

Virtually every sponsorship mentioned in this book created coparents. Frankish sources make clear that coparents were expected to be united by the bonds of brotherly affection, but among the Anglo-Saxons the creation of coparenthood and its social consequences were rarely mentioned. For the early period, the silence is understandable. When an adult Christian king sponsored an adult pagan king, the latter's father was usually dead and so no coparenthood was created. But between the ninth and the eleventh centuries, most accounts of sponsorship explicitly mentioned godparent/godchild bonds and only rarely told the reader that the adults also became coparents.

Coparents are not entirely absent. The *Chronicle* reported that the Viking Hæsten ravaged the territory of Ealdorman Æthelred of Mercia, whom it identified as his *cumpæder*.[54] In 966, Bishop Oswald of Worcester

52. Osbern, *Vita sancti Elphegi archiepiscopi cantuariensis,* in *Anglia Sacra,* ed. Henry Wharton (London, 1691), p. 2:141: "Accurens autem quidam, quem et ipsum de sacro fonte susceperat, cum videret virum in confinio mortis diutius laborantem, impia pietate motus, securim capiti illius infixit. Qui statim in aeterna pace requiescens, victorem spiritum cum triumpho dirigit ad coelum."

53. John of Worcester, *The Chronicle of John of Worcester,* s.a. 1012, ed. R. R. Darlington and P. McGurk and trans. Patricia Bray and P. McGurk (Oxford, 1995), p. 470: "Ad ultimum quidam Thrum nomine, quem confirmarat pridie, impia motus pietate, securim capiti illius infixit."

54. *ASC(A)*, s.a. 893, p. 57.

leased land to Eadric, whom he identified as his *compater*.[55] In the early eleventh century, Archbishop Wulfstan lamented that coparents (*godsybbas*) sometimes killed one another, which they should not do.[56] And the York bidding prayer explicitly requested that the congregants pray for their cofathers (*godsybbas*) and comothers (*cumæðran*).[57] The Peterborough continuation of the *Anglo-Saxon Chronicle* reported that in 1093, Moræl of Bamburgh, who was both the steward of Earl Robert of Northumbria and the cofather (*godsibb*) of King Malcolm of Scotland, killed the king, who was raiding in England.[58] But the weight of evidence suggests that coparenthood was less important than godparenthood in the Anglo-Saxon version of the godparent complex.

The bonds that linked godparents and godchildren were a permanent feature of Anglo-Saxon Christianity, just as they were of Frankish and Byzantine Christianity. In addition to their religious duties, godparents had significant social duties that might last a lifetime. They gave their godchildren gifts, protected them, and acted as their patrons at law. In Alfred's Wessex, godfather and godson from baptism and confirmation were assimilated to blood kin and were due compensation from the slayer of their respective spiritual kin. Godchildren owed respect in return for patronage. Coparenthood certainly existed, although the admittedly unsatisfactory sources suggest that it was acknowledged only after the mid-ninth century. There was yet another social function of sponsorship, its use in diplomacy, which is distinct enough to be treated in the next chapter.

55. *Cartularium Saxonicum,* 1182 (S 1310), (London, 1893), 3:445.

56. Wulfstan, *Homily* 20 (*Sermo Lupi*), in all three versions, Wulfstan wrote: "And godsibbas and godbearn to fela man forspilde wide geond þas þeode"; see p. 258, lines 72–73, p. 263, lines 83–84; and p. 270, lines 78–79.

57. William H. Stevenson, "Yorkshire Surveys," *EHR* 27 (1912), 10.

58. *ASC, The Peterborough Chronicle,* s.a. 1093, p. 20.

CHAPTER 12

Sponsorship in Anglo-Saxon Diplomacy

From one perspective, sponsorship for diplomatic purposes was just another "social" use of a common Christian institution, but it is in fact important and distinct enough to warrant separate treatment. Early medieval rulers had many diplomatic instruments available, including the exchange of women in marriage, written treaties, adoptions, oaths, the exchange of hostages, the payment of tribute, the giving of gifts, and of course, brute force. The choice of diplomatic strategy varied by circumstances, including the relative strength of the opponents and the ends sought. From the sixth century, some Christian rulers used sponsorship and spiritual kinship in their dealings with one another and with pagan "outsiders." A decision to sponsor a fellow ruler or his child made sense because sponsorship was deeply rooted in Christian societies, whose leaders knew from their own experience how godparents, godchildren, and coparents ought to behave. Spiritual kinship had the potential to sacralize political relationship that might otherwise be based on power alone.

Arnold Angenendt has been a pioneer in the study of sponsorship in early medieval diplomacy. In articles and a fundamental monograph, he has written of the complicated interplay among sponsorship, diplomacy, and missionary activity in the early Middle Ages. He demonstrated that Christian rulers, especially Byzantine and German emperors, regarded the conversion of their pagan neighbors as a god-given task, which had earthly benefits as well. Conversion might pacify a dangerous people and bring them into the sphere of influence of the Christian power from which the missionaries came. Sponsorship was sometimes a key instrument in diplomatic and missionary policies, which were closely intertwined. If a Christian ruler could arrange for the baptism of a foreign ruler, whom he then sponsored, he became that man's spiritual and political father and opened his spiritual son's realm to Christian missionaries. The sponsorship of a ruler, his family, and his main followers often marked publicly both the beginnings of the conversion of a people and their new political orientation.[1]

The Byzantine Empire, the most diplomatically sophisticated of the Christian powers in the early Middle Ages, was equipped with such things as a diplomatic service and archival records of treaties. The Byzantines used calculated displays of wealth and power to impress foreign visitors, and they propagated an ideology that arranged foreign rulers into a "family" whose "father" was the Byzantine emperor.[2] Baptismal sponsorship was one of the Byzantine diplomatic tools for integrating rulers into the emperor's "family." Either in person or by proxy, Byzantine emperors received kings or chiefs from the baptismal font and made them their spiritual sons.[3] During the feasting and gift giving after the sponsorship, the emperor/godfather might bestow on his godson Byzantine titles, marriage alliances, and wealth, which could in fact be veiled tribute or a subsidy to strengthen the position of the ruler/godson among his own people. When a ruler accepted baptism, he was expected to open the way for the conversion of his people and their incorporation into the Byzantine sphere of influence. The political subordination, which was at the heart of the relationship, was softened and masked by the sacred and honorable bond of spiritual kinship.

The sixth-century chronicler John Malalas reported that in about 522, Ztathios, king of the Lazi, abandoned his subordination to the Persians and asked Emperor Justin (518–527) to recognize him as ruler of the Lazi. Justin invited Ztathios to Constantinople, where he sponsored him at baptism, gave him a highborn Byzantine woman as a wife, crowned him a king, and gave him impressive symbolic gifts.

> He was received by the emperor [Justin], baptized and having become a Christian, married a Roman wife named Valeriana, the granddaughter of

1. Arnold Angenendt, "Taufe und Politik im frühen Mittelalter," *FS* 7 (1973); "Das geistliche Bündnis der Päpst"; and *Kaiserherrschaft.*

2. Evangelos Chrysos, "Byzantine Diplomacy, A.D. 300–800: Means and Ends," in *Byzantine Diplomacy,* ed. Jonathan Shepherd and Simon Franklin (Aldershot, Great Britain, 1992); Franz Dölger, "Die 'Familie der Könige' im Mittelalter," *Historisches Jahrbuch* 60 (1940), and reprinted in *Byzanz und die europäische Staatenwelt* (Ettal, 1953).

3. On Byzantine practices, see Dölger, "Die 'Familie der Könige'" (1953) pp. 56–60, and "Der Bulgarenherrscher als geistlicher Sohn des byzantinischen Kaisers," in *Byzanz.* See also Isrun Engelhardt, *Mission und Politik in Byzanz: Ein Beitrag zur Strukturanalyse byzantinischer Mission zur Zeit Justins und Justinians* (Munich, 1974), esp. pp. 80–90; and Angenendt, *Kaiserherrschaft,* pp. 5–11, and "Die Karolingern und die 'Familie der Könige,'" *Zeitschrift des aachener Geschichtsvereins* 96 (1989).

> Nomos the patrician and he took her back with him to his own country. He had been crowned by Justin, the emperor of the Romans, and had put on a Roman imperial crown and a white cloak of pure silk. Instead of the purple border it had the gold imperial border; in its middle was a true purple portrait medallion with a likeness of the emperor Justin. He also wore a white tunic, a *paragaudion,* with gold imperial embroideries, equally including the likeness of the emperor. . . . He received many gifts from the emperor Justin, as did his wife Valeriana.[4]

The alliance worked. Justinian, Justin's nephew and successor, answered Ztathios's request for military help against the Persians in 528, though the expedition itself was a failure.[5] The practice of imperial sponsorship remained a permanent feature of Byzantine diplomacy.[6]

The western Germanic successor states to the Roman Empire also practiced diplomacy, though generally in a less sophisticated way than the Byzantines. Margret Wielers studied the many forms of alliance used by the early medieval Franks.[7] They had techniques for creating *pax* and *amicitia,* "peace" and "friendship," some of which imitated parent/child kinship.[8] The cutting of a young boy's hair, for example, could be the occasion for a form of adoption. Charles Martel, the Frankish mayor of the palace, sent his son Pepin to the Lombard king Liutprand, who cut the boy's hair and "was made a father (*pater*) to him and sent him back to his father (*genitor,* i.e., Charles Martel) enriched with many royal gifts."[9] A second way to adopt was by equipping a teen-aged boy with his first weapons, an ancient Germanic ceremony attested by Tacitus in the first century. By the

4. John Malalas, *Chronicle,* cc. 412–13, in *The Chronicle of John Malalas,* trans. E. Jeffries, M. Jeffries, and Roger Scott (1986), pp. 233–34. Other evidence from John Malalas on imperial sponsorships is gathered in Roger Scott, "Diplomacy in the Sixth Century: The Evidence of John Malalas," in *Byzantine Diplomacy,* ed. Jonathan Shepherd and Simon Franklin (Aldershot, Great Britain 1992), pp. 162–63. See also Engelhardt, *Mission,* pp. 80–82.

5. John Malalas, *Chronicle,* c. 427, p. 236.

6. Other early medieval sponsorships by Byzantine emperors include Justinian and Grod, the king of the Crimean Huns in ibid., c. 431, p. 250; Justinian and Grepes, king of the Heruli, in ibid., cc. 427–28, p. 247; Justinian and Askoum the Hun, *magister militum per Illyricum,* in ibid., c. 438, p. 254. Heraclius (610–641) sponsored a Bulgarian ruler in 619, in Nicephorus, *Opuscula historica,* ed. C. de Boor (Leipzig, 1880), p. 12; Leo IV (775–780) sponsored Telerigos, lord of the Bulgars, in Theophanes, *Chronographia,* ed. C. de Boor (Leipzig, 1883), 1:451. On such sponsorships at Byzantium, see Angenendt, *Kaiserherrschaft,* pp. 5–11; Engelhardt, *Mission,* pp. 80–90; Dölger, "Die Familie der Könige," pp. 56 ff.

7. Margret Wielers, *Zwischenstaatliche Beziehungsformen im frühen Mittelalter: Pax, Foedus, Amicitia, Fraternitas* (Münster in Westphalia, 1959).

8. Ibid., pp. 47–59.

9. Paul the Deacon, *Historia Langobardorum,* 6.3, ed. L. Bethmann and G. Waitz, *MGH SRG* 48 (Hanover, 1878), p. 237.

sixth century, the rite had become an adoption *per arma,* which might involve two adults, as when the Byzantine emperor Zeno (474–491) adopted the Ostrogothic king Theoderic (489–526) through a bestowal of weapons.[10]

Some of the Germanic Christian peoples used baptismal sponsorship in their search for friendships (*amicitiae*). In the Merovingian period, the Franks, whose activities are relatively well documented, used sponsorship among their own people to strengthen existing kinship ties or to create new kinlike bonds. Some Frankish aristocrats sought their peers or charismatic holy men as sponsors for their children. The Merovingian kings sought sponsors within their family and from among important Frankish bishops. So far as the sources reveal, however, the Merovingian rulers did not create spiritual kinship with non-Franks, and they sponsored only at baptism.[11]

The early Carolingians—Pepin, Charlemagne, and Carloman—whose family replaced the Merovingian line after 751, generally sought sponsors for their children outside their family and, like their Merovingian predecessors, often among important churchmen. The chronicle of the abbots of Fontanelles reported that Archbishop Raginfrid of Rouen (739–755) was the *compater* of Pepin, hence must have sponsored one of his children. They had a falling out, and Pepin deposed Raginfrid in 755.[12] The greatest bishop of the west was the pope, with whom the early Carolingian rulers created formal pacts in which spiritual kinship played a central role. Angenendt traced the series of unprecedented sponsorships of Carolingian children by popes between 754 and 781.[13]

Although Carolingian rulers never sought foreign rulers—unless popes are to be regarded as foreign rulers—to sponsor their children, they did break with Merovingian practice and begin a long tradition of sponsoring foreign leaders with whom they wanted peaceful diplomatic relations or whom they wanted to draw into their sphere of influence.[14]

10. Tacitus, *Germania,* c. 13, in *Tacitus: The Agricola and the Germania,* trans. H. Mattingly and S. A. Handford (Harmondsworth, 1970); Wielers, *Zwischenstaatliche,* pp. 47–49; Eckhardt, "Adoption," pp. 257–58; Angenendt, *Kaiserherrschaft,* pp. 9–10; E. Eichmann, "Die Adoption des deutschen Königs durch den Papst," ZSSRG, Germanistische Abteilung 37 (1916), 295, on adoption *per arma* in the fifth and sixth centuries. Althoff, *Verwandte,* p. 89.

11. Lynch, *Godparents,* pp. 163–204; Jussen, *Patenschaft,* pp. 168–228, treated bishops as sponsors. For an instance of two great aristocrats related by sponsorship, see Fredegar, *Fourth Book of the Chronicle,* Continuation 2, p. 82: Ebroin, former mayor of the palace, killed Leudesius, the present mayor of the palace, who was his *conpater.*

12. *Gesta abbatum Fontanellensium,* c. 12, ed. S. Loewenfeld, *MGH SRG* 28 (Hanover, 1886).

13. Angenendt, "Das geistliche Bündnis," pp. 32–94.

14. Angenendt, *Kaiserherrschaft,* pp. 196–259, treated the Carolingian diplomatic sponsorships of the later-eighth and ninth centuries.

Anglo-Saxon Diplomatic Sponsorship

The Roman missionaries, who were Byzantine subjects, and the Frankish missionary bishops were aware of the practices in their respective homelands and must have suggested to their royal converts the usefulness of sponsorship. Anglo-Saxon kings actually preceded the Franks by more than a century in the use of sponsorship for diplomatic, as opposed to what might be called domestic, purposes. The Anglo-Saxon world of small, unstable kingdoms, with power repeatedly shifting from one to another, had a great need for diplomatic means to lessen violence. The introduction of Christianity was soon followed by baptismal sponsorship, which may be regarded as "diplomatic" because it involved independent kings, who happened to be Angles or Saxons.[15]

Within a generation after the arrival of the Roman missionaries, baptismal sponsorship was mingled with diplomacy. The missionaries encouraged newly converted Anglo-Saxon kings to spread Christianity, which they did in a variety of ways. Some Christian kings urged their pagan fellow kings to accept Christianity; others made the acceptance of Christianity a condition for a dynastic marriage; and some imposed it as a condition of peace.[16] For example, King Oswiu agreed to allow Peada, king of the Middle Angles, to marry his daughter Alhflæd only if Peada became a Christian. When Peada agreed, Bishop Finan baptized him and his entourage at one of King Oswiu's estates—Bede's account did not name the sponsor. King Peada then took four priests to his kingdom, who preached the new religion, "and they were heard gladly and every day many of the nobles and lesser folk, having renounced the filth of idolatry, were washed in the font of faith."[17] King Edwin of Northumbria successfully persuaded King Eorpwold of East Anglia to be baptized along with his people.[18]

Some Anglo-Saxon rulers must have perceived conversion as risky, a dangerous experiment that might anger the gods. King Rædwald of East Anglia converted briefly but then hedged his bets by having a Christian altar and an altar for pagan sacrifices in the same temple. Bede saw him as an apostate, but we might call him a syncretist, who added Christ to his pantheon.[19] Some Anglo-Saxon royal families seem to have put off the baptism of a son or sons when their father converted. The young men could keep

15. Ibid., pp. 176–96.
16. On the role of Christian kings in the conversion of pagan kings, see Chaney, *Cult of Kingship*, pp. 156–73.
17. Bede, *HE*, 3.21, pp. 278–80.
18. Ibid., 2.15, pp. 188–90.
19. Ibid., pp. 189–90.

the royal family's bonds to the gods just in case Christianity failed to bring prosperity and victory.[20]

When Christian Anglo-Saxon kings were successful in encouraging or forcing their pagan peers to accept baptism, as they often were, their efforts must usually have been capped by sponsorships—although for most of them no records survive.[21] We can safely assume that every Anglo-Saxon king who converted to Christianity in the seventh century had a sponsor. Bede, the *Anglo-Saxon Chronicle*, the *Liber Eliensis*, and perhaps the anonymous *vita* of Pope Gregory I recorded the names of four kings who sponsored subordinate kings at baptism. King Oswald of Northumbria, whom Bede listed as one of the dominant kings (the so-called Bretwalda),[22] sponsored King Cynegils of Wessex, whose daughter he subsequently married: Oswald was both godfather and son-in-law to Cynegils.[23] King Wulfhere of Mercia sponsored King Æthelwealh of the South Saxons.[24] King Æthelwald of East Anglia sponsored King Swithhelm of Essex.[25] The case of King Cenwealh of Wessex is less clear. Bede reported that Cenwealh spent three years in exile at the court of King Anna of East Anglia, where he was baptized.[26] The *Chronicle* reported *sub anno* 646 that "in this year Cenwealh was baptized."[27] The *Liber Eliensis*, composed in the twelfth century but with Anglo-Saxon sources, added that Bishop Felix carried out the baptism, and King Anna of East Anglia received Cenwealh from the font.[28] Perhaps the author of the *Liber* had a now-lost source for his assertion. I think it likely, however, that he drew it from reading Bede's account: if Cenwealh accepted Christianity at Anna's court, the latter must have been the sponsor at baptism.

Sometimes a king who accepted Christianity wanted to avoid becoming the "son," and hence the subordinate, of a more powerful king. In such cases, the convert might have sought sponsorship from a bishop, which

20. Angenendt, *Kaiserherrschaft*, pp. 179–81; Angenendt developed more fully his views on the delay in baptizing Anglo-Saxon kings' sons in "Conversion of the Anglo-Saxons," esp. pp. 747–54.

21. Angenendt, *Kaiserherrschaft*, pp. 176–96, treated political use of sponsorship among the seventh-century Anglo-Saxons.

22. Bede, *HE*, 2.5, pp. 148–50: Oswald of Northumbria is the sixth king, and his brother Oswiu is the seventh, to hold a preeminence over the other Anglo-Saxon kingdoms. On the Bretwaldas, see Fanning, "Bede, *Imperium*, and the Bretwaldas."

23. Bede, *HE*, 3.7, p. 233.

24. Ibid., 4.13, p. 372.

25. Ibid., 3.22, p. 285.

26. Ibid., 3.7, pp. 232–34.

27. *ASC*(*A*), s.a. 646, p. 29.

28. *Liber Eliensis*, ed. E. O. Blake, Camden Third Series 92 (London, 1962), p. 18: "Baptizatus est rex Chenuualla in eadem provincia a Felice episcopo, quem de fonte sacro Rex Anna suscepit."

had parallels in the contemporary Frankish kingdom. Anglo-Saxon sources record one instance in which a bishop sponsored a king and three other cases in which a bishop might have done so. I shall outline the recorded diplomatic sponsorships of early Anglo-Saxon history briefly as follows:

627	Bishop Paulinus baptized and *may* have sponsored King Edwin of Northumbria.[29]
635	King Oswald of Northumbria sponsored King Cynegils of Wessex.[30]
639	Bishop Birinus baptized and sponsored Cuthred, son of King Cwichelm of Wessex.[31]
646	King Anna *may* have sponsored King Cenwealh of the Gewisse.[32]
661	King Wulfhere of Mercia sponsored King Æthelwealh of the South Saxons.[33]
660s	King Æthelwald of the East Angles sponsored King Swithhelm of the East Saxons.[34]
689	Pope Sergius baptized, renamed, and *may* have sponsored King Cædwalla.[35]
c. 705	Bishop Wilfrid made young King Osred of Northumbria his "son," although we do not know the means used to carry out the "adoption."[36]

Between the early eighth and the late ninth centuries, there are no more records of baptismal sponsorships uniting Anglo-Saxon royal houses. The success of Christianity may have ended the opportunity: after King Æthelwealh of the South Saxons was baptized, probably in the 660s, there were no more adult pagan Anglo-Saxon kings.[37] Thereafter, the caution about not angering the old gods was also gone, and Anglo-Saxon royal children were probably baptized soon after birth, as were children in every Christian society. Of course kings might have invited other rulers to sponsor their newborn children, but sponsorship of infants across the boundaries of kingdoms might have become less politically significant or less feasible. But

29. *Vita sancti Gregorii,* c. 15, p. 96.
30. Bede, *HE,* 3.7, p. 232; *ASC(A)*, s.a. 635, p. 28.
31. *ASC(A)*, s.a. 639, in *Anglo-Saxon Chronicle,* trans. Whitelock, p. 18.
32. *Liber Eliensis,* p. 18.
33. Bede, *HE,* 4.13, p. 373; *ASC(A)*, s.a. 661, p. 30.
34. Bede, *HE,* 3.22, p. 284.
35. Ibid., 5.7, pp. 468–73.
36. Eddius Stephanus, *Vita Wilfridi,* c. 59, p. 128: "et regnavit pro eo puer regius, cui nomen erat Osred, filius Aldfrithi regis, et sancto pontifici nostro filius adoptivus factus est."
37. Bede *HE,* 4.13, pp. 370–76.

it is likely that the lack of records is not due to the end of the practice but to the poor state of the sources themselves—there is nothing even remotely comparable to Bede's *History*, finished in 731, until the late-ninth-century *Anglo-Saxon Chronicle*. For much of the eighth and early ninth centuries, Mercia was the dominant Anglo-Saxon kingdom, under its three long-lived and effective kings, Æthelbald (716–757), Offa (757–796), and Cenwulf (796–821).[38] Few sources survive from Mercia during that period—no saints' lives, no annals, no learned works, and only a few charters.[39] Because of that dearth of sources, there can be no certainty whether or not the Mercian or other Anglo-Saxon kings practiced diplomatic sponsorship during the eighth and ninth centuries.

With the composition of the A-Version of the *Chronicle* in about 892 (and its continuations), the record of diplomatic sponsorships begins again. In these later sources, there are three features of sponsorship which did not appear earlier. First, changes in the liturgy between the seventh and the ninth century created more occasions for sponsorship: catechumenate, baptism, confirmation, and the *crismlysing*. Second, whereas there was no early record of sponsorship between an Anglo-Saxon king and a non–Anglo-Saxon ruler, in the later Anglo-Saxon sources, Vikings and Celts predominate as the persons sponsored by Anglo-Saxon kings. Third, when a Viking or Celtic ruler was already a Christian, the Anglo-Saxon king might sponsor his child at baptism or the ruler himself at confirmation.

Contemporary Frankish practices are an illuminating introduction to later Anglo-Saxon diplomatic sponsorships. Eighth-, ninth- and tenth-century Carolingian kings attempted to deal with their northern and eastern pagan neighbors/enemies—Saxons, Avars, Danes, and other Vikings—by the use of sponsorship at baptism and confirmation, in conjunction with other means. Religious difference was a major obstacle to trust and cooperation between the Franks and their neighbors. When pagan enemies accepted Christianity, a new relationship was possible, not necessarily friction free but potentially more reliable and peaceful. Acceptance of baptism was the outward expression both of a new political alignment and of a new religious allegiance. A major political realignment of the Saxons took place after 785, for example, when Widukind, who had led the Saxon resistance for more than a decade, and his son-in-law Abbi were baptized at Attigny, where Charlemagne was their sponsor.[40]

38. Patrick Wormald, "The Age of Bede and Æthelbald" and "The Age of Offa and Alcuin," in *The Anglo-Saxons,* ed. James Campbell (Oxford, 1982).

39. Wormald, "Age of Offa and Alcuin."

40. *Annales regni Francorum,* s.a. 785, (1968), 48, reported the baptism of Widukind and Abbi but said nothing of Charlemagne's sponsorship, which was mentioned in *Annales Mosellani,* s.a. 785, p. 497.

Because all the Germanic peoples were eventually converted to Christianity, it is tempting to assume that conversion was inevitable. The conversion of Germanic or Viking rulers was, however, neither easy nor automatic. Many were devoted to their gods and to their independence from Christian powers: as long as they were successful in war, there seemed no reason to abandon their gods. In fact it was probably seen as dangerous to repudiate gods who proved themselves effective in war. It was often in the wake of military defeat, as with the Continental Saxons in the late eighth century or the Danish Viking Guthrum in 878, that conversion became an option or even a political necessity.

Between the late eighth and eleventh centuries, the Anglo-Saxons had dangerous neighbors—sometimes the same ones as the contemporary Franks. The greatest menace came from the Vikings, who poured out of Scandinavia in successive waves. Peter Sawyer identified two Viking ages in Anglo-Saxon history, the first coinciding generally with the ninth century and the second, quite distinct from the first, beginning about 980.[41] The first Viking age opened in the late eighth century when Scandinavian raiders attacked exposed monasteries in the British Isles. After 835, the raids on Anglo-Saxon England became more widespread and destructive. In the 850s, the Viking attackers began to spend the winter in England, a change with ominous implications for the future of the Anglo-Saxon kingdoms. The next step was to conquer and colonize parts of England.

Sixty years of struggle with Viking invaders dramatically changed the political and cultural map of Anglo-Saxon England. When the Danish "Great Army" landed in 865, there were four independent Anglo-Saxon Kingdoms—Mercia, East Anglia, Northumbria, and Wessex. Between 865 and 869, the Great Army under the leadership of King Ivarr the Boneless defeated and killed Osberht and Ælla, rival kings of Northumbria, as well as King Edmund of East Anglia. King Burgred of Mercia fled overseas and died at Rome. The Danes appointed puppet Anglo-Saxon kings in those kingdoms. By 871, only Wessex was independent of Danish control and ruled by a member of its ancient native dynasty, King Alfred.[42]

The reappearance of narrative sources, especially the *Chronicle,* reveals that Alfred and his successors used sponsorship as an element of their strategy to resist, tame, or expel the pagan invaders. They also used sponsorship in their relations with Christian Celtic rulers. The following are the recorded "diplomatic" sponsorships of late Anglo-Saxon history:

41. Peter Sawyer, "The Two Viking Ages of Britain: A Discussion," *Mediaeval Scandinavia* 2 (1969).
42. Smyth, *Scandinavian Kings,* pp. 170–213; Stenton, *Anglo-Saxon England,* p. 243.

853	Pope Leo IV (or Pope Benedict III) sponsored Alfred at Rome in confirmation.
878	King Alfred sponsored the Danish king Guthrum at baptism, and Ealdorman Æthelnoth sponsored him at the *crismlysing.*
c. 893	King Alfred sponsored Anarawd of Gwynned at confirmation.
893	King Alfred sponsored the son of the Viking chief Hæsten at baptism.
893	Æthelred, the ealdorman of Mercia, sponsored another son of Hæsten at baptism.
927	King Athelstan sponsored the son of Constantine, king of the Scots, at baptism.
c. 931 (or before 924)	King Athelstan sponsored Alan Barbatorta, the future duke of Brittany, at baptism.
943	King Edmund sponsored King Olaf Sihtricson at baptism.
943	King Edmund sponsored King Rægnald at confirmation.
994	King Æthelred sponsored Olaf Tryggvason at confirmation.
c. 1017–1035	King Cnut may have sponsored a son of King Malcolm II of Scotland.

Each of these diplomatic sponsorships needs to be analyzed.

King Æthelwulf of Wessex (839–858)

In Chapter 6, I treated the controversial episode recorded in the *Anglo-Saxon Chronicle,* s.a. 853: "King Æthelwulf [of Wessex] sent his son Alfred to Rome. The lord Leo [IV] was then pope at Rome, and he consecrated him king and stood sponsor to him at confirmation."[43] Æthelwulf was apparently a man of diplomatic ambitions, who traveled to Rome and who married a Frankish Princess, Judith, daughter of Charles the Bald.[44] If he sent or took Alfred to Rome for confirmation by the pope, he might have done so in an effort to enhance his own prestige by imitating Charlemagne, who became cofather to Pope Hadrian in 781. Whatever was in-

43. *ASC(A)*, s.a. 853, p. 45: "þy ilcan geare sende Ethelwulf cyning Elfred his sunu to Rome. þa was domne Leo papa on Rome and he hine to cyning gehalgode and hiene him to biscepsuna nam."

44. Michael J. Enright, "Charles the Bald and Æthelwulf of Wessex: The Alliance of 856 and Strategies of Royal Succession," *Journal of Medieval History* 5 (1979), argued that the alliance was directed against Æthelwulf's rebellious son Æthelbald.

tended in the 850s, the events at Rome took on a new meaning when Alfred unexpectedly outlived his brothers and became king in 871. The ceremonies he experienced at Rome were reinterpreted or even falsified in retrospect. When the *Chronicle* was composed about 892, Alfred was portrayed, perhaps correctly, as the confirmation godson of a pope and, unlikely as it seems historically, as having been prophetically anointed king by a pope.

King Alfred (871–899)

After a hiatus of about 150 years, records of diplomatic sponsorships began again with the reign of King Alfred. Bishop Asser, Alfred's biographer, explained what an alliance with Alfred meant. "Nor did all these rulers gain the king's friendship in vain. For those who wished to increase their worldly power were able to do so; those who wished an increase in wealth obtained it; those who wished to be on more intimate terms with the king achieved such intimacy; and those who desired each and every one of these things acquired them. All of them gained support, protection and defense in those cases where the king was able to defend himself and all those in his care."[45]

Alfred and Guthrum

The greatest danger to Wessex came from Vikings, who were generally but not always pagans.[46] In 874, the Danish Great Army, which had invaded England in 865, split into two parts, one of which settled in Northumbria and the other attacked the south. Wessex was hard pressed to resist when the invaders, reinforced by a second army under the Danish king Guthrum, turned on it in 877. King Alfred and the royal family fled into the swamps of the Isle of Athelney. In a remarkable reversal of fortune, Alfred defeated Guthrum's army in May 878 at Edington.[47] The *Anglo-Saxon Chronicle* recorded the consequences of that victory.

45. Asser, c. 82, in *Alfred the Great,* ed. Simon Keynes and Michael Lapidge (Harmondsworth, 1983), p. 96.
46. Loyn, *Vikings in Britain,* pp. 44–67. For a list of Vikings known to have accepted Christianity during the ninth century on the Continent, see Ian Wood, "Christians and Pagans in Ninth-Century Scandinavia," in *The Christianization of Scandinavia,* ed. Brigit Sawyer, Peter Sawyer, and Ian Wood (Alinesas, Sweden, 1987), p. 50, nn. 84 and 86.
47. Dorothy Whitelock, "The Importance of the Battle of Edington," in *Report for 1975, 1976, and 1977 of the Society of Friends of the Priory Church of Edington, Wiltshire,* and reprinted in *From Bede to Alfred: Studies in Early Anglo-Saxon Literature and History* (London, 1980), art. xiii.

And then the enemy gave him preliminary hostages and great oaths that they would leave his kingdom, and promised also that their king should receive baptism, and they kept their promise. Three weeks later King Guthrum with 30 of the men who were the most important in the army came [to him] at Aller, which is near Athelney, and the king stood sponsor to him at his baptism there (*his se cyning þær onfeng æt fulwihte*); and the unbinding of the chrism (*crismlising*) took place at Wedmore. And he was twelve days with the king, and he honored him and his companions greatly with gifts.[48]

The account of Alfred's sponsorship of Guthrum contains or implies the key elements of diplomatic sponsorship as Christian rulers had practiced it for about three centuries. Alfred defeated King Guthrum in battle and compelled him to submit, though Guthrum remained a formidable foe. Smyth argued that Guthrum had his own reasons for seeking peace: the Danish farmers who composed his army had been in the field for years and pressured him to give them land for settlement.[49] To initiate a truce, Guthrum gave hostages and swore oaths to his native gods on a sacred iron ring. He agreed to be baptized along with thirty (or perhaps twenty-nine)[50] of his leading warriors: the conversion of a ruler was almost always accompanied by the baptism of his important followers. King Alfred received Guthrum from the font and gave him a baptismal name (*fulluht nama*) to accompany his new status, which was the aristocratic West Saxon name Athelstan. Although the *Chronicle* does not say so, Guthrum's warriors were certainly sponsored by someone, perhaps leading Anglo-Saxon thanes. Kings Alfred and Guthrum and their retinues feasted for twelve days, and Alfred made rich gifts to the new Christian, which could be interpreted as traditional baptismal gifts, although they may also have been tribute to Guthrum and his warriors. As noted earlier, Æthelnoth, ealdorman of the Mercians, may also have created a spiritual bond with Guthrum when he removed the chrism band from his forehead at Wedmore (*crismlysing*).[51] The peacemaking was successful. As Smyth noted,

His [Guthrum's] new life as a landed king in England, and as a Christian, would help in his relations with his powerful neighbor in Wessex who had

48. *ASC(A)*, s.a. 878, p. 51; *Anglo-Saxon Chronicle,* trans. Whitelock, pp. 49–50. Smyth, *Scandinavian Kings,* pp. 240–54, treated the entire episode.
49. Smyth, *Scandinavian Kings,* pp. 252–53.
50. See *Anglo-Saxon Chronicle,* trans. Whitelock, p. 15, n. 11, on interpreting Anglo-Saxon numbers.
51. Æthelweard, *Chronicon,* p. 42.

> just defeated him in war. The new relationship between the two kings was symbolized by Alfred standing sponsor to Guthrum at the font at Aller. No longer would Danes swear on their sacred ring while Alfred swore on the relics of saints during their mutual treaty negotiations. Both sides would henceforth be bound by the laws of the church to which they both belonged.[52]

Guthrum settled with his followers in East Anglia and maintained relatively good relations with his godfather. There is a surviving treaty concluded between them, although it does not mention their spiritual relationship.[53] Guthrum issued coins modeled on those of Alfred, and significantly, he used on them his Christian baptismal name, Athelstan.[54] In the entry for 890 (891 in the C-Version), the *Chronicle* recorded that "the northern King, Guthrum, whose baptismal name was Athelstan (*þæs fulluht-nama wæs Eþelstan*), died. He was King Alfred's godson (*se wæs Elfredes cyninges godsunu*), and he lived in East Anglia and was the first to settle that land."[55]

There is a striking Frankish parallel to Alfred's sponsorship of Guthrum. At Mainz or Ingelheim in 826, Louis the Pious (814–840) sponsored the Danish royal pretender Heriold. In a careful expression of earthly hierarchies, the empress Judith sponsored Heriold's wife; Louis's eldest son Lothar sponsored Heriold's son; Frankish nobles sponsored Heriold's noble followers; and Frankish commoners sponsored the remaining Danes. Louis clothed his godson in the white robes of a neophyte and subsequently gave him Frankish clothing made of expensive materials and decorated with jewels and precious metals. Each of the other godparents gave gifts of clothing suitable to the rank both of the sponsor and of the baptizee. After the religious service, Emperor Louis presided at a lavish banquet for the new Christians. Some days later, the emperor and his new godson concluded an alliance, renewing a bond that had existed since 814.[56] The unfolding of events in 826 helps us to understand what happened fifty-two years later when Alfred sponsored Guthrum. The accord with Guthrum, capped by baptism, sponsorship, renaming, and a godparental relationship, was the most successful of Alfred's sponsorships, probably because Guth-

52. Smyth, *Scandinavian Kings,* p. 253.
53. *EHD,* 416–17.
54. Smyth, *Scandinavian Kings,* p. 254.
55. *ASC(A)*, s.a. 890, p. 54; Stenton, *Anglo-Saxon England,* pp. 255–57.
56. Ermoldus Nigellus, *Poème sur Louis le Pieux et épîtres au Roi Pépin,* ed. and French trans. Edmond Faral (Paris, 1932), pp. 171–81; *Annales regni Francorum,* s.a. 814 and 826 (1968), pp. 106 and 144.

rum settled down in East Anglia and, as Smyth noted, it was in his interest to maintain peace.

Alfred and Hæsten

Alfred also tried, and apparently failed, to use sponsorship to deal with a second Viking chief, called Hæsten in the *Chronicle.*[57] Hæsten was a formidable figure on both sides of the English Channel. There was probably a saga literature about him which survives mostly in Latin texts, such as the first book, titled *Hastingus,* of Dudo of St. Quentin's history of the early Norman dukes, written in Normandy about 1015–1026.[58] For Dudo of St. Quentin, Hæsten was the model of the bad Viking, who among his many treacheries feigned conversion to Christianity. He contrasted Hæsten with Rollo, the good Viking who converted sincerely to Christianity and founded the Norman ducal family.[59]

Dudo's account of Hæsten throws interesting light on the role of sponsorship and baptism in dealing with Viking raiders. Dudo wrote that Hæsten set out with his warriors to conquer the city of Rome. Instead they attacked the city of Luna on the Italian coast, which they thought was Rome. When the count and bishop defended the city, Hæsten, whom Dudo depicted as wily and unscrupulous, decided on a ruse. His messengers told the authorities at Luna that he had been blown off course by unfavorable winds and meant the city no harm. They said their leader was ill and wished to be baptized and, if he died, to be buried in the city. The Christians took him at his word, and the bishop prepared for the baptism. Dudo continued: "The faithless one [Hæsten] enters the font, washing only his body. The wicked man receives baptism to the death of his soul. He is received from the very holy baptism by the bishop and the count. He is led as if ill and is anointed with the holy chrism and oil."[60] Hæstan then returned to the ship, where the next stage of his plan was set in motion.

57. *ASC(A)*, s.a. 893, pp. 55–58; Ruth Waterhouse, "The Haesten Episode in 894 *Anglo-Saxon Chronicle,*" *Studia Neophilologica* 46 (1974), analyzed the rather "muddled" account of Hæsten's stay in England.

58. Frederic Amory, "The Viking Hasting in Franco-Scandinavian Legend," in *Saints, Scholars, and Heroes: Studies in Medieval Culture in Honor of Charles W. Jones,* vol. 2 (Collegeville, Minn., 1979); Wilbur C. Abbott, "Hasting," *EHR* 13 (1898). Dudo of St. Quentin, *De moribus et actis primorum Normanniae ducum,* ed. Jules Lair, *Mémoires de la Société des Antiquaires de Normandie* 23/2 (1865).

59. Dudo, *De moribus,* 2, *Mémoires,* pp. 138–75, which is titled "Rollo."

60. Ibid., 1.6, p. 133: "Intrat perfidus fontes, corpus tantum diluentes. Suscipit nefarius baptismum, ad animae suae interitum. Suscipitur de sacrosancto baptismate ab episcopo et comite. Deducitur quasi infirmus, sacro chrismate oleoque delibutus."

His emissaries informed the bishop and count that their godson had died. They said that Hæsten offered rich deathbed gifts to the church and wished to be buried in a monastery within the city. Hæsten, feigning death, was brought into the city on a bier. The bishop celebrated mass for his godson. Just before burial was to take place, Hæsten rose from his bier, sword in hand, and killed the bishop personally, the ultimate bad godson. After much slaughter and looting of the city, the Vikings returned to Francia.[61]

The Viking raid on Luna may be historical, although the rich details in Dudo's account cannot be verified and seem mythological. The trickery built around baptism and sponsorship, whether or not it happened, was however based in reality. Other sources confirm that Vikings knew that Christians were eager to have them convert and that the agreement to be baptized and become godsons, however insincere, could cause Christian foes to let down their guard or at least to give gifts to the new converts.[62]

It is not easy to separate the mythologized Hæsten from the historical. The historical Hæsten may have fought, raided, and ravaged Frankish territory from 866. He entered the service of a Frankish king in the 880s but continued his search for booty. King Arnulf defeated him in 891 at the battle of the Dyle, and a famine in 892 drove the experienced warrior and his army from Francia to Anglo-Saxon England, where he posed a serious threat to King Alfred.[63]

A relatively long entry in *Anglo-Saxon Chronicle* recounted his stay in England:

> When the king [Alfred] heard that, he turned west towards Exeter with the whole army, except for a very inconsiderable portion of the people (who continued) eastwards. They went on until they came to London, and then with the citizens and with the reinforcements which came to them from the west, they went east to Benfleet. Hæsten had then come there with his army which had been at Milton, and the large army which had been at Appledore on the estuary of the Lympne had then also come there. Hæsten had previously built that fortress at Benfleet; and he was then out on a raid, and the

61. Ibid., 1.5, pp. 132–35. Henry G. Leach, *Angevin Britain and Scandinavia* (Cambridge, Mass., 1921), pp. 349–50, noted other examples of Vikings feigning death to capture a fortified place.
62. See Notker Balbulus, *Gesta Karoli* (1969), pp. 420–22. The *Annales Bertiniani,* s.a. 876, ed. Georg Waitz, *MGH SRG* 5 (Hanover, 1883), and reprinted in *Ausgewählte* 6 (Darmstadt) (1969), 244, recorded that some Northmen were baptized by the abbot/margrave Hugh and were brought before Emperor Charles the Bald, who gave them gifts and sent them home. "And just as before the baptism, so afterwards they behaved as Northmen in a pagan way."
63. *Annales Vedastini,* s.a. 892, ed. B. von Simpson, *MGH SRG* 12 (Hanover and Leipzig, 1909), and reprinted in *Ausgewählte* 6 (Darmstadt) (1969), 324; Amory, "Viking Hasting."

> large army was at home. Then the English went there and put the enemy to flight, and stormed the fortress and captured all that was within, both goods, and women and also children, and brought all to London; and they either broke up or burnt all the ships, or brought them to London or to Rochester. And Hæsten's wife and two sons were brought to the king; and he gave them back to him, because one of them was his godson, and the other the godson of Ealdorman Ethelred. They had stood sponsor to them before Hæsten came to Benfleet, and he had given the king oaths and hostages, and the king had made him generous gifts of money, and so he did also when he gave back the boy and the woman. But immediately they came to Benfleet and had made that fortress, Hæsten ravaged that kingdom, that very province which Ethelred, his son's godfather (*cumpæder*), was in charge of; and again, a second time, he had gone on a raid in that same kingdom when his fortress was stormed.[64]

The chronology of Hæsten's activities in England is not immediately clear in this chronicle entry and requires some disentangling. Almost as soon as Hæsten arrived in England, Alfred tried to make peace in the usual ways, exchanging hostages, oaths, and gifts. Circumstances favored sponsorship as well, because Hæstan had two unbaptized sons. Each of them was sponsored by an important Anglo-Saxon leader, one by King Alfred and the other by Alfred's powerful son-in-law, Æthelred, the ealdorman of Mercia. Such a double sponsorship had also been used with Guthrum in 878, when Alfred sponsored at baptism and Ealdorman Æthelnoth sponsored at the *crismlysing* (and perhaps at confirmation). Alfred did not sponsor Hæsten himself—why not? Probably Hæsten had already been baptized during his long career on the Continent, which included a period of alliance with a Frankish king.

Alfred's effort to find a modus vivendi with Hæstan failed. Unlike Guthrum, who had his own reasons to make peace, Hæsten was a rootless raider who had no intention of settling down. Neither oaths, nor gifts nor spiritual kinship tamed him. As soon as he had built a fortified camp at Benfleet, east of London, he began to raid "that very province which Ethelred, his cofather (*cumpæder*), was in charge of."[65] While Hæsten was absent from his camp on a raid, Alfred's army stormed the stronghold of his cofather "and captured all that was within, both goods, and women and also children, and brought all to London; and they either broke up or

64. *ASC(A)*, s.a. 893, pp. 55–58; *Anglo-Saxon Chronicle*, trans. Whitelock, p. 55.

65. *ASC(A)*, s.a. 893, p. 65, with the change that whereas Whitelock translated *cumpaeder* as "son's godfather," I translated it literally as "cofather," which retains the emphasis given by the chronicler.

burnt all the ships, or brought them to London." In contrast to Hæsten's treachery, the chronicler portrayed Alfred as scrupulous in his observance of the requirements of spiritual kinship. Among the captives were Hæsten's wife and two sons, whom Alfred returned to Hæsten "because one of them was his godson (*godsunu*), and the other the godson of Ealdorman Æthelred. They had stood sponsor to them before Hæsten came to Benfleet, and he had given the king oaths and hostages, and the king had also made him generous gifts of money."[66] The *Chronicle* actually said that Alfred returned only one son, but the thrust of the passage implies both. The *Chronicle* made the point that Alfred faithfully observed the duties of a spiritual kinsman when he released to his cofather his godson and the woman who was his comother. We do not know if Alfred's act of kindness to his cofather, comother, and godson had any effect because Hæsten disappeared from the historical record after 894, although he survived in legends primarily from northwestern France.[67]

Alfred and Anarawd of Gwynedd

At least once in dealing with Celtic Christians, King Alfred used sponsorship at confirmation to cement a political alliance. The Kingdom of Wessex was bounded on the west by Christian Welsh rulers who were themselves hard pressed by the Vikings who controlled York. Anarawd (c. 878–916), the son of King Rodri Mawr, the Christian ruler of the Kingdom of Gwynedd in northern Wales, was allied with the Vikings. About 893, Anarawd wished to escape his Viking alliance, "from which he had no good but rather loss. Carefully seeking the friendship of the king [Alfred], he came into his presence."[68] Because the British rulers of the Kingdom of Gwynedd were Christian, Anarawd had certainly been baptized, but apparently his confirmation was put off, as Alfred's had been a generation earlier. Or perhaps the Celtic liturgy in which Anarawd had been baptized omitted confirmation. Or maybe for political convenience Anarawd chose to be confirmed again. In any case, Alfred sponsored him at confirmation.

This situation reveals the usefulness of sponsorship at confirmation when dealing with rulers who were already Christians. The prevalence of speedy infant baptism meant that only occasionally was there an unbaptized child available to serve as the focal point for creating a spiritual bond between Christian rulers. But confirmation could provide an opportunity

66. *ASC(A)*, s.a. 893, p. 57.
67. Amory, "Viking Hasting"; Abbott, "Hasting."
68. Asser, *De rebus gestis Ælfredi*, c. 80, pp. 66–67.

to use the same person for a second sponsorship. Anarawd came to Alfred, "and when he was honorably received by the king and was accepted as a confirmation son (*filium confirmationis*) at the hand of a bishop and was enriched with very great gifts, he [Anarawd] submitted himself with all his people to the rule of the king under the same condition: that in all things he would be obedient to the royal will."[69]

King Athelstan (924–939)

King Athelstan and King Constantine

Alfred stabilized the political situation, and his successor, Edward, laid the groundwork for the resurgence of the Kingdom of Wessex. Alfred's grandson, King Athelstan, had an aggressive foreign policy. He conquered the Vikings of Northumbria; he imposed alliances by force or show of force on the rulers of Scotland, Strathclyde, and Wales. He also created a web of diplomatic alliances through marriage, fosterage, and sponsorship with rulers in the British Isles, Brittany, the Frankish kingdom, and the German Empire. One sister was married to the Frankish king Charles the Simple, and Athelstan sheltered Charles's heir and his own nephew, Louis, until the latter could be restored to the Carolingian throne in 936. Athelstan's sister, Eadhild, was married to Hugh, duke of the Franks, and his daughter Edith to Henry the Fowler's son Otto I.[70]

Athelstan's remarkable network of alliances extended temporarily to the Viking kingdom centered at York, before he conquered it. It is a complicated story with too many Olafs. In 926, one of Athelstan's sisters married Sihtric, the Danish king of York, who died unexpectedly in 927. Sihtric's heir was a young child named Olaf, born of Sihtric's earlier union. The child's rule was shaky, and his uncle, Guthfrith, king of the Irish Norsemen, came from Dublin to support him. When King Athelstan defeated both the boy and his uncle, young Olaf Sihtricson fled to Ireland and his uncle Guthfrith to Scotland. Athelstan's emissaries demanded that Constantine, king of the Scots, and Eugenius, king of the Cumbrians, turn over Guthfrith. But Guthfrith escaped captivity, gathered an army, and unsuccessfully attacked York. In desperation he surrendered to Athelstan, spent

69. Ibid.; David Dumville, "The "Six" Sons of Rhodri Mawr: A Problem in Asser's *Life of King Alfred*," *Cambridge Medieval Celtic Studies* 4 (1982), discussed the politics of the diplomatic realignment.

70. Stenton, *Anglo-Saxon England*, pp. 344–49; Michael Wood, "The Making of King Athelstan's Empire: An English Charlemagne?" in *Ideal and Reality in Frankish and Anglo-Saxon Society*, ed. Patrick Wormald, D. A. Bullough, and R. Collins (Oxford, 1983).

four days at his court, where he was treated honorably, and was permitted to return to his ships, "old pirate" (*vetus pirata*) that he was.[71]

Because Viking power had collapsed in Northumbria, the kings of the Scots and the Cumbrians needed to make amends with Athelstan. They came to him and "gave themselves along with their kingdoms to the king of the Angles [Athelstan]."[72] King Constantine happened to have an unbaptized son, who was used to seal the new relationship: "For the sake of that treaty (*in cujus pacti gratia*), he [Athelstan] ordered the son of Constantine to be baptized [and] he received him from the holy font."[73] King Constantine was a reluctant ally, and in 934, King Athelstan attacked him again. The twelfth-century chronicler John of Worcester reported that Constantine surrendered and gave a son to Athelstan as a hostage. If that boy was Athelstan's godson, he might have been about seven years old.[74] The peacemaking with the northern kings was unsuccessful in the long run because of Athelstan's ambitions. An alliance of Norse and Celts, including King Constantine, fought him at Brunanburgh in 937, where they were soundly defeated.[75]

King Athelstan and Alan, Duke of Brittany

King Athelstan used sponsorship for diplomatic purposes on another occasion. Between 919 and 937, Vikings operating in the Loire Valley disrupted Brittany and occupied Nantes. Matheudoi, the Breton count of Poher, and many of his followers fled to the Anglo-Saxon royal court in Wessex. Alan, known in later life as "Twisted Beard" (*Barbatorta*), was born from Count Matheudoi's marriage with a daughter of Alan the Great, the last duke of all of Brittany. Alan Barbatorta might have been born in England. Whether he was or not, at some time before Athelstan became king in 924, he sponsored the boy in baptism. Alan grew up at the Anglo-Saxon court as Athelstan's godson/foster son. Athelstan may also have been foster father to Hakon, son of Harold Fairhair, king of Norway.[76] After Athelstan

71. William of Malmesbury, *De gestis regum anglorum libri quinque,* 2.134, ed. William Stubbs (London, 1887), 1:146–47.
72. Ibid., p. 147.
73. Ibid., p. 147: "In cujus pacti gratia filium Constantini baptizari jussum ipse de sacro fonte suscepit."
74. John of Worcester, *Chronicle,* s.a. 934, p. 390.
75. William of Malmesbury, *De gestis,* 2.131, pp. 142–44. On these events, see Stenton, *Anglo-Saxon England,* pp. 342–43. In his introduction to *The Battle of Brunanburgh* (London, 1938), pp. 43–80, editor Alistair Campbell laid out the political events that led to the battle.
76. Stenton, *Anglo-Saxon,* pp. 348–49. See Lesley Abrams, "Anglo-Saxons," p. 217, n. 22, for the late-twelfth-century texts that identify Hakon as Athelstan's foster son.

became king, he remained Alan's strong patron. The *Chronicle of Nantes* recorded that "on account of the closeness (*familiaritas*) and friendship (*amicitia*) of this [baptismal] rebirth, the king [Athelstan] had great confidence in him [Alan]."[77] In 936, Alan led his followers back to Brittany and drove out the Vikings, with the military help of his godfather/foster father.[78]

King Edmund (939–946) and the Two Olafs

Athelstan's successor, Edmund, also used sponsorship in his dealings with Vikings. As mentioned earlier, in 927, King Athelstan had driven the young Olaf Sihtricson out of Northumbria into exile in Ireland. When Athelstan died in 939 and was succeeded by his eighteen-year-old brother Edmund, the exiled Vikings saw an opportunity to reestablish themselves in northern England. Olaf Guthfrithson, who was Olaf Sihtricson's cousin, reconquered much of Northumbria between 939 and 941. When he died in that year, Olaf Sihtricson became again king of the York Vikings. When he was defeated by King Edmund, the Northumbrian Vikings expelled him and chose as their king Rægnald, brother of Olaf Guthfrithson and cousin of Olaf Sihtricson.

As Olaf Sihtricson and Rægnald maneuvred against one another, each approached King Edmund, who became spiritual father to both. Because their religious statuses differed, so did Edmund's sponsorships. Olaf Sihtricson was a pagan, and in 943, King Edmund sponsored him at baptism.[79] Rægnald was already a Christian, and Edmund sponsored him at confirmation.[80] But control of York by either of these Norse rulers was unacceptable to Edmund. Within a year he had expelled both his godsons and taken possession of York.[81]

77. *Chronicon Namnetense*, c. 27, in *La Chronique de Nantes, 570 environ–1049*, ed. René Merlet, CTSEEH 19 (Paris, 1896), pp. 82–83: "quem et ipse rex Angliae Adelstannus jam prius ex lavacro sancto susceperat. Ipse rex pro familiaritate et amicitia hujus regenerationis magnam in eo fidem habebat."

78. Ibid., pp. 88–89. See also Flodoard, *Annales*, s.a. 936: "Brittones a transmarinis regionibus, Alstani regis praesidio, revertentes, terram suam repetunt," cited by Merlet, ibid. On the importance of the combination of godfather and foster father in some Celtic saints' lives, see François Kerlouegan, "Essai sur la mise en nourriture et l'éducation dans les pays celtique d'après le témoinage des textes hagiographiques latins," *Etudes Celtiques* 12 (1968–1969), 120–21. On Anglo-Saxon fosterage, see Roeder, *Über die Erziehung*.

79. *ASC(C)*, undated entry, p. 48: "Her Eadmund onfeng Onlafes cinges æt fulwihte."

80. Ibid.: "and þy ilcan gere embe tela micelne ferst he onfeng Rægnoldes cinges æt bisceopes handa."

81. *ASC(C)*, s.a. 944, p. 48; Stenton, *Anglo-Saxon England*, pp. 356–58.

King Æthelred II Unræd (978–1016) and Olaf Tryggvason

The second Viking age began about 980 with the resurgence of Viking invasions. In 994, Olaf Tryggvason, a descendant of the kings of Norway, entered an unstable alliance with Swein Forkbeard, son of the king of Denmark, to raid and plunder England. They ravaged much of southern and southeastern England, but their attack on London was unsuccessful. King Æthelred II could not defeat the combined armies and bought them off with food and sixteen thousand pounds of silver. In addition, he sought to split the Norwegians from the Danes as a way to weaken their power.[82] He sent Ealdorman Æthelweard (the chronicler) and Bishop Ælfheah of Winchester to arrange a separate peace with Olaf Tryggvason, who was already a Christian. "Then the king sent Bishop Ælfheah and Ealdorman Æthelweard for King Olaf, and hostages were given to the ships meanwhile. And they then brought Olaf to the king at Andover, with much ceremony, and King Ethelred stood sponsor to him at confirmation, and bestowed gifts on him royally. And then Olaf promised—as also he performed—that he would never come back to England in hostility."[83] Supported by his share of the sixteen thousand pounds of silver from his godfather Æthelred's tribute, Olaf left England and seized the Norwegian throne. Between 995 and 1000, he promoted the conversion to Christianity of his realms—Norway, the Orkney Islands, Iceland, and Greenland.[84]

King Cnut (1017–1035) and the Scottish King

Rodulfus Glaber (c. 980–c. 1046) composed a history of his times in five books.[85] He was not well informed about events in northern Britain, but King Cnut was his contemporary—he may even have seen him at Rome when Conrad II was made emperor in 1027/28. Rodulfus recorded that Cnut attacked King Malcolm II of Scotland (1005–1034):

82. Theodore M. Andersson, "The Viking Policy of Ethelred the Unready," *Scandinavian Studies* 59 (1987).
83. *ASC(C)*, s.a. 994, p. 54; *Anglo-Saxon Chronicle*, trans. Whitelock, p. 83.
84. Peter Sawyer, "Ethelred II, Olaf Tryggvason, and the Conversion of Norway," *Scandinavian Studies* 59 (1987), argued that Æthelred neutralized Olaf by his strategy of payments and sponsorship. See also Stenton, *Anglo-Saxon England*, pp. 376–78. Simon Keynes, "Andover 994," *Lookback at Andover: The Journal of the Andover History and Archaeology Society* 1 (1993), has a brief account of Olaf's confirmation.
85. Rodulphus Glaber, *Historiarum libri quinque*, pp. 1–253.

> After this Cnut set out with a great army to subjugate the Scots, whose king was called Malcolm. Malcolm was a great warrior, but, more importantly, he was a truly Christian king whose faith was reflected in his acts. When he realized that Cnut was seeking to invade his realm he gathered together the whole army of his own people and resisted mightily. In his pride Cnut continued the strife for a long time, but at last he ended his barbarous behaviour for the love of God on the advice of Duke Richard of Rouen and his sister, and mending his ways he lived in peace. Indeed he sought the friendship of the King of the Scots, receiving his son at the font of baptism.[86]

Rodulfus is not the best source for Cnut's activities in northern England; yet the account has an air of verisimilitude. The precedents noted above, including Athelstan's sponsorship of the son of King Constantine, argue for a cautious acceptance of the substance of the report.

Success and Failure

Sponsorship was not developed for the sake of diplomacy. It was a "domestic" institution of Christianity, arising out the intersection of liturgy, theology, and social need. But its importance inside Christian societies led to its use outside them, in what might be called foreign policy. Sponsorship did not always have the desired results, whether inside or outside Christian societies. Alliances failed or were repudiated when circumstances changed. But that did not make sponsorship unique. No tool of diplomacy was immune to failure, not marriage alliances, written treaties, oaths, other forms of adoption, nor even military victories. Power and circumstances determined whether any form of alliance would be long lasting.

Whether an act of sponsorship would create a durable political alliance varied from one situation to another. We can look at the matter from two points of view, that of the ruler who was sponsoring and that of the ruler, pagan or Christian, who was being sponsored. The royal sponsor viewed the matter from within his society, where kinship, spiritual or otherwise, was a powerful binding force. Although in messy reality, some kinsmen quarreled and even killed one another, kinship as it *ought* to function had a powerful hold on the emotions. The images of kinsmen fighting on one another's behalf, feuding for one another, advising one another in life's

86. Ibid., 2.3, pp. 54–57. The passage is difficult to date and explain; see John France's remarks in n. 1, pp. 56–57. On Malcolm II, see Benjamin T. Hudson, "Cnut and the Scottish Kings," *EHR* 107 (1992), which does not mention a sponsorship.

great moments, promoting one another's material welfare, and praying for one another after death animate imaginative literature as well as sober chronicles and charters. For a king, as for anyone else, circumstances beyond his control determined who his blood kin would be, but he could make more kin by choices at marriage, by forms of adoption, and by sponsorship. Because Christian rulers shared the same thought world as their Christian subjects, it was quite sensible for them to attempt to bring a pagan ruler or a foreign Christian ruler into some sort of kinship in the hope that he would adopt the outlook and behavior appropriate for a spiritual kinsman. Unlike some other techniques, which might be regarded as "pagan," sponsorship was Christian, rooted in God's sacramental grace, and sacred in a special way that no conferring of weapons or cutting of hair could be. When one ruler sponsored another, he may have hoped that a state of hostility or a harsh political arrangement of subordination could be softened by a bond that was at once personal and holy.

Rulers who were sponsored or whose children were sponsored probably saw the matter differently. Some might have been forced to accept baptism or confirmation for themselves or their children as a condition of making peace with their conqueror, like the Continental Saxons, who were forced to the baptismal font by military defeat. Such an alliance was often grudging and insincere, even if the sponsored ruler was already Christian. If pagan, there was the added problem that he probably did not share the sponsor's understanding of the theology of rebirth, of spiritual parenthood, and of spiritual childhood, which lay at the heart of spiritual kinship's success inside Christian societies. The records of baptized rulers who subsequently rebelled or attacked again point to such a scenario. The chances of lasting success through sponsorship seemed most remote when the pagan ruler was a raider without settled home, as were many of the Vikings and nomadic peoples of central and eastern Europe. But even settled rulers, such as those of the Celts on the western borders of the Anglo-Saxon kingdoms, threw off domination when they had the opportunity. In any case, the sponsoring bond was personal and lasted only for the lifetime of participants. The next generation of rulers might feel no obligation to honor the spiritual kinship, in which they did not automatically share.

But there were reasons why a pagan ruler might want to be sponsored by a Christian king or emperor. When invaders settled in a particular territory, they often wanted to regularize their relations with neighboring Christian powers and with the Christian subjects who inhabited the land they had conquered. Guthrum, for example, shared a border with an able Christian king; his Scandinavian followers lived among Christians. If Guthrum and his followers were to remain permanently in East Anglia, it was in their interest to accept Christianity and baptism, with Alfred as the king's godfather.

Some pagan rulers, especially those in the Byzantine and German spheres of influence, accepted Christianity because an alliance with the Byzantine or Ottonian emperor, who recognized their claims to power over their own people, strengthened their position within their own society. Alfred's alliance may have strengthened Guthrum's status in East Anglia, if not in the eyes of the Danes then in the eyes of the native Christian population. In central Europe, the introduction of Christianity fostered state building to the profit of anointed Christian kings and at the expense of independent aristocrats. In places such as Hungary and Poland, the conversion of a king had long-lasting effects in part because it opened the way for those respective peoples to take their place in a European/Christian world of kingdoms. But rulers often wanted to avoid political and religious subordination to the German emperors. To achieve that, they sought Christianity directly from the pope, to whom they "gave" themselves and from whom they gained archbishoprics independent from the German church.[87] Sponsorship remained a recurring feature of medieval diplomacy because a powerful godfather or cofather was a political asset of importance. Like their Christian counterparts on the Continent, Anglo-Saxon kings shared in that view and acted accordingly for more than four centuries to achieve diplomatic aims.

87. Angenendt, *Kaiserherrschaft,* pp. 296–310.

Epilogue

Since at least the sixth century, Greek and Latin Christians had cultivated forms of sacramental sponsorship which in their eyes created a new relationship, a spiritual kinship purer and more altruistic than physical kinship. In spite of many differences in detail, baptismal sponsorship, the oldest form, had the same basic structure everywhere—an adult Christian presented the candidate (usually an infant) for baptism; answered on the candidate's behalf, if necessary; "lifted" or "received" the person from the font after baptism; dried him or her off, and took the baptizee to Mass and first communion; and thereafter regarded the baptizee as a spiritual child and the baptizee's parents as coparents.

In aspiration, Christianity was a universal religion, but in operation it was profoundly local in the early medieval west. No council, pope, king, or emperor had "created" spiritual kinship, which was rooted in the theology of baptism. The widely felt desires to gain more spiritual kinsmen and to give religious sanction to human relationships led to a proliferation of occasions for sponsorship, which was a flexible institution, open to local conditions. Orthodox Christianity, which prevailed in the Byzantine Empire and elsewhere in the east, always carried out Christian initiation in a single, unified ceremony, which needed only one sponsor, called the *anadoxos.* In the west, the complex rituals of initiation "disintegrated" during the early Middle Ages into ceremonies that could be quite separate from one another—in the minister who performed them, their timing, their theology, and the sponsor who helped the candidate at each stage of initiation. Three occasions for sponsorship—the catechumenate, baptism, and confirmation—gradually became universal in the western churches, although the

Gallican liturgy and the related Celtic liturgies had no required episcopal confirmation before the eighth century. Local customs encouraged the creation of more occasions for sponsorship, such as the *crismlysing* in England or the five or six acts of sponsorship in parts of Norway, which never gained official approval but were observed in some places nonetheless.

Sponsorship created a family. There was an unmistakable spontaneity and, to use a much misused word, a "popular" dimension to the origin of this spiritual family. Clergy told participants in a baptism that they were participating in the second, spiritual birth of the baptizee. The participants drew the conclusion that just as a carnal birth creates a family, so a spiritual birth creates a new, spiritual family. It took centuries for the spiritual family to take shape, with its full range of expectations and taboos. Once it had become part of Christian religious and social life, however, the authorities in church and state tried to shape some aspects of it. There was a long tradition of exhortation and legislation on two matters, the duty of a godparent to instruct a godchild and the prohibition of marriage between people related by spiritual kinship. But sponsorship had other consequences in which the authorities were apparently not interested. Godparents had not only religious duties but also practical, secular duties toward their godchildren: they gave them gifts, protection, and advice, and they expected respect in return. In contrast to godparenthood, coparenthood was remarkably unnoticed and unregulated in early medieval sermons, conciliar canons, and laws, except for the abiding concern that coparents not marry each other. And yet coparenthood functioned in a multitude of practical ways. It is not an exaggeration to say that in Frankish society it was a central personal relationship among adults, where ritual, theology, and social need came together.

Although there was a shared framework of liturgy and theology, local traditions led to the emergence of different "godparent complexes" in early medieval Europe just as they have in modern Latin America and southern Europe. The early medieval sources do not permit the fine distinctions scholars can make among modern godparent complexes, but we can discern certain broad differences even in early medieval versions. In the early Middle Ages, there was a Byzantine/Italian version that placed great emphasis on the sexual consequences of spiritual kinship and defined the spiritual family in remarkably broad terms, to include even spiritual siblings. There was a Frankish version, which stressed the coparenthood that bound adults together in socially useful alliances while also recognizing godparenthood and, eventually, sexual taboos.

There was a third recognizable godparent complex in the west. When the Roman and Frankish missionaries brought Christianity to the pagan

Anglo-Saxons, they inevitably brought baptism, sponsorship, and spiritual kinship as well. The introduction of new forms of human relationship set in motion a centuries-long process of adaptation. When viewed against the wider backdrop of Christian practice, the Anglo-Saxon forms of sponsorship were variations on a Christian theme: they appear quite normal—there was nothing particularly "Germanic" about them, as some have argued.[1] But the Anglo-Saxon version of the godparent complex had features that set it off from others. It is striking that the sexual taboos associated with spiritual kinship, which were so prominent in Byzantium and Italy and in the Frankish realms, appeared very late in Anglo-Saxon history. Unlike the situation in Byzantium and Frankish Gaul, Anglo-Saxon godparents were never forbidden to marry their godchildren because the native practice of same-sex sponsorship cut off that possibility. The ban on marriage between coparents is found primarily in documents associated with Archbishop Wulfstan of York (996–1023). It is indeed possible that Wulfstan, a churchman deeply immersed in Carolingian normative texts, was the conduit through which the ban on the marriage of coparents reached the Anglo-Saxons. Aside from a few legal and homiletic texts of the early eleventh century, the sexual taboos had no discernible popular resonance in Anglo-Saxon England, as they certainly did in Byzantium and Francia. It is only after the Norman Conquest that one can say with some assurance that the sexual taboos associated with sponsorship functioned in England.

Another feature of the Anglo-Saxon godparent complex was its stress on godparenthood, which was conceptualized as a kind of adoption and assimilated to preexisting Anglo-Saxon practices, such as fosterage and the demand for wergild if a spiritual relative was killed. In England, godparenthood was certainly more widespread than fosterage. The latter might have been practiced primarily in the higher levels of Anglo-Saxon society, but every nonemergency baptism created a new parent-child bond, which was accessible to every Christian. No source said that sponsorship at the catechumenate, confirmation, or *crismlysing* created coparenthood. The Anglo-Saxons cultivated such forms of sponsorship for their ability to create the much desired parent-child bond.

The slow emergence of coparenthood, which is not attested for the first three centuries of Anglo-Saxon history, is also a distinct feature of the Anglo-Saxon complex, which set it apart from Frankish spiritual kinship in which coparenthood loomed large from the sixth century. But in the last 150 years of Anglo-Saxon history, coparenthood became visible in the

1. Ursula Perkow, *Wasserweihe, Taufe, and Patenschaft bei den Nordgermanen* (Hamburg, 1972).

sources, perhaps because the need for bonds with other adults made it more socially useful.

Thus far, I have stressed the ways in which the Anglo-Saxon godparent complex was more truncated than the Byzantine, Italian, and Frankish versions. But the Anglo-Saxon godparent complex is not to be understood primarily by what it did not have. In light of the fragmentary sources for early medieval history, it is bold to be too certain about when and where a social or religious custom originated. But the evidence points to a pioneering role for the Anglo-Saxons in the proliferation of forms of sponsorship. They might have created sponsorship at the catechumenate and at the *crismlysing,* for both of which the oldest evidence is Anglo-Saxon. They were also precocious in their interest in sponsorship at confirmation, which they might also have created. It is certain that the eighth-century Anglo-Saxon missionaries were important in disseminating sponsorship at confirmation among the Franks and, through them, to the western church.

Why might Anglo-Saxons have been interested in new forms of spiritual kinship? At least two factors were at work, one religious and one social. The sacramental origin of spiritual kinship set it apart from most other forms of relationship available to the laity. The Holy Spirit created the bond in a solemn religious setting and sustained it by divine grace. It was expected to be, and often was, more altruistic than carnal kinship.

But the word *spiritual* should not be confused with ethereal or ineffective. Spiritual kinship was a desirable kind of friendship, which created trust and put restraints on behavior in the face of deep-rooted social structures that made Anglo-Saxon society rather violent. The history of the Anglo-Saxon kings in the seventh and eighth centuries is marked by depositions, exiles, assassinations, and deaths in battle. The customs for royal succession invited strife among members of the *stirps regia,* the royal clan. Within the numerous royal lineages, every male of suitable age and battle worthiness could potentially be king. Violence was common in the succession to kingship.[2] Warfare was also endemic among the relatively small, often unstable early Anglo-Saxon kingdoms. For the rest of society, the feud was a morally sanctioned institution, and private vengeance, a part of life. In response, the Anglo-Saxons tried, not always successfully, to deter violence by creating personal bonds and group loyalties. Within a generation of the arrival of the missionaries, Anglo-Saxons used sponsorship to create kinlike bonds between rulers and, we may suppose, between other people.

2. Chaney, *Cult of Kingship,* pp. 7–42, on the *stirps regia,* the royal lineage, from which kings were chosen.

Over the course of its 450 years of existence, Anglo-Saxon society changed. Violence and instability were perhaps not more severe in the tenth and eleventh centuries than they had been in earlier times, but the sources reveal them more clearly. W. G. Runciman listed conditions that did not begin in late Anglo-Saxon England but did accelerate then: "internal warfare, external invasion, land reclamation and settlement, urbanization, the expansion of manufacture and trade, the introduction of coinage, the increasing sophistication of government, the spread of Christianity and monasticism, the revival of learning, and the progressive evolution of new forms of social differentiation."[3] He argued that these developments promoted social mobility but also increased anxiety and the need for new forms of association. Simon Keynes has made the point that tenth-century kings had difficulty in keeping peace and order in the face of corrupt reeves, overmighty subjects, and popular resistance.[4] The Viking invasions of the ninth century and their resurgence in the late tenth worsened the violence and instability. Some contemporaries thought that the Viking attacks contributed to the breakdown of traditional bonds of loyalty, which included kinship. Archbishop Wulfstan's *Sermo Lupi,* probably composed in 1014, took as one of its themes the disruption of moral and social order in the face of the Danish invaders. Wulfstan lamented the violation of traditional social bonds: parent to child, among kinsmen, lords and followers, slaves and masters. He included spiritual kinship among those social bonds whose failure he lamented: "And too many coparents and godchildren have killed one another far and wide throughout this people."[5] His call, of course, was not to abandon such bonds but to respect them.

But it was not only the Vikings who disrupted late Anglo-Saxon society. Internal changes remade human relationships. Two aggressive institutions, lordship and kingship, undermined traditional patterns of association based on kinship and community. Frank Stenton stressed that, in the last century of the Anglo-Saxon kingdom, older forms of personal and communal independence were giving way before the power of the richest thanes, who set themselves apart from and dominated other social groups.[6] The free farmers fell increasingly into subjection to powerful landlords.

3. W. G. Runciman, "Accelerating Social Mobility: The Case of Anglo-Saxon England," *Past and Present* 104 (1984), p. 3.

4. Simon D. Keynes, "Crime and Punishment in the Reign of King Æthelred the Unready," in *People and Places in Northern Europe: Essays in Honour of Peter Hayes Sawyer,* ed. Ian Wood and Niels Land (Woodbridge, England, and Rochester, N.Y., 1991), pp. 69–73.

5. Wulfstan, *Homily* 20, p. 258, lines 72–73.

6. Stenton, *Anglo-Saxon England,* pp. 490–91.

Malcolm Godden also emphasized the importance of wealth as a source of power. He argued that the growing disparity in wealth within the thanely group threatened the status and independence of the lesser thanes.[7] Within this context of violence and growing social differentiation, the need for bonds to promote loyalty and to serve as social glue was keenly felt. Voluntary, personal bonds grew in importance as a way to compensate for the relative decline of older forms of association. Such bonds might include commendation to a lord, membership in a gild or confraternity, and spiritual kinship. Godparenthood continued to be important as it had been since the seventh century, but coparenthood found a role it had not possessed in earlier Anglo-Saxon society, because it explicitly united adults.

Political alliances shared many of the characteristics of personal relationships. Consequently, sponsorship met the "diplomatic" needs of Anglo-Saxon kings, who in the early days had to deal with one another and in later times with foreign rulers, both Christian and pagan. The Anglo-Saxon kings were like their early medieval contemporaries, the Byzantine emperors, the Carolingian kings and emperors, and the German emperors, in using sponsorship to make foreign rulers their "sons" or "brothers" in order to enmesh them in alliances both religious and political.

In Anglo-Saxon England, as in the rest of the Christian world, church ritual and social life were not compartmentalized. Like other early medieval Christians, Anglo-Saxons found in sponsorship a flexible, religiously sanctioned personal relationship that became a permanent part of the social landscape. In it, liturgy, theology, social structures, and political culture intersected to create a "godparent complex," which shared its basic features with the rest of western Christianity but was adapted to the needs and structures of Anglo-Saxon society.

7. Malcolm Godden, "Money, Power, and Morality in Late Anglo-Saxon England," *ASE* 19 (1990).

Bibliography

Primary Sources

Actuum praeliminarium Synodi primi Aquisgranensis commentationes sive Statuta Murbacensia. Edited by Josef Semmler. In *Corpus consuetudinum monasticarum.* 1, *Initia consuetudinis Benedictinae,* edited by Kassius Hallinger, 442–50. Siegburg, 1963.

Adam of Bremen. *Gesta Hammaburgensis ecclesiae pontificum.* 3d ed. by Bernhard Schmeidler. *MGH SRG* 2. Hanover, 1917.

Adhemar of Chabannes. *Chronicon.* Edited by Jules Chavanon. CTSEEH 30. Paris, 1897.

Admonitio synodalis. In "Une 'Admonitio synodalis' de l'époque carolingienne: Etude critique et édition," edited by Robert Amiet. *Mediaeval Studies* 26 (1964): 12–82.

Adso of Montier-en-Der. *Vita sancti Bercharii.* In *Acta sanctorum,* October, 7/2, 1010–18.

Ælfric. *Ælfric's Catholic Homilies: The Second Series: Text.* Edited by Malcolm Godden. EETS SS 5. London, 1979.

———. *Ælfric's Lives of Saints.* 4 vols. Edited and translated by Walter W. Skeat. EETS OS 76, 82, 94, 114. London, 1881–1900; reprinted in 2 vol., 1966.

———. *Die Hirtenbriefe Ælfrics in altenglischer und lateinischer Fassung.* Edited by Bernhard Fehr. BAP 9. Hamburg, 1914.

———. *Homilies of Ælfric: A Supplementary Collection.* 2 vols. Edited by John C. Pope. EETS OS 259 and 260. London, 1967–68.

———. *Letter to Sigeweard.* In *The Old English Version of the Heptateuch,* edited by S. J. Crawford, 15–75. EETS OS 160. London, 1922; reprinted with additions by N. R. Ker, 1969.

——. *Sermones Catholici: First Series.* In *The Homilies of the Anglo-Saxon Church.* Vol. 1, edited by Benjamin Thorpe. London, 1844; reprinted New York, 1971.

——. *Sermones Catholici: Second Series.* In *The Homilies of the Anglo-Saxon Church,* vol. 2, edited by Benjamin Thorpe. London, 1846; reprinted New York, 1971.

Ælheah, Will of. In *Anglo-Saxon Wills,* edited and translated by Dorothy Whitelock, 22–24. Cambridge, 1930.

Æthelberht. *Dooms.* In *Die Gesetze der Angelsachsen,* edited by Felix Liebermann, 1:3–8. Halle, 1903; reprinted Aalen, 1960.

Æthelgifu, Will of. In *The Will of Æthelgifu,* edited by Dorothy Whitelock and N. R. Ker. Roxburghe Club. Oxford, 1968.

Æthelred, *Laws "ad Eanham."* In *Die Gesetze der Angelsachsen,* edited by Felix Liebermann, 1:247–59. Halle 1903; reprinted Aalen, 1960.

Æthelweard. *Chronicon.* In *The Chronicle of Æthelweard,* edited and translated by Alistair Campbell. London, 1962.

Æthelwulf. *De abbatibus.* Edited by Alistair Campbell. Oxford, 1967.

Alcuini sive Albini epistolae, edited by Ernst Dümmler. *MGH Epistolae* 4. Berlin, 1895.

Aldhelm. *Aldhelmi opera omnia.* Edited by Rudolph Ehwald. *MGH AA* 15. Berlin, 1919. Translated by Michael Lapidge and Michael Herren, *Aldhelm: The Prose Works,* Cambridge, 1979, and Michael Lapidge and James Rosier, *Aldhelm: The Poetic Works,* Cambridge, 1985.

Alfred the Great. Edited by Simon Keynes and Michael Lapidge. Harmondsworth, 1983.

Allocutio sacerdotum de coniugiis inlicitis ad plebem. In L. Machielsen, "Fragments patristiques non-identifiés du ms. Vat. Pal. 577," *Sacris Erudiri* 12 (1961): 533–35.

Die althochdeutschen Glossen. Edited by Elias von Steinmeyer and Eduard Sievers. 5 vols. Berlin, 1879–1922.

Angelsächsische Homilien und Heiligenleben. Edited by Bruno Assmann. BAP 3. Kassel, 1889.

The Anglo-Saxon Chronicle. Revised Translation edited by Dorothy Whitelock, with David C. Douglas and Susie I. Tucker. New Brunswick, N.J., 1962.

The Anglo-Saxon Chronicle:

A-Version. Edited by Janet Bately. Vol. 3 of *The Anglo-Saxon Chronicle: A Collaborative Edition.* General editors, David Dumville and Simon Keynes. Cambridge, 1986.

B-Version. Edited by Simon Taylor. Vol. 4 of *The Anglo-Saxon Chronicle: A Collaborative Edition.* General editors, David Dumville and Simon Keynes. Cambridge, 1983.

C-Version. Edited by Harry August Rositzke. *The C-Text of the Old English Chronicles.* Beiträge zur englischen Philologie 34. Bochum, 1940.

D-Version. Edited by G. B. Cubbin. Vol. 6 of *The Anglo-Saxon Chronicle: A Collaborative Edition.* General editors, David Dumville and Simon Keynes. Cambridge, 1996.

E-Version. Edited by Charles Plummer. *Two of the Saxon Chronicles Parallel,* on the basis of the edition by John Earle. Vol. 1. Oxford, 1892.

F-Version. Edited by Benjamin Thorpe. *The Anglo-Saxon Chronicle.* 2 vols. Rolls Series. London, 1861.

G-Version. Edited by Angelika Lutz. *Die Version G der Angelsächsischen Chronik.* Münchener Universitäts-Schriften, Philosophische Fakultät, Texte und Untersuchungen zur Englischen Philologie 11 Munich, 1981.

The Peterborough Chronicle, 1070–1154. 2d ed. by Cecily Clark. Oxford, 1970.

Annales Bertiniani. Edited by Georg Waitz. *MGH SRG* 5. Hanover, 1883. Reprinted in *Ausgewählte* 6 (Darmstadt) (1969): 11–287.

Annales Mosellani. Edited by J. M. Lappenberg. *MGH Scriptores* 16, 494–499. Hanover, 1859.

Annales regni Francorum. Edited by Friedrich Kurze. *MGH SRG* 6. Hanover, 1895. Reprinted in *Ausgewählte* 5 (Darmstadt) (1968): 10–155.

Annales Vedastini. Edited by B. von Simpson. *MGH SRG* 12, 40–82. Hanover and Leipzig, 1909. Reprinted in *Ausgewählte* 6 (Darmstadt) (1969): 290–337.

Asser. *De rebus gestis Ælfredi.* In *Asser's Life of King Alfred Together with the Annals of Saint Neots, Erroneously Ascribed to Asser,* edited by William Henry Stevenson. Oxford, 1904.

Augustine. *Confessionum libri xiii.* Edited by L. Verheijen, *CCSL* 27. Turnhout, 1981. Translated by Henry Chadwick. *Confessions.* Oxford, 1991.

——. *De catechizandis rudibus.* Translated by Joseph P. Christopher. *St. Augustine, First Catechetical Instruction.* Ancient Christian Writers 2. Westminster, Md., 1946.

——. *Epistulae.* In *S. Aureli Augustini hipponiensis episcopi epistulae,* edited by A. Goldbacher. *CSEL* 34. Vienna, 1895.

Aurelian. *Regula ad monachos.* In *PL* 68, cols. 385–98.

——. *Regula ad virgines.* In *PL* 68, cols. 399–406.

The Battle of Brunanburgh. Edited by Alistair Campbell. London, 1938.

Bede. *Epistola ad Ecgbertum episcopum.* In *Venerabilis Baedae opera historica,* edited by Charles Plummer, 1:405–23. Oxford, 1896.

——. *Historia abbatum.* In *Venerabilis Baedae opera historica,* edited by Charles Plummer, 2:364–387. Oxford, 1896.

——. *Historia ecclesiastica gentis Anglorum.* In *The Ecclesiastical History of the English People,* edited and translated by Bertram Colgrave and R. A. B. Mynors. Oxford, 1969.

——. *In Marci evangelium expositio.* Edited by D. Hurst. *CCSL* 120, 427–648. Turnhout, 1960.

——. *The Old English Version of Bede's Ecclesiastical History of the English People.* Edited and translated by Thomas Miller. EETS OS 95, 96, 110, 111. London, 1890–1898; reprinted 1959–1963.

——. *Vita sancti Cuthberti.* In *Two Lives of Saint Cuthbert,* edited and translated by Bertram Colgrave, 142–307. Cambridge, 1940.

Berthold von Regensburg. *Vollständige Ausgabe seiner Predigten.* 2 vol. Edited by Franz Pfeiffer. Vienna, 1862–1880.

Bertram of Le Mans. *Testamentum.* In *Actus pontificum Cenomannis in urbe degentium,* edited by Gustave Busson and Ambroise Ledru. *Archives Historiques du Maine* 2 (1901): 102–41.

Bidding Prayer. In W. H. Stevenson, "Yorkshire Surveys and Other Documents of the Eleventh Century in the York Gospels," *EHR* 27 (1912): 1–25.

The Blickling Homilies. Edited by R. Morris. EETS OS 58, 63, 73. London, 1874–1880; reprinted in 1 vol. London, 1967.

Boniface. *Epistolae.* In *S. Bonifatii et Lullii epistolae, MGH Epistolae selectae* 1, edited by Michael Tangl. Berlin, 1916. Translated by Ephraim Emerton. *The Letters of Saint Boniface.* Records of Civilization 31. New York, 1940.

Boniface, Pseudo-. *Capitula.* In *PL* 89, cols. 821–24.

——. *Sermones.* In *PL* 89, cols. 843–79.

Brotanek, Rudolf. *Texte und Untersuchungen zur altenglischen Literatur und Kirchengeschichte.* Halle, 1913.

Burchard of Worms. *Decretum.* In *PL* 140, cols. 537–1058.

Caesarius of Arles. *Regula monachorum.* In *Sancti Caesarii episcopi Arelatensis opera omnia,* edited by Germain Morin, 2:149–55. Maredsous, Belgium, 1942.

——. *Sermones.* In *Sancti Caesarii episcopi Arelatensis opera omnia,* 2 vols, edited by Germain Morin. Maredsous, Belgium, 1937 and 1942. Reprinted in *CCSL* 103 and 104. Turnhout, 1953.

——. *Statuta sanctarum virginum.* In *Sancti Caesarii Arelatensis episcopi Regula sanctarum virginum aliaque opuscula ad sanctimoniales directa,* edited by Germain Morin. Florilegium patristicum 34. Berlin, 1933. Translated in Mary Caritas McCarthy. *The Rule for Nuns of Saint Caesarius of Arles: A Translation with a Critical Introduction.* CUA Studies in Mediaeval History, new ser. 16. Washington, D.C., 1960.

Canones sancti Gregorii pape urbis Romae. In *Die Canones Theodori Cantuariensis und ihre Überlieferungsformen,* edited by Paul W. Finsterwalder, 253–70. Untersuchungen zu den Bussbüchern des 7., 8., und 9. Jahrhunderts. Weimar, 1929.

The Canons of Edgar. In *Councils and Synods with Other Documents Relating to the English Church,* vol. 1, A.D. *871–1204,* pt. 1: 871–1066, edited by Dorothy Whitelock, Martin Brett, and C. N. L. Brooke, 313–38. Oxford, 1981. Also edited by Roger Fowler. *Wulfstan's Canons of Edgar.* EETS OS 266. London, 1972.

Capitularia regum Francorum. 2 vols. Edited by A. Boretius and V. Krause. *MGH Leges,* 2. Hanover 1883 and 1897.

Cartularium Saxonicum. 3 vols. Edited by Walter de Gray Birch. London, 1885–1893; reprinted New York and London, 1964.

Chrodegang of Metz. *The Old English Version, with the Latin Original, of the Enlarged Rule of Chrodegang.* Edited by A. S. Napier. EETS OS 150. London, 1916.

Chronicon Namnetense. In *La Chronique de Nantes, 570 environ–1049,* edited by René Merlet. CTSEEH 19. Paris, 1896.

The Civil Law, including the Twelve Tables, the Institutes of Gaius, the Rules of Ulpian, the Opinions of Paulus, the Enactments of Justinian, and the Constitutions of Leo. 17 vols. Translated by S. P. Scott. Cincinnati, 1932.

Claudius Pontifical I. In *The Claudius Pontificals (from Cotton Ms. Claudius A.iii in the British Museum),* edited by D. H. Turner, 1–88. HBS 97. Chichester, 1971.

Codex Carolinus. Edited by Wilhelm Gundlach. *MGH Epistolae* 3, 476–657. Berlin, 1892.

Codex Iustinianus. In *Corpus iuris civilis,* vol. 2, edited by Paul Krueger. Berlin, 1895.

Collectio vetus Gallica. In *Kirchenrecht und Reform im Frankenreich: Die Collectio Vetus Gallica, die älteste systematische Kanones-sammlung des fränkischen Gallien,* edited by Hubert Mordek. Beiträge zur Geschichte und Quellenkunde des Mittelalters 1. Berlin and New York, 1975.

Concilia aevi Karolini. Edited by Albert Werminghoff. *MGH Concilia* 2/1–2. Hanover, 1906.

Concilia Galliae, A. 314–A. 506. Edited by Charles Munier. *CCSL* 148. Turnhout, 1963.

Concilia Galliae, A. 511–A. 695. Edited by Carlo de Clercq. *CCSL* 148A. Turnhout, 1963.

Confessionale Pseudo-Egberti. In *Das altenglische Bussbuch (Sog. Confessionale Pseudo-Egberti): Ein Beitrag zu den kirchlichen Gesetzen der Angelsachsen,* edited by Robert Spindler. Leipzig, 1934.

Constitutiones et acta publica imperatorum et regum. Vol. 1. Edited by L. Weiland. *MGH Legum* 4. Hanover, 1893.

Councils and Ecclesiastical Documents Relating to Great Britain and Ireland. 3 vols. Edited by Arthur Haddan and William Stubbs. Oxford, 1869–1878.

Councils and Synods with Other Documents Relating to the English Church. Vol. 1/1, A.D. *871–1066.* Vol. 1/2, A.D. *1066–1204.* Edited by Dorothy Whitelock, Martin Brett, and C. N. L. Brooke. Oxford, 1981.

Cyprian of Carthage. *Epistolae.* In *S. Thasci Caecili Cypriani opera omnia,* edited by Guilelmus Haertel. *CSEL* 3/2. Vienna, 1871.

De infantibus. In A. S. Napier, "Ein altenglisches Leben des heiligen Chad," *Anglia* 10 (1888): 154–55.

Dhuoda. *Manuel pour mon fils.* Edited by Pierre Riché and French translation by Bernard de Vregille and Claude Mondésert. *SC* 225. Paris, 1975.

Didascalia et Constitutiones Apostolorum. Edited by F. X. Funk. 2 vols. Paderborn, 1905.

Discipulus Umbrensium. *Canones Theodori.* In *Die Canones Theodori Cantuariensis und ihre Überlieferungsformen,* edited by Paul W. Finsterwalder, 285–334. Untersuchungen zu den Bussbüchern des 7., 8., und 9. Jahrhunderts. Weimar, 1929.

Dobbie, E. V. K. *The Anglo-Saxon Minor Poems.* Anglo-Saxon Poetic Record 6. New York, 1942.

Donatus of Besançon. *Regula ad virgines.* In *PL* 87, cols. 273–98.

Donatus of Metz. *Vita Trudonis confessoris Hasbaniensis.* Edited by Wilhelm Levison, 273–98. *MGH SRM* 6. Hanover, 1913.

Dudo of St. Quentin. *De moribus et actis primorum Normanniae ducum,* edited by Jules Lair. Caen, 1865. Also in *Mémoires de la Société des Antiquaires de Normandie* 23/2 (1865): 115–301.

Ecloga: Das Gesetzbuch Leons III und Konstantinos V, edited by Ludwig Burgmann. Forschungen zur byzantinischen Rechtsgeschichte 10. Frankfort am Main, 1983.

Ecloga. In *A Manual of Roman Law: The Ecloga Published by the Emperors Leo III and Constantine V of Isauria,* translated by Edwin H. Freshfield. Cambridge, 1926.

Eddius Stephanus. *Vita Wilfridi episcopi Eboracensis.* In *The Life of Bishop Wilfrid by Eddius Stephanus,* edited and translated by Bertram Colgrave. Cambridge, 1927.

Egeria. *Itinerarium.* Edited by A. Franceschini and R. Weber. *CCSL* 175, 29–103. Turnhout, 1965. English translation by John Wilkinson. *Egeria's Travels.* London, 1971.

Egil's Saga. Translated by Gwyn Jones. Syracuse, N.Y., 1960.

Einhard. *Vita Karoli Magni.* 6th ed. by Oswald Holder-Egger. *MGH SRG* 25. Hanover, 1911. Reprinted in *Ausgewählte* 5 (Darmstadt) (1968): 164–211.

Eligius of Noyon. *Predicacio sancti Eligii episcopi.* Edited by Bruno Krusch, 751–61. *MGH SRM* 4. Hanover and Leipzig, 1902.

Encomium Emmae reginae. Edited by Alistair Campbell. Camden Third Series 72. London, 1949.

English Historical Documents. Vol. 1, *c. 500–1042.* 2d ed. by Dorothy Whitelock. London and New York, 1979.

Ermoldus Nigellus. *Poème sur Louis le Pieux et épîtres au Roi Pépin.* Edited and French translation by Edmond Faral. Les classique de l'histoire de France au Moyen Age 14. Paris, 1932.

Eusebius Gallicanus. *Collectio homiliarum.* Edited by Fr. Glorie. *CCSL* 101. Turnhout, 1970.

Excerptiones Egberti. In "The Latin Canonical Tradition in Late Anglo-Saxon England: The *Excerptiones Egberti,*" edited by Robin Aronstam. Ph.D. dissertation, Columbia University, 1974.

Exhortatio ad plebem Christianam. In *Denkmäler deutscher Poesie und Prosa aus dem VIII–XII Jahrhundert,* edited by K. Müllenhoff and W. Scherer, 1:200–201. Berlin, 1892.

Felix. *Vita sancti Guthlaci.* In *Felix's Life of Saint Guthlac,* edited and translated by Bertram Colgrave. Cambridge, 1956.

Ferreolus of Uzès. *Regula.* In *PL* 66, cols. 959–76.

Flodoard. *Annales de Flodoard.* Edited by Philippe Lauer. CTSEEH 39. Paris, 1905.

———. *Historia Remensis ecclesiae.* Edited by J. Heller and G. Waitz, 409–599. *MGH Scriptores* 13. Hanover, 1881.

Fredegar, pseudo-. *Chronicle.* In *The Fourth Book of the Chronicle of Fredegar with Its Continuations,* edited and translated by J. M. Wallace-Hadrill. London, 1960.

Frostathing, Older Law of the. In *Norges gamle love indtil 1387,* edited by R. Keyser and P. A. Munch, 1:121–258. Christiania, 1846. Translated by Laurence M. Larson. *The Earliest Norwegian Laws, Being the Gulathing Law and the Frostathing Law,* 213–403. Records of Civilization 20. New York, 1935.

Gelasian Sacramentary. In *Liber sacramentorum Romanae Ecclesiae,* edited by H. A. Wilson. Oxford, 1894.

George, Bishop of Ostia. Letter to Pope Hadrian I. In *Alcuini sive Albini epistolae,* edited by Ernst Dümmler, 19–29. *MGH Epistolae* 4. Berlin, 1895.

Die Gesetze der Angelsachsen. 3 vols. Edited by Felix Liebermann. Halle, 1903–1916; reprinted Aalen, 1960.

Gesta abbatum Fontanellensium. Edited by S. Loewenfeld. *MGH SRG* 28. Hanover, 1886.

Ghaerbald of Liège. *Die Kapitulariensammlung Bischof Ghaerbalds von Lüttich.* Edited by Wilhelm A. Eckhardt. Germanenrechte. Neue Folge, Deutschrechtliches Archiv 5. Göttingen, 1955.

——. *Second Diocesan Statute.* Edited by Peter Brommer, 26–32. *MGH Capitula episcoporum* 1. Hanover, 1984.

Grágás. In *Laws of Early Iceland: Grágás: The Codex Regius of Grágás with Material from Other Manuscripts,* translated by Andrew Dennis, Peter Foote, and Richard Perkins, 23–238. University of Manitoba Icelandic Studies 3. Winnepeg, 1980.

Gratian. *Decretum.* In *Corpus iuris canonici,* Vol. 1, edited by Emil Friedberg. Leipzig, 1879; reprinted Graz, 1955.

Gregory I. *Dialogi libri iv.* In *Dialogues,* 3 vols., edited by Adalbert de Vogüé and French translation by Paul Antin. *SC* 251, 260, 265. Paris, 1978–1980.

——. *Epistolae.* In *S. Gregorii Magni Registrum epistularum,* 2 vols., edited by Dag Norberg. *CCSL* 140 and 140A. Turnhout, 1982.

——. *Old English Dialogues.* In *Bischof Wærferths von Worcester Übersetzung der Dialoge Gregors des Grossen,* edited by H. Hecht. BAP 5. Leipzig and Hamburg, 1900–1907.

Gregory II. *Old English Version of the Council of 721.* In *Die altenglischen Version des Halitgar'schen Bussbuches* (*Sog. Poenitentale Pseudo-Ecgberti*), edited by Joseph Raith, 71–72. BAP 13. Hamburg, 1933.

Gregory of Tours. *Historia Francorum* 2d ed. by Bruno Krusch, Wilhelm Levison, and Walther Holtzmann. *MGH SRM* 1/1. Hanover, 1951. Translated by O. M. Dalton. *The History of the Franks by Gregory of Tours.* 2 vols. Oxford, 1927.

Gulathing, Older Law of the. In *Norges gamle Iove indtil 1387,* edited by R. Keyser and P. A. Munch, 1:3–118. Christiania, 1846. Translated by Laurence M. Larson. *The Earliest Norwegian Laws, Being the Gulathing Law and the Frostathine Law,* 35–210. Records of Civilization 20. New York, 1935.

Haito of Basel. *Capitula.* Edited by Peter Brommer, 210–19. *MGH Capitula episcoporum* 1. Hanover, 1984.

Herard of Tours. *Capitula.* In *PL* 121, cols. 763–74.

Hincmar of Reims. *Vita Remigii episcopi Remensis.* Edited by Bruno Krusch, 250–341. *MGH SRG* 3. Hanover, 1896.

Hippolytus. *The Apostolic Tradition.* In *La Tradition Apostolique d'après les anciennes versions,* 2d ed. by Bernard Botte, *SC* 11bis. Paris, 1968.

Homilia de sacrilegiis. In *Eine Augustin fälschlich beilegte Homilia de sacrilegiis,* edited by C. P. Caspari. Christiania, 1886.

Hrabanus Maurus. *Epistolae.* Edited by Ernest Dümmler, 381–515. *MGH Epistolae* 5. Berlin, 1899. And *Appendix ad Hrabanum epistolarum Fuldensium fragmenta ex octava nona et decima centuriis ecclesiasticae historiae,* ibid., 517–30.

Huneberc. *The Hodoeporicon of St. Willibald.* In *The Anglo-Saxon Missionaries in Germany,* translated by C. H. Talbot, 152–77. New York, 1954.

Ine, King of Wessex. *Institutiones.* In *Die Gesetze der Angelsachsen,* edited by Felix Liebermann, 1:89–133. Halle, 1903; reprinted Aalen, 1960.

Instituta Cnuti. In *Die Gesetze der Angelsachsen,* edited by Felix Liebermann, 1:279–367. Halle, 1903; reprinted Aalen, 1960.

The Irish Penitentials. Edited and translated by Ludwig Bieler with Appendix by D. A. Binchy. Scriptores Latini Hiberniae 5. Dublin, 1965.

Iudicia Theodori Greci et episcopi Saxonum. In *Die Canones Theodori Cantuariensis und ihre Überlieferungsformen,* edited by Paul W. Finsterwalder, 239–52. Untersuchungen zu den Bussbüchern des 7., 8., und 9. Jahrhunderts. Weimar, 1929.

Iudicium de penitentia Theodori episcopi. In *Die Canones Theodori Cantuariensis und ihre Überlieferungsformen,* edited by Paul W. Finsterwalder, 271–84. Untersuchungen zu den Bussbüchern des 7., 8., und 9. Jahrhunderts. Weimar, 1929.

John Chrysostom. *Huit catéchèses baptismales inédites.* Edited by Antoine Wenger. *SC* 50. Paris, 1957.

John the Deacon (sixth century). *Epistola Iohannis Diaconi ad Senarium.* In "Un florilège carolingien sur la symbolisme des cérémonies du baptême, avec un Appendice sur la lettre de Jean Diacre," in *Analecta Reginensia,* 153–79. *ST* 59. Vatican City, 1933.

John the Deacon (ninth century). *Vita sancti Gregorii Magni.* In *PL* 75, cols. 59–242.

John the Deacon (eleventh century). *Chronicon venetum et gradense.* In *Cronache veneziane antichissime,* edited by Giovanni Monticolo, 59–171. Fonti per la storia d'Italia 9. Rome, 1890.

John Malalas. *Chronicle.* In *The Chronicle of John Malalas,* translated by E. Jeffries, M. Jeffries, and Roger Scott. Byzantina Australiensia 4. Melbourne, 1986.

John Skylitzes. *Synopsis historiarum.* Edited by Johannes Thurn. Corpus fontium historiae byzantinae 5. Berlin, 1973.

John of Worcester. *The Chronicle of John of Worcester.* Vol. 2. Edited by R. R. Darlington and P. McGurk and translated by Patricia Bray and P. McGurk. Oxford Medieval Texts. Oxford, 1995.

Jonas, pseudo-. *Vita Uulframni episcopi Senonici.* Edited by Bruno Krusch and Wilhelm Levison, 657–73. *MGH SRM* 5. Hanover and Leipzig, 1910.

Lacnunga. In *Anglo-Saxon Magic and Medicine,* edited by J. H. G. Grattan and C. Singer, 96–204. Publications of the Wellcome Historical Medical Museum, new ser. 3. London, 1952.

The Laws of the Earliest English Kings. Edited by F. L. Attenborough. Cambridge, 1922.

Leo III and Constantine V. *Novella.* In Dieter Simon, "Zur Ehegesetzgebung der Isaurier." In *Fontes minores,* vol. 1, Forschungen zur byzantinischen Rechtsgeschichte 1, 16–35; text of the *Novella,* 21–30. Frankfurt am Main, 1976.

The Leofric Missal. Edited by F. E. Warren. Oxford, 1883.

Liber Eliensis. Edited by E. O. Blake. Camden Third Series 92. London, 1962.

Liber historiae Francorum. Edited by Bruno Krusch. *MGH SRM* 2, 238–328. Hanover, 1888. Translated by Bernard S. Bachrach. *Liber historiae Francorum.* Lawrence, Kans., 1973.

Liber Pontificalis. 2d ed. by Louis Duchesne. 3 vols. Paris, 1955–1957.

Liber sacramentorum Romanae aecclesiae ordinis anni circuli (*Sacramentarium Gelasianum*). Edited by L. C. Mohlberg, L. Eizenhöfer, and P. Siffrin. Rerum ecclesiasticarum documenta, Ser. maior 4. Rome, 1960.

Liber sacramentorum Romanae ecclesiae. Edited by H. A. Wilson. Oxford, 1894.

Liutprand, King. *Leges Liutprandi regis.* Edited by Fr. Bluhme. *MGH Leges* 4: *Leges Langobardorum,* 96–175. Hanover, 1868. Translated by Katherine F. Drew. *The Lombard Laws,* 137–214. Philadelphia, 1973.

Machielsen, L. "Fragments patristiques non-identifiés du ms. Vat. Pal. 577." *Sacris Erudiri* 12 (1961): 488–538.

Manuale et Processionale ad usum insignis Ecclesiae Eboracensis. Edited by W. G. Henderson. Surtees Society 63. London, 1875.

Martin of Braga. *De correctione rusticorum.* In *Martini episcopi Bracariensis opera omnia,* edited by Claude Barlow, 183–203. Papers and Monographs of the American Academy in Rome 12. New Haven, 1950.

Medieval Handbooks of Penance. Translated by John T. McNeill and Helena Gamer. Records of Civilization 29. New York, 1938.

Memorials of the Church of S. S. Peter and Wilfrid, Ripon. Surtees Society 74. Durham, 1882.

The Missal of New Minster, Winchester. Edited by D. H. Turner. HBS 93. London, 1962.

The Missal of Robert of Jumièges. Edited by H. A. Wilson. HBS 11. London, 1896.

The Missal of Saint Augustine's, Canterbury. Edited by Martin Rule. Cambridge, 1896.

Mone, F. J. *Quellen und Forschungen zur Geschichte der teutschen Literatur und Sprache.* Vol. 1. Aachen and Leipzig, 1830.

Napier, A. S. "Contributions to Old English Literature. 1, An Old English Homily on the Observance of Sunday." In *An English Miscellany Presented to Dr. Furnivall in Honour of His Seventy-Fifth Birthday,* edited by W. P. Ker, A. S. Napier, and W. W. Skeat, 355–62. Oxford, 1901.

———. *Old English Glosses.* Anecdota Oxoniensia, Medieval and Modern Series 11. Oxford, 1900.

———. *Wulfstan.* Sammlung Englischer Denkmäler 4. Berlin, 1883; reprinted with appendix by K. Ostheeren, 1967.

Napier, A. S., and William H. Stevenson. *The Crawford Collection of Early Charters and Documents Now in the Bodleian Library.* Anecdota Oxoniensia, Medieval and Modern Series 7. Oxford, 1895.

Nicephorus. *Opuscula historica.* Edited by C. de Boor. Leipzig, 1880.

Nicholas I. *Epistolae.* Edited by E. Perels. *MGH Epistolae* 6, 257–690. Hanover, 1925.

Nornageststhåttr. In *The Saga of the Völsungs,* translated by George K. Anderson. Newark, Del., 1982.

The Northumbrian Priests' Law. In *Councils and Synods with Other Documents Relating to the English Church,* vol. 1/1, A.D. *871–1066,* edited by Dorothy Whitelock, Martin Brett, and C. N. L. Brooke, 449–68. Oxford, 1981.

Das northumbrische Priestergesetz. Edited by Hans P. Tenhaken. Düsseldorfer Hochschulreihe 4. Düsseldorf, 1979.

Notker Balbulus. *Gesta Karoli.* Edited by Hans F. Haefele. *MGH SRG,* nova series 12. Berlin, 1959. Reprinted with German translation in *Ausgewählte* 7 (Darmstadt) (1969): 322–427.

Oda, Archbishop of Canterbury. *Constitutiones.* In *Councils and Synods with Other Documents Relating to the English Church,* vol. 1/1, A.D. *871–1066,* edited by Dorothy Whitelock, Martin Brett, and C. N. L. Brooke, 67–74. Oxford, 1981.

Old Gelasian Sacramentary. Edited by H. A. Wilson. In *Liber sacramentorum Romanae ecclesiae.* Oxford, 1894.

Les ordines Romani du Haut Moyen Age. 5 vols. Edited by Michel Andrieu. Spicilegium Sacrum Lovaniense 11, 23, 24, 28, 29. Louvain, 1931–1961.

Ordo ad visitandum et unguendum infirmum. In "Altenglische Ritualtexte für Krankenbesuch, heilige Ölung und Begräbnis," edited by Bernhard Fehr, In *Texte und Forschungen zur englischen Kulturgeschichte: Festgabe für Felix Liebermann,* ed. M. Förster and K. Wildhagen, 46–67. Halle, 1921.

Osbern. *Vita sancti Elphegi archiepiscopi cantuariensis.* In *Anglia Sacra,* edited by Henry Wharton, 2:122–42. London, 1691.

Page, R. I. "Old English Liturgical Rubrics in Corpus Christi College, Cambridge, MS 422." *Anglia* 96 (1978): 149–58.

Passio beatae Margaretae virginis et martyris. In *The Old English Lives of St. Margaret,* edited by Mary Clayton and Hugh Magennis, 152–71. CSAE 9. Cambridge, 1995.

Paul the Deacon. *Historia Langobardorum.* Edited by L. Bethmann and G. Waitz. *MGH SRG* 48. Hanover, 1878.

——. *Vita Gregorii.* In *PL* 75, cols. 41–60.

The Peterborough Chronicle. See under *Anglo-Saxon Chronicle.*

Pirminius. *Dicta abbatis Pirminii de singulis libris canonicis scarapsus.* In *Der heilige Pirmin und sein Pastoralbüchlein,* edited by G. Jecker and translated by Ursmar Engelmann. Sigmaringen, 1976.

Poenitentiale Cummeani. In *The Irish Penitentials,* edited by Ludwig Bieler, 108–35. Scriptores Latini Hiberniae 5. Dublin, 1963.

Poenitentiale Ecgberti. In *Quellen und Forschungen zur Geschichte der teutschen Literatur und Sprache,* vol. 1, edited by F. J. Mone, 500–528. Aachen and Leipzig, 1830.

Poenitentiale Martenianum. In "Bussbücherstudien. 1, Das sog. poenitentiale Martenianum," edited by Walther von Hörmann. ZSSRG, Kanonistische Abteilung 4 (1914): 358–483.

Poenitentiale Pseudo-Egberti. In *Die altenglische Version des Halitgar'schen Bussbuches* (*Sog. Poenitentiale Pseudo-Egberti*), edited by Josef Raith. BAP 13. Hamburg, 1933.

Poenitentiale Theodori. In *Quellen und Forschungen zur Geschichte der teutschen Literatur und Sprache,* edited by F. J. Mone, 1:532–42. Aachen and Leipzig, 1830.

Pontificale Lanaletense (*Bibliothèque de la Ville de Rouen A.27 Cat. 368*): *A Pontifical Formerly in Use at St. Germans, Cornwall.* Edited by G. A. Doble. HBS 74. London, 1936.

The Pontifical of Egbert. In *Two Anglo-Saxon Pontificals* (*The Egbert and Sydney Sussex Pontificals*), edited by H. M. J. Banting. HBS 104. London, 1989.

Le Pontifical Romano-germanique du dixième siècle. 2 vols. Edited by Cyrille Vogel and Reinhard Elze. *ST* 226 and 227. Vatican City, 1963.

Procopius. *The Anecdota or Secret History.* Edited and translated by H. B. Dewing. Loeb Classical Library 6. London and Cambridge, Mass., 1935.

Quadripartitus. In *Die Gesetze der Angelsächsen,* edited by Felix Liebermann, 1:529–46. Halle, 1903; reprinted Aalen, 1960.

Regino of Prüm. *Libri duo de synodalibus causis et disciplinis ecclesiasticis.* Edited by F. G. A. Wasserschleben. Leipzig, 1840.

Regula Tarnantensis. In Fernando Villegas. In "La 'Regula Monasterii Tarnantensis': Texte, sources, et tradition," *RB* 84 (1974): 7–65.

Remigius of Reims. *Testamentum.* In Hincmar, *Vita Remigii episcopi Remensis,* edited by Bruno Krusch, 336–47. *MGH SRM* 3. Hanover, 1896.

Rimbert. *Vita Anskarii.* Edited by Georg Waitz. *MGH SRG* 55. Hanover, 1884.

Robert Grosseteste. *Epistolae.* Edited by Henry Luard. Rolls Series 25. London, 1861.

Rodulfus Glaber. *Vita domni Willelmi abbatis.* In *Rodulfi Glabri Historiarum libri quinque,* edited by Neithard Bulst and translated by John France and Paul Reynolds, 254–99. Oxford, 1989. Also in Neithard Bulst, "Rodulfus Glabers Vita domni Willelmi abbatis: Neue Edition nach einer Handschrift des 11. Jahrhunderts (Paris, Bibl. nat. lat. 5390)." *DAEM* 30 (1974): 450–87.

Rushworth Gospels. In *The Four Gospels in Anglo-Saxon, Northumbrian, and Mercian Versions,* 4 vols., edited by W. W. Skeat. Cambridge, 1871–1887.

The Sarum Missal Edited from Three Early Manuscripts. Edited J. Wickham Legg. Oxford, 1916.

The Sidney Sussex Pontifical. In *Two Anglo-Saxon Pontificals* (*The Egbert and Sydney Sussex Pontificals*), edited by H. M. J. Banting. HBS 104. London, 1989.

Stowe Missal. 2 vols. Edited by G. F. Warner. HBS 31 and 32. London, 1906–1915.

Sulpicius Severus. *Vita sancti Martini.* In *Vie de Saint Martin,* 3 vols., edited by Jacques Fontaine. *SC* 133–35. Paris, 1967–1969.

Tacitus, *Germania.* In *Tacitus: The Agricola and the Germania,* translated by H. Mattingly and translation revised by S. A. Handford, 101–41. Harmondsworth, 1970.

Tertullian. *De baptismo.* Edited by R. F. Refoulé in collaboration with M. Drouzy. *SC* 35. Paris, 1952. Edited and translated by Ernest Evans. *Tertullian's Homily on Baptism.* London, 1964.

Theodore of Canterbury. In *Die Canones Theodori Cantuariensis und ihre Überlieferungsformen,* edited by Paul W. Finsterwalder. Untersuchungen zu den Bussbüchern des 7., 8., und 9. Jahrhunderts. Weimar, 1929.

Theodulf of Orléans. *First Synodal Statute.* Edited by Peter Brommer, 102–42. *MGH Capitula episcoporum* 1. Hanover, 1984. Old English translations edited by Hans Sauer. *Theodulfi Capitula in England.* Munich, 1978.

Theophanes. *Chronographia.* 2 vols. Edited by C. de Boor. Leipzig, 1883–1885.

Thietmar of Merseburg. *Chronicon.* Edited by Robert Holtzmann and reprinted with a German trans. by Werner Trillmich, *Ausgewählte* 9 (Darmstadt) (1957).

Trent, Council of. In *Decrees of the Ecumenical Councils,* translated by Norman Tanner, 2:657–800. London, 1990.

Trullo, Council in. In *Iuris ecclesiastici Graecorum historia et monumenta,* vol. 2, edited by J. B. Pitra, 4–75. Rome, 1868.

Twelfth-Century Homilies in MS. Bodley 343. Edited by A. O. Balfour. EETS OS 137. London, 1909; reprinted 1962.

Vercelli Homilies. In *The Vercelli Homilies and Related Texts,* edited by D. G. Scragg. EETS OS 300. Oxford, 1992. Also Paul Szarmach. *Vercelli Homilies IX–XXIII.* Toronto, 1981.

Vita sanctae Balthildis, recensiones A and B. Edited by Bruno Krusch. *MGH SRM* 2, 475–508. Hanover, 1888.

Vita Bertini. Edited by Bruno Krusch and Wilhelm Levison. *MGH SRM* 5, 729–86. Hanover, 1910.

Vita Ceolfridi. In *Venerabilis Baedae opera historica,* edited by Charles Plummer, 2:388–404. Oxford, 1896.

Vita Cuthberti episcopi Lindisfarnensis. In *Two Lives of Saint Cuthbert,* edited and translated by Bertram Colgrave, 59–139. Cambridge, 1940.

Vita Dagoberti III regis Francorum. Edited by Bruno Krusch. *MGH SRM* 2, 511–24. Hanover, 1888.

Vita beate Genovefae virginis. Edited by Bruno Krusch. *MGH SRM* 3, 215–38. Hanover, 1896.

Vita sancti Gregorii. In *The Earliest Life of Gregory the Great by an Anonymous Monk of Whitby,* edited and translated by Bertram Colgrave. Lawrence, Kan. 1968.

Vita Hucberti episcopi Traiectensis. Edited by Wilhelm Levison. *MGH SRM* 6, 482–96. Hanover, 1913.

Vita Lupi episcopi Senonensis. Edited by Bruno Krusch. *MGH SRM* 4, 179–87. Hanover and Leipzig, 1902.

Vita sancti Machuti. In *The Old English Life of Saint Machutus,* edited by David Yerkes. Toronto, 1984.

Vita sancti Rumwoldi. In *Three Eleventh-Century Anglo-Latin Saints' Lives: Vita S. Birini, Vita et Miracula S. Kenelmi, and Vita S. Rumwoldi,* edited by Rosalind Love, 91–115. Oxford, 1996.

Wærferth. *Bischofs Wærferth von Worcester Übersetzung der Dialoge Gregors des Grossen.* Edited by Hans Hecht. BAP 5. Leipzig, 1900.

Walafrid Strabo. *Libellus de exordiis et incrementis quarundam in observationibus ecclesiae. MGH Capitularia* 2, 473–516. Hanover, 1897.

Whitaker, E. C. *Documents of the Baptismal Liturgy.* London, 1960.

Whitelock, Dorothy. *Anglo-Saxon Wills.* Cambridge, 1930.

William of Malmesbury. *De gestis regum Anglorum libri quinque.* Edited by William Stubbs. Rolls Series 90, in 2 parts. London, 1887–1889.

——. *Vita Wulfstani. The Vita Wulfstani of William of Malmesbury,* edited by R. R. Darlington. Camden Third Series 40. London, 1928. Translated by Michael Swanton. In *Three Lives of the Last Englishmen,* 89–140. Garland Library of Medieval Literature, ser. B, 10. New York and London, 1984.

The Winchcombe Sacramentary (*Orléans, Bibliothèque municipale, 127* [*105*]). Edited by Anselme Davril. HBS 109. London, 1995.

Wulfric Spott, Will of. In *Anglo-Saxon Wills,* edited and translated by Dorothy Whitelock, 47–51. Cambridge, 1930.

Wulfstan of Winchester. *Vita sancti Ethelwoldi.* In *The Life of Saint Æthelwold,* edited by Michael Lapidge and Michael Winterbottom. Oxford, 1991.

Wulfstan of York. *The Homilies of Wulfstan.* Edited by Dorothy Bethurum. Oxford, 1957.

——. *Institutes of Polity, Civil and Ecclesiastical.* Edited by Karl Jost. Schweizer Anglistische Arbeiten 47. Bern 1959.

——. *Sermo Lupi ad Anglos.* Rev. ed. by Dorothy Whitelock, Exeter, 1976. Also in *The Homilies of Wulfstan,* edited by Dorothy Bethurum, 261–275. Oxford, 1957.

Zachary, Pope. Letter to Theodore of Pavia. In *Epistolae Langobardicae collectae,* edited by Wilhelm Gundlach. *MGH Epistolae* 3, 710–11. Berlin, 1892.

Zeno of Verona. *Tractatus.* In *Zenonis Veroniensis Tractatus,* edited by Bengst Löfstedt. *CCSL* 22. Turnhout, 1971.

Secondary Sources

Aarts, F. G. A. M. "The Pater Noster in Medieval English Literature." *Papers on Language and Literature* 5 (1969): 3–16.

Abbott, Wilbur C. "Hasting." *EHR* 13 (1898): 439–63.

Abrams, Lesley. "The Anglo-Saxons and the Christianization of Scandinavia." *ASE* 24 (1995): 213–49.

Aland, Kurt. *Did the Early Church Baptize Infants?* Translated by G. R. Beasley-Murray. London, 1961.

Althoff, Gerd. *Verwandte, Freunde, und Getreue: Zum politischen Stellenwert der Gruppenbindungen im früheren Mittelalter.* Darmstadt, 1990.

Amory, Frederic. "The Viking Hasting in Franco-Scandinavian Legend." In *Saints, Scholars, and Heroes: Studies in Medieval Culture in Honor of Charles W. Jones,* edited by Margot H. King and Wesley M. Stevens, 2: 265–86. Collegeville, Minn., 1979.

Andersson, Theodore M. "The Viking Policy of Ethelred the Unready." *Scandinavian Studies* 59 (1987): 284–95.

Angenendt, Arnold. "Bonifatius und das Sacramentum initiationis: Zugleich ein Beitrag zur Geschichte der Firmung." RQCAKG 72 (1977): 133–83.

——. "The Conversion of the Anglo-Saxons Considered against the Background of the Early Medieval Mission." In *Angli e Sassoni al di qua e al di là del Mare, SSAM* 32, Spoleto, 1986, 747–81.

——. "Das geistliche Bündnis der Päpste mit den Karolingern, 754–796." *Historisches Jahrbuch* 100 (1980): 1–94.

——. *Kaiserherrschaft und Königstaufe: Kaiser, Könige, und Päpste als geistliche Patrone in der abendländischen Missionsgeschichte.* Arbeiten zur Frühmittelalterforschung 15. Berlin, 1984.

———. "Die Karolingern und die 'Familie der Könige.' " *Zeitschrift des Aachener Geschichtsvereins* 96 (1989): 5–33.

———. "Taufe und Politik im frühen Mittelalter." *FS* 7 (1973): 143–68.

Archbishop Theodore: Commemorative Studies on His Life and Influence. Edited by Michael Lapidge, CSAE 11. Cambridge, 1995.

Aronstam, Robin. "The Latin Canonical Tradition in Late Anglo-Saxon England: The *Excerptiones Egberti.*" Ph.D. dissertation, Columbia University, 1974.

———. "Recovering Hucarius: A Historiographical Study in Early English Canon Law." *Bulletin of Medieval Canon Law* 5 (1975): 117–22.

Aubrun, Michel. *La paroisse en France des origines au xv*[e] *siècle.* Paris, 1986.

Bäck, Hilding. *The Synonyms for 'Child,' 'Boy,' 'Girl,' in Old English: An Etymological-Semasiological Investigation.* Lund Studies in English 2. Lund, 1934.

Banks, R. A. "A Study of the Old English Versions of the Lord's Prayer, the Creeds, the Gloria, and Some Prayers Found in British Museum Ms. Cotton Galba A.XIV, Together with a New Examination of the Place of the Liturgy in the Literature of Anglo-Saxon Magic and Medicine." Ph.D dissertation, University of London, 1968.

Barlow, Frank. *Edward the Confessor.* Berkeley and Los Angeles, 1970.

Bastiaensen, A. A. R. *Observations sur le vocabulaire liturgique dans l'Itineraire d'Egérie.* Latinitas Christianorum primaeva 17. Nijmegen and Utrecht, 1962.

Battaglia, Francis J. "Anglo-Saxon Chronicle for 755: The Missing Evidence for a Traditional Reading." *Publications of the Modern Language Association* 81 (1966): 173–78.

Bedard, Walter. *The Symbolism of the Baptismal Font in Early Christian Thought.* CUA Studies in Sacred Theology, 2d ser. 45. Washington, D.C., 1951.

Bennett, Michael. "Spiritual Kinship and the Baptismal Name in Traditional European Society." In *Principalities, Powers, and Estates: Studies in Medieval and Early Modern Government and Society,* edited by L. O. Frappell, 1–13. Adelaide, 1978.

Betz, Werner. "Karl der Grosse und die Lingua Theodisca." In *Karl der Grosse: Lebenswerk und Nachleben.* Vol. 2, *Das geistige Leben,* edited by Bernhard Bischoff, 300–306. Düsseldorf, 1965.

Bischoff, Bernhard, and Michael Lapidge. *Biblical Commentaries from the Canterbury School of Theodore and Hadrian.* CSAE 10. Cambridge, 1994.

Blair, John. "Anglo-Saxon Minsters: A Topographical Review." In *Pastoral Care before the Parish,* edited by John Blair and Richard Sharpe, 226–66. Leicester, 1992.

———. "Debate: Ecclesiastical Organization and Pastoral Care in Anglo-Saxon England." *EME* 4 (1995): 193–212.

Bolton, W. F. *A History of Anglo-Latin Literature, 597–1066.* Vol. 1, *597–740.* Princeton, N.J., 1967.

Bono, Francesco del. "La letteratura catechetica di lingua tedesca." In *La conversione al cristianesimo nell'Europa dell'alto medioevo,* 697–741. *SSAM* 14. Spoleto, 1967.

Bostock, J. Knight. *A Handbook on Old High German Literature.* 2d ed. rev. by K. C. King and D. R. McLintock. Oxford, 1976.

Bosworth, Joseph. *An Anglo-Saxon Dictionary, Based on the Manuscript Collections of Joseph Bosworth.* Edited by Thomas N. Toller. Oxford, 1882–98. *Supplements* by Thomas N. Toller, issued in three parts, 1908–21, with revisions and enlarged addenda by Alistair Campbell. London and New York, 1973.

Botte, Bernard. "Le vocabulaire ancien de la confirmation." *La Maison-Dieu* 54 (1958): 5–22.

Bouhot, J.-P. "Explications du rituel baptismal à l'époque carolingienne." *Revue des Etudes Augustiniennes* 24 (1978): 278–301.

Boynton, Mark, and Susan Reynolds. "The Author of the Fonthill Letter." *ASE* 25 (1996): 91–95.

Braude, Jacob. *Die Familiengemeinschaften der Angelsachsen.* Rechtsgeschichtliche Abhandlungen 3. Leipzig, 1932.

Brückmann, J. "Latin Manuscript Pontificals and Benedictionals in England and Wales." *Traditio* 29 (1973): 391–458.

Brundage, James A. *Law, Sex, and Christian Society in Medieval Europe.* Chicago, 1987.

Brunner, Heinrich. "Sippe und Wergeld nach niederdeutschen Rechten." ZSSRG, Germanistische Abteilung 3 (1882): 1–101.

Brusselmans, Christianne. "Les fonctions de parrainage des enfants aux premiers siècles de l'Eglise, 100–550." Ph.D. dissertation, CUA, Washington, D.C., 1964.

Buisson, Ludwig. "Formen normannischer Staatsbildung, bis 11. Jahrhundert." In *Studien zum mittelalterlichen Lehenswesen,* 95–125. Vorträge und Forschungen 5. Lindau and Konstanz, 1960.

Cabié, Robert. *La lettre du pape Innocent Ier à Décentius de Gubbio, 19 Mars 416* Bibliothèque de la Revue d'histoire ecclésiastique 58. Louvain, 1973.

Cambridge, Eric, and David Rollason. "Debate: The Pastoral Organization of the Anglo-Saxon Church: A Review of the 'Minster Hypothesis.' " *EME* 4 (1995): 87–104.

Campbell, James. "The First Christian Kings." In *The Anglo-Saxons,* edited by James Campbell, 44–69. Oxford, 1982.

———. "Observations on the Conversion of England." *Ampleforth Journal* 78 (1973): 12–26. Reprinted in his *Essays in Anglo-Saxon History,* 69–84. London, 1986.

Campbell, J. K. *Honour, Family, and Patronage: A Study of Institutions and Moral Values in a Greek Mountain Community.* Oxford, 1962.

Cattaneo, Enrico. "Il battistero in Italia dopo il mille." In *Miscellanea Gilles Gerard Meersseman,* 171–95. Italia Sacra 15. Padova, 1970.

Chaney, William A. *The Cult of Kingship in Anglo-Saxon England: The Transition from Paganism to Christianity.* Berkeley and Los Angeles, 1970.

Charles-Edwards, Thomas. *Early Irish and Welsh Kinship.* Oxford, 1993.

———. "The Penitential of Theodore and the *Iudicia Theodori.*" In *Archbishop Theodore: Commemorative Studies on His Life and Influence,* edited by Michael Lapidge, 141–74. CSAE 11. Cambridge, 1995.

Chavasse, Antoine. *Le sacramentaire gélasien (Vaticanus Reginensis 316): Sacramentaire presbytéral en usage dans les titres romains au viie siècle.* Bibliothèque de Théologie, sér 4, Histoire de la Théologie 1. Paris and Tournai, 1958.

Chrysos, Evangelos. "Byzantine Diplomacy, A.D. 300–800: Means and Ends." In *Byzantine Diplomacy,* edited by Jonathan Shepherd and Simon Franklin, 25–39. Aldershot, Great Britain, 1992.

Cleasby, Richard. *An Icelandic-English Dictionary.* Enlarged by Gudbrand Vigfusson, 2d ed. with a supplement by William A. Craigie. Oxford, 1957.

Collingwood, William G. "Christian Vikings." *Antiquity* 1 (1927): 172–80.

Cook, Albert. "The Evolution of the Lord's Prayer in English." *American Journal of Philology* 12 (1891): 59–66.

——. "New Texts of the Lord's Prayer and Hymns." *Modern Language Notes* 7 (1892): 21–23.

Corblet, Jules. *Histoire dogmatique, liturgique, et archéologique du sacrement de baptême.* 2 vols. Paris, 1881.

Corrain, Clito, and Pierluigi Zampini. *Documenti etnografici e folkloristici nei sinodi diocesani italiani.* Bologna, 1970.

Cramer, Peter. *Baptism and Change in the Early Middle Ages, c. 200–c. 1150.* CSMLT 4 ser., 20. Cambridge, 1993.

Crawford, Samuel J. "The Worcester Marks and Glosses of the Old English Manuscripts in the Bodleian Together with the Worcester Version of the Nicene Creed." *Anglia* 52 (1928): 1–25.

Crehan, Joseph. *Early Christian Baptism and the Creed: A Study in Ante-Nicene Theology.* London, 1950.

Cross, James E., and Andrew Hamer. "Ælfric's *Letters* and the *Excerptiones Ecgberhti.*" In *Alfred the Wise: Studies in Honour of Janet Bately on the Occasion of Her Sixty-fifth Birthday,* edited by Jane Roberts and Janet L. Nelson with Malcolm Godden, 5–13. Cambridge, 1997.

Cubitt, Catherine. *Anglo-Saxon Church Councils, c. 650–c. 850.* London and New York, 1995.

——. "Pastoral Care and Conciliar Canons: The Provisions of the 747 Council of Clofesho." In *Pastoral Care before the Parish,* edited by John Blair and Richard Sharpe, 193–209. Leicester, 1992.

Dalbey, Marcia. "The Good Shepherd and the Soldier of God: Old English Homilies on St. Martin of Tours." *Neuphilologische Mitteilungen* 85 (1984): 422–34.

Daly, William M. "Caesarius of Arles: A Precursor of Medieval Christendom." *Traditio* 26 (1970): 1–28.

——. "Clovis: How Barbaric, How Pagan?" *Speculum* 69 (1994): 619–64.

Danielou, Jean, and Henri Marrou. *The First Six Hundred Years.* Translated by Vincent Cronin. London, 1964.

Deanesly, Margaret. "Canterbury and Paris in the Reign of Æthelberht." *History* 26 (1941): 97–104.

——. *The Pre-Conquest Church in England.* New York, 1961.

——. *Sidelights on the Anglo-Saxon Church.* London, 1962.

Delabriolle, Pierre. "Papa." *Archivum Latinitatis Medii Aevi* (*Bulletin du Cange*) 4 (1928): 65–69.

Delahaye, Hippolyte. "Note sur la légende de la lettre du Christ tombée du ciel." *Bulletins de l'Académie Royale de Belgique,* Classe des lettres (1899): 171–213. Reprinted in his *Mélanges d'hagiographie grecque et latine,* 150–78. Subsidia hagiographica 42. Brussels, 1966.

Dick, Ernst. "Das Pateninstitut im altchristlichen Katechumenat." *Zeitschrift für Katholische Theologie* 63 (1939): 1–49.

A Dictionary of Medieval Latin from British Sources. Edited by R. E. Latham. Oxford, 1975– .

Dictionary of Old English [microform]. Edited by Angus Cameron, Antonette Di Paolo Healey et al. Toronto, 1986– .

Dölger, Franz. "Der Bulgarenherrscher als geistlicher Sohn des byzantinischen Kaisers." In *Byzanz und die europäische Staatenwelt,* 183–96. Ettal, 1953.

——. "Die 'Familie der Könige' im Mittelalter." *Historisches Jahrbuch* 60 (1940): 397–420. Reprinted in his *Byzanz und die europäische Staatenwelt,* 34–69. Ettal, 1953.

Dondeyne, A. "La discipline des scrutins dans l'Eglise Latine avant Charlemagne." *RHE* 28 (1932): 5–32, 751–87.

Dujarier, Michel. *A History of the Catechumenate: The First Six Centuries.* New York, 1979.

——. *Le parrainage des adultes aux trois premiers siècles de l'Eglise: Recherche historique sur l'évolution des garanties et des étapes catéchuménales avant 313.* Paris, 1962.

Dumville, David. "The Importation of Mediterranean Manuscripts into Theodore's England." In *Archbishop Theodore: Commemorative Studies on His Life and Influence,* edited by Michael Lapidge, 96–119. CSAE 11. Cambrdige, 1995.

——. "Liturgical Books from Late Anglo-Saxon England: A Review of Some Historical Problems." In *Liturgy and the Ecclesiastical History of Late Anglo-Saxon England,* 96–152. Woodbridge, England, 1992.

——. "The "Six" Sons of Rhodri Mawr: A Problem in Asser's *Life of King Alfred.*" *Cambridge Medieval Celtic Studies* 4 (1982): 5–18.

Earle, John. *A Hand-book to the Land-Charters and Other Saxonic Documents.* Oxford, 1888.

Eckhardt, Karl A. "Adoption." In *Studia Merovingica,* 240–61. Bibliotheca rerum historicarum 11. Aalen, 1975.

Eichmann, E. "Die Adoption des deutschen Königs durch den Papst." ZSSRG, Germanistische Abteilung 37 (1916): 291–312.

Ellis, Henry. *A General Introduction to Domesdaybook.* 2 vol. London, 1833.

Engelhardt, Isrun. *Mission und Politik in Byzanz: Ein Beitrag zur Strukturanalyse byzantinischer Mission zur Zeit Justins und Justinians.* Miscellanea Byzantina Monacensia 19. Munich, 1974.

English-Icelandic Dictionary. 3d ed. by G. T. Zoega. Reykjavik, 1954.

Enright, Michael J. "Charles the Bald and Æthelwulf of Wessex: The Alliance of 856 and Strategies of Royal Succession." *Journal of Medieval History* 5 (1979): 291–302.

Essays in Anglo-Saxon Law. Boston, 1905.

Evans, Angela Care. "Late Roman and Byzantine Silver, Hanging-Bowls, Drinking Vessels, Cauldrons and Other Containers, Textiles, the Lyre, Pottery Bottle, and Other Items." In *The Sutton Hoo Ship-Burial,* edited by Rupert Bruce-Mitford, 3:125–46. London, 1983.

——. *The Sutton Hoo Ship-Burial.* London, 1986.

Fanning, Stephen. "Bede, *Imperium,* and the Bretwaldas." *Speculum* 66 (1991): 1–26.

Farmer, Sharon A. *Communities of Saint Martin: Legend and Ritual in Medieval Tours.* Ithaca, N.Y., 1991.

Ferro, Karen. "The King in the Doorway: The Anglo-Saxon Chronicle, A.D. 755." In *Kings and Kingship,* edited by Joel Rosenthal, 17–30. Acta 11. Binghamton, N.Y., 1986.

Fichtenau, Heinrich. *Living in the Tenth Century: Mentalities and Social Orders.* Translated by Patrick J. Geary. Chicago, 1991.

Finberg, H. P. R. *The Early Charters of Wessex.* Studies in Early English History 3. Leicester, 1964.

Fine, Agnès. *Parrains, marraines: La parenté spirituelle en Europe.* Paris, 1994.

Finn, Thomas M. *Early Christian Baptism and the Catechumenate: Italy, North Africa, and Egypt.* Collegeville, Minn., 1992.

——. *Early Christian Baptism and the Catechumenate: West and East Syria.* Collegeville, Minn., 1992.

——. *The Liturgy of Baptism in the Baptismal Instructions of St. John Chrysostom.* CUA Studies in Christian Antiquity 15. Washington, D.C., 1967.

Fischer, Andreas. *Engagement, Wedding, and Marriage in Old English.* Anglistische Forschungen 176. Heidelberg, 1986.

Fisher, J. D. C. *Christian Initiation: Baptism in the Medieval West: A Study in the Disintegration of the Primitive Rite of Initiation.* Alcuin Club Collections 47. London, 1965.

Foot, Sarah. "Anglo-Saxon Minsters: A Review of Terminology." In *Pastoral Care before the Parish,* edited by John Blair and Richard Sharpe, 212–25. Leicester, 1992.

——. " 'By Water in the Spirit': The Administration of Baptism in Early Anglo-Saxon England." In *Pastoral Care before the Parish,* edited by John Blair and Richard Sharpe, 171–92. Leicester, 1992.

Förster, Max. "Die altenglischen Bekenntnisformeln." *ES* 75 (1942–43): 159–69.

——. "Die Bedeutung von AE Gebisceopian und ihre Sippe." *Anglia* 66 (1942): 255–62.

Foster, George. "Cofradriá and Compadrazgo in Spain and Spanish America." *Southwestern Journal of Anthropology* 9 (1953): 1–28.

Frantzen, Allen J. *The Literature of Penance in Anglo-Saxon England.* New Brunswick, N.J., 1983. Revised by the author and translated by Michel Lejeune as *La littérature de la pénitence dans l'Angleterre anglo-saxonne,* Studia Friburgensia, nouvelle série 75. Fribourg, 1991.

Freisen, Joseph. *Geschichte des kanonischen Eherechts bis zum Verfall der Glossenliteratur.* 2d ed. Paderborn, 1893.

Fritze, Wolfgang. "Die fränkische Schwurfreundschaft der Merowingerzeit: Ihr Wesen und ihre politische Funktion." ZSSRG, Germanistische Abteilung 71 (1954): 74–125.

Fritzner, Johan. *Ordbog over det gamble norske Sprog.* Edited by Didrik Seip and Trygve Knudsen. 3 vols. Oslo, 1954.

Gatch, Milton McC. *Preaching and Theology in Anglo-Saxon England: Ælfric and Wulfstan.* Toronto, 1977.

Gelis, J. "La mort du nouveau-né et l'amour des parents. Quelques réflexions à propos des pratiques de répit." *Annales de Demographie Historique* (1983): 23–32.

Gerberding, Richard. *The Rise of the Carolingians and the Liber historiae Francorum.* Oxford, 1987.

Gillmann, Franz. "Das Ehehindernis der gegenseitigen geistlichen Verwandtschaft der Paten?" *AKKR* 86 (1906): 688–714.

Gneuss, Helmut. *Lehnbildungen und Lehnbedeutungen im Altenglischen.* Berlin, 1955.

——. "Liturgical Books in Anglo-Saxon England and Their Old English Terminology." In *Learning and Literature in Anglo-Saxon England: Studies Presented to Peter Clemoes on the Occasion of His Sixty-fifth Birthday,* edited by Michael Lapidge and Helmut Gneuss, 91–141. Cambridge, 1985.

Godden, Malcolm. "Money, Power, and Morality in Late Anglo-Saxon England." *ASE* 19 (1990): 41–65.

Goody, Jack. *The Development of the Family and Marriage in Europe.* Cambridge, 1983.

The Greatest Englishman: Essays on St. Boniface and the Church at Crediton. Edited by Timothy Reuter. Exeter, 1980.

Greenfield, Kathleen. "Changing Emphases in English Vernacular Homiletic Literature, 960–1225." *Journal of Medieval History* 7 (1981): 283–97.

Greenfield, Stanley B., and Daniel G. Calder. *A New Critical History of Old English Literature.* New York, 1986.

Gretsch, Mechtild. "The Language of the 'Fonthill Letter.' " *ASE* 23 (1994): 57–102.

Guchteneeëre, Bernard de. "Le parrainage des adultes aux ive et ve siècles de l'Eglise." Excerpta ex dissertatione ad Lauream in Facultate Theologica Pontificiae Universitatis Gregorianae, Louvain, 1964.

Gy, Pierre-Marie. "Du baptême pascal des petits enfants au baptême Quamprimum." In *Haut Moyen-Age: Culture, éducation, et société: Etudes offerts à Pierre Riché,* edited by Claude Lepelley and Michel Sot, 353–365. La Garenne-Colombe, 1990.

——. "Quamprimum: Note sur le baptême des enfants." *La Maison-Dieu* 32 (1952): 124–28.

Hanawalt, Barbara. *Growing Up in Medieval London: The Experience of Childhood in History.* Oxford, 1993.

Harris, Joseph, and Thomas D. Hill. "Gestr's 'Prime Sign': Source and Signification in *Norna-Gests Þáttr.*" *Arkiv för Nordisk Filologi* 104 (1989): 103–22.

Hartmann, Wilfried. *Die Synoden der Karolingerzeit im Frankenreich und in Italien.* Konziliengeschichte: Reihe A: Darstellungen. Paderborn, 1989.

Hattenhauer, Hans. "Observantia christianitatis: St. Dunstan und das Eherecht." In *Vom mittelalterlichen Recht zur neuzeitlichen Rechtswissenschaft,* edited by N. Brieskorn, P. Mikat, D. Muller, and D. Willoweit, 31–57. Rechts- und Staatswissenschaftliche Veröffentlichungen der Görres-Gesellschaft, Neue Folge 72. Paderborn, 1994.

Hazeltine, Harold D. "Geschichte der Eheschliessung nach angelsächsischen Recht." In *Festgabe für Dr. Bernhard Hübler . . . zum 70. Geburtstag am 25. Mai 1905 von ehemaligen Schülern,* 249–84. Berlin, 1905.

Head, Constance. *Justinian II of Byzantium.* Madison, Wis., 1972.

Herlihy, David. "Making Sense of Incest: Women and the Marriage Rules of the Early Middle Ages." In *Law, Custom, and the Social Fabric in Medieval Europe: Essays in Honor of Bryce Lyon,* edited by Bernard S. Bachrach and David Nicholas, 1–16. Studies in Medieval Culture 28. Kalamazoo, Mich., 1990.

Herrin, Judith. *The Formation of Christendom.* Princeton, N.J., 1987.

Higham, N. J. *The Convert Kings: Power and Religious Affiliation in Early Anglo-Saxon England.* Manchester and New York, 1997.

Hildebrandt, Reiner. "Germania Romana im deutschen Wortatlas. 2, Die Bezeichnungen der Patenschaft." In *Deutscher Wortschatz: Lexikologische Studien Ludwig Erich Schmitt zum 80. Geburtstag von seinen Marburger Schülern,* edited by H. H. Munske, P. von Polenz, O. Reichmann and R. Hildebrandt, 661–76. Berlin, 1988.

Hill, Rosalind. "Marriage in Seventh Century England." In *Saints, Scholars, and Heroes: Studies in Medieval Culture in Honor of Charles W. Jones,* edited by Margot H. King and Wesley M. Stevens, 1:67–75. Collegeville, Minn., 1979.

Hill, Thomas D. "Gestr's 'Prime Sign': Source and Significance in *Norna-Gests Þattr.*" *Arkiv för Nordisk Filologi* 104 (1989): 112–17.

Hillgarth, Jocelyn N. "Modes of Evangelization of Western Europe in the Seventh Century." In *Irland und die Christenheit/Ireland and Christendom,* edited by Próinséas Ni Chatháin and Michael Richer, 311–31. Stuttgart, 1987.

Hoffmann, Hartmut, and Rudolf Pokorny. *Das Dekret des Bischofs Burchard von Worms: Textstufen, Frühe Verbreitung, Vorlagen. MGH Hilfsmittel* 12. Munich, 1991.

Holthausen, Ferdinand. *Altenglisches Etymologisches Wörterbuch.* 2d ed. Heidelberg, 1963.

——. "Eine ae Interlinearversion des athanasischen Glaubensbekenntnisse." *ES* 75 (1942–43): 230–54.

Hope, D. M., and G. Wolfenden. "The Medieval Western Rites." In *The Study of Liturgy,* 2d ed., by Cheslyn Jones, Geoffrey Wainwright, Edward Yarnold, and Paul Bradshaw, 264–85. London, 1992.

Hopper, Paul J. "Some Observations on the Typology of Focus and Aspect in Narrative Language." *Studies in Language* 3 (1979): 37–64.

Hudson, Benjamin T. "Cnut and the Scottish Kings." *EHR* 107 (1992): 350–60.

Jedin, Hubert. "Le origini dei registri parrochiale e il concilio di Trento." *Il Concilio di Trento* 2 (1943): 322–36. German translation in Hubert Jedin, *Kirche des Glaubens: Kirche der Geschichte: Ausgewählte Aufsätze und Vorträge,* 2:526–39. Freiburg, 1966.

Jeremias, Joachim. *Infant Baptism in the First Four Centuries.* Translated by David Cairns. Philadelphia, 1962.

Jones, A. H. M., P. Grierson, and J. A. Crook. "The Authenticity of the 'Testamentum S. Remigii.' " *Revue Belge de Philologie et d'Histoire* 35 (1957): 356–73.

Jones, Charles W. *Saints' Lives and Chronicles in Early England.* Ithaca, N.Y., 1947.

Jones, Gwyn. "Egill Skallagrimsson in England." *Proceedings of the British Academy* (1952): 127–44.

Jong, Mayke de. "To the Limits of Kinship: Anti-Incest Legislation in the Early Medieval West, 500–900." In *From Sappho to De Sade: Moments in the History of Sexuality,* edited by Jan Bremmer, 36–59. London, 1989.

Jost, Karl. *Wulfstanstudien.* Schweizer anglistische Arbeiten 23. Bern, 1950.

Jungmann, Joseph. *Missarum Solemnia.* 5th ed. 2 vols. Vienna, 1962.

Jussen, Bernhard. "Le parrainage à la fin du Moyen Age: Savoir publique, attentes théologiques, et usages sociaux." *AESC* 47 (1992): 467–502.

——. *Patenschaft und Adoption im frühen Mittelalter: Künstliche Verwandtschaft als soziale Praxis.* Veröffentlichungen des Max-Planck-Instituts für Geschichte 98. Göttingen, 1991.

Kahle, Bernhard. "Die altnordische Sprache im Dienste des Christentums. Teil1, Die Prosa." *Acta Germanica* 1 (1890).

Kaske, Robert. "The Silver Spoons of Sutton Hoo." *Speculum* 42 (1967): 670–72.

Käsmann, Hans. *Studien zum kirchlichen Wortschatz des Mittelenglischen, 1100–1350.* Buchreihe der Anglia, Zeitschrift für englische Philologie 9. Tübingen, 1961.

Keefe, Susan A. "Baptismal Instruction in the Carolingian Period: The MS Evidence." Ph.D. dissertation, University of Toronto, 1981.

——. "Carolingian Baptismal Expositions: A Handlist of Tracts and Manuscripts." In *Carolingian Essays,* edited by Ute-Renate Blumenthal, 169–237. Washington, D.C., 1983.

Keefer, Sarah Larratt. "Manuals." In *The Liturgical Books of Anglo-Saxon England,* edited by Richard W. Pfaff. *Old English Newsletter,* Subsidia 23 (1995): 99–109.

Kelly, Fergus. *A Guide to Early Irish Law.* Early Irish Law Series 3. Dublin, 1988.

Kelly, Henry Ansgar. *The Devil at Baptism: Ritual, Theology, and Drama.* Ithaca, N.Y., 1985.

Ker, N. R. *Catalogue of Manuscripts containing Anglo-Saxon.* Oxford, 1957.

Kerlouegan, François. "Essai sur la mise en nourriture et l'éducation dans les pays celtiques d'après le témoinage des textes hagiographiques latins." *Etudes Celtiques* 12 (1968–1969): 101–46.

Keynes, Simon. "Andover 994." *Lookback at Andover: The Journal of the Andover History and Archaeology Society* 1 (1993): 58–61.

——. "Crime and Punishment in the Reign of King Æthelred the Unready." In *People and Places in Northern Europe: Essays in Honour of Peter Hayes Sawyer,*

edited by Ian Wood and Niels Lund, 67–81. Woodbridge, England, and Rochester, N.Y., 1991.
——. "The Fonthill Letter." In *Words, Texts, and Manuscripts: Studies in Anglo-Saxon Culture Presented to Helmut Gneuss on the Occasion of His Sixty-fifth Birthday,* edited by Michael Korhammer, 53–97. Cambridge, 1992.
Kirby, D. P. *The Earliest English Kings.* London, 1991.
Klapisch-Zuber, Christiane. "Compérage et clientélisme à Florence, 1360–1520." *Ricerche Storiche* 15 (1985): 61–76.
——. "Parrains et filleuls: Une approche comparée de la France, l'Angleterre, et l'Italie médiévales." *Medieval Prosopography* 6 (1985): 51–77.
Klingshirn, William E. *Caesarius of Arles: The Making of a Christian Community in Late Antique Gaul.* CSMLT 4th ser. 22. Cambridge, 1994.
Knowles, David. *The Monastic Order in England.* 2d ed. Cambridge, 1963.
Kottje, Raymund. *Die Bussbücher Halitgars von Cambrai und des Hrabanus Maurus.* Beiträge zur Geschichte und Quellenkunde des Mittelalters 8. Berlin, 1980.
Labriolle, Pierre de. "Papa." *Archivum Latinitatis Medii Aevi (Bulletin du Cange)* 4 (1928): 65–69.
Lange, Wolfgang. *Studien zur christlichen Dichtung der Nordgermanen, 1000–1200.* Palaestra 222. Göttingen, 1958.
Lanoë, Guy. "Les évêques en Angleterre 597–669." *Le Moyen Age* 89 (1983): 333–55.
Lapidge, Michael. "The School of Theodore and Hadrian." *ASE* 15 (1986): 43–72.
——. "The Study of Greek at the School of Canterbury in the Seventh Century." In *The Sacred Nectar of the Greeks: The Study of Greek in the West in the Early Middle Ages,* edited by Michael H. Herren and S. A. Brown, 169–94. King's College London Medieval Studies 2. London, 1988.
Latte, Robert de. "Saint Augustin et le baptême: Etude liturgico-historique du rituel baptismal des adultes chez Saint Augustin." *QLP* 56 (1975): 177–223.
——. "Saint Augustin et le baptême: Etude liturgico-historique du rituel baptismal des enfants chez Saint Augustin." *QLP* 57 (1976): 41–55.
Laughlin, J. Laurence. "The Anglo-Saxon Legal Procedure." In *Essays in Anglo-Saxon Law,* 183–305. Boston, 1905.
Laurent, V. "L'oeuvre canonique du concile *in Trullo* 691–692, source primaire du droit de l'église orientale." *Revue des Etudes Byzantines* 23 (1965): 7–41.
Laurin, Franz. "Die geistliche Verwandtschaft in ihrer geschichtlichen Entwicklung bis zum Rechte der Gegenwart." *AKKR* 15 (1866): 216–74.
Lawson, M. K. *Cnut: The Danes in England in the Early Eleventh Century.* London, 1993.
Leach, Henry G. *Angevin Britain and Scandinavia.* Harvard Studies in Comparative Literature 6. Cambridge, 1921.
Lécuyer, Jacques. "La confirmation chez les pères." *La Maison-Dieu* 54 (1958): 24–33.
Lees, Clare A. "The 'Sunday Letter' and the 'Sunday Lists.' " *ASE* 14 (1985): 129–51.
Levin, Eve. *Sex and Society in the World of the Orthodox Slavs, 900–1700.* Ithaca, N. Y., 1989.

Levison, Wilhelm. *England and the Continent in the Eighth Century.* Oxford, 1946.

Liebermann, Felix. "Über die Gesetze Ines von Wessex." In *Mélanges d'histoire offerts à M. Charles Bémont par ses amis et ses élèves* 21–42. Paris, 1913.

Lohaus, Annethe. *Die Merowinger und England.* Münchener Beiträge zur Mediävistik und Renaissance Forschung 19. Munich, 1974.

Love, Rosalind, ed. *Three Eleventh-Century Anglo-Latin Saints' Lives: Vita S. Birini, Vita et miracula S. Kenelmi, and Vita S. Rumwoldi.* Oxford, 1996.

Loyn, H. R. *The Vikings in Britain.* London, 1977.

Lynch, Joseph H. "Baptismal Sponsorship and Monks and Nuns, 500–1000." *American Benedictine Review* 31 (1980): 108–29.

———. *Godparents and Kinship in Early Medieval Europe.* Princeton, N.J., 1986.

———. "*Spiritale Vinculum:* The Vocabulary of Spiritual Kinship in Early Medieval Europe." In *Religion, Culture, and Society in the Early Middle Ages: Studies in Honor of Richard E. Sullivan,* edited by Thomas F. X. Noble and John J. Contreni, 181–204. Studies in Medieval Culture 23. Kalamazoo, Mich., 1987.

MacDonald, Frederick Charles. *A History of Confirmation.* London, 1938.

Macrides, Ruth. "The Byzantine Godfather." *Byzantine and Modern Greek Studies* 11 (1987): 139–62.

Magoun, Francis P. "Cynewulf, Cyneheard, and Osric." *Anglia* 57 (1933): 361–76.

Martimort, Amié-Georges. *Les "ordines," les ordinaires, et les cérémoniaux.* Typologie, fascicule 56. Turnhout, 1991.

Maurer, Konrad. *Vorlesungen über altnordische Rechtsgeschichte.* 5 vol. Leipzig, 1907–38; reprinted Osnabrück, 1966.

McKillop, S. "A Romano-British Baptismal Liturgy?" In *The Early Church in Western Britain and Ireland,* edited by S. M. Pearce, 35–48. Oxford, 1982.

McKitterick, Rosamond. *The Frankish Church and the Carolingian Reforms, 789–895.* London, 1977.

McTurk, R. W. " 'Cynewulf and Cyneheard' and the Icelandic Sagas." *Leeds Studies in English,* new ser. 12 (1981): 81–127.

Meaney, Audrey. "Ælfric and Idolatry." *Journal of Religious History* 13 (1984): 119–35.

Meyvaert, Paul. "Bede's Text of the *Libellus responsionum* of Gregory the Great to Augustine of Canterbury." In *England before the Conquest: Studies in Primary Sources Presented to Dorothy Whitelock,* edited by Peter Clemoes and Kathleen Hughes, 15–33. Cambridge, 1971.

———. "Diversity within Unity: A Gregorian Theme." *Heythrop Journal* 4 (1963): 141–62.

A Microfiche Concordance to Old English. Compiled by Richard L. Venezky and Antonette di Paolo Healey. Newark, Del., 1980.

Middle English Dictionary. Ann Arbor, Mich., 1952– .

Mikat, Paul. *Die Inzestgesetzgebung der merowingisch-fränkischen Konzilien, 511–626/27.* Rechts- und Staatswissenschaftliche Veröffentlichungen der Görres-Gesellschaft, Neue Folge 74. Paderborn, 1994.

Mitchell, Leonel L. *Baptismal Anointing.* Alcuin Club Collections 48. London, 1966; reprinted Notre Dame, Ind., 1978.

Mittellateinisches Wörterbuch bis zum ausgehenden 13. Jahrhundert. Munich, 1967–.

Moorman, Charles. "The Anglo-Saxon Chronicle for 755." *Notes and Queries* 199 (1954): 94–98.

Morin, Germain. "Textes inédits relatifs au Symbole et à la vie chrétienne." *RB* 22 (1905): 505–24.

Morris, R. "Baptismal Places: 600–800." In *People and Places in Northern Europe: Essays in Honour of Peter Hayes Sawyer,* edited by Ian Wood and Niels Lund, 15–24. Woodbridge, England, 1991.

Napier, A. S. "Old English Notes:" *Modern Philology* 1 (1903–4): 303–8.

Nelson, Janet. "The Problem of King Alfred's Royal Anointing." *Journal of Ecclesiastical History* 18 (1967): 145–63.

——. "Reconstructing a Royal Family: Reflections on Alfred, from Asser, Chapter 2." In *People and Places in Northern Europe: Essays in Honour of Peter Hayes Sawyer,* edited by Ian Wood and Niels Lund, 47–66. Woodbridge, England, 1991.

Nelson, Janet, and Richard Pfaff. "Pontificals and Benedictionals." In *The Liturgical Books of Anglo-Saxon England,* edited by Richard W. Pfaff. *Old English Newsletter,* Subsidia 23 (1995): 87–98.

Niermeyer, J. F. *Mediae latinitatis lexicon minus.* Leiden, 1976.

Nutini, Hugo, and Betty Bell. *Ritual Kinship: The Structure and Historical Development of the Compadrazgo System in Rural Tlaxcala.* 2 vols. Princeton, N.J., 1980–84.

Oppenheim, Philipp. "Mönchsweihen und Taufritus." In *Miscellanea liturgica in honorem L. Cuniberti Mohlberg,* 259–82. Bibliotheca "Ephemerides liturgicae" 22. Rome, 1948.

Ostheeren, Klaus. "Bibliographischer Anhang." In A. S. Napier, *Wulfstan,* 319–67. Sammlung englischer Denkmäler 4. Berlin, 1883; reprinted 1967.

Oxford English Dictionary. 2d ed. J. A. Simpson and E. S. C. Weiner. 20 vols. Oxford, 1989.

Oxford Latin Dictionary. Edited by P. G. W. Glare. Oxford, 1982.

Pappenheim, Max. "Über künstliche Verwandtschaft im germanischen Rechte." ZSSRG, Germanistische Abteilung 29 (1908): 304–33.

Patlagean, Evelyne. "Christianisation et parentés rituelles: Le domaine de Byzance." *AESC* 33 (1978): 625–36.

Payer, Pierre J. *Sex and the Penitentials: The Development of a Sexual Code, 550–1150.* Toronto, 1984.

Pepperdene, Margaret. "Baptism in the Early British and Irish Churches." *Irish Theological Quarterly* 22 (1955): 110–23.

Perkow, Ursula. *Wasserweihe, Taufe, und Patenschaft bei den Nordgermanen.* Hamburg, 1972.

Pfaff, Richard W. "Massbooks: Sacramentaries and Missals." In *The Liturgical Books of Anglo-Saxon England,* edited by Richard W. Pfaff. *Old English Newsletter,* Subsidia 23 (1995): 7–34.

Pfleger, A. "Zur Taufe toter Kinder: Ein Beitrag zur religiösen Volkskunde." *Archiv für Elsassische Kirchengeschichte* 15 (1941–42): 211–26.

Philpotts, Bertha. *Kindred and Clan.* Cambridge, 1913.

Pitsakis, Constantin G. "Le droit matrimonial dans les canons du concile in Trullo." *Annuarium Historiae Conciliorum* 24 (1992): 158–85.
Pitt-Rivers, Julian. "The Kith and the Kin." In *The Character of Kinship,* edited by Jack Goody, 89–105. Cambridge, 1973.
———. "Ritual Kinship in Spain." *Transactions of the New York Academy of Sciences,* 2d ser., 20 (1958): 424–31.
Priebsch, Robert. "The Chief Sources of Some Anglo-Saxon Homilies." *Otia Merseiana* 1 (1899): 129–47.
———. *The Letter from Heaven on the Observance of Sunday.* Oxford, 1936.
Puniet, P. de. "La liturgie baptismale en Gaulle avant Charlemagne." *Revue des Questions Liturgiques,* nouvelle série 28 (1902): 382–423.
Richard, Jean. "La donation en filleulage dans le droit bourguignon." *Mémoires de la Société pour l'Histoire du Droit et des Institutions des Anciens Pays Bourguignons, Comtois et Romands* 16 (1954): 139–42.
Richards, Jeffrey. *Consul of God: The Life and Times of Gregory the Great.* London, 1980.
Richardson, H. G., and G. O. Sayles. *Law and Legislation from Æthelberht to Magna Carta.* Edinburgh University Publications, History, Philosophy, and Economics 20. Edinburgh, 1966.
Riché, Pierre. *Education and Culture in the Barbarian West.* Translated by John J. Contreni. Columbia, S.C., 1976.
Richter, Michael. "Practical Aspects of the Conversion of the Anglo-Saxons." In *Ireland und die Christenheit/Ireland and Christendom,* edited by Próinséas Ni Chatháin and Michael Richter, 362–76. Stuttgart, 1987.
Riley, Hugh M. *Christian Initiation: A Comparative Study of the Interpretation of the Baptismal Liturgy in the Mystagogical Writings of Cyril of Jerusalem, John Chrysostom, Theodore of Mopsuestia, and Ambrose of Milan.* CUA Studies in Christian Antiquity 17. Washington, D.C., 1974.
Rivière, Ernest-M. "La lettre du Christ tombée du ciel." *Revue des Questions Historiques* 79 (1906): 600–605.
Roeder, Fritz. *Über die Erziehung der vornehmen angelsächsischen Jugend in fremden Häusern.* Halle, 1910.
Ross, Margaret Clunies. "Concubinage in Anglo-Saxon England." *Past and Present* 108 (1985): 3–34.
Runciman, W. G. "Accelerating Social Mobility: The Case of Anglo-Saxon England." *Past and Present* 104 (1984): 3–30.
Sandholm, Åke. *Primsigningsriten under nordisk Medeltid.* Acta Academiae Aboensis, Series A: Humaniora, vol. 29/3. Åbo, Finland, 1965.
Sawyer, Birgit, and Peter Sawyer. *Medieval Scandinavia: From Conversion to Reformation, circa 800–1500.* Nordic Series 17. Minneapolis, 1993.
Sawyer, Peter. "Ethelred II, Olaf Tryggvason, and the Conversion of Norway." *Scandinavian Studies* 59 (1987): 299–307.
———. "The Process of Scandinavian Christianization in the Tenth and Eleventh Centuries." In *The Christianization of Scandinavia,* edited by Birgit Sawyer, Peter Sawyer, and Ian Wood, 68–87. Alingsas, Sweden, 1987.

——. "The Two Viking Ages of Britain: A Discussion." *Mediaeval Scandinavia* 2 (1969): 163–76, 203–7.

Schach, Paul. "The Theme of the Reluctant Christian in the Icelandic Sagas." *Journal of English and Germanic Philology* 81 (1982): 185–203.

Schieffer, Theodor. *Winfrid-Bonifatius und die christliche Grundlegung Europas.* Freiburg, 1954; reprinted with updated bibliography, Darmstadt, 1972.

Schlutter, Otto B. "Weitere Beiträge zur altenglischen Wortforschung." *Anglia* 37 (1913): 41–53.

Schnell, B. "Himmelsbrief." *Verfasserlexicon.* Zweite Auflegung, 4 (1982): 28–33.

Schwarz, Helga. *Das Taufgeld: Ein Beitrag zur historischen Entwicklung der Taufbräuche.* Graz, 1950.

Scott, Roger. "Diplomacy in the Sixth Century: The Evidence of John Malalas." In *Byzantine Diplomacy,* edited by Jonathan Shepherd and Simon Franklin, 159–65. Aldershot, Great Britain, 1992.

Scragg, D. G. "The Corpus of Vernacular Homilies and Prose Saints' Lives before Ælfric." *ASE* 8 (1979): 223–77.

Seebohm, Frederic. *Tribal Custom in Anglo-Saxon Law.* London, 1902.

Sheehan, Michael. *The Will in Medieval England: From the Conversion of the Anglo-Saxons to the End of the Thirteenth Century.* Studies and Texts 6. Toronto, 1963.

Sherlock, D. A. "Saul, Paul, and the Silver Spoons from Sutton Hoo." *Speculum* 47 (1972): 91–95.

Signorini, Italo. *Padrini e compadri: Un'analisi antropologica della parentela spirituale.* Turin, 1981.

Simon, Dieter. "Zur Ehegesetzgebung der Isaurier." In *Fontes minores,* vol. 1. Forschungen zur byzantinischen Rechtsgeschichte 1, 16–43. Frankfurt am Main, 1976.

Sisam, Kenneth, *Studies in the History of Old English Literature.* Oxford, 1953.

Smyth, Alfred P. *King Alfred the Great.* Oxford, 1995.

——. *Scandinavian Kings in the British Isles, 850–880.* Oxford, 1977.

Spencer, Mark. "Dating the Baptism of Clovis, 1886–1993." *EME* 3 (1994): 97–116.

Stancliffe, Claire E. "Kings and Conversion: Some Comparisons between the Roman Mission to England and Patrick's to Ireland." *FS* 14 (1980): 59–94.

——. "Kings Who Opted Out." In *Ideal and Reality in Frankish and Anglo-Saxon Society: Studies Presented to J. M. Wallace-Hadrill,* edited by P. Wormald, D. A. Bullough, and R. Collins, 154–76. Oxford, 1983.

Stenton, Frank M. *Anglo-Saxon England.* 3d ed. Oxford 1971.

Stevenson, Jane. "Introduction" to Frederick E. Warren, *The Liturgy and Ritual of the Celtic Church,* ix–cxxvii. Reprinted Woodbridge, 1987.

Stevenson, William H. "Yorkshire Surveys and Other Documents of the Eleventh Century in the York Gospels." *EHR* 27 (1912): 1–25.

Stryker, W. G. "The Latin–Old English Glossary in Ms. Cotton Cleopatra A.III." Ph.D. dissertation, Stanford University, 1951.

The Study of Liturgy. Rev. ed. by Cheslyn Jones, Geoffrey Wainwright, Edward Yarnold, and Paul Bradshaw. New York and London, 1992.

Tessier, Georges. *Le baptême de Clovis.* Paris, 1964.

Thacker, Alan. "Monks, Preaching, and Pastoral Care in Early Anglo-Saxon England." In *Pastoral Care before the Parish*, edited by John Blair and Richard Sharpe, 137–70. Leicester, 1992.

Thomas, Charles. *Christianity in Roman Britain to AD 500*. London, 1981.

Thurston, Herbert. "Clerical Celibacy in the Anglo-Saxon Church." *Month* 542 (1909): 180–94.

Towers, Tom H. "Thematic Unity in the Story of Cynewulf and Cyneheard." *Journal of English and Germanic Philology* 62 (1963): 310–16.

Trahern, Joseph. "Caesarius of Arles and Old English Literature: Some Contributions and a Recapitulation." *ASE* 5 (1976): 105–19.

Troianos, Spyros N. "Die Wirkungsgeschichte des Trullanum (Quinisextum) in der byzantinischen Gesetzgebung." *Annuarium Historiae Conciliorum* 24 (1992): 95–111.

Vaillant, A. "Une homélie de Méthode." *Revue des Etudes Slaves* 23 (1947): 34–47.

Van Buchem, L. A. *L'homélie pseudoeusébienne de Pentecôte: L'origine de la confirmatio en Gaule Méridionale et l'interprétation de ce rite par Fauste de Riez.* Nijmegen, 1967.

Van der Meer, F. *Augustine the Bishop.* Translated by Brian Battershaw and G. R. Lamb. London, 1961.

Van Esbroeck, Michel. "La lettre sur le dimanche, descendu du ciel." *Analecta Bollandiana* 107 (1989): 267–84.

Varrentrapp, Eleonore. *Über den Zusammenhang von Taufe und kirchlichen Unterweisung in der christlichen Frühzeit Deutschlands.* Marburg, 1946.

Vogel, Cyrille. *La discipline pénitentielle en Gaule des origines à la fin du viie siècle.* Paris, 1952.

——. "Les échanges liturgiques entre Rome et les pays francs jusqu'à l'époque de Charlemagne." In *Le chiese nei regni dell'Europa occidentale e i loro rapporti con Roma sino all'800,* 185–295. *SSAM* 7/1 Spoleto, 1960.

——. *Les "Libri paenitentiales."* Revised by Allen J. Frantzen. Typologie 27. Turnhout, 1985.

——. *Medieval Liturgy: An Introduction to the Sources.* Translated and revised by William G. Storey and Niels K. Rasmussen. Washington, D.C., 1986.

Vollrath, Hanna. *Die Synoden Englands bis 1066.* Konziliengeschichte, Reihe A: Darstellungen. Paderborn, 1985.

——. "Taufliturgie und Diözesaneinteilungen in der frühen angelsächischen Kirche." In *Irland und Christenheit/Ireland and Christendom,* edited by Próinséas Ni Chatháin and Michael Richter, 377–86. Stuttgart, 1987.

Wallace-Hadrill, J. M. "The Franks and the English in the Ninth Century: Some Common Historical Interests." In *Early Medieval History,* 201–16. New York, 1976.

Warren, Frederick E. *The Liturgy and Ritual of the Celtic Church.* Oxford, 1881. Reprinted Woodbridge, England, 1987.

Waterhouse, Ruth. "The Haesten Episode in 894 *Anglo-Saxon Chronicle.*" *Studia Neophilologica* 46 (1974): 136–41.

——. "The Theme and Structure of 755 Anglo-Saxon Chronicle." *Neuphilologische Mitteilungen* 70 (1969): 630–40.

Whitaker, E. C. *Documents of the Baptismal Liturgy.* London, 1960.

Whitby, Michael. *The Emperor Maurice and His Historian: Theophylact Simocatta on Persian and Balkan Warfare.* Oxford, 1988.

White, Stephen D. "Kingship and Lordship in Early Medieval England: The Story of Cynewulf and Cyneheard." *Viator* 20 (1989): 1–18.

Whitelock, Dorothy. *The Beginnings of English Society.* Pelican History of England 2. Harmondsworth, 1974.

——. *History, Law, and Literature in 10th–11th Century England.* Collected Studies Series 128. London, 1980.

——. "The Importance of the Battle of Edington." In *Report for 1975, 1976, and 1977 of the Society of Friends of the Priory Church of Edington, Wiltshire,* 6–15. Reprinted in *From Bede to Alfred: Studies in Early Anglo-Saxon Literature and History.* Collected Studies Series 121. London, 1980.

——. "Wulfstan and the Laws of Cnut." *EHR* 63 (1948): 433–52.

——. "Wulfstan and the So-Called Laws of Edward and Guthrum." *EHR* 56 (1941): 1–21.

——. "Wulfstan's Authorship of Cnut's Laws." *EHR* 70 (1970): 72–85.

——, ed. *Sermo Lupi ad Anglos.* Revised ed. Exeter, 1976.

Wielers, Margret. *Zwischenstaatliche Beziehungsformen im frühen Mittelalter Pax, Foedus, Amicitia, Fraternitas.* Münster in Westphalia, 1959.

Willis, G. G. *Further Essays in Early Roman Liturgy.* Alcuin Club Collections 50. London, 1968.

Wilson, David R. *Anglo-Saxon Paganism.* London and New York, 1992.

Wilson, James H. "Cynewulf and Cyneheard: The Falls of Princes." *Papers on Language and Literature* 13 (1977): 312–17.

Wood, Ian. "Christians and Pagans in Ninth-Century Scandinavia." In *The Christianization of Scandinavia,* edited by Birgit Sawyer, Peter Sawyer, and Ian Wood, 36–67. Alingsas, Sweden, 1987.

——. *The Merovingian Kingdoms, 450–751.* London, 1994.

——. "The Mission of Augustine of Canterbury to the English." *Speculum* 69 (1994): 1–17.

Wood, Michael. "The Making of King Athelstan's Empire: An English Charlemagne?" In *Ideal and Reality in Frankish and Anglo-Saxon Society,* edited by Patrick Wormald, D. A. Bullough and R. Collins, 250–72. Oxford, 1983.

Wormald, Patrick. "Æthelred the Lawmaker." In *Ethelred the Unready: Papers from the Millenary Conference,* edited by David Hill. *British Archaeological Reports,* British ser. 3 (1978): 47–80.

——. "The Age of Bede and Æthelbald." In *The Anglo-Saxons,* edited by James Campbell, 70–100. Oxford, 1982.

——. "The Age of Offa and Alcuin." In *The Anglo-Saxons,* edited by James Campbell, 101–31. Oxford, 1982.

——. "In Search of Offa's 'Law-Code.' " In *People and Places in Northern Europe: Essays in Honour of Peter Hayes Sawyer,* edited by Ian Wood and Niels Lund, 25–45. Woodbridge, England, 1991.

——. " 'Quadripartitus.' " In *Law and Government in Medieval England and Normandy: Essays in Honour of Sir James Holt,* edited by George Garnett and John Hudson, 111–47. Cambridge, 1994.

Wrenn, C. L. "A Saga of the Anglo-Saxons." *History* 25 (1940): 208–15.

Yarnold, E. J. "Initiation: The Fourth and Fifth Centuries." In *The Study of Liturgy,* revised ed. by Cheslyn Jones, Geoffrey Wainwright, Edward Yarnold, and Paul Bradshaw, 129–44. New York, 1992.

Ysebaert, J. *Greek Baptismal Terminology: Its Origin and Early Development.* Graecitas Christianorum primaeva 1. Nijmegen, 1962.

Zachariä von Lingenthal, Karl Eduard. *Geschichte des griechisch-römischen Rechts.* 3d ed. Berlin, 1893; reprinted Aalen, 1955.

Index